FIFTH EDITION

THE STAGES

OF HUMAN EVOLUTION

C. Loring Brace
University of Michigan

Prentice Hall

Library of Congress Cataloging-in-Publication Data

Brace, C. Loring.
    The stages of human evolution / C. Loring Brace. —5th ed.
        p.   cm.
    Includes bibliographical references and index.
    ISBN 0-13-125485-5
    1. Human evolution.   2. Man, Prehistoric.   3. Anthropology,
    Prehistoric—History.   I. Title.
    GN281.B67   1995
    573.2—dc20   94-35681
                                                         CIP

Acquisitions Editor: Sharon Chambliss
Production Editor: Alison Gnerre
Copy Editor: Lynn Buckingham
Cover design: Carol Ceraldi
Buyer: Mary Ann Gloriande

To Mimi

whose contributions are even more than those
that are so graphically apparent.

 © 1995, 1991, 1988, 1979, 1967 by Prentice-Hall, Inc.
A Simon & Schuster Company
Englewood Cliffs, New Jersey 07632

Printed in the United States of America
10   9   8   7   6   5   4   3   2   1

ISBN 0-13-125485-5

Prentice-Hall International (UK) Limited, *London*
Prentice-Hall of Australia Pty. Limited, *Sydney*
Prentice-Hall Canada Inc., *Toronto*
Prentice-Hall Hispanoamericana, S.A., *Mexico*
Prentice-Hall of India Private Limited, *New Delhi*
Prentice-Hall of Japan, Inc., *Tokyo*
Simon & Schuster Asia Pte. Ltd., *Singapore*
Editora Prentice-Hall do Brasil, Ltda., *Rio de Janeiro*

Contents

7

Evolutionary Principles

8

Prehominids

9

Culture as an Ecological Niche

10

The Australopithecine Stage   *119*

11

The Pithecanthropine Stage   *150*

12

The Pithecanthropine to Neanderthal Transition   *173*

13

The Neanderthal Stage   *192*

14

The Modern Stage   *242*

15

Epilogue/Summary   *299*

Sources Cited   *305*

Index   *359*

Preface

Looked at from this point of view, the Neandertal and Pithecanthropus skulls stand like the piers of a ruined bridge which once continuously connected the kingdom of man with the rest of the animal world.

William J. Sollas 1908[1]

Of all the subjects that have provoked the play of human curiosity, few equal our concern with our own prehistoric origins. At the same time, few subjects have been the target for so much unprofessional speculation. Although the present work does not reduce the quantity of speculations (quite the reverse), it is my hope that they can, technically at least, bear the label of *professional* speculations. Part of the reason for the less-than-abundant work on human origins is that, in this material world, such efforts can produce little measurable gain. Physics can produce bigger and more expensive explosions, basic biology can introduce medical breakthroughs, geology and economics can contribute to our mineral and monetary well-being.

But prehistoric anthropology, in contrast, can reveal only the humble nature of human beginnings, and this has dubious value as a marketable commodity. Many have regarded it as an interesting hobby, but few have been tempted to treat it as a serious career and devote lifelong concentration to its advancement. Even at the professional level, the competition to qualify has often been less than it is for other fields. Consequently there are fewer jobs and hence fewer practitioners, and those who cultivate its pursuits have access to only modest amounts of research support, with the result that ad-

[1] W. J. Sollas, 1908: 337.

vances and accomplishments have been far less spectacular than has been the case with, for instance, genetics or electronics. The subject is fascinating nevertheless, and for the professionals its pursuit is quite satisfying in and of itself.

As I have revised this book periodically over the last quarter of a century, I have stuck pretty much by the original aim of writing for the interested undergraduate reader. This is still the principal focus of the present revision, but, this time, I have added a separate dimension for the instructors and the interested graduate students in the field. In effect, it is now two parallel books. The main text of chapters 1 through 14 runs much as it did before, although augmented and brought up to date in a number of ways. What is significantly different, however, is the addition of notes to each chapter in which the statements in the text are amplified, with references to the primary documentation in the professional literature. The main practicing specialists in paleoanthropology have largely ignored the ideas that have appeared on the pages of the previous editions—presumably because they were not properly documented. In the present edition, I have added that documentation, and this plus some of the other treatment in the notes should pique the interest of the professional and possibly of the general readers as well.

The book is not intended to be a compendium of paleoanthropology where every fossil fragment ever found receives mention. Instead, the focus is on the major trends that have characterized the course of human evolution and the circumstances that contributed to the changes that took place. Significant representative specimens are dealt with without going into great detail. The most important of these are represented graphically, and the points they illustrate are described in brief. The hard-core professional will object that this or that specimen is not mentioned, and that the trivia in which they delight are largely left out. The beginning student on the other hand, will surely feel that more than enough material is included. Instead, I have concentrated on the actual mechanisms that have produced human form. These are discussed in the light of the particular morphological changes that they have engendered. It is an approach that deals with those aspects of ourselves and our fossil predecessors that have the greatest evolutionary significance and in consequence should be of the greatest interest.

It is the purpose of the present volume to communicate a modicum of this interest to the reader, young or old; perhaps to kindle the spark of what might grow to be another professional career; and to add a possible modifying influence, however minor, to the understandable human tendency to magnify our present accomplishments to the point that we are inclined to forget how precarious was the very existence of our predecessors until the recent past—and how uncertain it may become again in the impending future.

C. Loring Brace

chapter one

Interpreting Human Evolution

SCIENCE AND RELIGION

As a general rule, there need be no conflict between science and religion. Many scientists are deeply religious people and, although occasionally their manifestations of religious belief are on the unorthodox side, they are frequently of one or another traditional denominational stance. The Darwinian theory of evolution also is not viewed as being incompatible with the vast majority of organized religious systems, even when evolutionary expectations are applied to the human condition. The largest Christian denomination, the Roman Catholic church, has faced the matter squarely and has published the results of its deliberations in a series of key papal encyclicals—*Providentissimus Deus* and *Divina Afflante Spiritu,* in 1943, and *Humani Generis,* in 1950. In these, Pope Pius XII declared that the Bible is a religious and moral document and was not intended as a discourse on geology and natural history. He concluded that evolution is a perfectly valid hypothesis, and that evolutionary research and teaching are perfectly valid enterprises that do not conflict with or overlap the concerns of the church as long as they do not presume to deal with matters of morality and the human soul.[1]

Most scientists and members of the clergy are perfectly content to leave it at that, but people in some denominations find aspects of science—partic-

1

ularly those that deal with human evolution—in conflict with their basic beliefs. Among these are certain "fundamentalist" Christian groups who declare that the words of the Bible recount literal truth, and anything else therefore is wrong by definition. According to them, evolution is in conflict with their religion. I can do nothing to help readers with such a starting presumption, other than to say that this book is not for them.

Those who start from such a position also start with something of a conundrum, because at the very beginning of the Bible, 1 Genesis lists a very different order for creation than 2 Genesis. If indeed the words of the Bible are to be taken literally, then 2 Genesis must be wrong because it contradicts 1 Genesis. But if the Bible "cannot be wrong," then two successive chapters that say opposite things must both be right even if that is logically impossible.

Although this "most ingenious paradox" may worry the literal-minded theologian, it is beyond the realm of science. So, too, is that contradiction in terms, "creation science," which is offered by fundamentalist Christians as deserving equal time in the classroom with evolutionary biology. The interpretations offered by evolutionary biologists can be put to the test by experiment and the collection of relevant data, and, if they are found wanting, they are discarded. "Creation science," on the other hand, cannot be tested in such a way, and its proponents will not accept the possibility that crucial experiments or collected data could lead to its rejection. For this reason, "creation science" cannot be science. The United States District Court judge, William R. Overton, who presided in the 1982 "balanced treatment" court decision in Arkansas, ruled that "creation science" not only failed to qualify under the definition of science—it "has no scientific merit"—but that it owed its tenets and promotion solely to denominational religious conviction. He concluded that "the evidence is overwhelming that both the purpose and effect" of the legislation attempting to seek equal time in the curriculum "is the advancement of religion in the public schools," which is expressly forbidden by the Constitution of the United States of America.[2]

GOD AND THE GAPS

The fossil record is admittedly incomplete because the vast majority of the creatures that lived in the past have died without leaving a trace. The appearance of change as one ascends the picture in superimposed strata tends to be discontinuous, with gaps of varying length between the earlier and the later sections. The different appearance of sequential forms has been taken by some to be a proof for the existence of God.

This, however, has to be about as demeaning a criterion for demonstrating Divine Existence as one can imagine, and it does little credit to those who accept such a test. It purports, in fact, to use human ignorance as a proof of Divinity. When gaps are filled in, as is being done year by year, what does this do for the nature of the God who was postulated to account for them? To use gaps in our knowledge as proof for the existence of God is, in effect, to deify ignorance.[3]

We are finite creatures, and our knowledge will always have its limits. But to deny the efforts of scientists and scholars to try to extend those limits, and to glory instead in our imperfections, is to do less than justice to our potential capacity to learn about the endless variety and mechanics of the natural world—itself something that is far more worthy of the designation "Divine."

EVOLUTIONARY EXPECTATIONS

Few among the educated and no serious scholars doubt that *Homo sapiens* evolved by natural means from a creature which today would not be considered human. From this initial point of agreement, the thinking of those who are considered qualified to judge diverges to such a degree that many feel we do not have a basis which is adequate enough to warrant any interpretation at all. Yet schemes have been constructed that attempt to arrange the prehistoric evidence and account for the course of human evolution. The pages that follow present and discuss the strengths and weaknesses of a number of these.

Since it is generally agreed that evolutionary thinking should be applied to the course of prehistoric human development, it would seem unnecessary at first glance to consider the nonevolutionary or even antievolutionary views of pre-Darwinian thought. As we shall see, however, the differences between several of the attitudes discernible at the present time can be traced in part to the continuing influence of currents of thought that have specific pre-Darwinian sources.[4] Once these have been identified and the historical connections have been traced, the reasons for the differences between the major opposing interpretations will become obvious and we shall have some basis for making a choice between them.

Interpretations of the human fossil record can be arranged along a spectrum between two polar and opposed approaches. At one extreme is the school that takes all the known hominid fossils, arranges them in a lineal sequence, and declares that this is the course which human evolution has pursued. The other extreme is the school which declares that the great majority, if not all, of the available fossil record has nothing to do with the actual course of human evolution. In this view, the probability that any given fossil has descendants that are still alive is so vanishingly small that to declare otherwise is to be guilty of the unscientific stance of "ancestor worship."[5] Furthermore, the course of evolution is never a straight, unbranching line—witness the diversity of related forms in the organic world today—and we should expect to find branches and specializations among human fossils. This latter view tends to regard the differing fossil hominids as "specializations" away from the main line of human evolution, which eventually became extinct without issue. And, because the chance is almost nonexistent that a given remote fossil was literally ancestral to anything still alive, it can be completely discounted. Countering this is the argument that, although indeed any given prehistoric individual is unlikely to have living descendants, the *population* to which it belonged certainly may be ancestral to continuing populations.

People are invariably fascinated by investigating the skeletons in their closets. In the field of human evolution, we could say that this is *literally* the case. This fascination has led many people, amateur and professional, to write about the human fossil record. Some people have not been fully qualified and have failed to perceive the nature of the two schemes just mentioned. As a result, many authors prefer some hazy middle ground because they feel that both schemes have some merit. Consequently, only a few authors today represent the poles in fully developed form.

In the first edition of this book, one of the extreme positions was specifically defended—the linear scheme mentioned previously—not because there was conclusive proof for it, but in an effort to follow the principles expounded by the medieval logician, William of Occam (sometimes spelled Ockham [1280–1349]), for whom the best explanation was always the simplest. At the time, it appeared that the complexities of the most widely accepted interpretive schemes were more a product of the minds of their advocates than they were the necessary result of the available facts. Simplification, however, can be pushed too far, and the wealth of discoveries over the last twenty-five years has clearly shown that a rigid unilinear interpretation is, in fact, an oversimplification. It is still true, nonetheless, that the simplest interpretation that accounts for all of the facts is the one that should be accorded top preference.[6] And, as we shall see, the one offered here is the simplest one available. Certainly the student will discover that it is the easiest one to learn.

More of this later, but first it should be instructive to sample the various other current views on the course of human evolution. First among these, and generally regarded as most traditional, is the view that the different forms in the human fossil record are the results of the adaptive radiation of the basic human line. At present several versions are being stressed. One suggests that the entire human fossil record is made up of divergent "specialized" lines, most of which became extinct without issue.[7] Another concentrates on the earlier parts of the record where various "specializations" are supposed to have occurred.[8] The last concentrates on the latter part of the record, where the Neanderthals are identified as "specializations" on their way to extinction.[9] Running through all of these is the tendency to deny possible ancestral status to any fossil that differs from modern form to any marked extent. To some degree, then, these schemata focus more on assertions concerning how human evolution presumably did *not* occur than on trying to find out what actually was going on.

TIME, GEOLOGY, AND FOSSILS

To understand these applications and the criticisms that can be made of them, it is first necessary to gain some sort of perspective on the time scale in question, the fossils concerned, and the principles involved. Briefly, it has become apparent that the span during which the events of human evolution occurred was not just 300,000 or 800,000 years, as was once believed, but somewhat more than 3 million years in duration. Previous estimates were based largely upon guesswork involving sedimentation rates and stratum thicknesses. This recent reappraisal is derived from the work of geophysicists who have utilized the known and constant rates by which radioactive elements decay into their stable end products, for example the decay of radioactive Potassium 40 into Argon. The Potassium/Argon (K/Ar) proportion in ancient volcanic rocks is directly related to the length of time since they have cooled. Although many pitfalls are connected with the use of this technique to date strata in the recent past (keeping in mind that 3 million years is "recent past" in the full perspective of geological time), it is becoming increasingly apparent that the duration of the human line has been sufficient that we need not invoke an unusual rate of evolution to account for all the changes revealed by the human fossil record.[10]

The geological period during which human form did most of its evolving is called the Pleistocene, which extended from nearly 2 million years ago to just over 10,000 years ago—if indeed it can properly be considered to have ended.[11] The oldest of our close fossil relatives are found in the Pliocene, well over 3 million and more years ago, and are referred to as Australopithecines.[12] These flourish for a span of about 2 million years, during which time they display a diversity of size, form and robustness that has been the subject of some vigorous scholarly disagreements. The size spectrum runs from the modern human average for bulk and stature down to creatures only half as large. The earliest ones appear to be small, and the most robust ones appear to be late, but it is abundantly clear that little ones continued to exist at the same time that big ones flourished. Aside from their sometimes different bulk, the most dramatic points of distinction between the Australopithecines and modern humans are in the head and face. Simply stated, the Australopithecine head is smaller—the brain is scarcely more than a third the size of the modern human average—while the faces and teeth are enormous.

At the moment, there is much professional debate over what the various Australopithecines should be called and how the various robust and gracile forms related to each other and to the larger continuing picture of human evolution. A solution to the controversy is suggested later in this book, but for now this initial brief sketch is offered so that the reader can have some framework on which to arrange the arguments that follow.

Another cluster of hominid fossils, which can be called Pithecanthropines, dates from near the beginning of the Lower Pleistocene, over 1.5 million years ago.[13] Among these fossils, brain size is double that of the Australopithecine and about two-thirds that of the Modern norm. Molar tooth size has dropped markedly from Australopithecine levels, and a remarkably robust skeletomuscular system is maintained. In the Upper Pleistocene, immediately prior to the appearance of people of recognizably modern form, there is a fossil group that has been called the Neanderthals. These are characterized by the achievement of fully modern levels of brain size while preserving many of the remaining characteristics of the Middle Pleistocene Pithecanthropines. To be sure, other fossils are unevenly scattered, in both the geographical and temporal sense, providing the basis for much of the disagreement that still surrounds any attempt to develop a systematic view of human evolution. But the foregoing should provide a useful outline to remember while the discovery of the human fossil record is being recounted.

The scheme that is developed in later chapters essentially takes these major blocks of fossil hominids, arranges them in temporal sequence, and explores the evolutionary logic that can be used to show how the earlier ones evolved into the later ones. These major groups form the evolutionary Stages through which one can suggest that the human line passed. Yet it should also be remembered that the identification of these "Stages" is largely dependent upon the accident of discovery. A few rich sites have provided concentrated evidence for particular forms of human fossils, and it is not only possible but extremely likely that, had these rich sites involved different time levels, then the identification and number of important Stages in human evolution would have been rather different. On the other hand, the Stages visible in the evidence at hand are adequate to represent the changes involved, and their consideration can be justified in terms of their utility.[14]

Ultimately, when the entire time spectrum of human existence is documented by an as-yet-unforseeable abundance of fossil evidence, the picture should be one of a completely gradual continuum of accumulating change, with no visible breaks between what are here considered as Stages. Even this, however, is vigorously disputed by one currently popular set of theoretical expectations, but this will be treated in a later chapter. In contrast, the view presented here is that human evolution has been continual in the past, it continues in the present, and it will continue in the future. The focus of this book, however, is with the changes that have taken place in the past. One of the principal objectives of this book, then, is to attempt to apply Darwinian principles to a field that has often honored his name while neglecting the use of his perspective.

The first concern, however, is to examine the sequence of discoveries and interpretations that led us to the position in which we now find ourselves. Interpretations of the major pieces of evidence are heavily conditioned by the attitudes prevalent at the time and place of their discovery. Traditions of interpretation, once established, tend to continue whether or not subsequent evidence provides justification. The story of how we became aware of the evidence for our predecessors, who made the discoveries, and what they thought it all meant is a fascinating one in itself. And in its telling, we can come to see how the various modern interpretations arose. This, then, is the purpose of Chapters 2 through 6.

CHAPTER ONE NOTES

[1]Andrew Dickson White's classic two-volume study, *A History of the Warfare of Science With Theology in Christendom* (1896), locates the well-known tension between religion and science in the systems of "theology" created by human beings for their own purposes. In his mind, the pursuit of knowledge only strengthened real religious feeling. The social and religious backgrounds of American scientists have been tabulated by Kenneth R. Hardy (1974).

[2]W. R. Overton, 1982.

[3]A. C. Hardy, 1975; R. D. Alexander, 1978. Opposition to the very idea of evolution is recorded in John C. Whitcomb and Henry M. Morris's *The Genesis Flood: The Biblical Record and Its Scientific Implications* (1961), and in *Evolution: The Challenge of the Fossil Record* (1985) by Duane T. Gish. Morris is director of the Institute for Creation Research in San Diego, and Gish is the associate director. The extent to which their views are an attempt to substitute Fundamentalist Christian dogma for testable science is clearly indicated by Dorothy Nelkin in *The Creation Controversy: Science or Scripture in the Schools* (1982), and in Laurie Godfrey (ed.), *Scientists Confront Creationism* (1983).

[4]The continuing strength of a pre-Darwinian and basically medieval mind-set in paleoanthropology was specifically noted before the third edition of this book was published (Brace, 1981a; 1988), but the Aristotelian stamp of the medieval scholastics still maintains its grip on most of those whose writings represent the outlook of professional students of human evolution—for example, Eldredge and Tattersall (1982); Groves (1989); and Stringer and Gamble (1993).

[5]For example, some of the most strict adherents to the Aristotelian outlook have refused to recognize ancestry as a legitimate concern of paleontological and evolutionary scholarship (Schaeffer et al., 1972; Eldredge and Cracraft, 1980). As one amused observer has remarked, "for them, `ancestor' is a `dirty word'" (Dawkins, 1986:283).

[6]Occam's style of thinking is well treated by E. A. Moody (1935). His opposition to the creation of unnecessary categories has been called "Occam's razor" (Wittgenstein, 1922:57), sometimes referred to as the "law of parsimony" (Singer 1950:421), and it led him into a conflict with the papacy and to expulsion from the Franciscan order in 1331. The problems that can arise from an overly zealous application of his minimalist logic have been treated in some very thoughtful discussions (Eco, 1983; Barth, 1986).

[7]Boule and Vallois, 1957.

[8]Groves, 1989; Rightmire, 1990.

[9]Howells, 1993; Stringer and Gamble, 1993.

[10]The variety of sophisticated techniques for establishing the antiquity of prehistoric strata has increased in numbers and sophistication over the twenty-five plus years since the first edition of

this book was written. Even the excellent work by Stuart Fleming, *Dating in Archaeology* (1977), is now far out of date. The general outlines of the geological time scale have been pretty well settled (Badash, 1989), and recently a roster of ingenious means of establishing the date of many key human fossils has greatly aided our ability to locate things in the past (Aitken et al., 1993).

[11]There are a considerable number of specialists who feel more comfortable with seeing the beginning of the Pleistocene located somewhere about a million-and-a-half years ago. Geoffrey Pope, speaking for this group, suggests a date of some 1.6 million years running to 12,000 years ago (Pope, 1989:52). More recent work synthesizing dates over the last 80 million years has presented evidence for establishing the beginning of the Pleistocene between 1.98 and 1.75 million years ago (Walter et al., 1991:148–49; Cande and Kent, 1992:13,933). That is the date used here.

[12]The first specimen to be discovered was called *Australopithecus africanus* by its describer, the late Professor Raymond A. Dart (1893–1988) (Dart, 1925), and that name has been used ever since for similar specimens.

[13]The name "Pithecanthropines" comes from the genus name given by the first discoverer, the Dutch physician Eugene Dubois, a century ago in Java (Dubois, 1894). Currently, most anthropologists do not accept such specimens as generically distinct from *Homo*, but, given the other disagreements surrounding the interpretation of such fossils, Pithecanthropines seems sufficiently neutral to be used as a general designation.

[14]The term "Stage" is used here in the sense of evolutionary grade where this entails the possession of a set of biological characteristics that indicate adaptation to a particular way of life or survival strategy. The late Sir Julian Huxley (1877–1975) introduced the term grade as "a secondary terminology aimed at delimiting steps of anagenetic advance" (1958:27), and it has been viewed with approval by Ernst Mayr for its recognition of an adaptive component in evolution (Mayr 1974:107). Huxley (1958) and Simpson (1961) used the concept of grade to refer to such major adaptive configurations as prosimians, monkeys, apes, and humans. The further division of humans into Australopithecines, Pithecanthropines, Neanderthals, and Moderns corresponds to what Huxley referred to as *subgrades* (Huxley 1958:38), and it is essentially this that is meant by the use of the term Stages in the present context. The most prolonged and consistent attempt to view human evolution in terms of "Stages" was made by the late Franz Weidenreich (1873–1948) (Weidenreich, 1928:59–61; 1936a:46;1939:85;1940:380;1947a:201). Recently, Krishtalka (1993:342) recommended dividing an "anagenetic" lineage into "either numbered stages or lineage segments," and, with Weidenreich's earlier example clearly in mind, this is what I have done here as in the previous editions of this book. Krishtalka's concern, however, was with an evolving lineage through time that showed successive change below the species level. In the picture of hominid evolution treated in this book, however, change goes beyond the specific to the generic level—not only *africanus* to *erectus* to *sapiens,* but *Australopithecus* to *Homo.* That is why I have given the segments of the lineage names rather than numbers.

chapter two

Fact and Fancy Before 1860

BEFORE THE NINETEENTH CENTURY

The earliest recognition of a fossil human was accorded a skull fragment discovered in the year 1700 at Cannstatt, near Stuttgart, in western Germany.[1] At this early date, however, there was not even the remotest suspicion that modern living forms, including human ones, might have evolved by natural means from earlier forms ultimately quite different in appearance. Nor was there any faint hint of the vistas of geological antiquity that research was to reveal in the subsequent century. The Cannstatt skull was accepted by some as evidence for human existence in ancient times, but its form was not different from that of modern human form, and "ancient times" were measured in terms of a total span since creation—thought to be somewhat less than 6,000 years.[2]

As late as the middle of the seventeenth century, the vision of such antiquity was considered somewhat daring, although it had received a certain amount of religious sanction in the work of the biblical scholar James Ussher, the Anglican Archbishop of Armagh in northern Ireland. Computing from the named generations recorded in the Bible, Ussher arrived at the conclusion that creation had occurred in the year 4004 B.C. To this, the Reverend Dr. John Lightfoot, vice-chancellor of Cambridge University, added the pronouncement that ". . . heaven and earth, centre and circumference, were created all together in the same instant, and clouds full of water. This work took place and man was created by the Trinity on October 23, 4004 B.C. at nine o'clock in the morning."[3]

By the end of the eighteenth century, 150 years later, appraisals of geological processes and the accumulating knowledge of the structure and strata of the earth led to the suspicion, on the part of some people, that the earth was really much older. Fossil remains of extinct and different animals had been discovered, and scholars were becoming aware that the world had been a very different place in ages gone by, and that great changes had occurred. A few people even noted that the shaped pieces of flint discovered in prehistoric strata might be human tools made before the discovery of metallurgy, and certainly historians and students of human institutions were aware that the human world had changed even in the recent past.[4]

Early in the nineteenth century, the French biologist Lamarck tried to promote a view that continuous and accumulating change was the normal condition. He really was a thoroughgoing evolutionist, but the mechanism that he proposed to account for organic change was invested with an element of unscientific mysticism and his position has subsequently been generally rejected.[5] The initial reason for this rejection was the fact that many people were emotionally unprepared to accept change as the normal expectation. The traditional view that the world was created fixed and changeless had both social and religious support, and a scheme proposing the normality of constant change was regarded as a threat to the established order. Yet change could be seen in the geological record of the remote past, and some sort of explanation was demanded.

CUVIER AND CATASTROPHISM

An acceptable solution was proposed by another French scholar, Georges Cuvier, who was a younger contemporary of Lamarck (see Figure 2–1). The English philosopher of science, William Whewell, coined the term "catastrophism" to describe Cuvier's scheme.[6] It claimed that the various geological layers had been deposited as the result of a series of cataclysms that had overwhelmed the planet periodically, extinguishing all previously living organisms. In the minds of many who accepted this scheme, the last of these cataclysms was equated with the biblical flood, which meant that human remains should not be discoverable in earlier layers.[7] Cuvier is credited with the statement: "Fossil man does not exist." Indeed, in the early nineteenth century there was very little known evidence to contradict such a position.[8]

Cuvier was somewhat vague concerning the origin of the new animals that appeared in the strata overlying the supposed evidence for his various supposed cataclysms. Such cataclysms need not have been worldwide, he

FIGURE 2–1. Georges Cuvier (1769–1832), zoologist, comparative anatomist, paleontologist, and unwitting influence on many of the subsequent attempts to interpret the human fossil record. (Brown Brothers.)

noted, since the detailed geological sequence in one part of the world tended to differ from the specifics of sequences in other parts of the world. Following the presumed cataclysm that eliminated the living forms in one given area, then, he suggested that the ones that had continued to live in places not so affected might just migrate into that now-empty region. Ultimately, however, in order to account for the disappearance of all former types of organisms and the continued emergence of the new and different, Cuvier's stance gave support to a philosophy of successive creations.[9] With the development of Darwinian evolutionary theory in the middle of the nineteenth century, the view of supernaturally caused extinctions, migrations, invasions, and successive creations was superseded as a general explanation. Yet, because of a variety of historical accidents, something of this has survived into the present in the traditions of paleontology—especially that part of paleontology particularly concerned with the matter of human origins: paleoanthropology.[10]

The discovery of the fossil and archaeological evidence for human evolution was the result of the fieldwork of people who had very little concern for the research that developed the evolutionary explanation for the origin of organic diversity and organic change, yet both realms of activity have parallel careers extending back into the eighteenth century. Archaeological and paleontological work could and did go on without much concern for theoretical implications. Even though Cuvier was specifically opposed to evolution, he can be regarded as the founder of paleontology, a discipline that, ironically, provides the most direct evidence in support of evolutionary theory.[11] His intellectual descendants (and other unrelated antiquarians and archaeologists) pursued their diggings right up into the twentieth century, often with quite incorrect assumptions concerning their interpretations. Today these figures are the principal sources of the other interpretations of the human fossil record that we will discuss in later chapters. Darwin, on the other hand, used relatively little paleontological evidence to support his major insights. This was partly because of the very incomplete nature of knowledge concerning the fossil record, and partly because his concern was focused on the attempt to explain diversity in the world of *living* organisms.

DARWIN AND *THE ORIGIN*

Although it has remained for the twentieth century to attempt a synthesis of the study of the present with the study of the past, scholars in both areas have been aware of the implications each has had for the other, and the public has been sensitive to this from the beginning. This still shows in the common misconception concerning the title of Darwin's most famous book, *On the Origin of Species*. From the time of its appearance in 1859 right up to the present, people who are not thoroughly familiar with the book have assumed that it suggests a common ancestry for apes and people, and that the "species" in the title refers to humanity itself. This latter assumption is so strong that the title is frequently misquoted, being rendered as *The Origin of* **"the"** *Species*. Actually, only one brief sentence at the very end makes any reference to humans at all, and this is thoroughly noncommittal.[12] Darwin's concern for human evolution was reserved for another book, *The Descent of Man*, published more than a decade after his *On the Origin of Species*. Even in his later book, however, his reference to the skimpy fossil and archaeological record of human prehistory is brief in the extreme.[13]

ARCHAEOLOGY

The trickle of accumulating evidence had been growing, however, with prehistoric skeletons and stone tools brought forth even during Cuvier's life-

FIGURE 2–2. Charles R. Darwin (1809–1882), author of *On the Origin of Species* and acknowledged father of evolutionary thinking. (National Portrait Gallery, London.)

time. During the 1820s, human skeletal material was discovered in association with extinct animals and ancient stone tools on the coast of Wales, in France, and in Belgium, but none of it attracted much attention. Late in the 1840s, Boucher de Perthes, a customs inspector at Abbeville in northwestern France, published the results of his prehistoric investigations over the previous 15 years at both Abbeville and St. Acheul. In the gravels of the Somme river terraces, Boucher de Perthes had discovered flints of such a regular shape that they could only be the products of human manufacture. Yet they obviously were deposited during the course of the formation of the terraces where they were found, which suggested an age for their makers far in excess of anything granted by even the most liberal supporters of human antiquity. Similar stone tools have since been discovered in prehistoric strata elsewhere in Europe, Africa, India, and Asia. Today the name Acheulean is used to refer to the type of artifact first recognized by Boucher de Perthes at St. Acheul.[14] (Figure 2–3 is an example of this type of artifact.)

FIGURE 2–3.
A biface from St. Acheul in northwestern France, the location that gave its name to a whole category of Middle Pleistocene tools. (Drawn by M. L. Brace from a specimen given to Charles L. Brace by Sir Charles Lyell.)

GIBRALTAR

Relegation to unimportant obscurity was very nearly the fate of the archaeological discoveries of Boucher de Perthes. Contemporary French scholars were so scornful of his claims that they never even bothered to visit his diggings or investigate his work firsthand, but simply remained in Paris and denounced him from a distance. Had it not been for the curiosity of a group of English scientists who visited his sites and confirmed his findings, these artifacts would have had as little influence on the study of human origins as had the Gibraltar skull found just a year later, in 1848, in a quarry on the north face of the Rock of Gibraltar (see Figure 2–4). The discovery of this skull, which we now recognize as a representative of the Neanderthal Stage of human evolution, was recorded by the Gibraltar Scientific Society. A slow 14 years later, after the skull had found its way to England, it was shown to, at best, mildly interested scholars at meetings of the British Association for the Advancement of Science, and at an anthropological congress.[15] Just 20 years after its discovery it was presented, pretty much as a curiosity piece, to the Museum of the Royal College of Surgeons in London where it remained, almost forgotten, until after the turn of the century.[16] Because its importance went unappreciated for more than half a century following its exhumation, it played no part in the development of the study of human evolution, which is rather a pity since it differs markedly from the stereotype of the heavily buttressed, muscle-marked, and robust image that is conjured up in so many minds when the name Neanderthal is invoked. The Gibraltar skull, as it happens, is that of a female in a stage where male-female differences are more marked than is now usually true.

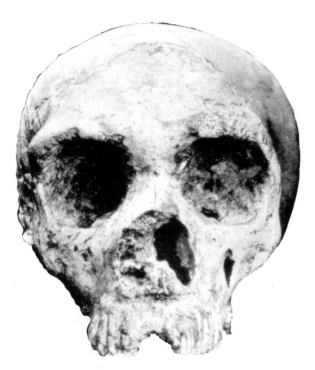

FIGURE 2–4.   The Gibraltar discovery—a skull of European Neanderthal form.

NEANDERTHAL

By a remarkable set of historical coincidences, the late 1850s saw the discovery of the skeletal remains of what could be identified as an earlier stage in human evolution, the recognition of the archaeological evidence for human antiquity, and the development of an intellectual framework within which these new facts could be encompassed. The specific timing of these events was a little less fortunate, because the discovery of the skeletal remains occurred first, and they were the subject of skeptical comments that have influenced interpretations ever since. The skeleton was discovered in 1856 during quarry operations in a limestone gorge through which flows the Düssel, a tributary of the lower Rhine. The gorge lies in the area between Elberfeld and Düsseldorf and bears the name of Neanderthal. By giving its name to the skeleton discovered there, it has provided a designation for the entire Stage of evolutionary development immediately prior to the emergence of Modern human form.

The skeleton had evidently been a burial in a small cave in the limestone cliffs, and had probably been complete. In the course of being recovered, however, it was somewhat battered. The skeleton, along with the dirt in which it lay, was unceremoniously shoveled out over the terrace and down to the valley floor sixty feet below by marble quarry workers who were cleaning out the cave to get at the rock. Its human nature was only recognized later by Dr. Johann Karl Fuhlrott (1803–1893), a natural science teacher at the high school in Elberfeld, who assured its preservation. Fuhlrott, with the aid of Hermann Schaaffhausen (1816–1893), a professor of anatomy at Bonn, promoted the view that this was an early human form, but this interpretation received no support until very nearly the end of the nineteenth century.[17] Possibly because of the mode of excavation, the face was not recovered. The head was represented by the skullcap, from the ridges over the eye sockets and extending to the back of the skull but minus the base. The limb bones were extraordinarily robust and the brow ridges of the skull enormous, but, lacking the face, jaws, and teeth, the evidence for clear difference from modern form was subject to debate.

And debate there was. Enough peculiarities were present to suggest all sorts of explanations, from derogatory hints that the specimen was an "old Dutchman" (Holländer), an ancient Celt of "low type" similar to the modern Irish, to suggestions that it was an idiot, a freak, the victim of rickets, or the residue of the Mongolian Cossacks who had chased Napoleon back from Russia in 1814.[18] The most authoritative opinion was delivered by one of Germany's leading scientists, Rudolf Virchow, a founder of German anthropology and, as the originator of the field of cellular pathology, the most outstanding pathologist of the day.[19] After careful examination, Virchow pronounced the skull "pathological" and sought to explain all of its peculiarities in that fashion. The weight of his judgment has been such that Neanderthal morphology has been regarded as "aberrant" from that day to this, and a majority of authorities even today refuse to accept Neanderthals as representative of the ancestors of modern human beings. In contrast to all of this, the argument will be developed in a later chapter of this book that Neanderthal form represents just what we would expect to find prior to Modern emergence, and that European Neanderthals are the most logical representatives of the ancestors of Modern Europeans.

In 1858, the year following the first discussion of the Neanderthal discovery, a delegation from the Royal Society of Great Britain visited the excavations of Boucher de Perthes in northern France. They returned and, convinced of the significance of his work, reported their findings to the British scientific world. Then, in 1859, Darwin's book *On the Origin of Species* appeared. From then on, human attitudes toward the world of nature and their own position within it were permanently altered. No longer could people regard themselves as the epitome of existence in a world created solely for their own benefit. Of course, many people could not accept the implications of this presentation. However, over time acceptance has become nearly universal, and it is apparent that the consequent enforced humility has done people no harm. The upshot of the entire matter is that no area of human behavior and philosophy has escaped the impact of the consequent revolution in attitudes.[20]

CHAPTER TWO NOTES

[1]Schwalbe, 1906:192.

[2]Its contemporaneity with extinct animals was taken for granted, for example see Quatrefages and Hamy (1882:6) and Schwalbe (Das Schädelfragment von Cannstatt, in Schwalbe, 1906:185–228), but it may well have been a recent human from the Middle Ages or Roman times (Gieseler, 1953:80).

[3]White, 1896(I):9.

[4]John Frere, an eighteenth century "country gentleman" in East Anglia, sent an assortment of flint tools to the Secretary of the Society of Antiquaries in London in 1797 described as "weapons of war fabricated and used by a people who had not the use of metals." These had been found in undisturbed deposits twelve feet beneath the surface, and Frere correctly identified them as prehistoric implements (Grayson, 1983:55–57; Daniel, 1986:1015).

[5]The most recent biographical treatment of Lamarck has been by Burkhardt (1977) and by Barthélemy-Madaule (1982). The assessment of his contributions from the perspective of modern evolutionary biology is recorded in Mayr (1982:359).

[6]Whewell, 1832:126.

[7]The biblical imagery was read into Cuvier's formulations mainly by English geologists who were far more concerned with reconciling apparent discrepancies between the scriptural accounts and the observable world. This was a kind of Protestant compulsion that was largely absent in the Catholic world. Although Cuvier was actually a Protestant himself, he functioned within a largely Catholic society and clearly was less driven to produce the kinds of rationalization that motivated his English readers (Rudwick, 1972:134; Grayson, 1983:59; Hallam, 1983:41). Although French paleontology and paleoanthropology have tended to simply accept the incomplete fossil record as evidence for categorical change, the more extreme exemplars of catastrophism were always their followers in the English-speaking world. This remains particularly evident in the field of "modern" paleoanthropology (e.g., Stringer and Gamble, 1993).

[8]Again, posterity has the pragmatic Cuvier declaiming in more dogmatic fashion than was his custom in print. He may very well have said "L'homme fossile n'existe pas" as has been claimed (de Mortillet, 1883:10), but if he did so it was off the cuff. Actually, Cuvier's only published words on the subject appear as a marginal note to his *Research on Fossil Bones*, where he commented laconically, "Il n'y a point d'os humains fossiles"—'There are no fossil human bones" (1826:65). This was literally true when he wrote those words. In the text beside which this note appears he wrote, "on n'a pas encore trouvé d'os humains parmi les fossiles," which means, "human bones have not yet been found among fossils."

[9]By 1849, Cuvier's protégé Alcide d'Orbigny (1802–1857) had identified 27 faunal and geological periods requiring an equal number of catastrophes and creations (Coleman, 1964:185).

[10]Brace, 1962b; 1964; 1981a.

[11]Simpson, 1961:43; Coleman, 1964:2, 114.

[12]Darwin wrote, "Light will be thrown on the origin of man and his history" (Darwin, 1859:488). In subsequent editions, this was modified to read "Much light will be thrown . . . ."

[13]Darwin, 1871.

[14]Boucher de Perthes's work provided the impetus for a reassessment of human antiquity based on archaeological evidence, and this was personally checked by Sir Charles Lyell. The story is well told in Lyell's *Antiquity of Man* (1863). The import of those archaeological discoveries was phrased by Boule and Vallois in words that are as true today as when they were first written: "In spite of all their imperfection, these rude stones prove the existence of Man as surely as a whole Louvre would have done" (Boule and Vallois, 1957:14).

[15]Only minor public notice was taken of the find in England (Busk, 1864, 1865).

[16]The first real recognition of the importance of Gibraltar was by the Strassburg anatomist, Gustav Schwalbe (Schwalbe, 1906:154ff.). With this as a stimulus, the Oxford geologist, William J. Sollas, finally gave Gibraltar the full comparative treatment that it deserved (Sollas, 1908:321ff.).

[17]Fuhlrott, 1857; Schaaffhausen, 1858; Cunningham, 1895; von Eickstedt, 1937:128; Potonie, 1958:277; Bürger, 1956.

[18]Pruner-Bey, 1863, 1864a, b; Dawson, 1863; Mayer, 1864; Wagner, 1864; Virchow, 1872.

[19]Ackerknecht, 1953.

[20]The latest effort at recounting the discovery and interpretations of the Neanderthal remains is by Erik Trinkaus and Pat Shipman, *The Neandertals* (1992). As one might guess from their insistence on what could be called "orthographic correctness" in using a modernized spelling of Neanderthal, they are not fully successful in seeing things from the perspective of the times about which they write. Although they make some major historiographic gaffes, they have tried to do their homework, and, even though they sometimes get overwhelmed by their subject, they tell a fascinating story.

chapter three

The Picture Up to 1906

CRO-MAGNON

The vindication of Boucher de Perthes and the intellectual revolution going on in Britain was a great stimulus to prehistoric research. During the late 1850s and 1860s, basic work on discovering the characteristics of human cultures prior to the discovery and use of metal was undertaken. In France, particularly in the Dordogne region and the Vézère River valley of the Southwest, excavations at La Madeleine, Solutré, Aurignac, and Le Moustier uncovered the evidence for prehistoric stone tool-making traditions. These were named Magdalenian, Solutrean, Aurignacian, and Mousterian, and are now known to be roughly 15, 20, 30, and 40 and more thousand years old, respectively.[1] It was suspected that they dated from a period more recent than those discovered by Boucher de Perthes, but no one then imagined that the difference was actually more than 100,000 years. Then, most exciting of all, in 1868, human skeletal remains were discovered in the same stratigraphic level with tools of Aurignacian type.[2] To the interest as well as the relief of the public, these remains indicated that the individuals in question were not markedly different from Modern human form. In fact, their appearance has been portrayed in an idealized manner and with a glowing enthusiasm not entirely warranted by their somewhat fragmentary condition.

The human skeletal remains that we have been discussing, representing some five individuals, were discovered in the years following the construction of the railroad through Les Eyzies, in the aforementioned Dordogne region of southwestern France. The removal of fill for use in local road construction revealed a long-hidden rock shelter, near an eminence called Cro-Magnon, within which the skeletons and artifacts were found (Figure 3–1). Competent geologists were on hand to verify the antiquity and the stratigraphic associations, and the study of human fossils was finally given its first solidly documented specimens.[3] Stature of the male skeleton is regularly reported as being close to six feet, which is tall in comparison to present or previous worldwide general averages.[4] Calculations based on actual measurements of the preserved long bones yield figures of 5 feet, $8\frac{1}{2}$ inches for males and an

FIGURE 3–1.   The male Cro-Magnon, from Les Eyzies, Dordogne, France. (Courtesy of the Musée de l'Homme, Paris.)

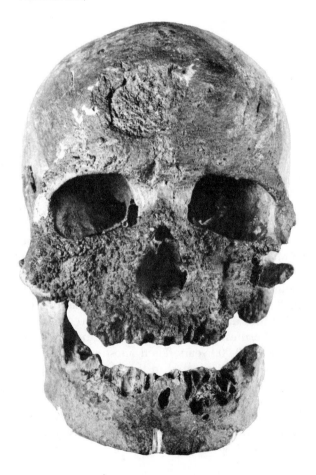

inch shorter for females, although the rugged long bones suggested a robust and muscular people.[5] The face was vertical rather than projecting, and possessed a prominent chin, although these features have been stressed to a greater extent than the evidence warrants, considering that the large male cranium was toothless at discovery.

Still, the Cro-Magnon finds were recognizably of Modern form and provide the basis for the still valid assertion that the Upper Paleolithic tool-making traditions—Aurignacian, Solutrean, Magdalenian, and others— were the products of people not unlike more recent Europeans and their descendants. Associated artwork in the form of carvings and engravings on bone and ivory revealed a degree of sophistication in these Upper Pleistocene hunters, which was quite gratifying from the point of view of those who were beginning to accept these Upper Paleolithic people as ancestral to more recent humanity. The following decades witnessed the discovery of much additional support for the picture outlined in the discoveries at Cro-Magnon, and it was some time before the unearthing of more ancient remains again forced people to face the issues of human evolution: the possibility that humans had arisen from something quite different from their present form.

SPY

Exactly thirty years after the original discovery in the Neanderthal, and long enough later for the controversy to have died down, two human skeletons were found buried in a Mousterian level in a cave in the commune of Spy (pronounced Spee) in the Province of Namur, Belgium.[6] The form of both skeletons was recognizably similar to that of the original Neanderthal; the skull Spy I, in fact, was of practically identical shape. No longer was it possible to expound with such certainty the supposed pathological features of the individual from the Neanderthal. However, the adamant Virchow refused to back down and, although the Spy discoveries confirmed the Neanderthaler as a valid human type, the implications of abnormality and peculiarity tended to remain. Indeed, to this day they have not been fully shaken off. Nevertheless, the Neanderthals could now be regarded as a "type" associated with a definite tool-making tradition, and given a definite age.

EUGENE DUBOIS AND *"PITHECANTHROPUS"*

The scene was shortly to shift to another part of the world and involve another, possibly even more dramatic, form of human fossil. The German naturalist Ernst Haeckel, greatly excited by the implications of Charles Darwin's work, was communicating his enthusiasm for the evolutionary viewpoint to a rising generation of students on the German academic scene. Pushing evolutionary logic to its conclusion, Haeckel drew a hypothetical family tree linking modern humans to a common ancestry with the living apes and monkeys. He further suggested that somewhere in between the two, back in the remote past, there must have been a form which was neither one nor the other—a completely transitional stage. This, he suggested, should be referred to as *"Pithecanthropus alalus,"* that is, ape-man without speech.[7] The popular press, borrowing a label from an earlier intellectual controversy, quickly christened it the "missing link," a term which remains a firm item of popular folklore.[8]

Whereas Darwin had suggested that Africa was the most likely place to search for the earliest human ancestor, believing that the gorilla and the chimpanzee were our closest living relatives, Haeckel and others in Germany stressed Southeast Asia, since they claimed that the detailed morphology of the gibbon's skull was more akin to the human than was that of the African anthropoid apes. Today it appears that Darwin's suspicions were much sounder, although the discoveries of the 1890s made Haeckel's guess seem little short of inspired.

Fascinated by Haeckel's hypothetical portrayal of human ancestry, a young Dutch doctor, Eugene Dubois, went to Southeast Asia with the avowed intention of finding the "missing link." At the time, this seemed like a ridiculous thing to do. Not only did Dubois have to give up a promising career as a teacher of anatomy at Amsterdam, but also there was virtually no shred of evidence in support of his scheme. Nevertheless, fortune smiled on Dubois and he did indeed find what he was looking for. The improbability of his venture can be compared to the only other instance in which theoretical expectations launched an expedition to demonstrate the locale of human origins, claimed by one eminent scholar to be somewhere in eastern Asia, the result of which was the discovery of dinosaur eggs in the Mongolian desert![9]

Plagued by a lack of funds—his project sounded so absurd that no one was willing to back him—Dubois signed on as a health officer in the Dutch colonial forces in Indonesia, which was then referred to as "the Dutch East Indies." He was first assigned to Sumatra, where he spent several years hunting fossils. A variety of circumstances led him to suspect that Java was a more likely area, and in 1889 he managed to transfer there. He remained in Java for the next five years, making the discoveries for which he will always be remembered. In 1890, he discovered a small fragment of a lower jaw whose importance was only recognized later. In 1891, his excavations unearthed a skullcap with such a low forehead and heavy brow ridge, and with such marked constriction between the brow and the brain case, that he attributed it to a chimpanzee. In 1892, some 50 feet away, he found a femur (thighbone) that was practically indistinguishable from the femur of a modern human being. This, Dubois claimed, belonged to the individual represented by the skull, and for a while he believed that he had discovered an ancient erect walking chimpanzee. His comparative studies and measurements forced him to alter his opinion because the skull, however primitive or apelike it appeared to be, was half way between that of a human and that of a chimpanzee in gross size. It possessed a brain that fell within the lower limits of the normal modern range of variation. This he realized was indeed his "missing link," but, in contrast to the semi-erect posture which had been attributed to the Spy and Neanderthal finds, it was an erect walking "missing link." So Dubois slightly modified Haeckel's designation and, in his monograph of 1894, christened his discovery *"Pithecanthropus" erectus*.[10] This still serves as the type specimen for our Pithecanthropine Stage, although it is no longer regarded as a valid separate genus.

Dubois's admirable monograph created an international sensation, and when he returned to Europe in 1895, he was an immediate celebrity. At the International Zoological Congress meeting at Leyden in 1895, Dubois and his *"Pithecanthropus"* were the focus of attention of an unparalleled gathering of famous scholars. After prolonged argument, three schools of thought emerged. One, siding with Dubois, felt that *"Pithecanthropus"* was neither an ape nor a human but a genuine transitional form. Another felt that it was on the human side of the boundary—primitive, perhaps, but hominid nevertheless. The third group, headed by the aged Virchow, regarded it as being a giant form of gibbon, interesting and unusual, but only an ape after all.[11]

The controversy continued unresolved for many years, and it was not until the late 1920s and 1930s, when more Pithecanthropine skeletal remains were discovered in China near Beijing and also in Java, that general acceptance was possible. The Chinese Pithecanthropines, originally christened *"Sinanthropus pekinensis"* in 1927, were associated with stone tools and charcoal deposits once thought to be the remains of hearths, and this was accepted as evidence confirming the human status of the Pithecanthropines as a whole. Paradoxically, among the very few voices now raised in opposition to the human status of *"Pithecanthropus"* was none other than that of the elderly Dubois himself. Although he was willing to accept the newer discoveries in Java and China as genuine early human beings, he reverted to the opinion expressed by Virchow in 1895 that his own original discovery had been just a giant gibbon.[12]

GUSTAV SCHWALBE

While full confirmation for the significance of *"Pithecanthropus"* had to wait some 30 years after the original announcement, most scholars at and following the turn of the century came to feel that it could be regarded as an extremely primitive form of humanity. What with Pithecanthropines, Neanderthals, and Moderns established at different times, and at least the latter two associated with different archaeological traditions, it was possible during the first years of the twentieth century to suggest a logical evolutionary scheme containing all the known human fossils arranged in terms of relationships and chronology. This was done by Gustav Schwalbe (Figure 3–2), professor of anatomy at the University of Strassburg, who capped a series of papers and monographs in the late nineteenth and early twentieth centuries with his summary work, *Studies on the Prehistory of Man*, published in 1906. Schwalbe tentatively proposed a picture of human evolutionary history comprising three successive stages— "Pithecanthropus," Neanderthal, and Modern; he also allowed for the possibility of adjustments and modifications that future finds would make inevitable.[13]

Schwalbe's scheme was useful, flexible, and in accord with the evidence available at that time. With one major addition, it has proven to be valuable enough to provide the organizing principle behind the interpretations offered in the later chapters of this book. For reasons we consider in the pages that follow, however, it has been generally rejected and forgotten by the anthropological world.[14]

FIGURE 3–2. Gustav Schwalbe (1844–1916), Strassburg anatomist and physical anthropologist, who first arranged the known human fossils in an evolutionary sequence. (Courtesy Ashley Montagu.)

CHAPTER THREE NOTES

[1]L. G. Straus, 1985; P. Mellars, 1986; S. A. de Beaune, and R. White, 1993; P. A. Mellars et al., 1993; R. White, 1993.

[2]Broca, 1868; Lartet, 1868.

[3]Bouchud, 1965.

[4]Quennell and Quennell, 1922:126; Stringer and Gamble, 1993:183.

[5]Brennan, 1991:140.

[6]de Puydt and Lohest, 1886; Fraipont and Lohest, 1886.

[7]Haeckel, 1870:590, 597.

[8]A century earlier, many scholars assumed that the living creatures of the world were arranged in a "Great Chain of Being," ranging downward in perfection from God at the top to the inorganic at the bottom. There were two versions of this world view: one in which the chain was composed of discrete steps, and another in which one rank graded into another without break. The term "missing link" was coined in the service of this controversy, and, later, the American showman and "eminent practical psychologist" Phineas T. Barnum (1810–1891) gave the public many "missing links" for an admission fee (Lovejoy, 1936:236).

[9]Roy Chapman Andrews (1926) tells the story of how dinosaur eggs were found in the Gobi Desert. Dubois's biography is recounted in Theunissen (1989).

[10]Dubois, 1894.

[11]Dubois, 1895, 1896; Keith, 1895; Virchow, 1895.

[12]Black, 1927; Boule, 1929, 1937; Pei, 1930, 1931; Hrdlička, 1930; Teilhard and Pei, 1932; Dubois, 1935.

[13]Schwalbe, 1906.

[14]Schwalbe's own student and, briefly, successor at Strassburg, Franz Weidenreich (1873–1948), followed his teacher's lead as is discussed in Chapter 12 and subsequently. The American anthropologist Carleton Coon (1904–1981) claimed to have adopted Weidenreich's scheme (Coon, 1962), although it has been shown that he "seriously misrepresented" Weidenreich's actual position (Brace, 1981a:423). Neither Schwalbe nor Weidenreich attempted to use the perspective of evolutionary biology in formulating their stages, but it is perfectly possible to do so, and that is what I have tried to do in all of the editions of this book.

chapter four

Hominid Catastrophism

HEIDELBERG

In 1907, the year following Schwalbe's summary, a brief wave of excitement surrounded the discovery of an enormous hominid mandible in a gravel pit near the village of Mauer, not far from the city of Heidelberg in western Germany. Without the rest of the skull, interpretations were somewhat inhibited, although the primitive characteristics were obvious. Still, the stratigraphy was precisely documented, and it was associated with the earliest of the tool types found by Boucher de Perthes. All of this indicated that the Heidelberg jaw was, as it remains today, among the oldest of the human fossils discovered in western Europe (see Figure 4–1). It was a probable representative of the Pithecanthropines. Certainly it was a contemporary of those Far Eastern specimens that have given us our most detailed knowledge of the appearance of the Pithecanthropine stage of human evolution.[1]

LE MOUSTIER

In 1908, however, the scene of discovery shifted, and the tide of historical accident began that is so largely responsible for the present interpretations of

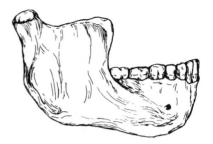

FIGURE 4–1.
The Heidelberg jaw. Until the rash of discoveries of the last few years, this had been the only Pithecanthropine known in Europe. (Drawn from a cast by M. L. Brace.)

human evolution in general and of the Neanderthals in particular. At Le Moustier in southwestern France—the same village that gave its name to the tool-making tradition associated with the Neanderthals—a genuine Neanderthal burial was discovered.[2] For a variety of reasons (initially related to the somewhat dubious activities of the discoverer, a Swiss dealer in antiquities who had been looting French archaeological sites and selling the booty to the highest bidder), the description was delayed for many years, and, as a result, the Le Moustier skeleton never received the attention it deserved.[3]

LA CHAPELLE-AUX-SAINTS, MARCELLIN BOULE, AND THE NEANDERTHAL CARICATURE

Later in the same year and not far from the same region in southwestern France, another and more complete Neanderthal skeleton was discovered in excavations near the village of La Chapelle-aux-Saints.[4] These remains were entrusted to Marcellin Boule, the renowned paleontologist at the National Museum of Natural History in Paris. During the next five years he produced a series of scholarly papers, climaxed by a massive monograph in three installments, appearing in 1911, 1912, and 1913.[5] Boule's portrayal of this, the most complete Neanderthal skeleton yet to have been discovered, formed the basis for the caricature of the cave man espoused by subsequent generations of cartoonists, journalists, and, alas, professional scholars.[6] The "Old Man" of La Chapelle-aux-Saints was depicted as being a creature structurally intermediate between modern humans and the anthropoid apes (see Figure 4–2).

The great toe was presumed to diverge, hinting that it still preserved a degree of opposability to the other toes, and, in so doing, it presumably forced the possessor to walk on the outer margins of the feet in the awkward manner of the modern orang. Details of the knee joint were taken to indicate that the leg could not be entirely extended, meaning that the Neanderthals were not completely erect and could do no better than to shuffle along with a "bent-knee gait." This also was supposed to indicate their similarity to modern apes, although since apes are perfectly capable of fully extending their legs, such

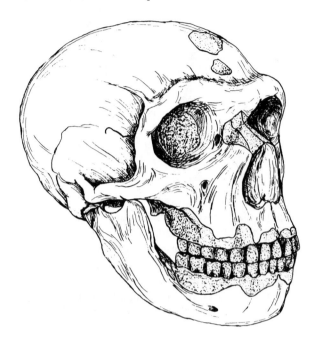

FIGURE 4–2.   The "Old Man" from La Chapelle-aux-Saints, Corrèze, southwestern France. An extreme example of the "classic" European Neanderthals. (Drawn by M. L. Brace from a cast and restoration.)

claims demonstrate an ignorance of the anatomy and functioning of the knee joint in apes as well as humans. Boule's reply to the critics who raised these points was that they were mere anatomists whose familiarity was only with living forms. For this reason, he suggested that they were not competent to assess form and function of skeletal remains from the remote past that his own experience as a paleontologist gave him the qualifications to judge.[7] The same issues had been raised concerning the Spy skeletons, and several detailed studies before the end of the nineteenth century demonstrated that they deserved serious consideration, but Boule chose to ignore these.[8]

In harmony with the semi-erect picture conjured up by his discussion of the feet and legs, Boule claimed that the reverse curves present in the human neck and lower back were absent, as in the modern apes, and that the whole trunk indicated a powerful but incompletely upright postural adaptation. On top of this scarcely human caricature was a head that hung forward instead of being balanced on top of the spinal column. A detailed study was made of the cast of the interior of the braincase, and this convinced Boule that the brain was inferior in organization to that of the modern human brain, particularly in the frontal lobes, which, since the days when phrenology had been respectable, everyone "knew" to be related to the higher functionings of the mind.[9]

The significance of continued and repeated use of words such as "ape-like," "primitive," and "inferior" was not lost on a fascinated public, which quickly invested the Neanderthals with a veritable hairy pelt and long simian arms, although there is no evidence concerning hair and the arms were actually relatively short. In the years since that time, it has been demonstrated that Boule was in error on each one of the foregoing points,[10] but the vision of the totality has not been altered, and the Neanderthals continue to shuffle through the pages of numberless books, slouch stupidly in countless cartoons, and get relegated to sterile oblivion in the majority of treatises on human evolution.[11]

Having produced this caricature, Boule then proclaimed that it could have nothing to do with the ancestors of modern *Homo sapiens*. As justification, he claimed that the Neanderthals and their culture came to an abrupt end and were suddenly replaced by full *Homo sapiens* who swept into Europe with their superior Upper Paleolithic technology. Furthermore, said he, people of modern form already existed during the time when the Neanderthals were the main occupants of the European scene. This latter claim has provided one of the main stimuli for subsequent activities in human paleontology because, within a year, the representative Boule cited to prove the existence for this ancient modern was disqualified.[12] From that time on, more than three subsequent generations of anthropologists have been searching for the as-yet-undiscovered *sapiens* of "modern" form in the Middle Pleistocene or even earlier.

One of the problems that has plagued this search is that many of the anthropologists who are well-versed in the study of human fossils have only the vaguest acquaintance with the nature of variation in living human populations. Another problem is the assumption that "modern" form emerged as a unit at one time and in one place for reasons that are never specified. As we shall see later on, the one thing that unites Modern humans is the possession of equivalent intellectual capabilities symbolized by a brain that is the same size relative to bodily bulk from one part of the world to another. In all other features, the various living populations of Modern *Homo sapiens* display varying degrees of reduction from their Middle Pleistocene ancestors. The reasons for those differences in reduction can be directly traced to the different lengths of time that specific aspects of selective force relaxation have been in effect in the various continuously inhabited portions of the world. This is treated in Chapters 13 and 14.

THE PILTDOWN FRAUD

Within the same year that the final installment of Boule's ponderous work appeared, an ingenious Englishman fabricated the famous Piltdown fraud, which confused the picture for a full forty years before being exposed.[13] Pilt-down turned out to be the fragments of a modern human cranium and part of the jaw of a modern female orang, stained to look ancient, appropriately broken and artificially worn, and mingled with a doctored collection of arti-facts and extinct animal bones acquired from all over the world before being scattered in a gravel pocket in southeastern England.

Also in the same year, Gustav Schwalbe published a review of Boule's monograph which, at 80 pages, was nearly a book in itself.[14] In this he yielded to the picture painted by Boule and abandoned his own former claims that the Neanderthals were the direct ancestors of modern human beings, even though he noted the errors in Boule's treatment of Neanderthal anatomy and the fact that the evidence did not support Boule's claim for the existence of ancient moderns. Schwalbe never abandoned Dubois's Java discovery, which he continued to regard as ancestral to all later human forms. Boule had indicated that he considered *both* the Pithecanthropine and Neanderthal groups to be branches off to the side of the mainstream of human evolu-tion—branches that became extinct without issue. It is an interesting com-mentary on the durability of intellectual traditions that, despite the continuing lack of evidence to support it, the interpretation proposed by Boule remains the majority view right up to the present day among profes-sional paleoanthropologists.

THE IMPACT OF WORLD WAR I

In 1914, the year after Boule's final publication on La Chapelle-aux-Saints, World War I burst upon Europe. Dislocation of human affairs and cessation of scholarly activity are inevitable companions of war, but in the field that pursues the study of human evolution, the legacy of this conflict has been more enduring if less clearly appreciated. Germany not only lost the war, but suffered a blow to its intellectual prestige that has had repercussions ever since. In the postwar era, Germany's intellectual recovery was progressively stifled by the rise of the Hitler regime, which, when it came to power, quickly extinguished what had managed to survive. This was particularly true for any scientific endeavors that attempted to make an objective and unbiased study of human beings. Anthropology and the other social sciences suffered se-verely. They have seen few contributions made and have played but a minor role in the subsequent general advances made in other countries. Little re-mains of the pre-World War I tradition in German anthropology and, while I can hear my colleagues muttering that this is really a good thing, the valuable parts have been eliminated along with the bad ones. It is to be regretted, for instance, that so little is remembered of the pre-Boule writings of Gustav Schwalbe.[15]

FIGURE 4–3. Aleš Hrdlička (1869–1943). Born in Czechoslovakia, raised in the United States, he was the first physical anthropologist at the Smithsonian Institution and one of the most distinguished representatives of the field in America. Hrdlička was one of the very few scholars who continued to view the Neanderthals as a Stage in human evolution. See his *The Skeletal Remains of Early Man,* 1930. (Courtesy of the Smithsonian Institution.)

HOMINID CATASTROPHISM

Before proceeding, it is of more than idle concern to note the source of Boule's orientation. Boule was a paleontologist, trained during the 1880s in an academic environment that had not accepted the Darwinian view of evolution. Although French paleontologists spoke of "evolution," they carefully distinguished it from "Darwinism." To them, evolution signified the appearance of successive organic forms, whereas Darwinism meant the development of later forms out of earlier ones by natural processes, and this they refused to accept.[16] When questioned concerning the source of the successive forms, they would evoke extinctions followed by invasions from elsewhere, and, ultimately, successive creations. This, then, was simply the survival of Cuvier's "catastrophism" relabeled "evolution," and this was what Marcellin Boule applied to the human fossil record. As he noted, Modern-looking humans appeared more recently than Neanderthals, so, following the tradition in which he was trained, he postulated Neanderthal extinction and subsequent Modern invasion. This, of course, presupposed the existence of Modern forms elsewhere, about which he, like Cuvier a century before, was relatively vague. This presupposition has caused his followers a considerable degree of mental anguish ever since, although it has been one of the main stimuli for continued efforts at research and discovery in paleoanthropology.

This view can be labeled hominid "catastrophism," and, because of the historical accidents of the second decade of the present century, it has continued to dominate interpretations of human evolution, although the recognition of its intellectual roots and original justification has been largely forgotten.[17] Following World War I, Boule treated the totality of the known human fossil record, presenting his scheme of hominid catastrophism—labeled "evolution"—in a single volume, *Fossil Men* (1921). This book continued to influence the field long after his death in 1942. It was revised by his student and follower, H. V. Vallois, after World War II and enjoyed considerable popularity in its English translation.[18] And recently the intellectual assumptions of pre-Darwinian paleontology and biology have gained a wide following in the guises of "cladistics" and "punctuated equilibria." This represents a resurgence of a medieval intellectual stance, and it has been referred to as "the great leap backwards."[19] We treat these matters later in Chapter 7, "Evolutionary Principles."

CHAPTER FOUR NOTES

[1]Schoetensack, 1908; Rust, 1956. The Heidelberg mandible has had a long and curious history, as might be expected of any interesting object that has been claimed as a souvenir by members of various contending armies (Wüst, 1951). Perhaps even more curious, however, is the reaction of various contending anthropological theoreticians. Somehow the idea got circulated that its teeth were within the expected range of variation of modern human teeth (Day, 1977:57), although, since Schoetensack published their dimensions, it is easy to see that they exceed the mean figures of even the largest-toothed living Australians. Not to be outdone in creative thinking, another recent anthropologist has attributed duplicates of the headless Heidelberg mandible to ancient jawless crania in southern France, Greece, and Africa, and has gone on to attribute their cranial characteristics to the missing Heidelberg head. The resulting construct, he suggests, warrants recognition as *Homo "heidelbergensis,"* which is somehow more real than the Pithecanthropine category that comfortably includes them (Rightmire, 1990:229).

[2]Hauser, 1909; Klaatsch and Hauser, 1909.

[3]Boule, 1915a; Weinert, 1925. Like the Heidelberg mandible, Le Moustier did not survive the consequences of war unscathed, although, even before that happened, its curious history of sales and multiple reconstructions had inflicted a substantial amount of damage (Hesse, 1966).

[4]Bouyssonie et al., 1908.

[5]Boule, 1913.

[6]The most recent and undiluted manifestation of this tradition is in Stringer and Gamble, 1993.

[7]Boule, 1915b.

[8]Manouvrier, 1893.

[9]Boule and Anthony, 1911.

[10]The studies demonstrating Boule's mistakes and misinterpretations are surveyed in Brace (1964).

[11]Keith, 1915; Boule, 1921; Quennell and Quennell, 1922; Hooton, 1946; Boule and Vallois, 1957; Howells, 1959, 1993; Eldredge and Tattersall, 1982; Mellars and Stringer (eds.), 1989; Diamond, 1992; Stringer and Gamble, 1993.

[12]Boule's examples of the contemporary of Neanderthals were the two skeletons found at one of the Grimaldi Caves, the Grotte des Enfants, on the border between France and Italy in 1901 (Boule, 1913:243). He actually knew that the archaeological evidence showed that they were burials from an overlying Aurignacian layer (1913:213–14), but he chose to ignore the stratigraphy (1913:229). In Schwalbe's long and admiring review, this, along with the anatomical errors Boule made in assessing the Neanderthal ankle and foot, was one of the few points of criticism indicated (Schwalbe, 1913:585, 599).

[13]The "discovery" was announced in 1912, but, even though there were some grumblings, no one really thought that it had been a deliberate fraud until physical and chemical tests in the early 1950s showed that the skull and jaw fragments were actually modern (Weiner et al., 1953). The full story of the exposure is delightfully told in Weiner (1955), but the identity and motives of the forger(s) were not identified. Obviously Charles Dawson (1864–1916), a local legal figure and amateur archaeologist in southern England, was involved somehow, but most commentators have felt that he could not have gotten the specimens with which the site was "salted" without the help and collusion of some highly placed people. Suspicion has been directed towards all kinds of people—the French Jesuit paleontologist/archaeologist, Teilhard de Chardin (Gould, 1979); Sir Arthur Keith (Spencer, 1990); and even Sherlock Holmes himself (Sackett, 1981)—but, in spite of the fun people have had with the case, none of these accusations have stood up under critical scrutiny (Thomson, 1991). The mammalian fossils found at Piltdown were remarkably similar in specific identity and in their trace element contents to fossils found during British Museum expeditions to several locales outside of England, so there are good reasons to suspect that paleontologists at the British Museum were somehow involved.

[14]Schwalbe, 1913.

[15]Sir Arthur Keith's view of the course of human evolution was almost exactly the same as that of Schwalbe prior to World War I, as can be seen in the little book he published in 1911, *Ancient Types of Man.* In that year, however, the first installment of Boule's monograph on La Chapelle-aux-Saints appeared in print, and it stimulated Keith to visit the famous archaeological sites in southern France. Years later he wrote of his conversion experience (Keith, 1946:141; 1950:319). By the time he produced his most influential book in 1915, his approach was exactly the same as that of Marcellin Boule, a switch that has been regarded as "puzzling" by the most recent recounters of those times who evidently did not read Keith's own reminiscences (Trinkaus and Shipman, 1992:196, 198–99, 219). This has been the intellectual starting point for almost all English-speaking writers on human "evolution" from that day to this (Brace, 1964, 1981a, 1992).

[16]The French hostility to Darwin during the nineteenth century has been well documented (Appel, 1987:233), and it has continued right up to the present, as has been clearly demonstrated (Stebbins, 1974; Boesiger, 1980).

[17]Brace, 1964.

[18]Boule, 1921; Boule and Vallois, 1957.

[19]Brace, 1988:133; 1989:444; and in press(a).

chapter five

Between World Wars

RAYMOND DART AND *AUSTRALOPITHECUS*

Over the years, far more fossils have been discovered than there is room even to begin to record in a treatment as brief as this. Some of these, although relatively important specimens, must be omitted because they have not met the criterion of contributing substantially to alterations in the overall picture. The next discovery that did measure up was made in 1924. Although it was but a little fossil for which only modest claims were made, in retrospect it can be regarded as a major portent of what was to come.

The scene was South Africa, where a small fossil skull was given to the young Professor Raymond Dart (see Figure 5–1) at the medical school of the University of the Witwatersrand in Johannesburg.[1] Dart had recently finished his training in medicine, anatomy, and physical anthropology in London, and was keenly aware that Africa, cited by Darwin as the possible source of the human line of development, had up to that time yielded no dated early human material. Only the single enigmatic and undated find of a Pithecanthropus-like skull in a mine shaft at Kabwe (then Broken Hill) in Zambia (formerly Northern Rhodesia) existed to demonstrate the presence of an earlier stage in human evolution.[2]

The little skull handed to Dart was that of an immature individual—approximately at the same stage of development as that of a modern six-year-

FIGURE 5–1. Raymond A. Dart (1893–1988), whose prophetic interpretation of *Australopithecus* went unappreciated for more than thirty years. (Photo courtesy of the late Professor Raymond A. Dart.)

old child—and it is risky to establish taxonomic affinity or evolutionary stage on the basis of specimens in which growth has not been completed. Still, Dart's study, published early in 1925, was able to demonstrate that his juvenile creature had a brain the size of an adult gorilla, that its head was balanced atop the spinal column instead of slung forward, that the palate was human rather than apelike in shape, and that, despite the great size of the teeth, the canines did not project beyond the level of the other teeth. Although Dart correctly noted that juvenile apes are less distinct from juvenile humans in more of these features than the adults of the various forms, he could state in summary that this South African fossil, blasted out of a quarry at Taung, presented a curious mixture of apelike and human features. He regarded it as an extinct ape—closer perhaps to the human line than any yet discovered, but an ape nevertheless—and christened it *Australopithecus africanus* (southern ape of Africa), as shown in Figure 5–2).[3]

    Dart's sober and relatively cautious appraisal was greeted by an outburst of patronizing scorn from the evolutionary and anatomical authorities back in England, several of whom were his former teachers. Chief among these

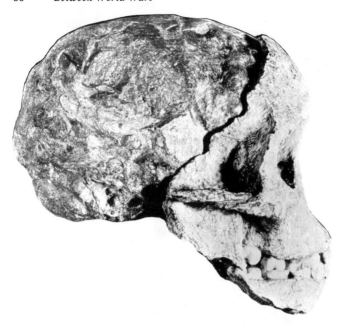

FIGURE 5–2. The first Australopithecine to be discovered, Dart's original *Australopithecus africanus.* (Courtesy of the American Museum of Natural History.)

was Sir Arthur Keith, champion of the Piltdown fraud, who repeatedly stated that Dart's claims were "preposterous." In fairness it should be pointed out that Keith was in no way to be blamed for the fraudulent facets of the Piltdown melange, since he was as badly—even tragically—misled by it as anyone. Yet of all the criticism offered of Dart's views, only a relatively trivial one remains: that he mixed Latin and Greek roots in a single term and used a substantive in place of an adjectival form in assigning the fossil its name.[4]

There seem to have been two sources for the reaction to Dart's claims. One was the feeling that the fossil should really have been turned over to the "proper authorities" (namely those back in England) for study. The second was based on the feeling that, with Dubois's Pithecanthropus finally accepted as the earliest possible form of human life (by all except Dubois himself), anything demonstrably more primitive, as *Australopithecus* was, even had it grown to adulthood, could not conceivably belong in the picture. Furthermore, that Dart, like Dubois, should make such an epochal discovery within just a few years of his arrival seemed just too much of a coincidence to be believable. Influenced by such considerations, "Dart's Child," as *Australopithecus* was deprecatingly designated, was relegated to the category of "just another fossil ape." Indeed, that alone should have been reason enough to attract attention since at that time fossil apes were—as they are even now—rare specimens indeed.[5]

FRANZ WEIDENREICH AND PITHECANTHROPINES IN CHINA

The excitement over *Australopithecus* was soon superseded by the discovery of Pithecanthropines in China, the so-called *"Sinanthropus"* remains, or "Pekin Man."[6] The first well-preserved skull was found by the Chinese paleontologist, Pei Wenzhong (W. C. Pei, 1904–1982) in 1929.[7] During the succeeding decade, fragments of more than forty individuals were retrieved from the limestone caves at Zhoukoudian (Choukoutien), a few dozen miles southwest of the Chinese capital, Beijing. Ultimately, these were the subject of a series of splendid monographs by Franz Weidenreich, a refugee from Hitler's Germany who was teaching anatomy at the Peking Union Medical School at the time, and who, by great good fortune, was one of the very few who perpetuated the outlook of his late teacher and colleague, Gustav Schwalbe.[8] (See Weidenreich in Figure 5–3.)

FIGURE 5–3. Franz Weidenreich (1873–1948) shown with Dr. G. H. R. von Koenigswald (1902–1982). (Courtesy of the American Museum of Natural History.)

War, with its inevitable disrupting influence, spelled final oblivion for the original Sinanthropus material. These were last seen on December 7, 1941, the day when the bombs fell on Pearl Harbor signalling the entry of the United States into the war that Japan had begun against China four years earlier. Casts of the hominid fossils had been sent to the United States previously, and the originals were in the process of being sent for safekeeping, but Japanese troops captured the American marine detachment escorting the material at the port of embarkation, Qin Huang Dao, and no trace of them has since been found.[9] However, during the brief time of their resurrection, excellent casts, drawings, and photographs had been made—all of which survive—and the exhaustive descriptions and comparisons in Weidenreich's splendid publications have removed all remaining doubts concerning the human status of the Pithecanthropines.

The 1930s also saw important discoveries in other parts of the world. A skull from Steinheim in Germany (1933)[10] and the back of a skull from Swanscombe in England (1935 and 1936)[11] partially served to portray the nature of the Western successors of the Zhoukoudian group, although interpretations are still the subject of a prolonged debate that owes more to the continuing reluctance to accept the implications of a Darwinian viewpoint than it does to the nature of the fossils themselves.

MOUNT CARMEL

More important, however, were discoveries made in the Middle East and again in South Africa. The Middle Eastern finds were the result of excavations on the slopes of Mount Carmel in Israel (then Palestine), just south of Tel Aviv and little more than a mile from the shore of the Mediterranean Sea. There, in the years 1931 and 1932, a joint Anglo-American archaeological expedition discovered the remains of at least a dozen fossil humans in two different caves. The one complete skeleton from the cave of Mugharet et-Tabūn was of a female, which was in other respects indistinguishable from the "classic" Neanderthals of Europe. (Figure 5–4 shows a female skull from this Mount Carmel site.) This at least demonstrated that the Neanderthals were not just a limited European phenomenon.[12] This point was also demonstrated by the simultaneous discovery of a series of skulls, approaching Pithecanthropine form but at the edge of the early Neanderthal spectrum, only twenty miles downstream from the site of the original Pithecanthropus discovery at Trinil in Java.[13] After World War II, more full Neanderthals were found at Shanidar cave in northern Iraq.[14] Further specimens found in Israel at Amud in 1961 and Kebara in 1983 attest to Neanderthal form and distribution.[15]

The second Mount Carmel Cave, Mugharet es-Skhūl, yielded the re-

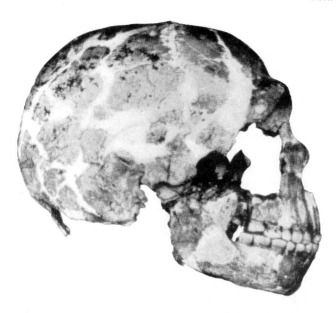

FIGURE 5–4. The skull of a classic Neanderthal female from the cave of Mugharet et-Tabūn, Mount Carmel, Israel. (Courtesy of the Clarendon Press, Oxford.)

mains of at least ten individuals, but rather than exhibiting fully Neanderthal form, they displayed characteristics that were halfway between Neanderthal and Modern form. This has earned them the designation of "Neanderthaloid"—that is, recalling the Neanderthals on the one hand, but not to a sufficient degree to separate them from moderns on the other.

By one of those little ironies that only fate can arrange, the major burden of description and interpretation fell to Sir Arthur Keith. He had been very critical of Dart's attempt to make sense out of a mixture of simian and human traits, and yet he was confronted with the task of interpreting a mixture of Neanderthal and modern traits. Unfortunately, his vacillations between alternate possibilities satisfied no one. To add to the confusion, opinion tended to regard both Mount Carmel sites as being dated to an interglacial before the onset of the last Pleistocene ice advance. If the dates were correct, that would have made them older than the "classic" Neanderthals of Europe. Under such circumstances the form of Tabūn made reasonable sense, but that of Skhūl would represent a dilemma. Keith tried to face the problem squarely, but he could not decide whether Skhūl indicated the hybridization of a fully Neanderthal population (represented by Tabūn) and the long-sought but as-yet-undiscovered modern one, or whether it was a Neanderthal population in the throes of rapid evolutionary change. He seemed to favor the latter explanation, although others have stressed the former.

QAFZEH

During the same time that work at Mount Carmel was underway, the French consul in Jerusalem, René Neuville, undertook excavations in caves on the east side of a valley running south from the biblical town of Nazareth. As a result of field seasons in 1933 and 1934, Neuville found the stone artifacts and the remains of their makers at the site that he referred to as Kafzeh—now generally spelled Qafzeh.[16] The tools were the same kind as those found at Skhūl, which have often been assumed to be the handiwork of Neanderthal sorts of makers. The human skeletal remains, however, looked even less like the known Neanderthals than the specimens found at Skhūl. These were duly forwarded to the laboratory of Marcellin Boule in Paris, where they remained essentially unstudied for approximately thirty years.

Then, starting in the mid-1960s, Bernard Vandermeersch, a student at the Sorbonne in Paris, got permission to resume excavations at Qafzeh and use the combined results as the basis for his doctoral dissertation. His work was an immediate success, and he was able to add more tools and human skeletal remains to the sample already assembled.[17] Instead of solving problems, however, the results have contributed to an ongoing professional argument about the course and timing of the emergence of "modern" human form. Both the Skhūl and Qafzeh discoveries have been promoted as "anatomically modern" *Homo sapiens* in somewhat simplistic typological fashion. Even further, they have been touted as "Proto-Cro-Magnon," although there are marked differences between the characteristics of the specimens at the two Israeli sites, and Qafzeh, at any rate, can be statistically removed from any tie with the actual form of Cro-Magnon or any more recent European.[18]

In the Skhūl groups, it is clear that the reduction towards recent levels of jaw and tooth size had already begun, while there still remained indications of Middle Pleistocene levels of robustness surviving in the cranial reinforcements and in other parts of the skeleton. Qafzeh, on the other hand, had retained Middle Pleistocene levels of tooth and jaw dimensions while tending toward recent manifestations of both cranial and post-cranial reductions in robustness. Each group represents a different trajectory towards the attainment of Modern human form, as illustrated by the different manifestations in Africa on the one hand and Europe on the other. What is surprising, however, is the date at which these changes had evidently begun. It would appear that these developments were proceeding while full-scale Neanderthal morphology continued to characterize the appearance of the inhabitants of the region running from Iraq in the East to the Atlantic coast of Europe in the West.

Over the years, attempts had been made to assess the antiquity of the deposits in Qafzeh and Skhūl by using radiocarbon analysis, but these attempts produced inconclusive results. The possibility of using radioactive elements as natural clocks was exploited after World War II, and radiocarbon—[14]C—has proven to be of great value in sorting out the ages of archaeological deposits of the last 40,000 years.[19] Radioactive elements decay into stable end products at a fixed rate, so that the amount of each in a given structure such as a crystal will be strictly in proportion to the length of time that structure has been an identifiable reality. As it happens, however, Qafzeh and Skhūl are too old to be reliably dated by [14]C. The amount of ^{14}C left in those deposits has reduced to such a level that it is no longer possible to get a reliable measure of it.

Radiation physicists, however, have developed a variety of techniques to exploit the same general principals. Some of these techniques have been applied to testing the antiquity of the Israel sites, and they turn out to be much older than had been anticipated. Based on the technique called Electron Spin Resonance—ESR—Qafzeh is at least 96,000 years and perhaps as old as 115,000 years.[20] Skhūl was dated by the related Thermoluminescence—TL—technique, and is dated at 119,000 years.[21] The various levels at Tabūn range from around 100,000 to maybe more than 300,000 years ago.[22] While these techniques may still be improved, we do not anticipate surprises in dating similar to those that have emerged as a result of the application of the new techniques of the last five years or so.

ROBERT BROOM AND MORE AUSTRALOPITHECINES

Because of the dating difficulties, a proper assessment of the fifty-year-old discoveries at Mount Carmel and Qafzeh has only recently become possible. Meanwhile, in 1936, old issues of another sort were reopened, and this time the evidence was sufficient to ward off attempts to ignore them. Just when it seemed that the furor over Dart's *Australopithecus* had been reduced to a memory, another fortunate explosion occurred. This particular blast took place in a limeworks quarry at Sterkfontein, some miles north of Johannesburg in the Transvaal area of South Africa. Fossil bones were discovered as a result and, by good fortune, were delivered into the hands of the venerable vertebrate paleontologist and physician, Dr. Robert Broom (1866–1951) (Figure 5–5).[23] Fragments of nearly a half-dozen creatures were included, among them a reconstructable adult skull. Broom immediately recognized the similarity of these to *Australopithecus*. Eventually he advocated an entire taxonomic subfamily, the "Australopithecinae," to include them all, but he believed that the new finds were different enough to warrant new generic and specific designations. In his first formal paper on his finds in 1936, Broom had called them *Australopithecus "transvaalensis,"* but, two years later, he had a change of heart and he rechristened them *"Plesianthropus transvaalensis."*[24] Time has shown that they are simply adult versions of *Australopithecus,* and so, for the present at least, we will simply refer to them as Australopithecines. Please note, however, that the resurgent medieval enthu-

FIGURE 5–5. Dr. Robert Broom (1866–1951), physician and paleontologist, with a cast of *"Plesianthropus."* (Courtesy of the American Museum of Natural History.)

siasm for multiplying generic and specific names has led to recent attempts to resurrect the formal designations given by Broom and others[25] (a position that this book does not support).

The upright carriage of the head and the extraordinarily human appearance of the distal end of a femur contributed to the suspicion that these creatures may have been erect walking bipeds, and it began to appear as though Dart had not been so rash as his detractors had claimed. Nor was this all. Two years later, in 1938, on a farm named Kromdraai some two miles from Sterkfontein, more Australopithecine remains were discovered and brought to the attention of Dr. Broom. Fragments of teeth and skull, jaw, arm, and foot bones suggested the presence of a similar but larger-toothed creature, which Broom, with his zeal for creating new designations, called *"Paranthropus robustus."* While these are similar enough to the Sterkfontein remains to be included among the Australopithecines, they clearly represent another kind of adaptation.[26] They are commonly referred to as the "robust" Australopithecines, while those from Sterkfontein, along with similar specimens elsewhere, are called "gracile" Australopithecines, even though the difference in relative degree of robustness may apply only to the molar teeth and not to the rest of the body.[27]

Now, with the backing of Broom combined with the quantity of accumulating evidence, the Australopithecines could no longer be overlooked. However, consistent with the principles of hominid catastrophism, modified or extreme, most anthropologists were convinced that fossils of modern form would yet be discovered in the early Pleistocene, and they continued to support the view that the Australopithecines were simply another side branch from the main stem of human evolution that had become extinct without issue. To be sure, a few anthropologists, notably the American student of the Neanderthals, Hrdlička, and that peripatetic refugee, Franz Weidenreich, complained that the human evolutionary tree portrayed by most scholars was, in effect, all branches and no trunk. Real qualms, however, did not develop until after World War II.[28]

G. H. R. VON KOENIGSWALD

With the close of the 1930s, war came to the West as it had earlier come to the East, and, as invariably happens under such circumstances, fossil hunting ceased and evolutionary studies were seriously impeded. Fortunately, the conflagration was delayed in Southeast Asia, and work continued for a while in Java. The last major find of that era was made by the German/Dutch paleontologist, G. H. R. von Koenigswald (1902–1982), who had been responsible for further Pithecanthropine finds in Java throughout the late 1930s. Just before the Japanese occupation in 1941, von Koenigswald found a small fragment of a rugged mandible with a few large but clearly human teeth to which he gave the relatively jawbreaking name, *"Meganthropus palaeojavanicus"* (see Figure 5–6).[29] A similar mandible was found in the same area in 1952, and for a while some anthropologists believed that these belonged to a genuine Australopithecine.[30] This, if true, would be the only example of that Stage of evolution found outside of Africa.

FIGURE 5–6. *"Meganthropus palaeojavanicus,"* a robust Pithecanthropine from the early Pleistocene of Java. (Courtesy of the late G. H. R. von Koenigswald.)

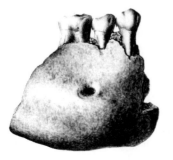 

As an interesting postscript, a recent comparative study by Andrew Kramer of the University of Tennessee has shown that the *"Meganthropus"* specimens possess a series of traits that are also found in subsequent Pithecanthropine fossils in Asia. As Weidenreich explicitly noted a half century ago, these same traits continue through time and can be found today in representatives of Modern *Homo sapiens* in Melanesia and Australia, providing support for the picture of regional continuity between the stages of human evolution that we shall be discussing in later chapters.[31]

CHAPTER FIVE NOTES

[1]Raymond Dart (1893–1988), with the aid of the journalist Dennis Craig, tells the story of his involvement with paleoanthropology in most engaging fashion in *Adventures with the Missing Link* (Dart and Craig, 1959). Dart's own life and career are admirably depicted by his own former student and successor, Phillip Tobias (Tobias, 1984).

[2]The magnificently robust skull from the Broken Hill Mine (see the picture in Chapter 11) was found on June 17, 1921 (Woodward, 1921; Hrdlička, 1926). The skull and some other associated fragments were entrusted to the authorities at the British Museum (Natural History) in London for formal description and interpretation—the same group that had handled the Piltdown material. The pieces of pelvis presumed to be associated were reconstructed to show that the individual could not stand upright, and the zoologist at the British Museum (Natural History) who wrote the technical description tried to use this to justify the name of *"Cyphanthropus,"* which means "stooping man" (Pycraft, 1928:49–50). As it happened, the describer was an ornithologist and not an anthropologist, and when a trained human anatomist had a chance to examine the material, the mistake was quickly corrected (Clark, 1928). There is no reason to expect that posture and locomotion differed in any significant respect from that of normal living human beings.

[3]Dart, 1925.

[4]Bather, 1925.

[5]Broom, 1950b:23; Clark, 1967:19–20.

[6]"Pekin" is the same as Beijing, but it is no longer politically correct to spell it that way. Incidentally, the "-jing" in Beijing is pronounced the same way it is in "jingle bells," and not with the French "j" affected by so many announcers in the media. The latter pronunciation sounds just as odd in Chinese as it does in English, but the Chinese are too polite to make an issue of it.

[7]Pei, 1930.

[8]An appraisal of Weidenreich's life and work along with a list of his publications is presented in the volume edited by Sherwood Washburn and Davida Wolffson (1950).

[9]Shapiro, 1974.

[10]Berckhemer, 1933; Weinert, 1936.

[11]Marston, 1935, 1936, 1938; Wymer, 1958; Ovey (ed.), 1964.

[12]McCown and Keith, 1939.

[13]Oppenoorth, 1932.

[14]Solecki, 1963, 1971.

[15]Suzuki and Takai (eds.), 1970; Arensburg et al., 1985.

[16]Köppel, 1935.

[17]Vandermeersch, 1966, 1969, 1970, 1981.

[18]The stress on the "modern" appearance of the specimens from the two sites is repeated in Bar-Yosef and Vandermeersch (1993), and the claim that they can be regarded as "Proto-Cro-Magnons" is offered by Vandermeersch in the published version of his doctoral dissertation (Vandermeersch, 1981:5). The one specimen that is complete enough to allow full comparative

statistical treatment is Qafzeh 6. Analysis based on fifteen craniofacial dimensions shows that it is vanishingly unlikely that it could be found in a recent European population (P=<0.000), but it cannot be distinguished from living sub-Saharan Africans (Brace, 1991:189–91, in press [d]). There is one recent claim that there is no evidence either from morphology or archaeology for an African ancestry (Frayer et al., 1993:38), but it is just a statement made in the absence of a consideration of the nature of African cranial form and the known archaeological record. The evidence for the use of Levallois flakes as projectile points at Qafzeh (J. Shea, 1988, 1989, 1992) is the same as the evidence for the use of Levallois flakes in the Middle Stone Age of Africa (Brooks, 1988; J. D. Clark, 1988). Finally, the microfauna at Qafzeh clearly indicates a major incursion from sub-Saharan Africa (Tchernov, 1988, 1992). The evidence for the African connection involving morphology, archaeology, and fauna is summarized in Brace (in press [d]). The Qafzeh dentition, on the other hand, is larger than that of any living human population and exceeds that of the "classic" Neanderthals (Brace, in press [b]). Neither Qafzeh nor Skhūl should be treated in the simplistic typological fashion that has generally been their fate. Each has aspects of the "modern" and aspects of the archaic, but they are not the same aspects. An analysis of both can help us understand where and why modern form emerged when it did. (see Chapter 14).

[19]Taylor, 1987.

[20]Schwarcz et al., 1988; Aitken and Valladas, 1993.

[21]Mercier et al., 1992; Aitken and Valladas, 1992.

[22]Mercier et al., 1992; Stringer and Gamble, 1993:121.

[23]Broom clearly was one of the great "characters" in paleontology. Born and educated in Scotland, he moved to Australia and then to South Africa, where he used the income from his medical practice to support his fieldwork. In favor of spiritualism, and opposed to Darwin and statistics, he had an extraordinary eye for modern art and available women. (Findlay, 1972:99).

[24]Broom, 1936, 1938b.

[25]Tattersall, 1986b; Grine, 1988a, 1988b; Groves, 1989.

[26]Broom, 1938a, 1939.

[27]McHenry, 1974, 1975b.

[28]These issues are discussed in Brace (1964, 1981a, 1992).

[29]von Koenigswald, 1949.

[30]Tobias and von Koenigswald, 1964.

[31]Weidenreich, 1943:249–50, 1945; Kramer, 1989, 1991.

chapter six

Recent Discoveries

STERKFONTEIN

In 1947, soon after peace made it possible once again to return to his prehistoric research, Dr. Broom, by that time more than eighty years of age but undiminished in energy, resumed his investigations at Sterkfontein. Within a short time he discovered quantities of Australopithecine remains, among which was a nearly complete half pelvis.[1] This bone was remarkably like a small modern human pelvis and, of all the Australopithecine fragments found to date, most clearly demonstrated their erect and bipedal mode of locomotion. Yet traditional anthropological doubts were raised, and it was hinted by some that perhaps the pelvic fragment properly belonged to the long-sought "true man" and had nothing to do with the Australopithecines. Possibly, it was hinted, "true man" was hunting the Australopithecines.[2] Variants of this argument continue to be offered concerning other fragments of evidence, but, like the cry of "pathological," which was repeatedly applied to early human fossils in the late nineteenth century, this has begun to sound more than a little strained.

MAKAPANSGAT

In 1947, too, Raymond Dart returned to the arena of Australopithecine research. His work was concentrated on a deserted lime-works dump near Makapansgat, some 200 miles northeast of Sterkfontein. This dump produced a wealth of Australopithecine fragments. These evidently belonged to the same sort of gracile Australopithecine as those of Taung and Sterkfontein, although Dart gave them a new specific name, *Australopithecus "prometheus."* Within two years Dart, like Broom, had also recovered substantial fragments of pelvis, which, if anything, were even more human in appearance than those from Sterkfontein.[3] Also in 1947, Sir Arthur Keith published a handsome and gracious apology, noting that it was he who had been rash and hasty in 1925, and that time and events had proven Dart's interpretation to be much more nearly correct than his own.[4]

SWARTKRANS

Starting in the succeeding year, 1948, Broom and his assistant, J. T. Robinson, began work at another site, Swartkrans, a short distance from Sterkfontein, where they soon found Australopithecines of the same robust sort that Broom had found at Kromdraai ten years earlier. Predictably, they created yet another species name for their new material, calling it *"Paranthropus crassidens."* Adding still another dimension to the Plio/Pleistocene fossil picture as seen in the Transvaal of South Africa, a pocket in the Swartkrans site produced another form of human fossil. The first fragment, a nearly complete jaw found in 1949, was initially given the name of *"Telanthropus capensis,"* but comparative study convinced Robinson and others that it is not distinguishable from the Pithecanthropines of Asia.[5] As such, it is a find of the greatest significance, and just a hint of what Africa was to produce in the years that have followed.

Dart and his assistants at Makapansgat and, following Broom's death in 1951, Robinson at Swartkrans and Sterkfontein, continued to recover fossil fragments of various kinds during the succeeding decade. More recently, after Dart and Robinson retired from active fieldwork, their lead has been followed by C. K. Brain at Swartkrans and Phillip V. Tobias at Sterkfontein, and the discoveries have continued to accumulate.

Confirming Expectations

During the decades since the end of World War II, human fossil remains from all corners of the Old World have been discovered that represent all of the stages of human evolution as well as an increasing fossil record of the prehuman ancestors dating back some tens of millions of years. So far, demonstrable Australopithecine finds have only been made in Africa, although there have been a lot of them. Variations on the Australopithecine theme have been found from Ethiopia, near the "Horn" of Africa, and down through Kenya, Tanzania, and South Africa. Crude tools of the same age have an even wider distribution in Africa, extending along the Mediterranean coast of North Africa and even across into Spain, with representatives in Israel and throughout the nonforested parts of the rest of the African continent.[6]

Specimens at the Pithecanthropine stage of development have been found at a number of places in Africa and Europe. An increasing number of similar specimens have been found in China, and in 1993 further discoveries were made in Java, adding to that already extraordinary collection.[7] The majority of the representatives of this stage are tropical or restricted to appearances in the Temperate Zone to those times not under the influence of glacial conditions. Furthermore, the time span with which they are associated is later than that of the Australopithecines and earlier than that of the Neanderthals. In these matters, they have conformed to the expectations attributed to the discoveries made from Dubois's original *Pithecanthropus* up to the first major applications of radiometric dating in the years following World War II.

Also conforming to these expectations is the essentially Neanderthal form of specimens that are of more recent date than the Pithecanthropines, but not so recent as the widespread presence of fully Modern humans. China has produced a fine Neanderthal at the eastern end of the range,[8] and Spain has given us several from the westernmost extent.[9] Again, as might have been expected, the Chinese Neanderthals possess characteristic features that continue to be identifiable in the modern inhabitants of eastern Asia, and the Spanish Neanderthals possess traits that continue to be characteristic of certain Europeans today, but not other populations.

In between, India has finally yielded its first fossil representative of a previous stage of evolution. This, the Narmada specimen of 1982, is not quite complete enough for definitive assignation to a given stage. On the other hand, it certainly is not Modern, nor is it convincingly Pithecanthropine.[10] Since its interpreters are inclined to call it *Homo sapiens*, it would seem to qualify for inclusion in the Neanderthal stage.[11] This would be consistent with the indications of date and associated tools and fossil animal bones, but with the uncertainty about whether it belongs in the earlier or more recent category, it is almost easier to place it simply between categories.

In contrast to these instances of confirmation, Israel continues to provide ammunition for conflicting interpretations. The evidently Neanderthal skeleton found in 1983 at another Mount Carmel cave—Kebara—is clearly younger than the non-Neanderthal specimens from Qafzeh and Skhūl.[12] The implications of this are treated in Chapters 13 and 14. Israel, in fact, sits right at the contact point between Africa, Europe, and Asia, and aspects of both cultural and biological developments associated with those different continental masses actually met at just that point at various times in the past, as they continue to do today. When these facts are taken into account, the meaning of the differences in appearance of the various near-contemporary fossils in Israel will become apparent.

MARY AND LOUIS LEAKEY AND OLDUVAI GORGE

Certainly one of the most dramatic facets of this historical review is the account of the East African discoveries initiated by the work of the late Dr. L. S. B. Leakey (1903–1972), and continued by his wife, Mary Leakey, at Olduvai Gorge, Tanzania (then Tanganyika). Olduvai Gorge is shown in Figure 6–1. Although the Olduvai finds which made them famous were not discovered until 1959,[13] the basis that makes these discoveries so important goes back more than a third of a century earlier to the time when Louis Leakey first started making expeditions to this area.[14] Leakey's general experience in East African prehistory goes back even further, but he first visited Olduvai Gorge in 1931 and shortly thereafter discovered stone tools of a type as crude as, or cruder than, those of any known tradition. Because of their location, these have been called Oldowan tools. They precede the Acheulean and are now regarded as constituting the oldest tool-making tradition in the world. The Leakeys' continued work in Olduvai Gorge has revealed the development of the Oldowan tradition through the ascending layers until it becomes the familiar Acheulean "handaxe" tradition recognized over a century ago by Boucher de Perthes at Abbeville and widely distributed throughout the Middle Pleistocene of the Old World.[15] Here, then, is the Lower Pleistocene parent of all subsequent human cultural traditions, including our own: a confirmation of Darwin's prediction made so long ago!

As if this were not enough of a contribution to have made during a lifetime, the Leakeys' continued persistence in the face of formidable financial and environmental obstacles finally rewarded them with the discovery of the manufacturers of the Oldowan tools—the bones of what must be our own ancestors as well as those of others who may have been collaterals, although there still is a good deal of uncertainty about which falls into what category. On July 17, 1959, they discovered their first fossil "man." [16] Initially they followed the annoying paleontological practice of giving it a new generic and specific name before it was systematically compared with anything else. They called it *"Zinjanthropus" boisei*, although it turns out to be nothing less than a robust Australopithecine (see Figure 6–2).[17] Their find was even more robust than the Swartkrans specimens from South Africa—so much more robust, in fact, that most specialists now regard the new species name of *boisei* to be fully warranted. This makes the name properly *Australopithecus boisei*, although some professionals are pushing hard to support their case for making it *"Paranthropus" boisei*.[18]

FIGURE 6–1. Olduvai Gorge, Tanzania. (Courtesy George H. Hansen.)

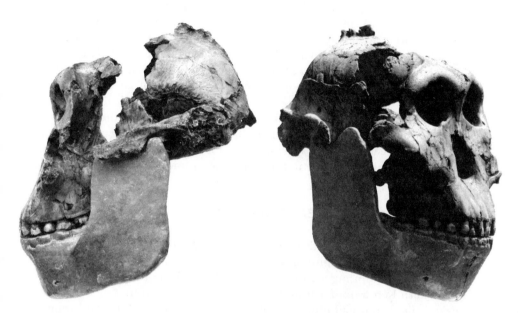

FIGURE 6–2.   The "Zinj" skull from Olduvai Gorge, a robust Australopithecine, with an artist's idea of what the mandible should look like. (Photo by R. I. M. Campbell, Nairobi, Kenya.)

The discovery of "Zinj," as it continues to be unofficially called, attracted worldwide attention and financial support, and it initiated a new era in paleoanthropology. Within just a few years, the Leakeys had uncovered the remains of gracile Australopithecines as well as Pithecanthropines at various levels in Olduvai Gorge. Although their work has been of the greatest value to students of human evolution, it has not been an unmixed blessing. Underlying Dr. Leakey's many productive years in the field was the unshaken conviction that nothing so crude as an Australopithecine could possibly have been ancestral to subsequent human forms. He seemed to feel that the only proper ancestor for modern humanity was none other than ancient "true man," and each new discovery was hailed as evidence for this patently nonevolutionary view until proper comparative study showed it to be one or another already known taxon. At one point, Dr. Leakey assembled a mixed collection of Australopithecine and Pithecanthropine material from Olduvai and tried to claim that this, which he called *"Homo habilis,"* was the long sought "true man" that was ancestral to ourselves.[19]

At the time I wrote the first edition of this book, I had felt that the Australopithecines could be lumped together as a single, if variable, Stage in human evolution that evolved as a group into the Pithecanthropines, and that if this were true, then representatives of those two distinct Stages could not have been present at the same point in time. And indeed, the various forms that he mixed in this claimed taxon came from very different time levels. Dr. Leakey, however, kept trying to show that this or that new find showed that different forms existed at the same level, always with the hope that one might be shown to be his "true man." Because each new piece of evidence always turned out to have some flaw, I became convinced that his actions were analogous to those of "the little boy who cried wolf." One of my colleagues reminded me, however, that in the old didactic story, eventually there actually *was* a wolf. And so there was in this case, as we shall see, but the confusions caused by his repeated claims remain with us, and, along with a return of the tradition of creating a new specific name for each additional scrap discovered, will continue to plague us for some time to come.[20]

RICHARD LEAKEY AND EAST TURKANA

Dr. Leakey's richly productive life came to an end in 1972, by which time he had seen the fruitful beginnings of the continuation of his work by his son Richard, in a promising area just east of Lake Turkana (then Lake Rudolf), in northern Kenya not far from the Ethiopian border. At that time, Richard Leakey's field crew had found a skull that was not quite a Pithecanthropine, but was certainly tending in that direction. This, the cranium ER-1470 (Figure 6–3), was half again as large as "Zinj" and nowhere near as heavily buttressed and flanged, but it was of roughly the same date.[21] Clearly

FIGURE 6–3. KNM ER-1470, a transitional Australopithecine/Pithecanthropine skull from east of Lake Turkana. (Drawn from a cast by M. L. Brace.)

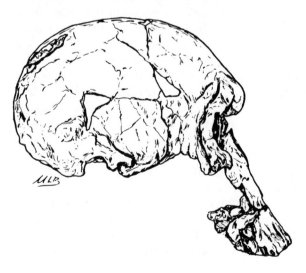

the transition that was to produce the Pithecanthropines from the Australopithecines was half accomplished. The face was still large and of Australopithecine form, but the braincase was definitely modified in a Pithecanthropine direction both in its external and its internal features. Unfortunately, it too was given the label *Homo "habilis"* so that, now, this "category" includes some specimens that are Australopithecine, some that are Pithecanthropine, and ER-1470, which is clearly in between. Actually, the difficulty in assigning ER-1470 to a known category illustrates just how arbitrary it is to divide an evolutionary continuum into pat stages, however useful these may be in general.[22]

But if one group of Australopithecines evolved into Pithecanthropines, another group evidently did not. Both forms are now shown to be contemporaries in the East Turkana area being worked by Richard Leakey and his associates. The skull ER-406, found at Ileret in 1969, is an obvious robust Australopithecine (brain size=510 cc.), and yet it is a contemporary of the 1.3 million year old of ER-3733 skull found at Koobi Fora in 1975 (also in the East Turkana area), which is an unmistakable Pithecanthropine (brain size=800–900 cc.).[23] (Figure 6–4 illustrates both ER-406 and ER-3733.) It was the discovery of ER-3733 that finally provided the evidence that some form of *Homo* lived at the same time as some form of *Australopithecus,* and one could argue that this is as close to the real "wolf" as we are likely to come.

DON JOHANSON AND ETHIOPIA

The continuing work of the Leakey family during the last few years has given us the pieces that suggest a rationale for how the Australopithecines ended and how the Pithecanthropines began. The same years have also produced evidence that helps us understand how the Australopithecines themselves began. Starting in 1972, a series of field seasons by a French-American group made significant discoveries in the Pliocene deposits in the badlands of the Afar Depression north of Addis Ababa in northern Ethiopia.

Conditions for pursuing research were considerably less than promising. The climate was and is harsh in the extreme: an unrelenting, blazing desert heat. And however unprepossessing it may seem, the area has been politically upset for years with intermittent sniping, raiding, armed forays, and out-and-out civil war. But the Pliocene strata lie flat and workable, filled with fossil bones, and datable by the K/Ar technique. So with ingenuity, persistence, and more than a little courage, the French geologist Maurice Taieb and the American anthropologist Donald C. Johanson led crews on yearly efforts until full-scale civil war drove them out in 1977.[24]

Their fieldwork was crowned with abundant success. Their most spectacular discoveries were a nearly complete Australopithecine skeleton late in 1974 and a group of over a dozen more Australopithecines at the end of the

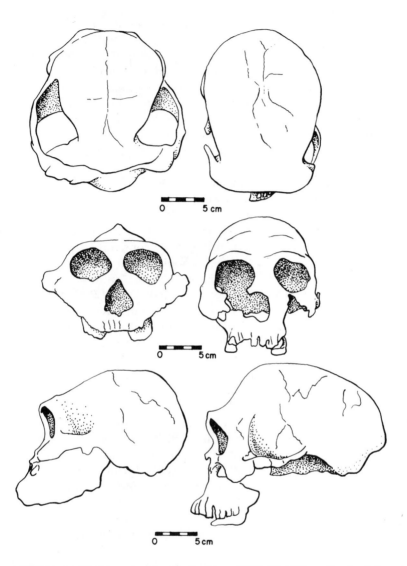

FIGURE 6–4.   ER-406, a robust Australopithecine, and ER-3733, a Pithecanthropine, both contemporaries in the East Turkana area of Kenya about 1.3 million years ago.

1975 field season.[25] They christened that first relatively complete specimen "Lucy," and what an interesting specimen she turns out to be. Lucy was barely $3\frac{1}{2}$ feet tall and fully bipedal, although her arms were relatively long in proportion to the length of her legs. Her jaws and teeth, like those of other specimens found there, display a series of features that are intermediate between an apelike and a human condition. With a date of well over 3 million years,

Lucy and her companions are among the earliest Australopithecines so far discovered. Given that degree of antiquity, a mixture of human, apelike, and transitional features is just what we would expect to find. Just to ensure that the collection will continue to be the focus of professional academic controversy, the specimens have been given yet another specific name—*Australopithecus "afarensis"*—and the claim has been put forth that these, and not the South African or Olduvai Australopithecines, are the "true" ancestors of later human populations.

CONTINUING FIELDWORK

These discoveries have led to further efforts in the field, and these efforts have been crowned by further success. In spite of the problems caused by nationalism, professional jealousies, and limited funds for fieldwork, hardly a year goes by without significant new discoveries. Because the early evidence for our evolutionary line is something that appeals to the imagination of the public at large, it is considered newsworthy, and each new find is reported in the popular press.

Unfortunately, while the press generally sees to it that those who are chosen to report on matters of art, poetry, literature, history, and politics actually know something about the fields on which they write, the same is not generally true for science. As a result, many of the news reports dealing with paleoanthropological discoveries display that mixture of misunderstanding and sensationalism that appears so regularly in the media when the topic is science. The headline "New Find Overturns All Previous Theories of Human Evolution" appears every few years in newspapers all over the world. One appeared within a week of the completion of the third edition of this book in the summer of 1986.[26] And now as the fifth edition is being written, new Pithecanthropine material has emerged as a result of the efforts of Donald E. Tyler of the University of Idaho and Sastrohamijoyo Sartono of the Institute of Technology in Bandung working at Sangiran in central Java (see Figure 6–5). This is creating a similar furor among journalists.[27]

The earlier discovery being hailed was an *Australopithecus boisei* specimen, WT 17000, found by Professor Alan Walker of Johns Hopkins University, a long-time collaborator with Richard Leakey (Figure 6–6).[28] The find, informally known as "the Black Skull," was actually made in August of 1985 southwest of Lake Turkana in northern Kenya, and it came from deposits 2.5 million years old. That is a full million years older than the previously known *boisei* specimens. The brain case is even smaller, and other aspects are more primitive. It is an important and dramatic find, and, in extending our knowledge in significant ways, it has raised a number of questions that could not even have been asked before.[29] But that is just how science works, and it hardly constitutes the overthrow of all previous theories of human evolution.

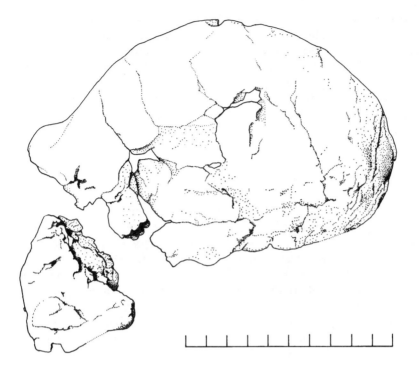

FIGURE 6–5.   Skull IX from Sangiran in central Java, discovered by a farmer in early May of 1993 with pieces confirmed in situ by Professor Donald E. Tyler shortly afterwards. Dating is probably in the one million year range, and it is clearly the skull of a Javanese Pithecanthropine, *Homo erectus*. (Drawn by Kay Clahassey from a photograph provided by Don Tyler.)

Barely a year later, in the summer of 1986, Professor Tim White of the University of California at Berkeley was surveying a portion of Olduvai Gorge in a collaborative project with Don Johanson, now director of the Institute of Human Origins in Berkeley, California. At Dik Dik Hill (DDH) on July 21, Tim White, and subsequently others, found fragments of a skeleton that rivals Lucy in interest. Given the fragmentary nature of fossils that old—and this was found in Bed I, which makes it in the million-and-a-half year range— it is rare indeed to find pieces of *both* the upper and lower limbs of the same individual. Their discovery, now formally catalogued as Olduvai Hominid (OH) 62, had pieces of both arm and leg bones, and the preliminary indications are that they have found an Australopithecine that is even smaller than Lucy, but which resembles her in having arms that are relatively large in proportion to leg size.[30] Evidently the Australopithecines, although well-adapted terrestrial bipeds, also engaged in activities that preserved relatively robust arms, and it has been suggested by some that they may have continued to use trees as a place of refuge at night or in times of stress.

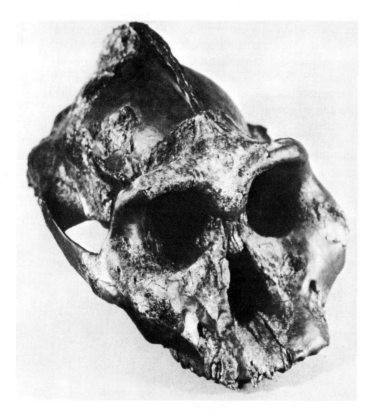

FIGURE 6–6. WT 17000, "the Black Skull," a 2.5 million year old specimen of *Australopithecus boisei.* (Photo A. Walker @ National Museums of Kenya.)

Just to ensure that confusion will continue, the specimen has been put into Leakey's grab bag category, *Homo "habilis,"* although the adaptive features that separate *Homo* from *Australopithecus* are either missing or not preserved on the specimen. The excitement caused by discoveries from west of Lake Turkana have not been confined to those of Australopithecines only. A remarkably complete skeleton of a youthful *Homo erectus* specimen was found at Nariokotome (it rhymes with frontal lobotomy) in northwestern Kenya.[31] It is the most complete single Pithecanthropine ever found, and it is already giving us considerable insight into aspects of the life cycle of the stage of human evolution immediately preceding the emergence of *Homo sapiens.* The Nariokotome specimen—WT 15000—has been nicknamed "Strapping Youth" since, by some estimates, he would have been well over six feet tall if he had lived to adulthood.

Because there is more informed interest in the past in Europe than in any other part of the Old World, it is not surprising that important discoveries are continuing to be made in European soil. Representatives of the last three Stages of human evolution have been added over the last quarter of a century, and there is even one tentative candidate for an Australopithecine at Orce in eastern Spain.[32] Starting in the early 1970s, the work of Henry and Marie-Antoinette de Lumley at the Cave of Arago in the eastern part of the French Pyrenees produced a quantity of material that can be associated with the Pithecanthropine Stage.[33]

In the summer of 1979 in the Charente-Maritime of southwestern France, a skeleton with face and teeth was found that some regard as a "good Neanderthal," and others, such as myself, see as being perfectly intermediate between Neanderthal and Modern form.[34] Even more recently, a series of Neanderthal skulls has been found in a cave in the Atapuerca Hills in north central Spain that show many of the cranial characteristics of the Modern inhabitants of central and eastern Europe.[35] We have spent enough time recounting what was found, when, and by whom, and what they have said about it—it is time now to get on to an assessment of what it all means.

CHAPTER SIX NOTES

[1]Broom, 1947; Broom and Robinson, 1947, 1950b.

[2]Washburn, 1957.

[3]Dart, 1948, 1949.

[4]After Keith declared that "Professor Dart was right and I was wrong" (1947:377), he then went on to suggest that the Australopithecines be called "Dartians" (1947:377, 1948:234). Privately, many Keith admirers felt that his apology was extreme. Keith, however, should be given full credit for having faced up to his initial mistake and recognizing the value of Dart's original interpretation. The name "Dartians," however, sounds a bit too much like Martians, and it never stuck.

[5]Broom and Robinson, 1949, 1950a.

[6]J. D. Clark, 1975, 1976, 1993; Gibert, 1992; Gibert et al., 1991, 1992; Tchernov, 1992.

[7]Sartono and Grimaud-Hervé, 1983a, b; Eijgenraam, 1993.

[8]Lü, 1984; Pope, 1988a, b.

[9]Arsuaga et al., 1993.

[10]Sonakia, 1985.

[11]Kennedy et al., 1991.

[12]Arensburg et al., 1985; Bar-Yosef et al., 1992.

[13]L. Leakey, 1959.

[14]Louis (pronounced "Lewiss" and not "Looey") Leakey was a flamboyant character who initiated and pursued a plethora of projects with an energetic enthusiasm that was almost more romantic than scientific. His own autobiographical account is somewhat bland (L. Leakey, 1974), but Sonia Cole has provided a splendid biography (Cole, 1975). His extraordinary life generated an endless series of anecdotes, and a further collection is delightfully presented by his friend, Phillip Tobias (1976). Still more are recounted in the straightforward and astonishingly candid autobiography of his equally remarkable wife, Mary Leakey (1984).

[15]L. Leakey, 1951; M. Leakey, 1971, 1979b; Clark, 1993.

[16]As was so often the case with some of their most momentous discoveries, it was actually Mary who found it. Louis was ill and had remained at the campsite. Mary was out walking with her two dalmatians when she correctly recognized the discovery for what it was (M. Leakey, 1979b:75).

[17]"Zinj" was the medieval Arabic name for the east coast of Africa. Because they knew immediately what a difference it was going to make in their lives, Mary and Louis Leakey privately referred to it as "Dear Boy." That portent is clearly exhibited by the extravagant label that Louis Leakey used to refer to it in his field notebook: *"Titanohomo mirabilis"* (Johanson and Shreeve, 1989:68).

[18]Grine, 1988a.

[19]L. Leakey at al., 1964.

[20]Leakey's biographer referred to the claim by one of his colleagues that *"habilis* had been launched mainly by the power of Louis's personality" (Cole 1975:256). The study of our own origins tends to bring out an element of the subjective in our assessments, and personality has often played a larger role than the strictly scientific. This remains as true today as it was during Leakey's life.

[21]Curtis and Hay, 1972; Curtis et al., 1975; R. Leakey, 1973; McDougall et al., 1980.

[22]Indicative of the confusion surrounding the purported "species" is the fact that one eminent anthropologist is quite happy to keep the name *"Homo habilis"* and yet consider it consistent with its placement within the "australopithecine grade of organization" (Wolpoff, 1980:165). Another has recognized it as "really an australopithecine" but "likely not to be *Australopithecus*" (Oxnard, 1987:235). A third anthropologist has referred to it as *Australopithecus habilis* (Walker, 1980, 1984:122, 126, 129).

[23]Leakey et al., 1971; R. Leakey and Walker, 1976.

[24]The story of Don Johanson's successful ventures in the field is engagingly told in Johanson and Edey (1981).

[25]Taieb et al., 1974, 1976; Johanson and Taieb, 1976.

[26]Wilford, 1987.

[27]For example, Eijgenraam (1993).

[28]Walker et al., 1986.

[29]Nothing displays the wondrously medieval mind-set of paleoanthropologists more pointedly than the wrangles that have been going on over the Black Skull. In 1967, a Plio/Pleistocene mandible was found in the Omo Valley, northeast of Lake Turkana in Ethiopia. Clearly it was an Australopithecine, but its distinction was enhanced by the suggestion that it might be a new species, so a name was duly created for it. The name was *Australopithecus "aethiopicus"* (Arambourg and Coppens, 1967). The possibility then was raised that this mandible might have belonged to the same kind of creature represented by the jawless skull found in southwestern Kenya and might be discovered to be of the same geological age. These presumptions led to the new name for the Black Skull, *A. aethiopicus* (Johanson, 1986).

[30]Johanson et al., 1987; Johanson and Shreeve, 1989.

[31]Brown et al., 1985; Walker, 1986.

[32]Gibert et al., 1992.

[33]de Lumley and de Lumley, 1971.

[34]Lévêque and Vandermeersch, 1980.

[35]Arsuaga et al., 1993.

chapter seven

Evolutionary Principles

Many approaches to the subject of human evolution are restricted to descriptions of the fossil evidence, or perhaps to the events surrounding the discovery of the major fragments.[1] However fascinating these may be (and here I suspect my own enthusiasm for the bony details of long defunct hominids may somewhat outrun that of the beginning student or general reader), they do not automatically ensure the full understanding of what is being described. Somewhere along the line, one should encounter a summary of the major principles of evolution in general, and the forces which act on humans in particular. Finally, these should be specifically applied to the human fossil record, and the role which they have played in the production of the specific noted changes should be delineated. This last will be the subject of the final chapters; meanwhile, we give a brief consideration to the major evolutionary principles that specifically apply to human evolution.

POPULATIONS VERSUS TYPES

The study of human evolution starts with the discovery of the fossil evidence. This is then arranged in temporal sequence, and the patterns that can be discovered are interpreted according to standard evolutionary principles. Al-

though nearly all of the current treatments discuss both evolutionary principles and the fossil evidence, one often gets the impression that the actual interpretations are being guided by unrecognized or at least unstated sets of
assumptions. To the average biologist trained in the Darwinian tradition, the
student of human evolution has often appeared to be marching to the beat
of a different drummer. Recently this has been made explicit in some treatments of paleontology,[2] and it has been particularly apparent in current paleoanthropology.[3]

We have seen how the lingering tradition of catastrophism has continued to be influential. Some other equally important vestiges of traditional
Western world views have continued to survive. One of these is our notion of
the "typical" or "ideal." Renaissance artists portrayed human form according
to what they felt were ideal proportions, and post-Renaissance biologists
stocked their museums with what they hoped were typical representatives of
the plants and animals of the world. In Platonic philosophy, the essence of
reality was a perfect idea that was reflected in less-than-perfect forms visible
in the material world.[4]

Dating from the time of Augustine in the fourth century A.D., currents of
Platonic thought, really Neoplatonism, were combined with Christian faith to
shape the way people thought. In this amalgamated intellectual tradition, the
essence of reality, as it had been to Plato, was a perfect idea, but in this case it
was an Idea in the Mind of God. Visible form can approach, but it cannot attain, that perfection, for to do so would be to equate it with divinity itself.[5]

As the Renaissance age of exploration and discovery revealed to Europeans the enormous variety of plants and animals that they assumed reflected
the manifold ideas in the mind of God, it became a kind of act of piety to list
and describe them. To a considerable extent, this provided the impetus for
the systematic pursuit of science. Whether it was Kepler working out the laws
of planetary motion or Linnaeus identifying the plants and animals of the
world, scientists believed they were discovering the dimensions of the mind
of God and thereby coming to understand God's plan for the way things
ought to be.[6] Not only that, the medieval Christian philosopher, Thomas
Aquinas, noted that the "goodness" of the world was best illustrated by recognizing a greater number of kinds of species, thereby demonstrating the
power, the glory, and the goodness of the Creator himself. This view, established by St. Thomas in the thirteenth century, is alive and well and creating
a veritable Babel of confusing names in paleoanthropology at the present
time, although it is not clear whether the greatness being demonstrated is
that of divine glory or merely the dimensions of the ego of the individual who
creates and defends the name(s) in question.[8]

Because all of these categories were thought to derive from a perfect,
eternal, and therefore changeless Deity, the assumption followed that these
ideal categories themselves were fixed, perfect, and eternal. The ideas of ash
tree and aster, lobster and lion, man, mouse, and all the rest had a reality that

not only derived from but proved the existence of God. To suggest that such might not be the case was tantamount to atheism or blasphemy or worse. Obviously when Darwin developed his demonstration that the only constant was change itself, operating in response to the interplay of the mechanics of impersonal natural forces, he was perceived by the pious traditionalists as an enemy to the assumed perfection and fixity of their revealed religion.[9]

Darwin's focus on change not only cast doubt on the validity of fixed and changeless types, but it also identified the source of that potential change in the naturally occurring variation visible among the individuals of any given species. Individual differences, then, were not just imperfect renderings of an intended ideal type. Instead they provided a vital demonstration of how species can adapt to changing circumstances.

As a result of Darwin's insights, evolutionary biologists now realize that it is at least as important to know the naturally occurring range of variation of a given group as it is to know its idealized average. Consequently, the typological thinking of pre-Darwinian science has tended to be replaced by the populational approach of modern biology.[10]

Old habits die hard, however, and, although it is often denounced in theory and unrecognized in fact, typological thinking is alive and well and continuing to flourish in the last quarter of the twentieth century. To an extent, it is unavoidable in practice. Just to talk about things we have to give them names, and because of the nature of the fossil record, single specimens, often quite incomplete, have to do duty for whole populations and long periods of time. Scholars gain recognition for key discoveries, and inevitably the names and descriptions they give acquire an importance that smacks of typological essence with overtones of sanctity.

Finally, as was noted in the chapter on hominid catastrophism, the field of paleontology in general and paleoanthropology in particular has strong roots in the scholarship of France of the late nineteenth and early twentieth centuries. The French not only rejected a Darwinian view of evolution, with its emphasis on populational thinking and the action of natural forces, but stressed a kind of Platonic essentialism and generally avoided a consideration of natural mechanisms at all.[11] The focus on the intricacies and nuances of form without any particular regard for function derives from a tacit assumption that detailed description can reveal a kind of teleological intent. Inevitably, a substantial portion of the typological approach survives in practice in modern anthropology. Recently there has been an increasing effort to provide some kind of theoretical justification, even though this runs counter to the expectations of Darwinian biology.[12]

HUMANS IN NATURE

This is a book about human evolution, and it takes it as factually demonstrable that human beings are a part of the animal world. Certainly to claim the contrary would qualify as irrational at best. The patterning of our limbs and bodies, the numbers of bones and segments in our appendages, and the way our joints work are repeated down to the last detail in millions upon millions of other accepted members of the animal world. The morphology of the neurons and axons of our nervous system, the chemistry of its synapses, and the transmission of its nerve impulses are absolutely identical. So, too, are the structural, functional, and chemical details of our skeletomuscular systems, our sensory organs, our circulatory systems, and the rest of our basic biological construction.[13] To be sure, we occasionally refer to those whom we consider to be uncommonly inert as "vegetables," but even as we use such a term of opprobrium we realize that the objects of our scorn are not really members of the plant kingdom. And yet we do share things with plants that also demonstrate a kinship, albeit more remote, that could not have been the result of accidental independent acquisition. The nucleate cell is the basic building block for plants and animals. The mechanics of cell division, the phenomenon of sexual reproduction, the control of heredity by DNA, and the roles of structural and enzymatic proteins are all essentially the same. We know vastly more about the details of these similarities between living organisms than Darwin did when he realized that a theory of descent from a common origin was the most likely way to account for all of this, and everything we have learned since has simply bolstered the credibility of his insight.

DISTINCTIONS

It is also obvious that there are aspects of difference as well as of similarity, and we should be able to use the enumerated differences as an indicator of time since that point of common origin. In both theory and practice, matters are considerably more complex than that, but the overall generalization remains true. Studying similarities and differences, then, can enable us to arrange the living creatures of the world into various inclusive and exclusive categories that reflect their relationships in terms of relative recency of descent from common ancestors.[14]

We recognize, for example, that house cats and lions have more in common with each other than cats and dogs. Cats and dogs, however, have more in common than either has with horses or cows, and cats and cows share more with each other than either does with frogs or fish—and so on. By systematic means, we can build up a classification of living things that should reflect their evolutionary history. Most biologists assume, then, that classification is a means of depicting the results of evolution.

But this was not always the case. Many of the traditions that have shaped the practice of classification date from an earlier time when it was assumed that its object was to demonstrate the categories and logic of God's created world. Of course, people have been classifying things since the dawn of recorded history, and, considering the elaborate accuracy of the classifications of nature by nonliterate people from Australia and New Guinea to the Arctic, it is certain that people have been engaged in classification at least since the beginnings of language itself.

LOGIC AND NATURE

The formal written traditions of our classifications of the natural world go back to Aristotle. Both his application and his logic were adopted by the scholars of the medieval Christian church. This, in turn, was adopted by Linnaeus, the eighteenth-century Swedish botanist whose system is universally used today. Our terms Class, Order, Family, *Genus,* and *species* were all used by Linnaeus, but these, in turn, were the very terms of medieval Aristotelian logic.[15] Medieval scholars assumed that God's world was rigidly logical and that all of its categories equivalent. These, in effect, were fixed and unchangeable essences determined by God's intent. Classification, then, could be accomplished by strictly logical means.

In practice, many biologists realized that the higher categories were determined by human decisions for our own convenience. Darwin even went so far as to recognize that species themselves, the basic building blocks of any classification, not only had an element of the subjective in their establishment but were also capable of changing through time. This was profoundly upsetting to many of his contemporaries, and has continued to be a sore subject for many biologists right up to the present day. "If species do not exist at all, . . . how can they vary?" was the anguished objection of one of his eminent contemporaries.[16] Even today, a powerful school of thought has sought to reject this aspect of Darwin's insight and return to the certainties of the Middle Ages, where species were considered to be fixed and their relationships could be determined by the strict application of Aristotelian logic.[17]

LOGIC AND COMPUTERS

It is no accident that the emergence of this modern movement coincides with the growth in use of that extraordinarily powerful and useful instrument, the digital computer. The computer is based upon elementary certainties: whether a datum exists or it does not, something is true or it is not true, an answer is yes or it is no. Inevitably an instrument that is so enormously convenient will lead its users to take maximum advantage of its capabilities, but there is a sometimes unrealized consequence. It just might seduce its users into structuring their expectations and the way they handle their data and their problems so that these will be compatible with what the computer does best. The result is that the computer—admittedly not by anything one could call "intent" on its part—will influence the way we think about things.[18]

It is just possible that the recent enthusiasm for the use of a rigid deductive logic to solve the problems of evolutionary relationships is an unconscious byproduct.

THE CATEGORIES OF CLASSIFICATION

Ever since the Middle Ages, there have been repeated attempts to arrange the elements of the living world in a hierarchy that has a completely logical structure. The Linnaean classification of the eighteenth century, now universally accepted, is one such attempt. Plants and animals are put into separate Kingdoms. Within each of these, further distinctions are made at the Phylum level. For example, humans are placed in the Phylum distinguished by the possession of a spinal cord located in the back: Phylum Chordata. Fish, reptiles, amphibians, birds, and mammals are distinguished at the Class level. Within the Class Mammalia, insectivores, bats carnivores, rodents, elephants, and many others are distinguished at the Order level. We belong in the Order Primates, along with lemurs, lorises, tarsiers, monkeys, and apes. We are separated from them at the Family level, where we are noted as belonging to Family Hominidae. The great apes belong to Family Pongidae, and the close affinity of humans and apes is recognized at what is called the Superfamily level, where we are included as Superfamily Hominoidea. In an informal sense this is recognized by the term "hominoid." The familial distinctions are informally recognized by the use of the terms "pongid" for apes and "hominid" for humans. The genus name for humans is *Homo,* and the species name is *sapiens.* This completes the full formal classification from our own anthropocentric point of view.[19] The complete classification of *Homo sapiens* is illustrated in Figure 7–1.

All major levels of classification can be lumped at the "super" level, or divided at the "sub" level, and further divided at the "infra" level, with more attention paid to dividing than lumping. We have Suborders, Infraorders, Superfamilies, subspecies, and so on. The professional arguments over classification are endless. Over two hundred years ago, the French biologist, Buffon,

FIGURE 7–1. The classification of *Homo sapiens.*

Kingdom	**Animalia**
Phylum	**Chordata**
Class	**Mammalia**
Order	**Primates**
Family	**Hominidae**
Genus	***Homo***
species	***sapiens***

declared that it was all arbitrary, since classification was practiced by human beings for their own purposes and none of the categories had any logically independent reality. Eventually he admitted the separate reality of species, but not of the higher categories. At an operational level, this has been the position of most biologists ever since.[20]

SPECIES AND REALITY

But even at the species level, none other than Darwin himself noted that categorization has an element of the arbitrary.[21] Many have found this a profoundly disturbing point and have refused to accept it. The arguments have raged back and forth, and recently there has been a resurgence of the stance that species do have a categorical reality. In part this may be a reflection of the human desire for elementary certainty akin to the medieval faith in the verity of the units of God's created world, and in part this may be a result of the pragmatic utility inherent in being able to take for granted the reality of the units the computer allows us to manipulate with such ease. And whether or not species are regarded as validly definable and strictly comparable units, virtually all modern biologists use them as though they were.

Many practitioners follow the lead of Ernst Mayr of Harvard, one of the most eminent of contemporary zoologists, who defined species as "groups of actually or potentially interbreeding natural populations which are reproductively isolated from other such groups."[22] While this works effectively enough when we are dealing with living plants and animals, it is impossible to tell whether representatives of prehistoric populations could interbreed with each other or not. For the foreseeable future, this appears to be an insuperable problem, and, once again, we can do no better than to follow the lead of Charles Darwin. Darwin advocated that, in determining whether a given form should be regarded as a separate species or not, "the opinion of naturalists having sound judgment and wide experience seems the only guide to follow."[23]

There is no objective means of determining which "naturalists" have suitable quantities of "sound judgment and wide experience," and the result is that the numbers and names of fossil species—especially fossil hominids—differ greatly from one account to another. Those who have been involved with the treatment of the fossil record tend to fall into one of two schools of thought: the "splitters" and the "lumpers." Splitters tend to accord each newly discovered fossil specimen a new specific name, while lumpers tend to include new specimens within the named groups already known. Those engaged in the actual work of excavation and discovery, often without much training in evolutionary theory and principles, tend to be splitters, while those who attempt to interpret the accumulating numbers of individual finds in a context of evolutionary dynamics tend to be lumpers. The late Louis

Leakey, an exemplar of the fieldworker par excellence, was characterized by one observer as "a lavish splitter in an age of lumpers,"[24] while the approach taken in this book tends towards the opposite end of the spectrum.

Over the recent past, an increasing number of workers have been engaged in actual field excavation. This has led to a wealth of new discoveries, and, inevitably, the discoverers have bequeathed new specific names on each new treasure. This, along with a rather widespread retreat from a concern with the evolutionary issues to which this chapter is devoted, has led to a resurgent enthusiasm for splitting.[25] New species are being recognized and old names resuscitated in a fashion reminiscent of the Middle Ages, when the discovery and naming of new categories was regarded as a demonstration of creative powers of Divinity itself.[26] We shall try to temper some of this exuberance in the pages that follow. Happily, the evolutionary theory that leads us to question the tendency to multiply genera and species also limits the names that the beginner has to commit to memory.

We add one final note on the matter of taxonomic names. The reader may have observed that we have often used quotation marks around particular italicized terms—for example, *"Zinjanthropus" boisei, "Paranthropus crassidens," Homo "habilis,"* or *"Meganthropus palaeojavanicus."* This is done whenever there is some doubt about whether the name was properly proposed in the first place or whether the specimen in question is sufficiently distinct to warrant having that particular formal generic or specific name.

SPECIES AND CHANGE

That species have descended from previous species is a fact upon which all are in agreement. How this occurred is a matter of profound and continuing disagreement. The source of that disagreement is based partly on the nature of the species with which the various investigators are most familiar, and partly on the different intellectual traditions in which those investigators were trained. This book is concerned with change in the human species, so the choice of interpretation in the ongoing arguments about the nature of specific change is obviously conditioned by a familiarity with the human biological evidence, present and past. The intellectual tradition on which the interpretation of that evidence is based is the one that was established with the publication of Darwin's *Origin* and which has grown with the addition of a genetic—especially a molecular genetic—perspective.

Given this basis, it is perfectly clear that change in the human line of development has been a slow, gradual phenomenon. This does not mean that it has always proceeded at the same rate, or that the traits that can be assessed were all undergoing change simultaneously. But even though this may be "perfectly clear" if looked at in this way, it is not the view of the majority who work in paleoanthropology. Why this should be so is a demonstration of the strength and continuity of the essentialist tradition stemming from medieval Neoplatonism.[27]

CLADES AND CLADISTICS

This continuing essentialist tradition is currently known by the name of "cladistics," or, as its proponents prefer, "phylogenetic systematics," and its guiding intellectual figure was the late German entomologist, Willi Hennig (1913–1976).[28] The basic unit, or clade, is simply the continuation of a given lineage or "monophyletic unit" through time, and cladistics is the use of particular kinds of traits for the formal assessment of the relationships and distinctions of clades. The results can be presented in a cladogram (Figure 7–2).

For example, the position of humans in relation to their closest primate relatives can be clearly seen in the cladogram presented here (see Figure 7–3). There is no assumption of length of time or rate of change in a cladogram, and there is no identification of a common ancestor. Relationship is based on the recency of the split in clades from an assumed common ancestor and is expressed in the sharing of recently evolved or "derived" traits—"apomorphies," to use the formal term. Similarities based on the retention of common "primitive" traits—"plesiomorphies"—cannot show closeness of relationship. The problem with this procedure is in determining which traits are primitive and which are derived. Another obstacle can

FIGURE 7–2.   A cladogram showing the relationships of the major groups of primates in terms of the relative recency of splitting from common ancestors.

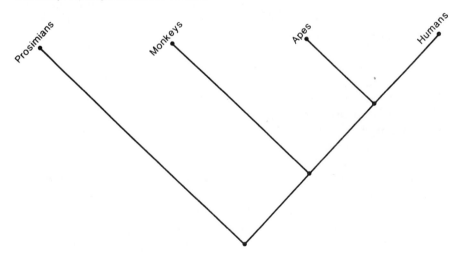

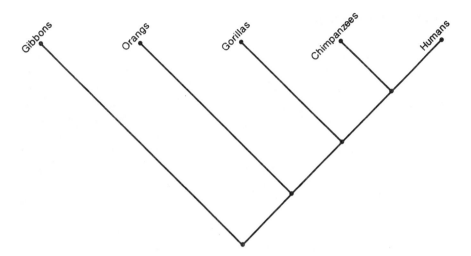

FIGURE 7–3. This cladogram shows the relationships between humans and the various members of the ape grade of primates, based on a combination of anatomical and DNA similarities and differences.

occur when what appear to be similar and recently derived traits in different organisms actually arose by "convergence" from somewhat different previous states.

Careful consideration and skeptical caution can overcome some of these problems and assure that a cladistic approach can yield valuable information on organic relationships. However, another assumption made by many practicing cladists cannot be dealt with so easily. As the field is constituted at present, it considers it to be axiomatic that a species *cannot* change gradually through time to the extent that it has to be granted new specific status. Evolutionary changes are assumed to occur only as a result of "speciation events" that are represented by the nodes or branch points of a cladogram. At this point, the parent species presumably ceases to exist, and two "sister" species of equivalent rank arise. Each of these then continues without change either to extinction or to a new branching point when two new sister species arise.

As a presentation of the nature of evolutionary change, this represents an assumption *a priori* that is simply taken on faith. In practice, there is no consideration of evolutionary process or the interplay of selective force and adaptive response. The result is remarkably like the picture presented by Cuvier's catastrophism early in the nineteenth century, which regards change as occurring suddenly, for undiscoverable reasons, and away from the region under examination. The new form, which spreads by migration, then prevails until the next sudden change.[29]

PUNCTUATED EQUILIBRIA

Closely related to cladistics but differing in some details is the theory of punctuated equilibria proposed by the New York paleontologist, Niles Eldredge,
and his Harvard colleague, Stephen Jay Gould.[30] This theory maintains that
the normal condition is the persistence of species unchanged throughout
their existence, a phenomenon referred to as "stasis." Gradual response to selective force is generally denied, and change, when it occurs, takes place suddenly at the isolated peripheries of the species range for reasons that are
largely unknown. The successful new species that results from this then per-
sists in unchanging equilibrium until the next punctuation.

Just as do orthodox cladists, punctuationists regard evolution as a thing
of fits and starts with long periods of stasis in between. Unlike cladists, they do
not insist upon the simultaneous emergence of two sister species and the disappearance of the parent species during the speciation event. A parent species
can persist after giving rise to a daughter species, and may even outlive it.

Some advocates of punctuated equilibria are not cladists in the strict
sense, then, but all cladists view the picture of organic life through time as
one of long periods characterized by the unchanging persistence of living
forms punctuated at intervals by sudden change. Inevitably, then, when dealing with the human fossil record, both cladists and punctuationists prefer the
traditional views previously described as hominid catastrophism. Adaptation
is ignored and extinctions and invasions are postulated, even though the archaeological and fossil record does not provide convincing support.

Needless to say, this is not the orientation of this present book. But that
does not mean that the stance taken by the punctuationists and the cladists is
always wrong. It is just not always right. We have to find out from the evidence itself whether and when stasis is the case; where speciation takes place
and whether it is the result of lineage splitting; and if adaptive response to selective force change can indeed account for gradual change through time. As
we shall see, all of these phenomena can be observed at one time or another
in the human fossil record.

GRADES

While clades represent lineages continuing through time, there is another
way of looking at organic forms in comparative perspective, and this is the
consideration of grades. Grades imply comparable levels of adaptive integra-
tion where similar traits allow the pursuit of similar life-ways.[31] Birds and bats
represent a flying vertebrate grade, although they are not linearly related.

Actually, bats themselves are an interesting example of the grade of flying mammal since they are not all that closely related to each other. The
insect-eating bats are really airborne insectivores, but the fruit bats, or "flying

foxes," may just be more closely related to true primates—a kind of lemur that has independently acquired the powers of flight.[32]

Within our own order, primates, there are four recognized grades—or five if the fruit bats are considered to count.[33] First, there is the *prosimian grade,* which includes the lemurs of Madagascar; the galagos of Africa; the lorises of Africa, India, and Southeast Asia; and perhaps the tarsiers of Indonesia and the Philippines. Prosimians retain many of the traits of their nonprimate ancestors. They possess sensory whiskers and a relatively acute sense of smell. Their vision tends to be less than fully binocular and stereoscopic, and brain size and manipulative capabilities are less well developed than in the other primate grades. But they are fully arboreal and can be considered slightly modified survivors of the first mammals that took to the trees and became primates.

Next there is the *monkey grade.* Like the prosimians, monkeys are basically arboreal quadrupeds, although some, such as baboons, have become secondarily terrestrial. Fully stereoscopic binocular vision has been achieved, the sense of smell is less important, brain size and manipulative capacity have increased, and the basic dietary focus is on the fruits, berries, nuts, and leaves that the tropical forest canopy produces in such abundance.

Beyond the monkey grade, there is the *ape grade.* The tendency for relative cerebral expansion is carried yet another step, and the normal primate tail disappears altogether. At the same time there is a general average increase in body size associated with a different habitual mode of locomotion. Instead of being an arboreal version of a terrestrial quadruped, full-scale quadrumanous (four-handed) climbing or clambering is the characteristic means of getting about. Arm hanging and hand-over-hand progression beneath the branches rather than quadrupedal running on top of them becomes more common. This is what allows for the development of a larger body size without limiting the apes to only the sturdier limbs and tree trunks, and it also improves access to the fruits and related edibles that grow at the tips of the smaller branches.

Finally, there is the *human grade,* which is characterized by further expansion of the brain, an erect-walking bipedal mode of locomotion, and the development of culture as a principal adaptation. Within the human grade are four gradelike levels of adaptation, which, for the purposes of this book, I have termed the "Stages of Human Evolution." These are the Australopithecine, the Pithecanthropine, the Neanderthal, and the Modern Stages, and each will be treated in its own chapter.

NATURAL SELECTION

The first and most important of the evolutionary principles is encompassed by the term "natural selection." In Darwin's own words, "This preservation of favourable variations and the rejection of injurious variations, I call Natural Selection."[34] Like many other basic principles in other areas of thought (culture for the anthropologist, or entropy for the physicist, for example), it is hard to define concisely, although natural scientists are virtually unanimous in its usage. Realizing that this is an oversimplification, one can regard natural selection as being the sum total of naturally occurring forces that influence the relative chances for survival and perpetuation of the various manifestations of organic life.

Darwin realized that populations were capable of multiplying much faster than the resources on which they depend. Furthermore, he was aware that the individual members of a population differed from each other and that those differences tended to be inherited. In the competition for the finite amount of resources, those individuals who were able to use those resources to sustain themselves for longer periods of time and leave more offspring would be contributing their inherited characteristics in greater proportions to the next generation. Those who were less successful in that regard, were less likely to see their inherited characteristics represented in future generations.

The model has been referred to as one of "selective retention."[35] With minor heritable changes occurring in each generation, those that are selectively retained will alter the nature of each succeeding generation so that, in the course of time, the species as a whole will be different from what it had been before. That by definition is evolution: the change through time of the species itself. The environment simply acts as an editor, allowing more favorable variants to survive at the expense of less favorable ones, and that, in essence, is natural selection.[36]

Charles Darwin deserves the credit for using this as the major explanatory principle necessary to account for the cumulative change apparent in the history of any given organic line. Occasionally the principle has been tersely expressed as "survival of the fittest," although it was not Darwin who first phrased it that way, and it has been justly criticized as being not quite accurate.[37] In the recent past it has been pointed out that evolutionary survival is determined more by reproductive success than by physical strength. The suggestion has been made that the phrase might be modified to read "the survival of the fit." Actually, a certain amount of verbal quibbling must inevitably surround any attempt to produce a precise definition—if fitness is described in terms of the production of viable offspring, then the fittest will obviously be those who produce the most and whose traits will be most frequently represented in subsequent generations.

As environmental forces change over time, the characteristics that have greatest survival value will not be those which had the most utility at an earlier age. However, in order that environmental forces may effect a change in the characteristic appearance of the species in question—that is, in order for natural selection to produce evolution—some source for the new traits must be postulated. In Darwin's day this source was unknown. On the basis of extensive observational experience, however, Darwin knew that the variants were always being produced, so he simply accepted their existence "on faith" without knowing where they came from.[38] Some of the most bitter attacks against him came from those who recognized that he did take it that way.[39]

Today we recognize that the faith Darwin had in his observation that variation occurs in the normal course of events was faith well-grounded. When developments in the field of genetics led to the recognition of mutations as the source of variation, it was soon explicitly realized that these provide "the raw material on which selection acts" to provide the observable reality of organic evolution.[40] As has been mentioned, this was the point where evolutionary thought and genetics joined to produce what has come to be called "the synthetic theory of evolution."[41]

THE PROBABLE MUTATION EFFECT[42]

At the very end of the Introduction to his *Origin,* Darwin wrote, "I am convinced that Natural Selection has been the main but not exclusive means of modification."[43] In effect, he had applied to biology the insights that Lyell and others had demonstrated in geology: that the form of the world we inhabit was entirely accounted for by the shaping effects of the everyday forces that we observe around us, applied over an enormously long period of time.[44] Long after Darwin's death, this was given full mathematical demonstration, and it has served as the cornerstone of modern biology.[45] Today, few qualified biologists doubt the primary role played by natural selection in shaping what we see in the living world.

Many leave it at that and concentrate strictly on natural selection as the object of their study, but Darwin had cagily left the door open to other possible sources of change and even provided some examples.[46] This is introduced here because there is reason to believe that the course of human evolution in the recent past has been increasingly influenced by matters that are not the result of natural selection. If there is one thing that distinguishes the human approach to survival in this world from that of the rest of its inhabitants, it is the persistent effort to avoid the effects of natural selection. We have invented clothing and shelter to shield us from the immediate elements, we have devised various medications to reduce the impact of diseases, we have concocted all sorts of devices to compensate for less than imposing muscular capabilities, and in general cooked up innumerable dodges that enable us to avoid the otherwise expectable consequences of facing the world without assistance.

The record of human cultural innovations provides clear evidence for human attempts to minimize the effects of some aspects of selection, and it is surely no accident that the relevant aspects of human physique have undergone marked reductions following the adoption of each such innovation.

With the single exception of the attainment and maintenance of the Modern brain, all of the other changes by which we can be distinguished from our immediate Middle Pleistocene ancestors are reductions in specific aspects of physical robustness. Although there have been attempts to claim that being weaker and more prone to dislocations and fractures is somehow "better" and therefore the result of natural selection in some incomprehensible sort of way,[47] it seems increasingly clear that the changes we have been able to document of that nature are the result of something other than positive selective forces.

If the summed forces of nature working on organic variability can be regarded as the most important principle in the production of evolutionary change, then the next most important dimension must be that which is determined by the nature and frequency of the sources of variation themselves. Simply stated, the nature of mutations, their frequency of occurrence, and the probable effect they have are of an importance second only to natural selection.

Although a discussion of genetics at the molecular level may seem rather a long way from the human fossil record, its importance will become quite clear during the treatment of all but one of the major changes that characterize the course of human evolution. In essence, the story goes like this: Recent research has identified the basic genetic material, demonstrated its structure, and suggested the mode of action whereby it controls organic form and function, as well as replicates itself. To say that the basic genetic material is DNA is true enough, but to say that a mutation is an error in the attempt by a DNA molecule to copy itself, while true, is not precise enough for our purposes. To appreciate the significance of the average mutation, one must first have some idea of how genetic control normally works.[48]

For the moment, we are concerned with two kinds of organic molecules: nucleic acids and proteins. Both are polymers—that is, they are chainlike structures whose links are called amino acids (in the case of proteins) and nucleotides (in the case of nucleic acids). The full nucleic acid molecule is a double chain composed of complementary or mirror-image halves. However, while the double chain of a nucleic acid is built up of only four different kinds of its basic building blocks—the nucleotides—the single chain protein molecules have more than twenty kinds of amino acids available for their construction.

Both kinds of molecules are of vital importance. Proteins not only form the structural components of which living organisms are constructed (bone, muscle, fiber), but they also constitute the organic catalysts called enzymes, hormones, and other such enabling molecules as hemoglobin, insulin, and adrenaline, without which normal metabolic functioning and growth could not occur. DNA, on the other hand, mostly remains within the nucleus of the cell where it provides a source of information for the construction of protein molecules. Figure 7–4 illustrates the DNA molecule.

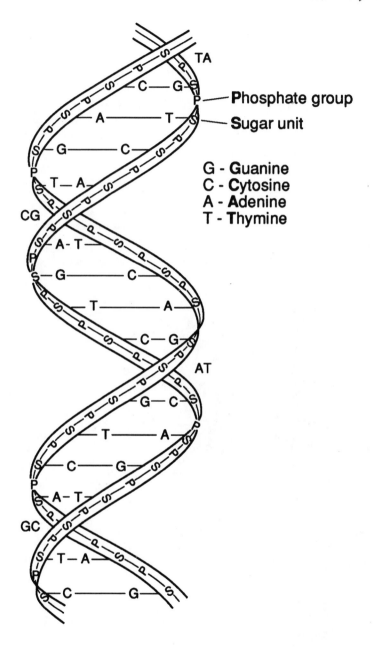

Phosphate group

Sugar unit

G - **Guanine**
C - **Cytosine**
A - **Adenine**
T - **Thymine**

FIGURE 7–4. The double helix, or Watson-Crick model of a DNA molecule.

At first it was not known how the four nucleotides of nucleic acids related to the twenty-plus amino acids of proteins. To simplify the rather complex process that subsequent research has shown to be involved, let us put it this way: Various sequences of nucleotides, taken three at a time, can specify (serve as the code for) given amino acids. The nucleotides, with the aid of specific enzymes, fasten together the amino acids by means of a phosphate energy bond. In the course of protein production, quantities of nucleotide triplets, called codons, attach themselves to free amino acids and tow them to the sites of protein synthesis within the cell, where they are lined up and snapped together (see Figure 7–5).

This brief and grossly oversimplified description is not intended to be

Figure 7–5.   Top left: Schematic representation of a protein molecule, made up of amino acid units in a chain, and of a nucleic acid molecule, made up of nucleotide units in a chain. Top right: Attachment of a specific amino acid to a particular nucleotide triplet (codon) with the aid of an enzyme especially constituted for that purpose. Bottom: Amino acids being towed by nucleotide triplets to the site where they are hooked together to form proteins.

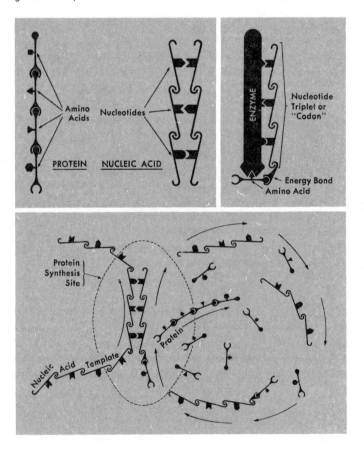

complete. The point to be made is that a sequence of three specific nucleotides acting as a unit (a codon) identifies one particular amino acid. If, by chance, an error is made in the replication of the nucleic acid molecule, the smallest identifiable change will be the modification of a single nucleotide. Although a single nucleotide does not correspond to an entire amino acid, the modification of any one nucleotide will indeed change the nature of the triplet to which it belongs, and in all likelihood this will code a different amino acid from what had previously been the case—if indeed it codes any. In the terms of classical genetics, this is the minimum definition of a mutation: that alteration in a portion of the DNA molecule which produces a single amino acid change in a protein.[49]

Two of the most likely changes at the single nucleotide level result in still further complications. The addition or deletion of a nucleotide will not only modify the triplet within which it occurs, but will also change the nature of the triplets that follow. Obviously, this means that more than one amino acid in the related protein will be changed, and it seems quite clear that the protein will not work in the way it was intended. A change in even one amino acid can drastically alter the function of the protein of which it is a part, as can be seen in sickle cell anemia and a variety of other deficiency diseases of an inherited nature.[50]

What we have been discussing forms the basis for the fact realized well over half a century ago: that the great majority of mutations will be disadvantageous to the organism in which they occur.[51] Actually, this statement, although correct, assumes a static picture in which environmental forces remain unchanged—that is, it assumes that any modification in an organism will be detrimental to it. To be sure, when an organism is well adapted to its environment, most alterations in its form that arise by chance will not be advantageous. But the environment itself may undergo a change, in which instance some structures that had previously been essential may become less important for the organism's survival. While this is not a major problem in evolution, it is one that continually arises, and, because it has apparently occurred in the course of human development, it deserves some attention.

When some major change occurs in a creature's environment, or when a creature enters an entirely new environment, it may suddenly find that it possesses some structures which, while not disadvantageous, are of no particular value to it. Because the structures in question are neither selected *for* nor selected *against*, they are at the mercy of random modifications in the genetic material that controls their appearance. It is now pertinent to ask what sort of variations are likely to occur. If we are dealing with a feature of gross morphology (teeth, horns, pigmentation), we must realize that these are the results of a period of growth during which development is influenced by the sequential interaction of a sizable series of enzymes. Since enzymes are protein molecules, evidently many of them will be subject to direct genetic control, with mutations affecting their amino acid constituents.

Normal..................DAD AND NAN CAN ADD DAN AND ANN

Mutated by

  addition of D..........[D]↘DDA DAN DNA NCA NAD DDA NAN DAN N

or,

  deletion of A..............↗[A] DDA NDN ANC ANA DDD ANA NDA NN

or,

  substitution

  of C for D..............[C]↘[D] CAD AND NAN CAN ADD DAN AND ANN

FIGURE 7–6. The effects of deletion, addition, and substitution on the "sense" of a phrase made up of three-letter words (codons) composed of only four kinds of letters (nucleotides) from the Roman alphabet. For purposes of illustration, alterations are made in the second position only of the first word, although in fact they could occur anywhere. As is evident, an addition or a deletion disrupts the subsequent sense of the message, which shows why the majority of "mutations" produce a reduction in the results of what is conveyed. Substitutions can produce a message that has some altered "sense" to it, as is shown in the adulterous implications of the little family scenario depicted here.

Random variation in a morphological feature usually occurs in modifications of this growth process, and the most common modification of the growth process is in the form of mutations affecting the controlling enzymes. At this level, the expected change is the alteration of a single amino acid, and almost invariably the result is either that the enzyme fails to work altogether, or that it does not work as well as it did in its unaltered form. If a growth enzyme fails to work, or works only to a reduced degree, then the structure that depends upon it either will fail to occur, or else will occur in reduced or only partially developed form.[52] Stated briefly, the most likely effect of the most likely mutation will be the reduction of a structure that depends upon it— that is, the result of the probable mutation effect is structural reduction. In a normally adapted organism, such reductions will, of course, be disadvantageous. On the other hand, whenever circumstances are altered so that a structure no longer has the same importance for survival that it previously had, one can predict that the probable mutation effect will produce its ultimate reduction.

GENETIC DRIFT

If the importance of the probable mutation effect is minor in comparison with that of natural selection, then the importance of genetic drift is practically negligible as far as the production of any significant evolutionary change is concerned.[53] Basically, genetic drift is the operation of chance as it influences the distribution of characteristics in a sequence of generations. This can easily be demonstrated by a simple example. Imagine a small, isolated band of Paleolithic hunters—say, six men and six women—encamped in a rock shelter at the edge of a game-filled valley. Hunting is good, and since they are the only people in that part of the world, their future seems well assured. A noticeable peculiarity among the men is that, whereas four of them have full heads of hair (as did their fathers, even in advancing age), the other two, having inherited a tendency to become prematurely bald, sport at best only thinning patches of what had once been long, healthy locks. On one unfortunate day, the roof of their rock shelter caved in, crushing most of the band of hunters—several of the women, and all but two of the men. As luck would have it, both the unscathed men were the balding ones. On the strength of this characteristic alone, one could safely predict that the future males of the band would tend to be bald as well. Actually, this little example portrays a particular form of genetic drift called "the founder effect," but it nevertheless suffices to illustrate the logic of the general principle.[54]

Evidently it was sheer chance that affected the future of the male contingent of our little group. Sheer chance is a much more important element in determining proportions in a small group than in a large group. In a population of several thousand, for instance, the accidental loss of four men will not appreciably affect the relative proportions of characteristics transmitted to future generations, as it did in our example. Chance occurrences of this or any other sort cannot impart any consistent direction to evolution or account for an evolutionary trend. Since all major evolutionary developments are the results of forces that operate over very long periods of time, genetic drift is clearly of only local or incidental importance.

There are two reasons for mentioning genetic drift. First, it has been frequently invoked to account for changes that appear to have no adaptive significance. Second, throughout much of prehistory, the characteristic human breeding population was just the sort of small semi-isolated group in which genetic drift could have had its greatest effect. While it is difficult to point with certainty to human features that owe their existence to the operation of genetic drift, it would be equally foolish to deny that it had played any role in human evolution.

As possible examples, we can cite some of the details in which human skeletal form differs from one part of the world to another. At the northwestern edge of Europe, for instance, the proportion of the height of the skull to both its length and its width is remarkably low. But the only role played by the major cranial bones is that of encasing the brain, and the important thing is not the gross shape of the enclosure but simply whether it is large enough to encompass its contents.[55] The length, width, and height proportions of the skull vary to a considerable degree between the living populations of the world, but the actual volume of the brain encompassed is strictly proportional to body size and nothing else, and the brain-to-body proportion is the same for all modern human groups. Evidently, the nuances of shape that regularly distinguish cranial form in the various regions of the world have no adaptive value whatever.[56] Regional differences, then, are simply the result of chance—genetic drift.

Even in those parts of the craniofacial skeleton where selection does play a discernible role, such as in the projection of the nose, which differs markedly between one region of the world and another, there are many details that are unrelated to the obvious effects of environmental selective forces. In the colder and drier parts of the world, nasal prominence is obvious among those peoples whose ancestors had lived there for some tens of thousands of years. But nasal prominence can be achieved by two very different means. The bony part of the cheek that lies right beside the nasal aperture can be drawn up into a substantially elevated beak and then capped with a narrow strip of the nasal bone itself. Or, at the other extreme, nasal elevation can be accomplished entirely by hypertrophy of the nasal bones alone. Both methods of developing nasal prominence are visible in different parts of the world, and, while the skeletal contributions are quite different, the flesh-clad noses of the living people can look remarkably similar and they are equally effective in moistening and warming the air inspired. The differences in the details of nasal construction, then, are not related to the action of the forces of selection. It seems likely that these have become distinct in their various areas simply as a result of chance—again, genetic drift.[57]

ORTHOGENESIS

Although orthogenesis is not really an evolutionary principle at all, it has been a prominent feature of former evolutionary schemes.[58] It is considered here only so that we can convincingly renounce it. In the past, when evolutionary principles were dimly understood and did not seem adequate to account for the developments that the fossil record and contemporary organic diversity revealed, it seemed to some scholars that the visible evolutionary trends could be explained only by invoking mystical principles of unknown or supernatural guidance. Whether the forces invoked were cited as being "vital principles" or simply "evolutionary momentum," the result was the continuation of evolutionary development in a given direction for no obvious or logical reason. Straight-line development of this kind is what "orthogenesis" means.

There is no reason why development cannot occur in a consistent direction, provided that the selective forces producing it continue to operate over long periods of time; clearly, this has happened in the evolutionary record. According to the modern synthetic theory of evolution, the main objection to orthogenesis is the inherent implication that there is an unknowable force involved, and that development, once started in a particular direction, will continue of its own momentum even after the initial stimulus has ceased to operate. As is now realized, evolution is completely opportunistic. It is simply the accumulation of organic responses to continuing environmental stimuli. When these stimuli cease, the adaptive responses cease as well. In this sense, then, we must deny that orthogenesis is a valid evolutionary phenomenon. At the point where selection disappears and adaptation stops as well, entropy takes over and the system starts to lose its organized appearance. This, however, is hardly what the proponents of orthogenesis had intended when they postulated a direction and momentum of evolution driven by something other than natural selection.

PREADAPTATION

Preadaptation also is not really an evolutionary principle, but it *is* a useful way of looking at things, and it lets us understand some aspects of evolution that otherwise would not make sense. Organic form is not redesigned from scratch for each aspect of adaptive radiation. For example, the fins of a whale, the wings of a bat, the paws of a bear, the flippers of a seal, and the arms of a man are built upon exactly the same number and kinds of bones.[59]

While these attain quite different end results, they are all achieved by modification of the same basic elements. It is obviously easier to redesign what is already there—even if there is some awkwardness and loss of functional efficiency—than to start over from scratch. The elements of the basic vertebrate limb, then, were already established in the limbs of the Paleozoic fish that served as the ancestor to the amphibians, which in turn gave rise to all of the reptiles and mammals that continue to exist today. That Paleozoic fish fin, then, was a preadaptation for the development of the arms and paws and flippers and wings of the ensuing adaptive radiation of the vertebrates.

Although preadaptation is the use of a structure that originally had been developed for one kind of use in a new situation (and for quite another kind of use), it must be stressed that there is absolutely no foreknowledge involved.[60] Evolution is completely opportunistic, and it can never foretell that the future will bring circumstances in which a previously adapted condition will prove to be of use in another context. If, in fact, this happens, all well and good; but nothing ever takes place with that kind of *intent*. For example, when primates first evolved binocular stereoscopic vision, it was specifically to help them cope with the problem of moving through the forest canopy where depth perception was literally of vital significance, but there was no presumption that their remote descendants would ultimately use that capability to direct the path of motorized conveyances, hurtling at high speeds, over the freeways of Los Angeles.

That example actually is simply a situational transfer rather than the modification of a pre-existing trait for use in a previously unforeseen set of circumstances, but it does serve to make the point. Our ancestral ape grade prehominid developed its quadrumanous clambering, suspensory locomotion, and arm-hanging for purposes of moving and feeding in the forest canopy. Kevin Hunt, of Indiana University, has recently demonstrated the importance of arm-hanging as a major feeding posture in modern chimpanzees. He has noted features that are present in the earliest hominids which suggest that either arm-hanging had continued to be of importance or it had been so in their immediate past.[61] Since it is hard to hang horizontally, one of the consequences was the development of a vertical body plan, which has left its stamp on all the descendants of that creature. This preadaptation determined that when a terrestrial life-way was subsequently resumed, the vertical body plan was retained.[62] The result was the bipedalism that freed our hands from locomotor duties and allowed them to get involved in the use and manufacture of the implements that have been the key to our survival ever since.

NEOTENY

Some aspects of human form recall the infantile. In all newborn mammals, the head is relatively large and the face is relatively small in comparison with their proportions when adulthood is finally reached. In the human adult, however, the head is still noticeably large and the face relatively underdeveloped if the standards of comparison are typical mammals such as horses, dogs, rats, or sheep. An adult who displays the features of infancy is said to exhibit "neoteny," which literally means "the retention of the new."

The newborn human is remarkably helpless by most mammalian standards, and the period of juvenile dependency is noticeably prolonged. It is during this long immature period of play and trial-and-error behavior that the growing human learns about the world. Human beings have carried a dependence upon learned behavior to the maximum, and, conversely, almost everything that could be considered instinctive behavior has been eliminated. If this is a slower way of producing an adult who can cope with its world, it also results in an adult who can handle the new and different in much more effective fashion. In human beings, the teachability of youth is extended throughout the rest of life.

Some scholars have tried to view these various human capacities and features as simple manifestations of neoteny, a biological rendering of the poet Wordsworth's vision of the child as father of the man.[63] The reliance on such imagery, however, encourages a tendency to confuse processes that are best treated separately. The adaptive advantage in the emphasis on braininess is obvious. The small human face—that is, small by prehuman or even Middle Pleistocene human standards—is not simply the product of retention of a supposedly advantageous juvenile condition, but rather the result of a failure to grow. Face development and brain development are under the control of completely separate sets of selective forces, and the proportion observed in comparing their relative development has no adaptive significance in itself. To invoke neoteny to account for that proportion, then, in fact explains nothing at all. When we look at the rest of the human body, it is obvious that the elongated legs and relatively short trunk of the human adult are actually the reverse of being neotenous. Applying the concept of neoteny to the human condition has tended to result in oversimplifications that have inhibited our ability to understand how modern human form has actually evolved.[64]

SEXUAL DIMORPHISM

Sensitivity to the normal range of variation is important to the student of evolution, but sometimes the unstated referent can inhibit a proper appreciation of what that normal range might be. For example, when we try to project a reconstruction of the range of variation of a fossil human population from a few scrappy specimens, we tend to do so with the model of the normal modern range in mind. To be sure, this is better than the approach that stresses the identification of an invariant typological ideal, but it does assume that the nature of human variation in the past was the same as it is in the present.[65] That in itself is a kind of teleological assumption, and it has created more than a little misunderstanding.

Obviously, variation was just as normal prehistorically as it is now, but that does not mean that the *nature* of variation was the same. In fact, there is considerable evidence to suggest that it was not. This can be appreciated by a quick consideration of crucial differences in life between Moderns and the people of remote antiquity.

In the postindustrial world, there are very few jobs that cannot be done equally well by males and females. Men are just as good at cooking and changing diapers as women are at driving bulldozers and laying bricks. Only in the physical acts of procreation and the mechanics of bearing offspring are there any evolutionary forces continuing to maintain the differences in male and female physiques.

This, however, was not true in the past. Before bottles and synthetic nipples were invented, a nursing mother was the sole source of nourishment for the infants upon whom the future of a population had to depend. In order to assure population continuity, the average human female spent her entire adult life either pregnant or lactating.[66] Inevitably, the burdens of group defense fell upon the males. Also inevitably, the unencumbered mobility necessary for systematic, large-mammal hunting restricted such activities to males. The different requirements of male and female roles reinforced the maintenance of those secondary sexual distinctions in size, shape, and muscularity that are still visible if no longer necessary for survival.

The difference between male and female roles also plays a part in maintaining sexual dimorphism in other animals as well. In flying predators, such as hawks and owls, it is the female that is systematically larger. Selection has stressed size in the female because of the problems of being an airborne hunter at the same time that the relatively large eggs are being developed in the maternal body.[67] In terrestrial predators such as lions, males are markedly larger than females, although they are much less effective as hunters. The size and strength of the male lion is used to defend the females and young against the incursions of other male lions, but they sacrifice something in speed and agility as a consequence. The females, on their part, hunt with sufficient effectiveness so that they can provide for all the members of the group including the young, who are their offspring, and the adult males, who can commandeer what they choose.

In other terrestrial carnivores, such as wolves, hunting is a communal or pack activity with both males and females participating. The greater male size and strength is not related to male-female differences in their activities as procurers of food but to the male role in maintaining the integrity of the pack against the potential incursions of other wolves. Because of the long-distance cooperative nature of wolf hunting, the male wolf, unlike the male lion, cannot sacrifice hunting ability in favor of the role of group maintenance (and unchallenged access to breeding opportunities with females).[68]

To return to the human example, the degree of male-female dimorphism now visible clearly survives from a time in the relatively recent past when male hunting, unaccompanied by women and children, played an important part in the subsistence activities of human groups. And if we project this kind of expectation back into the Pleistocene and beyond—to even simpler levels of technology—we should expect to find greater degrees of male-female distinction. At the very earliest Stage of hominid development, when tools were rudimentary, the role of group maintenance and defense must have led to the development of a degree of difference in size and muscularity between males and females that attained an order of magnitude not visible in the present or the recent past.

Among the terrestrial nonhuman primates—for example, baboons and gorillas—the selective pressure differences acting on the male involvement with group maintenance, as opposed to those acting on the female involvement with pregnancy and infant nurture, assured the development of a marked degree of male-female difference or sexual dimorphism. In both gorillas and baboons, males are literally double the size of females; they use that size and muscularity to ensure sexual access to as many females as they can control, thereby improving their chances at reproduction.[69] Because they lack tools to help them in their efforts at group maintenance, selection has stressed the development of enlarged canine teeth—especially in the males.

Since the evidence available suggests that sexual dimorphism among the earliest hominids was maintained to an extent that was quite beyond what a study of the modern range of variation would lead us to expect, we should be alert to the possibility that they may have been using reproductive strategies more like those found in modern primates where sexual dimorphism is more marked than what we normally find among those modern human groups who managed to maintain a hunting and gathering mode of subsistence.[70] But, unlike other terrestrial primates, the earliest hominids utilized tools in their various activities so that, although they may well have maintained a gorilloid degree of dimorphism in size and muscularity, this did not extend to the maintenance of a fully gorilloid degree of canine tooth-size dimorphism.

These considerations bring up a final matter that deserves some mention. If males and females differed to such a marked degree, then obviously any attempt to represent the group by a detailed description of only one specimen is going to constitute serious misrepresentation. In fact, it is just possible that some of the descriptions of different genera or species in the literature may be depictions of males and females of a single group. These points will all be kept in mind when we turn our attention to the actual fossil evidence for the stages of human evolution.[71]

MOSAIC EVOLUTION

Another matter that needs to be put into perspective is the question of coordinating change in the different anatomical components of the members of an evolving lineage. The various pieces of an organism are not only under the control of separate portions of the genome, they are also subject to the action of different and often unrelated selective forces. Brains, skin pigment, teeth, and feet, for example, serve very different functions and are important for very different and often quite unrelated reasons. It is only to be expected, then, that separate traits may well have separate and possibly independent evolutionary histories. This idea that an organism is made up of separate traits that evolve at different rates is what is meant by "mosaic evolution."[72]

It sounds simple enough when put this way, but it is something that the typologically committed cladists have great trouble dealing with.[73] The course of hominid evolution, however, is an absolutely classic case of mosaic evolution. From what we can see in the fossil record, it is obvious that bipedal locomotion of the Modern human pattern evolved while the brain was still barely distinguishable from that of an anthropoid ape. Then initial brain expansion occurred at the same time that there was a dramatic drop in molar tooth size, somewhere around a million-and-a-half years ago. Tooth size then remained the same for the next million years, while brain size slowly increased up to its modern levels.

Then starting from that point late in the Middle Pleistocene, Modern human form emerged as a result of a series of reductions from previous levels of robustness. These reductions, however, did not all proceed at the same rate in the various occupied portions of the world. "Modern" human form, then, emerged in a very uneven and mosaic fashion, and consequently still looks markedly different from one part of the world to another. The reasons for these differences in timing are due to the fact that the cultural dynamics that changed the nature of selective forces maintaining tooth size emerged first in the north and spread slowly elsewhere, while the technology that altered the forces maintaining post-cranial robustness arose first in Africa and only spread to inhabitants of other regions considerably later in time.[74]

It is the failure to appreciate the mosaic nature of the emergence of Modern form and the separate trajectories of its various components that is behind the endless recent wrangling in which paleoanthropologists have been engaged. The specifics of these matters are taken up in Chapters 13 and 14.

THE HUMAN ADAPTATION

Before embarking upon the final synthesis, wherein the foregoing insights are applied to the interpretation of the course of human evolution, we should give some attention to the age-old question, "What is man?"[75] Because of recent complaints about the sexism embedded in our language, it is no longer even regarded as legitimate to phrase the old biblical query in that form, but the sense of the question remains the same. What is this phenomenon called "humanity?" Definitions range from the realm of morality and philosophy to that of the pragmatic, functional, and physical. Depending on one's viewpoint, the more philosophical definitions can be characterized as displaying either dimensions of soaring insight or miasmas of vague verbalization. In any case, we leave this realm to other scholars with other purposes.

Attempts have been made to define humanity by means of specific, measurable, anatomical criteria, with the implication that such definitions are somehow "objective." As we have already seen, the recent revival of the approach of the medieval logicians has gained many adherents, although it continues to have the same kinds of problems that plagued its medieval exponents.[76] In the eighteenth century, an eminent Dutch naturalist claimed that the human condition was indicated by the lack of an intermaxillary bone;[77] and during the present century, anatomists have tried to claim that a brain capacity of at least 750 cc. is the minimum human criterion.[78] The trouble with such criteria is that inevitable exceptions can be found, and that ultimately there is no necessary relation between them and the condition of being human. Definitions are created by people for their own convenience and, although they are essential for practical purposes, we should always keep it in mind that, at bottom, they are arbitrary and subjective.

Viewed in evolutionary perspective, the most fruitful definition of humanity should be that which touches upon the most distinctive adaptation. Whereas arguments can be produced favoring the human brain in this regard, the social scientist can quickly counter this by pointing out that man does not survive by brain alone.[79] However valuable it may be, brain does not serve as a substitute for experience. The most characteristic part of being human is the ability to profit from the accumulated and transmitted experience of other human beings. This can be regarded as the most important human adaptation, and it is what the anthropologist means by the terms "culture."[80]

It is important to realize that culture, the primary human adaptive mechanism, is not a facet of human anatomy. In fact, some have referred to it as an "extra-somatic adaptation."[81] Evidently, any attempt to define humanity on the basis of anatomy alone will be doomed to failure. This is not to say that human anatomy is unrelated to culture. As we shall see, quite the reverse is the case. But the anatomical correlates that allow us to infer the presence of culture are reflections of an already existing dimension, and they must be regarded as occurring after the fact rather than as being of primary importance in and of themselves, a point that was quite missed by Trinkaus and Howells.[82] This is something we shall have to keep in mind when we look at the earliest hominids, where there is no preserved tangible evidence of culture, but where anatomical characteristics suggest to us that cultural attributes must have existed nonetheless.

This ability to transmit information and experience from one individual to another and from one generation to another is most clearly recognizable in languages and the records of their use. Unfortunately, however diagnostic language may be as an indicator of humanity, it leaves no trace in the archaeological or fossil record prior to the invention of writing. Since the vast majority of the happenings in human evolution occurred prior to this event, the prehistorian is put in the somewhat awkward position of trying to evaluate the humanity of our finds in the absence of the best criterion. Inevitably, the only tangible evidence for prehistoric human cultural capacity is prehistoric tools. This narrowing of the focus has even led some archaeologists to claim that the manufacture of tools should itself be the ultimate criterion of humanity, defining people as tool-making animals.[83] One consequence of this has been a heightened concern for the distinction between tool use and tool manufacture as a diagnostic criterion, and it is based on the feeling that a creature who merely selected suitably shaped natural objects as tools does not deserve to be called fully human. On the other hand, a creature who engaged in the regular modification of raw materials according to a set pattern could be appropriately elevated to the realm of the human. Contributing to this appraisal is the fact that prehistoric stone tools can be traced back to the point where the amount of shape modification is so rudimentary that they are little more than selected hunks of rock. Some archaeologists have felt that at this point we reach the boundary between the human and the prehuman.

There are several reasons why this latter assumption should be greeted with skepticism. First, field observation shows that modern chimpanzees engage in a little simple tool manufacture.[84] Next, merely because the prehistoric creature in question was not shaping stone does not necessarily mean that it was not shaping perishable materials, which are manifestly easier to modify. As we shall see later, when the earliest hominids are the focus of discussion, there is good reason to suspect that some of the aspects of the form they display could only have come about as a result of long-continued tool use, although there are no associated stone tools until much later. Finally, the dichotomy between the simple selection of appropriately shaped raw materials and tool manufacture artificially creates categories out of what should be a whole zone of transition that is unrelated to the question of whether or not the survival of the user depended on the accumulated and transmitted experience of previous generations.

Properly speaking, the mere presence of shaped or unshaped tools in the archaeological record is of symbolic value. To the prehistorian, such a presence symbolizes the fact that the user was employing a dimension of patterned behavior of an order of complexity that is too great to have been discovered anew each generation. Such behavior could be acquired only by enculturation: the process of growing up in a social environment conditioned by the accumulated and transmitted learning of previous generations.

Given no more than this, we must recognize that there almost certainly were rudimentary verbal clues in use that assisted in the enculturation process, but it is a much greater step to suggest that we are actually documenting the presence of even a simple form of what we would call language. Not too many years ago, it was fashionable to use the presence of tools as indicators of crude linguistic behavior, but the suspicion has recently grown that we were trying to read too much into the evidence. Early tools, in fact, remain remarkably similar through hundreds of thousands of years and over extensive geographic stretches.[85] Although language may not have been in the repertoire of their makers, we can certainly infer a creature who possessed the rudiments of culture in the anthropological sense and who could not have survived without it. Such a creature we can regard as a genuine hominid, but it might be stretching things a bit to call it a full human being. Hominids they may be, but there is no justification for including them in *Homo sapiens* as has recently been done.[86]

CHAPTER SEVEN NOTES

[1]For example, Day (1977), Rightmire (1990), Trinkaus and Shipman (1992), and Stringer and Gamble (1993).

[2]Gaffney, 1979; Eldredge and Cracraft, 1980; Nelson and Platnick, 1984.

[3]Eldredge and Tattersall, 1982; Groves, 1989; Rightmire, 1990; Eldredge, 1993; Kimbel and Martin, 1993.

[4]Lovejoy, 1936:147; N. White, 1979:186.

[5]Aquinas, 1923; Lurie, 1960:283; Moore, 1961:12; Mayr, 1982:92.

[6]Lindroth, 1973:380.

[7]Lovejoy, 1936:75; Aquinas, 1923 (vol. II):207

[8]Groves, 1989; Brace, in press (a).

[9]Wilberforce, 1860:135.

[10]Mayr, 1982:600, 1991:74.

[11]Broca, 1870:238; Boesiger, 1980:318–19.

[12]Eldredge and Tattersall, 1982; Kimbel, 1991; Kimbel and Rak, 1993.

[13]Romer, 1954; Romer and Parsons, 1986; Young, 1971; Kay, 1993.

[14]Simpson, 1961; Hennig, 1966.

[15]Larson, 1971:150).

[16]Agassiz, 1860:143.

[17]Hennig, 1966; Wiley, 1981; Groves, 1989.

[18]A possible example of this may very well have occurred in the recent past in regard to a highly publicized interpretation of a crucial part of human evolution—the origin and spread of Modern human form (Cann et al., 1987; Cann, 1988; Stoneking and Cann, 1989). The construction of an evolutionary tree based on mitochondrial DNA information from modern human populations used an established computer program without consideration for its various options. That picture was accepted by default as the definitive word of molecular biology (Stringer and Andrews, 1988; Stringer, 1990), in spite of the fact that it required abandoning what we knew about the fossil record, the evidence from archaeology, and what we should have expected from anthropology and evolutionary theory. As it happened, neither the molecular biologists nor the paleoanthropologists involved ever questioned whether the computer option chosen would

produce the only possible solution or even the best one available. When other computer options were explored, tens of thousands of different pathways were identified that accounted for Modern human emergence even more efficiently than the one that had been proposed as definitive (Hedges et al., 1992; Templeton, 1992, 1993).

[19]The approach taken here is basically the one used by the late A. S. Romer (1894–1973) (Romer, 1954) and G. G. Simpson (1902–1984) (Simpson, 1961, 1963). It was adopted by E. L. Simons (1972) and used in Brace and Montagu (1977:88) and Brace et al. (1979:11).

[20]Lovejoy, 1936:221–30; Mayr, 1982:336–37.

[21]Darwin 1859:52.

[22]Mayr, 1942:120. More recently, Mayr has revised this to produce the biological species concept: *"A species is a reproductive community of populations (reproductively isolated from others) that occupies a specific niche in nature* (Mayr, 1982:273).

[23]Darwin, 1859:47. While Simpson actually quoted Mayr's 1940 definition with approval (Simpson, 1961:150), his interest in the problem of identifying species in the past led him to advocate applying the same criteria to successive units in time that one could derive from comparing contemporary groups in order to determine whether the recognition of sequential as well as contemporaneous species' difference is warranted (Simpson, 1943:171–72). Later, Simpson offered his definition of an evolutionary species: "An evolutionary species is a lineage (an ancestral-descendant sequence of populations) evolving separately from others and with its own evolutionary role and tendencies" (Simpson, 1961:153). This is the logic that was used some years back to try to make sense out of the burgeoning names in the primate fossil record (Simons and Pilbeam, 1965:101).

[24]Gould, 1974:18.

[25]If the late Louis Leakey flourished during an age of lumpers, Russell Tuttle has given us fair warning: "Students, teachers, and paleophiles, beware! A new era of taxonomic splitting is upon us," which should prepare us for what he calls the "splitomania" that is at hand (Tuttle, 1988:397).

[26]Pondering the trends on the paleoanthropological scene, that inept versifier, I. Doolittle Wright, has left us his reactions in limerick form. He had toyed with the idea of calling it "Writhes and Splimpers: To Bleep Perchance to Scream," but he finally decided to refer to his production as:

Nominophilia

Consider the volatile splitter,
Excited and all of a twitter.
    At the fun in the game
    Of adding a name
For each little variant critter.

If you make up a different name,
For forms that just might be the same;
    You can use the confusion,
    To support the illusion
That the effort will add to your fame.

Combining a fragment of face,
With a jaw from a far-off place;
    They say they are able
    To warrant a label
Creating a whole new race.

But it's not always praxis that leads
To the multiplication of breeds;
    Nor the glory of God,
    But the conceit of the clod
With his ego-aggrandizing needs.

Now, a lumper's a different kind;
He thinks the world is designed,
    Of similar bits
    That won't addle the wits
In the limited scope of his mind.

Specify! somebody flutters;
Simplify! one of them mutters;
    The lumpers and splitters
    Will never be quitters,
So the field is a patchwork of splutters.

As names blossom forth anew,
There's much to be said for the view
    That puts its store
    In "less is more,"
And errs on the side of the few.

Quoted in Brace (in press[a]).

[27]Brace, 1964, 1981a, 1988, 1989, 1992, in press(a).

[28]Hennig, 1966.

[29]If Willi Hennig can be described as "the patron saint of cladistics" (Brace, in press [a]), one of his chief apostles is Edward O. Wiley, who added a corollary to a form of Simpson's definition of "evolutionary species" (Simpson, 1961:153): "No presumed separate, single, evolutionary lineage may be subdivided into a series of ancestral and descendant 'species'" (Wiley, 1978:21). Then he added, "This corollary is self-evident . . . (and) . . . This renders the concept of successional species unnecessary" (Wiley, 1981:34). However, there is nothing even faintly "self-evident" about it and the message is blatantly anti-Darwinian. Not only do the doctrinaire cladists deny that Darwinian evolution can occur, they say quite bluntly that "natural selection is not the driving force in evolution" (Wiley and Brooks, 1982:6–7). Since this is based on *a priori* reasoning and unexaminable faith in the fashion of medieval scholastics, it has been described as the "great leap backwards" (Brace, 1988:133, 1989:444; Brace et al., 1991:36). The absence of evolutionary thinking in paleoanthropology has been clearly perceived by one bemused archaeologist (G. A. Clark, 1988). Needless to say, the evidence marshalled in this book does not sustain that medieval faith.

[30]Eldredge and Gould, 1972; Eldredge, 1993. Nothing illustrates how far behind the times anthropological thinking on these matters is than the claim that, "The validity of the ontology that divorces pattern from process is a relatively new topic of discussion and debate in evolutionary biology" (Kimbel and Martin, 1993:541). In fact, it was Darwin himself who introduced the idea that pattern can only be understood as a product of process (Darwin, 1859; Ghiselin, 1969; Mayr, 1982, 1991). It is a measure of the backwardness of paleoanthropology that those who have tried to assume the role of cutting-edge theoreticians have yet to discover and understand the nature of what Darwin accomplished a century-and-a-half ago (Trinkaus and Shipman, 1992; Kimbel and Martin, 1993; Stringer and Gamble, 1993). There have been many attempts to provide an antidote for the theoretical vacuum that characterizes so much of the field (e.g., Brace, 1964, 1981a, 1988, 1992, in press [a]; Kellog, 1988; Rose and Bown, 1993; and Szalay, 1993).

[31]Huxley, 1958:27–28; Coon, 1962:306; Mayr, 1974:107, 1982:614. Defenders of cladistics, on the other hand, have no use for the concept of "grade." One cladist described the Great Chain of Being as "one of the greatest stumbling blocks to our understanding of human phylogeny" (Tattersall, 1986a: 316). Of course, if the natural world were amenable to the strict application of cladistic methodology, the automatic result would be the establishment of a hierarchy of relationships that would itself be a version of just that *scala naturae.*

[32]Pettigrew, 1986, 1991. Opposition has been vigorously expressed (Thewissen and Babcock, 1991; Baker et al., 1991), and there is a "caution against suggestions that the issue of bat relationships has been solved" (Simmons et al., 1991).

[33]Huxley, 1958:35–36.

[34]Darwin, 1859:81.

[35]Reed, 1978:204–5.

[36]Darwin's longtime friend and supporter, Thomas Henry Huxley (1825–1895), appointed himself as "Darwin's bull-dog" (Huxley [ed.], 1900, vol. I:391). When he first made himself fully familiar with Darwin's formulation, his reaction was, "How extremely stupid not to have thought of that!" (Huxley, 1887:551). In fact, it took an extremely sophisticated and subtle understanding of the world and the nature of species to be able to phrase things in such a way that the previously inconceivable became so obvious that it has often been regarded as just common sense (Ghiselin, 1969; Mayr, 1991; Williams, 1992). Huxley, for all his acclaimed "brilliance" and backing of Darwin, never completely comprehended the full nature of Darwin's revolutionary accomplishment (Ghiselin 1969:8, 1972:507; Reed, 1978:202; Mayr, 1982:544; di Gregorio, 1984:199). And in more peripheral professions such as paleoanthropology, this has yet to penetrate (e.g., Oxnard, 1987; Groves, 1989; Trinkaus and Shipman, 1992:10, 33, 81; Stringer and Gamble, 1993).

[37]It was Darwin's wordy friend Herbert Spencer (1820–1903) who coined the phrase, and Darwin, on the recommendation of Alfred Russel Wallace, inserted it into the fifth edition of his *Origin* in 1869 (Kennedy, 1978:78, 142). Neither Darwin nor Spencer foresaw that this would expose Darwin's formulation to the criticism of "tautology," although the most recent reputable philosopher to have resurrected that accusation (Popper, 1978b:171), on further reflection, took the opportunity of the first Darwin Lecture at Darwin College, Cambridge, to make his "recantation" (Popper, 1978a:344)

[38]Darwin actually knew as much about heredity as any of his contemporaries. He attended stock shows for years, corresponded with breeders, and carried out extensive tests in raising pigeons. This is extensively documented in his volumes on *Variation of Animals and Plants,* in which he actually proposes a particulate theory of heredity (Darwin, 1868). It was neither original nor correct (Mayr 1982:635), but it was essayed on the basis of a great deal of collected information.

[39]Mivart, 1871; Cope, 1887; Bateson, 1894; Morgan, 1916.

[40]Muller, 1927, 1928, 1929; Haldane, 1929, 1933.

[41]Dobzhansky, 1937; Mayr, 1942, 1982:569.

[42]This principle will not be found in standard works on evolutionary theory because of the overwhelming attention paid to natural selection at the expense of almost everything else except genetic drift (Gould and Lewontin, 1979). It was first suggested thirty years ago (Brace, 1963) and became part of an approach that was inappropriately called "non-Darwinian evolution" (Kimura, 1968; King and Jukes, 1969). Properly speaking, it is part of what has been termed "the neutralist theory" (Ayala, 1974:693) that has grown with the incorporation of the perspective of molecular genetics (Ohno, 1970; Kimura, 1983; Nei, 1987). The most detailed defense and application to human evolution is by Brace et al. (1991).

[43]Darwin, 1859:6.

[44]Ghiselin, 1969:14–15.

[45]Fisher, 1930.

[46]Darwin, 1859:134.

[47]Trinkaus, 1989; Trinkaus and Villemeur, 1991.

[48]In spite of the enormous advances made in molecular biology during the last several decades—or maybe because of them—the simplest and most comprehensible guide is the pioneering synthesis by Christian Anfinsen (1959). "Only with this . . . did the study of molecular evolution find its center of gravity" (Zuckerkandl, 1987:34).

[49]Hardman and Yanofsky, 1967.

[50]Stryer, 1988:166, 1989.

[51]Muller, 1929:488.

[52]Sewall Wright realized that the majority of mutations will tend to lead to "physiological inactivation" in the absence of selection (1931), and Haldane explicitly noted that structural reduction would be the consequence (1933:9).

[53]The theory behind genetic drift was articulated by Sewall Wright (1931, 1943, 1946), who realized that it just might be important in shaping human form since human prehistoric populations

were generally assumed to have lived in small, semi-isolated groups. Wright, however, did not assign it a large role in producing significant evolutionary change (1951).

[54]Neel (1989) provides other examples from actual field data.

[55]Brace, 1991.

[56]Brace and Hunt, 1990.

[57]Brace and Hunt, 1990; Brace and Tracer, 1992.

[58]One of the most eminent proponents was Henry Fairfield Osborn, long-time president of the American Museum of Natural History in New York, whose story is splendidly told by Rainger (1991). A survey of orthogenetically oriented biologists is offered by Mayr (1982:529, 853) although anthropology is left out. Anthropological orthogenesis was represented in the non-Darwinian outlook of Franz Weidenreich (1947b), and it is alive and well in the paleoanthropology of today, demonstrating once again how far out of touch the field has become with the outlook of modern biological science (e.g., Groves, 1989:54–55).

[59]Darwin, 1859:199–200.

[60]The term "preadaptation" has had a curious history, as is demonstrated by Mayr (1960:362–64). Recently, there has been an attempt made to substitute the term "exaptation" for what is usually meant by preadaptation (Gould and Vrba, 1982) just to get away from the implications of teleological intent presumed to be present. But "pre" does not imply intent, it simply indicates "prior to," and that is all that is meant.

[61]Hunt, 1989, 1991a, 1991b, 1992.

[62]There are other attempts to explain the development of upright bipedalism in the hominid line, and one of the more interesting involves the idea that the bipedal stance presents a significantly smaller amount of surface to the direct effects of the overhead tropical sun (Wheeler, 1984, 1985, 1990). The author does grant that some kind of preadaptation might have existed from a former habitat, which later proved to be advantageous in the savanna (Wheeler, 1993:66).

[63]That garrulously literate popularizer of science, Stephen Jay Gould, has written at length on neoteny, although about the only reason he can suggest for it being advantageous is that we think the neotenous is "cute" (Gould, 1977:350).

[64]The most recent assessment concludes that the only reason for the persistence of the concept is due to "anthropocentrism" (Shea, 1989:69), and that "the neoteny hypothesis is largely if not totally a bankrupt concept" (Shea, 1989:97).

[65]Bonnet, 1919:23–24; Schultz, 1963.

[66]Pickford, 1986.

[67]Earhart and Johnson, 1970:261–62. In fairness, it should be noted that this is not the reason for the reverse dimorphism noted by Earhart and Johnson, but their explanation of niche diversification seems even less likely.

[68]Mech, 1970; MacDonald, 1992.

[69]Alexander, 1979.

[70]Clutton-Brock, 1985a, b.

[71]Brace, 1973; 1979a.

[72]de Beer, 1954:48; Simpson, 1961:224; Mayr, 1982:613.

[73]Most practicing paleoanthropologists have rejected the principles of evolutionary biology for a faith in the essentialist certainties of cladistics, but "cladists have not been able to overcome the difficulties caused by mosaic evolution" (Mayr, 1974:120).

[74]Brace, in press (d).

[75]8 Psalms, 4 ff.

[76]Eco, 1984b:58, 68.

[77]The anatomist in question was Petrus Camper (1722–1789), and the relevant information is presented in Ashley-Montagu (1935:39).

[78]This was the famous "cerebral rubicon" of the late Sir Arthur Keith (1949:206).

[79]With apologies to Matthew 4:4.

[80]The significance of "Culture" in the anthropological sense is dealt with at greater length in Chapter 9. One recent English critic has called it "an unnecessary and not particularly useful concept" (Foley, 1987:790), and this, along with the fact that Darwin's insights are also missing from English paleoanthropology, may help to explain why paleoanthropology in England has failed to come to grips with the dynamics and course of human evolution. Those of us who not only find the concept "useful," but consider it essential to understanding how humans are able to survive, have accepted some derivative of the definition offered by Sir Edward Burnett Tylor (1832–1917): "Culture or Civilization, taken in its wide ethnographic sense, is that complex whole which includes knowledge, belief, art, morals, law, custom, and any other capabilities and habits acquired by man as a member of society" (Tylor, 181:1). The late Leslie White (1900–1975) referred to culture as our "extra-somatic adaptation" (White, 1959:8), and there is growing recognition that this is among those aspects of the traditions of social science "which social anthropologists have recently neglected at considerable cost" (Kuper, 1993:6).

[81]White, 1959:8.

[82]Trinkaus and Howells, 1979:127.

[83]The biographer of the celebrated Dr. Samuel Johnson, James Boswell, attributed this phrase to Benjamin Franklin (Hill, ed., 1887:33), and it has continued to enjoy recognition (Oakley, 1952, 1957).

[84]Goodall, 1964; Boesch and Boesch, 1981; McGrew, 1992.

[85]Howells speaks of a "general stagnation in Lower Paleolithic stonework, lasting more than a million years" (1993:118).

[86]Wolpoff, in press.

chapter eight

Prehominids

True hominids did not suddenly emerge by a punctuation event from a remote prehistoric pongid. Instead, we can trace the picture of their obvious predecessors, going back to ever more primitive primates, which in turn go back to the beginning of the Age of Mammals, 66 million years (myrs.) ago,[1] where they are visibly closer to a kind of generalized common mammalian stock than they are to the primates of today.[2]

DATING THE PAST

Geologists in the nineteenth century had no accurate way of judging the precise ages of the various segments of the earth. They could look at the layers of rocks that had been formed by deposition in prehistoric seas, and they knew that each layer was formed by the compacting of sediments that had been layed down stratum upon stratum. They could even calculate roughly how long it should have taken to deposit sediments that, when consolidated, would produce a given thickness of rock. Contemplating sections of stratified rock that measured their thicknesses in miles, the geologists realized that the earth had taken millions of years to form. They were absolutely right, of course, but they still had only hazy ideas about how many multiples of millions that involved.

They also began to develop a picture of what was older than which by the use of fossils characterized by a wide geographic spread but of short duration. A section with a series of such fossils in layers superimposed on each other could be used to provide a relative position for rocks found in other areas that contained only one or another of those particular "index fossils." The use of faunal correlations to establish the *relative* age of strata with regard to each other is still a key tool for the field geologist, but it cannot tell anything about the absolute age of the sediments in question.

While a variety of laborious techniques have enabled us to put accurate dates on otherwise unrecorded events over the last some thousands of years, the real breakthrough came with the use of radioactive elements to pinpoint the age of even the oldest of the rocks in the earth. A certain proportion of elements existing from the establishment of the earth at its beginning are radioactive. Each such element decays at a known rate—different for each such element—into a stable end product. When a radioactive element and its stable end product are bound in a single structure, such as a crystal in a volcanic rock or a calcite deposit, the proportion of one to the other is a direct indicator of just how long that crystal has been there.[3]

The realization that radioactive elements could be used as clocks to measure the strata of the earth goes back to the first decade of the twentieth century, but the technology that made such measurements possible did not become readily available until after World War II. Another useful technique for establishing the relations between sequences of formations in different parts of the world was also realized early in the century, but this, too, has only become of practical use in the last thirty years or so. This is the assessment of the polarity of prehistoric strata.

As it happens, the earth is one huge magnet with a positive and a negative pole, which is why compasses work the way they do—the north pole is the negative pole. But at periodic intervals in the past, the poles have reversed. It sounds a bit drastic, and there have even been some suggestions that, in between polar reversals, increased amounts of cosmic radiation may have altered the mutation rate of the organisms living at that time and accounted for the pulses that can be documented in the course of organic evolution. Now that the record of polarity reversals is known in better detail, it is clear that they are completely unrelated to any of the events in the evolution of life.

However, like the use of index fossils, the record of polarity in ancient deposits can be used to correlate strata that cannot otherwise be directly dated. Polarity cannot be measured in just any prehistoric sediment, however, and, like the other techniques used by geologists to provide information about the past, it has to be used with appropriate care. Volcanics are particularly useful because they start as molten masses, and then, when they cool and solidify, some of the elements that they contain will crystallize in alignment with the magnetic field of the earth at that time. Some of those volcanic rocks also contain crystals that can be radiometrically dated. Using a combination of these techniques, geophysicists have been able to build up a detailed picture of the polarity changes and times of deposition of the strata containing the fossil evidence for organic evolution.

If the field and laboratory details are sophisticated and complex in practice, the theory is relatively straightforward, and the results can be directly applied to unravelling the picture of organic evolution—including the evolution of the primates in general and the stages of human evolution in particular.[4]

THE GEOLOGICAL TIME SCALE

The major divisions of geological time, in which are preserved abundant evidence for prehistoric life, begin with the Paleozoic Era around 544 million years ago.[5] (Figure 8–1 outlines the major divisions.) There are fossils in the preceding Pre-Cambrian, but so much distortion has occurred by the warping, folding, and erosion which has subsequently taken place that most depictions of the course of organic evolution begin with the Paleozoic Era. During this time we can see the emergence of primitive and then more evolved fishes.[6] Some of these develop pelvic and pectoral fins with the same number and kind of bones in them as our own arms and legs. From these fish, full-fledged amphibians emerged.[7] By the end of the Paleozoic 249 myrs.

FIGURE 8–1. The division of geological time.

HOLOCENE	Recent	10,000 years
CENOZOIC	Pleistocene	2 million
	Pliocene	5 million
	Miocene	24 million
	Oligocene	34 million
	Eocene	55 million
	Paleocene	66 million
MESOZOIC		249 million
PALEOZOIC		544 million

ago, these had proliferated and diversified in the extensive swampy areas that produced the coal deposits that are of such importance today. Among those amphibians is one that is transitional in many respects to the reptiles.[8]

The Mesozoic Era is the second of the large geological divisions that contain the fossil evidence for organic evolution. This has been informally called the Age of Reptiles, a time when land-going adaptations were perfected.[9] Whereas the moist and permeable skin of the amphibians permits the evaporation of body fluids, the scaly skin that was acquired by the early reptiles allowed them to pursue a life that was no longer dependent upon proximity to the streams, ponds, and swamps, which were and still are the milieu of the amphibians. The other critical reptilian adaptation was the development of eggs with shells. Because these could be laid on land, this development marks the final separation from that dependence on the presence of standing water which characterizes the amphibian adaptation.

Within the Mesozoic we see the proliferation of the particular group of reptiles that has so captured the imagination of the public: the dinosaurs. The reptiles, in fact, go through a major adaptive radiation. Some forms returned to the sea and redeveloped adaptations for swimming; others developed the powers of flight; and many differentiated into various herbivorous and carnivorous terrestrial forms. Recently, a number of paleontologists have challenged the old assumptions that the dinosaurs and their kin were invariably cold-blooded, sluggish, and drab—adjectives that generally come to mind when the term "reptile" is invoked. From the structure of their limbs and bodies, it is clear that some were adapted for sustained and rapid running. Some paleontologists have suggested that this could only have been achieved by warm-blooded creatures characterized by an elevated rate of metabolism. Recent workers have shown that some dinosaurs exhibited maternal behavior and cared for their young after hatching, and they have interpreted some of the recent discoveries as indicating that some dinosaur groups may have engaged in seasonal migrations of large and socially integrated herds over considerable distances. To complete this revisionist picture, they have speculated that some of the Mesozoic reptiles may have presented more than the stereotypic muddy, gray-green surface to the world—possibly to the extent of being as brightly colored as many modern birds.[10]

One small member of the dinosaur group underwent an adaptation whereby its scales became transformed into feathers. Indeed it was intermediate in many respects between the class Reptilia and the class Aves, or true birds, and displayed a curious mosaic of the characteristics of both. It had the teeth, the bony tail, and hind limb structure of a small, lightly built Jurassic dinosaur, but the feathers and flight muscle attachments of a bird. There has been a long-continuing argument about whether this particular species, *Archaeopteryx lithographica,* had gained its evidently somewhat limited but real powers of flight by running along the ground and jumping up, as some have claimed,[11] or by climbing up trees and jumping down, as others have maintained.[12] In any case, all agree that *Archaeopteryx* clearly was a Jurassic (150 million-year-old) ancestor of modern birds.[13] In the Mesozoic also, the therapsid, or mammal-like, reptiles provided the source from which true mammals emerged to become the dominant form in the succeeding Cenozoic Era, which, appropriately, is known as the Age of Mammals.[14]

REPTILIAN EXTINCTIONS

What caused the extinction of the ruling reptiles is still a matter of much vigorous debate. Many forms of both marine and terrestrial life disappear at the Cretaceous/Tertiary boundary, which marks the transition from the Mesozoic to the Cenozoic 66 myrs. ago. Some have postulated that a comet or asteroid collided with the earth,[15] and that the ensuing dust cloud blocked out the rays of the sun long enough to cause the death of quantities of plants.[16] According to this scenario, animal forms from microorganisms to dinosaurs, dependent on those plants, died off in turn.[17]

Although it cannot be denied that such a sudden and dramatic catastrophe *could* have occurred, many geologists and paleontologists are skeptical and try to use a combination of more expectable means to account for the many extinctions that clearly took place late in the Cretaceous—the last period of the Mesozoic Era. Changes in the position of the major continents may have altered previously prevailing weather patterns. Increased volcanic activity accompanying that continental repositioning may also have had its effect.[18] In any case, whether the cause was extraterrestrial or the result of a configuration of less catastrophic geological phenomena, the result undoubtedly was the disappearance of many members of the previously ruling reptiles and the opening of a series of niches for exploitation by the emerging class of mammals.

PRIMATES

Among these were representatives of the order Primates. As mammals, these had fur for insulation, warm blood as an indication of a constant elevated metabolic rate, and produced live offspring nourished by milk from mammary glands. They are not differentiated from the rest of the mammals by any single characteristic, but rather by the configuration created by the combination of a series of retained primitive and emergent derived features.[19] Whereas in many mammals the numbers of fingers and toes are variously reduced, in the primates all five are retained on both the fore and hind limbs.

The grasping capabilities which this reflects are of use in manipulating food items and also in climbing activities. This emphasizes what it was that shaped the primates as an order distinct from the rest of the Mammalia—that is, a tree-going or arboreal way of life.

As the early Cenozoic mammals underwent their adaptive radiation, some became terrestrial herbivores, some became carnivores, one branch developed the capabilities of flight and gave rise to the bats of today, and others went back to the sea as whales and their relatives. The primates exploited the arboreal ecological niche. All of those retentions and developments reflect adjustments—adaptations—to the problems that face an arboreal animal, and the stamp of that arboreal heritage is visible in all of the primates alive today, including ourselves.

An arboreal environment puts different stresses on its inhabitants than does a terrestrial habitat, and the primates all show a series of consequent adaptations. There is a reduction in the reliance on the sense of smell, and the snout tends to be shortened as a result. Locating major supports and handholds at a distance tends to be done visually, and the importance of binocular stereoscopic vision for depth perception means that the eyes tend to be moved forward towards the front of the skull where their fields of vision overlap, rather than being laterally placed as in most animals.

Finally, movement through a forest canopy requires constant decision making. On the ground, even something as relatively witless as a rhinoceros can plod ahead, step after step, secure in the unreasoned faith that solid ground will continue to be there to support it. In a tree, however, the situation has to be constantly assessed and choices have to be made. Inevitably, the mechanism for making the choices—namely, the brain—tends to be enlarged beyond what is the case in nonarboreal creatures of comparable size. From early on in their history, primates have tended to have the largest brains when compared with other animals (even though a Paleocene primate would look rather underendowed in that respect compared with practically all comparably sized mammals today). But in the context of the Paleocene, the creatures we identify by these comparative means as primates clearly have a cerebral edge over the other representatives of the animal world.

In the latter stages of primate evolution, the hominid clade capitalized upon this cerebral expansion, ultimately using it as the device for the creation of a unique kind of adaptation—the cultural ecological niche—which, in turn, engendered selective pressures that led to further adaptive increases in brain size. This business of being able to use a trait developed for one set of circumstances to take advantage of a completely different situation is a classic example of preadaptation.[20] In this case, the presence of both an expanded brain and a developed grasping and manipulative capacity combined to produce the cultural milieu that has become the human ecological niche.[21]

PALEOCENE PRIMATES

In the Paleocene, which began 66 myrs. ago, there are a number of primitive kinds of primates, although there is some question as to which, if any, of the known forms gave rise to the primates of later periods. Fossils of a rat-sized primate, found in the Rocky Mountain area of the United States in the Early Paleocene and possibly the Late Cretaceous, have been identified as belonging to the genus *Purgatorius*.[22] Members of this group are both early enough and of general enough form to give us an idea of what the primate common ancestor must have looked like, whether or not *Purgatorius* actually is that common ancestor.

Other Paleocene primates, exemplified by the form *Plesiadapis*,[23] show traits which exhibit a convergence with the rodents, and it is probably no accident that they become extinct when the rodents subsequently undergo their own adaptive radiation. The rodents, as we know, are not only highly successful as gnawing, seed-eating creatures, but they are also capable of reproducing themselves in quantities and at a speed with which no primate can compete.

The primates of the Paleocene and the succeeding Eocene all qualify as belonging to the Prosimian Grade. Whichever particular form actually proves to be ancestral to the primates of more recent times, it is clear that it was some sort of prosimian that gave rise to the later monkeys, apes, and hominids.

EOCENE PRIMATES

During the Eocene, which started 55 myrs. ago,[24] there were several lemurlike primates related to the very first fossil primate to have been discovered, *Adapis,* described by Cuvier in 1821,[25] and a possible ancestor of the living prosimians.[26] The various different forms are regarded as being members of the family Adapidae, and informally we can call them "Adapids." Not only do some of these serve as good candidates for the ancestors of more modern primates, but we can also see them change through time and take on a slightly more modern aspect as they do so. For the past fifteen years and more, Philip D. Gingerich of the University of Michigan has been leading annual expeditions to the Bighorn Basin of Wyoming.[27] There among the thousands of Eocene fossils he and his co-workers have uncovered, Gingerich has found some hundreds of specimens of a primate of the genus *Cantius*.[28] This was a small, rat-sized creature that was comparable in overall form and general level of adaptation to a modern lemur; that is, somewhat less than a full-scale monkey but more than a nonprimate such as a tree shrew.

The Bighorn section is rich and detailed, and there are specimens representing *Cantius* from at least 20,000-year intervals in an unbroken sequence for several million years. This in itself is one of the more remarkable fossil demonstrations of mammalian continuity. But what makes it particularly interesting is that the *Cantius* specimens change from the bottom of the sequence on upwards until, by the top, they have to be regarded as an entirely different genus, *Notharctus*.[29]

Notharctus fossils have been known for more than a century, and, throughout that time, they have been recognized as candidates for just the sort of lemurlike creature from which monkeys, apes, and, ultimately, humans are derived. Whether or not *Notharctus* is that specific ancestral form, its emergence from the abundantly documented *Cantius* predecessors has given us a splendid picture of early primate evolution from its most primitive and almost insectivorelike origin up to the threshold of the monkey grade.[30]

OLIGOCENE PRIMATES

Although the Eocene primates (especially the early ones that represent the most likely candidates for the ancestors of the primates living today) are most abundantly represented in North American fossiliferous deposits, the Oligocene continuity is best demonstrated by the fossil record in Africa. The work done over the last thirty years by the American paleontologist Elwyn L. Simons in the Fayum region of Egypt west of the Nile has provided a rich assortment of Oligocene fossils.[31] The Oligocene extends from 33.7 myrs. ago to 24.3 myrs. ago.[32] The most justly famous and important of Simons's discoveries, dating from just over 33 myrs. ago, is *Aegyptopithecus zeuxis* (Figure 8–2).

Aegyptopithecus is a relatively heavy-bodied arboreal quadruped, about the size of a fox,[33] and it is clearly at what could be called the monkey grade of organization. Brain size has increased, relatively speaking, over what can be seen in *Notharctus*,[34] and the eye sockets have rotated more towards the front of the skull suggesting the development of overlapping stereoscopic vision.

Details in the crown patterns of the molar teeth clearly foretell the pattern that is later evident in the apes of the Miocene and of today, as well as the whole hominid line. But the presence of a well-developed tail and the clearly quadrupedal adaptation indicated by the form of the arms and legs keep *Aegyptopithecus* firmly anchored in the monkey grade.[35] It is a splendid representative of just what we would expect the monkey grade ancestor of subsequent apes and human beings to have looked like.

MIOCENE PRIMATES

The Miocene began 23.8 myrs. ago, and within the next 6 or 7 million years the continent of Africa moved north far enough so that the mammals that

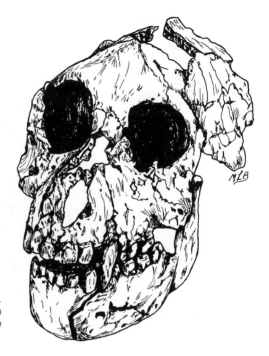

FIGURE 8–2.
Aegyptopithecus zeuxis, drawn by M. L.
Brace from a photograph furnished through
the courtesy of Prof. E. L. Simons of Duke
University.

had been evolving there could expand their ranges into the rest of what we now regard as a single entity: the Old World.[36] As the Miocene proceeded, apelike primates of evident African origin came to occupy a range all the way from Europe to China. Today their scattered remains can be found in the regions between, wherever there are fossil-bearing deposits of the right age.

The best candidate for the source of this group of Miocene primates is *Proconsul africanus* (Figure 8–3), another of the pivotal discoveries made by Mary and Louis Leakey.[37] The Leakeys found this in 1948 on Rusinga Island, located in Lake Victoria at the western edge of Kenya, in deposits that can be dated to 18 myrs.[38] Details of skull, face, jaw, and tooth form make this an ideal candidate to represent the ancestor of the subsequent apes, but the form of the arms, legs, and body shows that *Proconsul* was only at the threshold of, but not yet fully in, the ape grade of arm-hanging and quadrumanous clambering.

During the Middle Miocene, the widespread apelike forms all bear a noticeable resemblance to one of the very first prehistoric primates to have been discovered: the 1856 French find, *Dryopithecus fontani.*[39] Thirty years ago, Elwyn Simons and David Pilbeam, both then at Yale University, tried to reduce the proliferating confusion of different Miocene fossil apes and referred to them all as "Dryopithecines"; that is, members of a single related subfamily within the formal family Pongidae.[40] Included in the Simons and Pilbeam subfamily

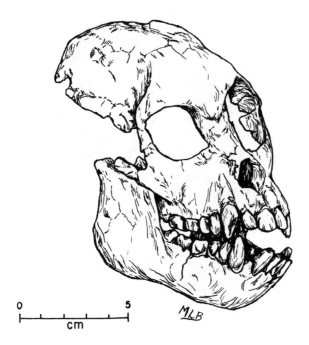

FIGURE 8–3. *Proconsul africanus,* drawn, from a cast, by M. L. Brace.

were *Graecopithecus* from Greece; *Ouranopithecus* from Hungary; *Ankarapithecus* from Turkey; *Sivapithecus* from Pakistan and India; a similar genus in China; and, arguably, even the original *Proconsul* as well as *Kenyapithecus* in Africa. It was an admirable attempt and there is much to be said in its favor, although the active players in the field have tended to ignore it in practice.[41]

As these names suggest, the local and national loyalties of the discoverers throughout this Eurasian expanse have led to the proliferation of new generic and specific designations, such as *Afropithecus, Heliopithecus, Lufengpithecus, Otavipithecus,* and *Victoriapithecus.*[42] In some instances we can even suspect that the ego of the discoverer is bound up in the proposal of a new and different name. In all too many cases, the names are given without adequate study and comparison to the obviously related fossils elsewhere in the geographic range where similar specimens have previously been found. Often, too, little or no consideration is given to the degree of individual difference or sexual dimorphism that one might expect to find in a given population of living (and also, by analogy, fossil) populations of similar primates. In more than one instance, restudy of specimens originally assigned to different genera has raised the suspicion that the different names were given to individuals that were really just males and females of a single taxonomic category.

In addition to the apelike Drypithecines, there are monkeylike fossil primates discovered in deposits ranging all the way from Africa to southwestern China.[43] Possibly because more effort and attention have been devoted to the fossiliferous localities in Kenya and adjacent areas, Africa has yielded the greatest variety and richness of these fossil primates. As in the case of Drypothecine discoveries, the influence of the "splitters" can be seen in the fact that each new discovery tends to be given a new genus and species name. We sympathize with the dismay felt by the general reader at the bewildering profusion of new fossil names that enters the technical literature each year. Discovery always precedes synthesis, however, and, at the moment, we are in a period where the rate of discovery has outstripped our ability to integrate the new material in a coherent framework.

The *Sivapithecus* discoveries from the late Miocene (8 myrs.) of Pakistan and related forms found in southern China are particularly interesting because the details of the anatomy of their facial skeleton and the way their teeth are implanted show obvious similarities to the recent southeast Asian orangs.[44] *Sivapithecus* is illustrated in Figure 8–4. Enough of the postcranial

FIGURE 8–4. *Sivapithecus indicus,* an 8 myr. old specimen from Pakistan, GSP 15000, drawn by M. L. Brace through the courtesy of Prof. D. R. Pilbeam of Harvard University.

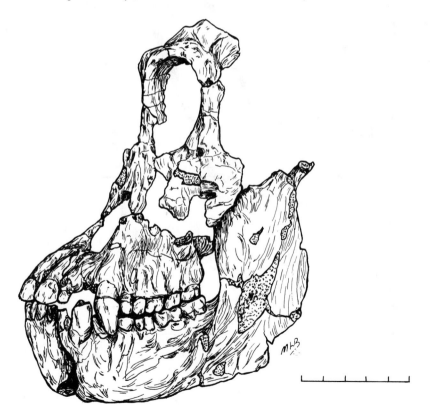

skeleton of *Sivapithecus* has been found to indicate that the elongation of the arms associated with arm hanging and the quadrumanous clambering mode of locomotion had already been achieved. *Sivapithecus* was fully in the ape grade, and is the obvious candidate for the ancestor of the modern orangutan of Sumatra and Borneo.

In Africa, the Dryopithecine descendants of *Proconsul* in the Middle Miocene show clear signs of being ancestral to both the modern African apes and the first true hominids (the Australopithecines), which means they can be considered ancestral to us. Although they are often called Miocene "apes," all those Miocene *Dryopithecus*-related or *Sivapithecus*-related forms named above in such profusion could best be referred to as "proto-apes" since most of them are not characterized by the suspensory arm-hanging behavior that is associated with attainment of the ape grade proper.[45] In the succeeding geo-

FIGURE 8–5. A phylogenetic tree showing the most likely course of primate continuity from the beginning of the Cenozoic, the Age of Mammals.

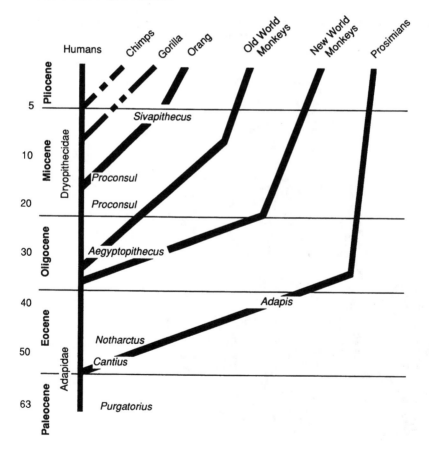

logical period, the Pliocene—which began 5 myrs. ago—there is a dearth of pongid fossil material, but by this time we do have the first full-scale hominids—the Australopithecines—and the continuity from that time on is relatively unbroken. This will provide the subject matter for the remaining chapters of this book.

CHAPTER EIGHT NOTES

[1]Cande and Kent, 1992:13,933.

[2]Simons, 1972; Martin, 1990: Chapters 3 and 4.

[3]Rona and Emiliani, 1969. The ratio of a radioactive element to its stable end product—for example, Uranium 235 to lead 207, written $^{235}U/^{207}Pb$—changes through time strictly in proportion to the speed of decay of the radioactive element in question. It takes 713 million years for half of a given amount of ^{235}U to decay into ^{207}Pb, and another 713 million years for half of the remaining ^{235}U to decay into lead, and so on until the amount left of the radioactive element is too small to measure. The time taken for half of the amount of a given radioactive element to decay into its stable end product is called its half-life. The half-life of Uranium 235 is 713 million years (Rona and Emiliani, 1969:66). If it takes 713 million years for half of a small amount of something to change, obviously it would be hard to make accurate measures of how much change there has been in the ratio between the radioactive and stable components after only a year or two. In fact, it is hard to detect much change in ten or twenty thousand years. Using $^{235}U/^{207}Pb$ ratios, then, is not going to help us determine the ages of events within the last 20,000 years very well, but elements with shorter half-lives can give us such answers. The most useful of these has been Carbon 14 (^{14}C), with a half-life of 5,730 years (Dyck, 1967; Gillespie et al., 1984; Taylor, 1987; Bowman, 1990). This has allowed us to date the end of the Pleistocene between 10,000 and 12,000 years ago (Stringer and Gamble, 1993:45). An element with a longer half-life, Potassium 40 can be used in the Potassium/Argon technique ($^{40}K/^{40}A$) to date older strata in the Pleistocene and earlier (the half-life of ^{40}K is 1.3 billion years). Elements such as Thorium 230 (^{230}Th with a half-life of 32,480 years) can help fill in the intervening dates (Schwarcz, 1993). Recently, it has been discovered that certain kinds of crystals will trap the products of radiation in proportion to the length of time they have been exposed, and the amount of trapped energy can then be measured by a series of techniques that will provide a measure of just how long that crystalline substance has been where it was found. The techniques of Thermoluminescence (TL) and Electron-Spin-Resonance (ESR) both are based on this phenomenon, and both have proved of enormous use in dating tools and fossils from human occupation sites over the last 200,000 years (Hillman et al., 1983; Aitken, 1985; Aitken and Valladas, 1993; Schwarcz and Grün, 1993).

[4]Fleming, 1977; Jacobs (ed.), 1987; Butler, 1991; Baksi et al., 1992.

[5]Cloud and Glaessner, 1982; Kerr, 1992; Bowring et al., 1993.

[6]Elliott, 1987.

[7]Jarvik, 1980.

[8]Renne and Basu, 1991.

[9]Romer, 1966.

[10]Bakker, 1986; Czerkas and Olson (eds.), 1987; Crompton and Gatesy, 1989; Krishtalka, 1989. Krishtalka (1989) does not focus only on dinosaurs; it includes stories about characters such as the abominable snow man and the legendary Big Foot of the American northwest.

[11]Ostrom, 1976, 1979.

[12]Feduccia, 1980, 1993.

[13]Wellnhofer, 1990; Wilford, 1993a.

[14]Crompton and Jenkins, 1973; Laurin and Reisz, 1990.

[15]Alvarez et al., 1984, 1990; Sharpton et al., 1993.

[16]Swisher et al., 1992.

[17]Raup, 1986.

[18]Hallam, 1987; Courtillot et al., 1988; Courtillot, 1990.

[19]Clark, 1950, 1960; Brace and Montagu, 1977:89; Martin, 1990:637–41.

[20]Refer back to the treatment in Chapter 7 (notes 59 and 60).

[21]This is given more extended consideration in Chapter 9.

[22]Szalay and Delson, 1979:41; Groves, 1989:161.

[23]Gingerich 1975b, 1976a, 1986. The possibility that *Plesiadapis* may not be a primate is considered by Gunnell (1986) and taken as being the case by Martin (1988) and by Wible and Covert (1987).

[24]Cande and Kent, 1992.

[25]Simons, 1972:126–27; Gingerich, 1975a.

[26]Rose and Walker, 1985.

[27]Gingerich, 1976b.

[28]Gingerich, 1977a; Gingerich and Simons, 1977.

[29]Gingerich, 1976b:16.

[30]Gingerich, 1977b.

[31]Simons, 1965, 1967, 1984, 1987, 1993.

[32]Cande and Kent, 1992:13,933.

[33]Simons, 1984:18.

[34]Radinsky, 1973.

[35]Simons, 1967, 1987; Fleagle et al., 1975.

[36]Pilbeam, 1984; Andrews and Martin, 1987; Groves, 1989:318.

[37]Leakey, 1948. As so often seemed to happen, it was Mary Leakey who made the key discovery. The story is well told by Sonia Cole (1975:173), but nothing can top the rendition of Mary Leakey herself. The discovery was made on October 2, 1948, and they both immediately realized that it was of truly great significance. As Mary put it: " . . . back in camp at Kathwanga, Louis and I wanted to celebrate. We were exhilarated and also utterly content with each other and we thought that quite the best celebration would be to have another baby. . . . In any case, that night we cast aside care and that is how Philip Leakey . . . came to join the family the following 21 June" (1984:99).

[38]Walker, 1983:6; Pilbeam, 1986:303.

[39]Lartet, 1856.

[40]Simons and Pilbeam, 1965.

[41]See note 38 above.

[42]Martin and Andrews, 1984; Wu and Xu, 1985; Fleagle et al., 1986; Leakey and Leakey, 1986a, b, 1987; Andrews and Martin, 1987; Conroy et al., 1992.

[43]Fleagle et al., 1986; Pan and Jablonski, 1987; Pan, 1988.

[44]Pilbeam, 1982; Ward and Kimbel, 1983; Ward and Brown, 1986; Wu and Oxnard, 1983; Wu and Xu, 1985.

[45]This designation was suggested to me by M. L. Brace as we discussed the revisions being made in this chapter for the fifth edition.

chapter nine

Culture as an Ecological Niche

THE PLEISTOCENE

With the presence of stone tools considered as sufficient to establish the existence of a culture-dependent creature—a genuine hominid—we must recognize the fact that some such form must have been in existence back in the Pliocene, well over two million years ago. Of course there are those who have stated that "there can be no such thing as culture without language and the socially determined sharing of meaning and value. It will therefore be misleading to talk of Culture for any hominids before fully modern humans."[1] For those who have articulated this *a priori* view, even the evidence for the construction of shelters and the regular manufacture of task-specific tools in the Middle Paleolithic has been denigrated as the mindless equivalent of instinctive nest-making in birds or beavers and not worthy of recognition as the manifestations of culture.[2]

From such a perspective, the hominids of the Late Pliocene up through the Middle Pleistocene are denied even the intellectual capabilities of chimpanzees where the socially determined sharing of learned subsistence activities differs from one part of Africa to another in such a way that can only indicate the presence of rudimentary regional cultural differences.[3] In the case of the early hominids, however, we can argue that their very survival was dependent on the activities symbolized by the presence of the stone tools they made. It is not at all clear that this is the case for chimpanzees, and it seems reasonable to suggest that it was this move in the direction of necessary dependence on the transmission of traditions of behavior learned by earlier generations that started the hominid line on its unique trajectory. The presence of stone tools from before the beginning of the Pleistocene on can be taken to indicate the beginnings and growth of a cultural milieu that has become an increasingly essential element in human survival. This is pursued at greater length in Chapter 10 and subsequently.

The Pleistocene is the geological period that contained the recently ended Ice Age. Since this was the period during which all of the major events of human evolution took place, it has necessarily been the focus of considerable attention on the part of the anthropological world. Recently, geophysicists have utilized a variety of ingenious techniques to establish the age of strata in the recent past.[4] Recognizing that various radioactive elements "decay" into stable end products at fixed rates, they have measured, in material taken from crucial geological layers, the ratio of certain of these radioactive elements to their stable end products.[5] Since the ratio discovered is proportional to the length of time during which the process has been going on, this serves as a measure of the time elapsed since the layer in question was formed. By these means, the Pleistocene has been calculated to extend from over 1.75 million down to some 10,000 to 12,000 years ago.[6]

Perhaps this makes Pleistocene dating seem simpler than it is. Actually, there are a great many knotty problems connected with it. For instance, finding suitable mineral specimens to use for this kind of analysis is beset with difficulties. Indeed, only a very limited number of layers have been pinned down in this way. The rest have been tentatively fitted in by extrapolations based on the fossil animals contained. As a result, a great deal of uncertainty still remains concerning such problems as the correlations and relative ages of layers in South Africa compared with those in Indonesia, or Europe with China. Despite all these uncertainties and inaccuracies, however, the temporal dimensions of the period during which humanity evolved are beginning to emerge.

During the Pleistocene there were periodic major onsets of glacial conditions in the northern hemisphere. Geologists used to regard the whole period as being taken up with glaciation, and they thought that there had been only four clear-cut Pleistocene glacial episodes. It has recently become apparent that episodes of glaciation have been recurring at 100,000 year intervals for at least the last million years, and that there may have been as many as a dozen of such demonstrable episodes.[7] The earlier part of the Pleistocene was characterized by milder climatic conditions, although there were indeed fluctuations between drier and better-watered periods of time in the areas inhabited by the early hominids. The accompanying chart (Figure 9–1) displays the divisions of the Pleistocene, their approximate duration, and the associated cultural stages displayed in the archaeological record.

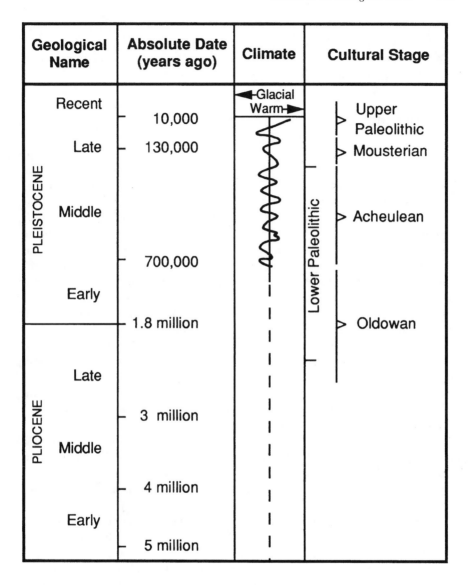

FIGURE 9–1. The divisions of the Pleistocene.

The most consistent and reliable evidence for hominid existence throughout this time is to be seen in the form of chipped stone artifacts. The tool-making traditions practiced during the Pleistocene have been given the label Paleolithic (old stone), and reveal the fact that the characteristic modes of subsistence were hunting and gathering. The change to a food-producing way of life did not begin to occur until after the Pleistocene was over. This was one of the most significant cultural events that ever occurred, and it has profoundly changed the nature of the selective forces acting on human populations during the last several thousand years. We shall return to a consideration of these matters in Chapter 14.

PALEOLITHIC TOOLS

The Paleolithic is further divisible into Upper, Middle (tentatively), and Lower segments of very unequal length. Ninety to ninety-five percent of the record is included in the Lower Paleolithic, during which cultural change was extremely slow and cultural diversity apparently at a minimum.[8] We say "apparently," since all we know of the Lower Paleolithic is the few stone tools remaining and the bones of the animals that people ate. While these indicate that the gross dimensions of human life were much the same from one end of the inhabited world to the other, it is perfectly possible, and even likely, that minor cultural differences of an unknown nature flourished in different areas. Stone tools form only a small component of the total cultural repertoire, which, one should remember, includes far greater quantities of perishable items and, even more important, dimensions of verbalization, knowledge, and social behavior that leave no record. Potential diversity of this sort notwithstanding, however, it is still possible to state that major and basic facets of human adaptation were substantially the same from one end of the Old World to the other. Whether in South Africa, Europe, Asia, or Indonesia, game was hunted by the same techniques and processed by chipped stone tools that were virtually identical over vast areas.

The increasing local diversity visible in the stone tools of the Middle and Upper Paleolithic will be treated later, but at the moment we are concerned with the Lower Paleolithic, and specifically with its earliest phases. According to current indications, the oldest cultural remains in the world, and consequently the earliest nonanatomical evidence for human existence, come from East and South Africa. The oldest reliably dated tools go back some 2.5 million years in Ethiopia.[9] The tools on which this judgment is based are of the crudest recognizable sort, and, were it not for the location in which they have been found, it would be almost impossible to prove that they were indeed the products of deliberate manufacture. But, occurring as they do by ancient lake margins and out on the plains miles from the nearest potential rock outcrop or natural source, we can only conclude that they were deliberately transported there. The discovery of such objects in a rocky stream bed or on a seashore among the countless thousands of pebbles or cobbles which natural water action has battered and fractured would attract no attention since, under such circumstances, such relatively simple forms could easily have been produced by natural processes. But found in a fine sedimentary deposit amidst the dismembered remains of extinct animals, they clearly indicate the activities of their ancient manufacturers.

Just what those activities were has been the subject of a great deal of debate, and this has led to some very interesting and fruitful research over the last decade and more. Well over twenty years ago, the distinguished pioneer in studies in the behavior and ecology of such varied creatures as gorillas, lions, tigers, and pandas, among others—George Schaller—presented a very plausible scenario suggesting that the earliest hominids might very well have carved out a life-way on the savannas of Africa as scavengers.[10] Subsequently, studies by a series of archaeologists and specialists in the analysis of carcass treatment showed that the remains of animal bones from Plio-Pleistocene tool-containing sites in East Africa provided evidence that offered support for Schaller's hypothesis. Analysis of the cut marks on the bones, using a scanning electron microscope and then comparing the results with experimental attempts to reproduce them, led to the realization that, while carnivore teeth may have produced some of those traces, a good many could only have been made by stone tools.[11]

The niche of scavenger may well have been exploited by the earliest hominids. Another student of this question has noted that, while there are no modern carnivores that are physically equipped to get through the skin of a recently defunct elephant or rhinoceros, it is not that difficult for a tool-using hominid to do so. The one prehistoric carnivore with the teeth and the musculature that would make this possible was the saber-toothed "tiger," and it is interesting to note that this creature disappeared from Africa when tool-wielding hominids became established. These saber-toothed cats survived longer in Europe, where human forms did not become permanent residents until later on in the Middle Pleistocene, and they survived in the western hemisphere until the first arrival of humans from Asia at the very end of the Pleistocene.[12] It is indeed possible that the early hominids became more efficient scavengers than the competing saber-toothed cats and ended by replacing them.

In their crudest form, those early "tools" resemble river pebbles from which a flake or two has been knocked off, creating an edge or point. This is the source of the type designation by which they are known: "pebble tools." Figure 9–2 shows samples of these tools. Because of the simple nature of the flaking, it is often impossible to say whether it was done deliberately, or whether it had occurred naturally and the ancient hominid had simply chosen the stone from among others for this reason. Furthermore, there is increasing reason to believe that the so-called pebble "tools" may not have been used as implements at all. Instead, it may well have been the flakes which had been removed that were the artifacts utilized. The items identified as "pebble tools" may simply have been the discarded cores of raw material from which the actual working tools themselves had been removed. Recent experimental

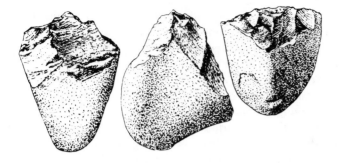

FIGURE 9–2.   Pebble "tools" of the Oldowan type from Bed I of Olduvai Gorge, Tanzania. (By courtesy of the British Museum of Natural History.)

work has shown that the flakes removed from suitably sized pebbles are considerably more effective in skinning and cutting up animal remains than the items originally identified as pebble tools.[13]

The controversy over the importance of tool manufacture as distinguished from tool use has been mentioned in a previous chapter. Although this controversy will probably never be resolved, the important thing to remember is that the presence of these tools, whether chosen or fashioned, signifies the presence of a creature whose life depended upon the behavioral complex of which these tools were a part—that is, whose survival depended upon the presence of culture.

There is another crucial fact to be realized: From the actual preserved pieces of material culture, there is evidence for no more than one basic cultural tradition in the early Pleistocene. By tracing this through time, we can see that this tradition is the direct ancestor of all succeeding cultural traditions, which makes it, among other things, the remote parent of this book. A single original cultural tradition strongly suggests that only one organism continued to rely on culture as a necessary condition for its survival.

CULTURE AND ECOLOGY

Ecology is "the study of environmental relations of organisms,"[14] and the total life-way of a given species can be called its ecological niche.[15] In the human case, virtually all aspects of life are conditioned by culture, and it is therefore justifiable to regard humans as inhabiting a cultural ecological niche.[16] By culture, the anthropologist means: *all those aspects of the learning and experience accumulated by previous generations that are acquired by virtue of being a member of a continuing society.*[17] The obvious advantage of not having to "reinvent the wheel" each generation gives those who can tap into the accumulated experience of their predecessors an enormous edge over those who cannot. But culture is not just an obviously tangible entity such as a tool that can be picked up and used at will. It has to be learned, and there must have been appreciable long-term selection acting to weed out those who could not, and preserve those who could, learn the ways of the group to which they belonged. Almost certainly it was the action of that kind of selection that led to the steady increase in hominid brain size from the Lower through much of the Middle Pleistocene. Among other things, a prolongation of the learning period will benefit those whose survival depends predominantly on the use of learned behavior, and this is clearly one of the reasons why human beings have the longest period of infant and juvenile dependency of all living animals.[18]

Today, obviously, the process of becoming "enculturated"—of learning one's own culture—is enormously assisted by the use of one aspect of that culture itself, namely language. The selective pressures leading to the development of a linguistic capacity must have been considerable in the past since virtually all living human groups possess this unique ability to an equal extent.[19] No other animal possesses anything remotely like a language, and even the efforts to teach the rudiments of linguistic understanding to our closest relative and that smartest of all nonhuman creatures, the chimpanzee, have been effective failures.[20] The shaping of the brain pathways that led to the capacity to use linguistic behavior obviously took a long time. Unfortunately, we have no fossilized evidence for the origin of language, but there are some very suggestive archaeological developments that occur after human brain size reached its modern levels around 200,000 years ago, and these are treated in the light of what they may indicate in Chapters 13 and 14.[21]

There is another ramification in the theory of evolutionary ecology that has been called the *"competitive exclusion principle."*[22] This states that no two "closely related (or otherwise similar) species" can continue to occupy the same ecological niche.[23] In a sense, this is stating the obvious, although, as in so much else, it is not always obvious until stated. The point is this: Culture, as known, comprises a single ecological niche within which one would expect to find only a single species.[24] Because early Pleistocene stone tools all belong to a single cultural tradition, the probability is greatly increased that there has been only one continuing hominid species since the beginning of that cultural record, and that the hominids at different time levels are lineally related.

But if culturally dependent creatures of different time levels are probably related, what about the occurrence of two different forms of hominid at the same time? How could that occur when competition within a niche—the cultural ecological niche in this case—tends to eliminate one of the competing forms? We can only guess that, at its earliest stages of development, culture was less effective and was consequently a less than all-pervasive determinant of the nature of the total life-way that it eventually came to dominate.[25] And even though the skeletal evidence from the very earliest hominids goes back more than a million years before the first stone tools, that skeletal evidence suggests that those hominids were dependent upon some aspects of culture—presumably of a perishable nature—for their survival.[26] From the Late Pliocene and Early Pleistocene skeletal remains, it would appear that more than one kind of hominid made an effort to enter the cultural ecological niche, but, in the long run, only one continued.

The term cultural ecological niche, then, is an abstraction that we can use for our own convenience. But as biologists have found when they have tried to define other kinds of ecological niches, one must be careful lest we raise a convenient abstraction to the level of a typological essence. The concept of ecological niche is a convenient way of generalizing about organic adaptation—and no more. We should not allow it to take on an idealized existence of its own. For making broad generalizations, such categorizations can be useful, but we must continue to be aware of the particular and separate factors that can exert very specific influences. If the general capacities of modern *Homo sapiens* have been conditioned by long-term adaptation to the cultural ecological niche, some obvious differences—skin color, nose form— are the product of regional differences in the intensity of selective forces that themselves are distributed without regard to human cultural capacities.[27]

Just as the evidence for cultural development can be viewed in terms of sequential stages, so the picture of human physical development can be treated in similar fashion, although its stages are considerably more tentative because of the fragmentary nature of the record and the long gaps between crucial specimens. For the earlier stages, the fossil evidence is spotty and widely separated, and the relative ages of the various localities are bitterly contested. For most of the later stages, the evidence is more complete, the dating more reliable, and the association with the cultural record more certain. In spite of this improvement, however, there are still many problems and disputed pieces of evidence, and many professional scholars are vehemently opposed to the implications of the solution about to be offered.[28] Speculation is rife, and since no interpretation can be more than that, the best justification for the interpretation that follows is that it treats the skeletal evidence for human evolution within a framework consistent with both cultural and evolutionary theory.

CHAPTER NINE NOTES

[1]Davidson and Noble, 1989:137.
[2]Stringer and Gamble, 1993:207–312.
[3]McGrew, 1992:14.
[4]Badash, 1989.
[5]See Chapter 8, note 3.
[6]Shackleton, 1975; Shackleton and Opdyke, 1976; Broecker and Denton, 1989, 1990; Walter et al., 1991; Cande and Kent, 1992.

[7]Shackleton and Opdyke, 1976:451; Broecker and Denton, 1990:50.

[8]Isaac, 1972:401; Klein, 1989b:212; Howells, 1993:118.

[9]Johanson, 1978:54; Johanson and Shreeve, 1989:259–60; Klein, 1983:26; Toth, 1987a, 1987b:114; Schick and Toth, 1993.

[10]Schaller, 1965, 1967, 1972, 1976; Schaller et al., 1985; Schaller and Lowther, 1969.

[11]Shipman and Rose, 1983; Shipman, 1986.

[12]Blumenschine, 1986, 1987; Blumenschine and Cavallo, 1992.

[13]Toth and Schick, 1983.

[14]Bates, 1960:547.

[15]Gause, 1934:19; Eldredge and Cracraft, 1980:328–29.

[16]Over forty years ago, one of the driving forces in trying to bring biological anthropology out of its persistently medieval mind-set, Sherwood L. Washburn, declared that "it is particularly the task of the anthropologist to assess the way the development of Culture affected physical evolution" (1951:69). Both particular and general attempts were made to follow up on Sherry Washburn's recommendation (Brace, 1962:343, 1964:14, 36, 1979a:287, in press [d]; Hulse, 1962:939, 1963: 687; Brace and Montagu, 1965:216, 1977:277; Alexander, 1990:6; Trinkaus and Shipman, 1992:352). Reactions have ranged from the skeptical feeling that culture should be regarded "as a form of adaptation rather than as a niche itself" (Alland, 1967:172), through a failure to understand its importance for human survival (Stringer and Gamble, 1993: 203), to a flat denial that it has any relevance at all (Foley, 1987:790).

[17]This, in effect, is a streamlined paraphrase of the famous definition of E. B. Tylor quoted in Chapter 7, note 77. The anthropological definition, then, encompasses the value-laden view associated with esthetics and literature framed by the famed Oxford poet and critic, Matthew Arnold (1822–1888), who defined "culture" as "the best which has been thought and said in the world" (Arnold, 1869:xi). In the anthropological version, culture is made up of all those aspects of learned behavior that survive and are transmitted from one generation to another because they work, whether they are judged to be "the best" or not.

[18]Harvey and Clutton-Brock, 1985; Falkner and Tanner (eds.), 1986.

[19]As anthropological linguists have discovered, all languages, regardless of the degrees of social and technical complexity of the speakers, are completely formed with equivalent grammatical and vocabulary elements and the same abilities to handle the concrete and the abstract (Swadesh, 1971:1). As one respected linguist put it, "No known languages are 'primitive'" (Hymes, 1964:104).

[20]Terrace et al., 1979.

[21]Swadesh, 1971:182–83; Hockett, 1978:249–54, 296–97. In contrast to those who have tried to deal with these matters in an evolutionary context, the catastrophist/creationist stance that dominates paleoanthropology at the present time makes it as an assertion that there can be no culture without language (Davidson and Noble, 1989:137), and that the development of language was an "all or nothing situation" resembling "the flick of a switch and *not* the slow upwards movement of a symbolic dimmer" (Stringer and Gamble, 1993:203–04). It is a classic comic book version of evolutionary thinking in which novel developments occur instantaneously like the light bulb that suddenly appears in a cartoon panel over the head of some momentarily inspired worthy with *IDEA* lettered across it. This is a splendid illustration of the situation described by Bickerton: "The fact that static formalism has prevented linguists from grappling with the origins of language has not, of course, prevented persons from other disciplines—with, unfortunately but inevitably, rather less understanding of all that language entails—from trying their hands at it" (1981:215). It is what Bickerton has called "the Flintstones approach to language origins (which) totally ignores the vast amount of preadaptation that was necessary before you could even get to that point, and equally ignores the vast amount of postadaptation that was necessary in order to get from that point to fully developed human language" *idem*. The Flintstones approach concentrates, "exclusively or almost so, on the moment when recognizable speech first emerged, when Ug first said to Og, '. . . . . ,' where '. . . . .' represents some kind of meaningful vocalized proposition" *idem*. Again, this is a just a further demonstration of just how remote "modern" paleoanthropology has become from a Darwinian perspective.

[22]Hardin, 1960. It has also been called "*Gause's principle* (after the Russian biologist who first confirmed the principle experimentally)" (Odum, 1971:214). See Gause, 1934:19.

[23]Gause, 1934:19; Odum, 1971:214.

[24]Mayr, 1951:116; Bartholomew and Birdsell, 1953:489; Brace, 1964:14.

[25]It was Sherwood Washburn himself who made this point in rebuttal to a presentation I had given at the 63rd annual meetings of the American Anthropological Association in Detroit, November, 1964, and he was absolutely right. It is a particular instance of the general complaint formulated by Francisco Ayala that the indiscriminate use of the competetive exclusion principle runs the risk of ignoring "the complexities of the biological world" (Ayala, 1972:355).

[26]Bartholomew and Birdsell, 1953:490; Brace and Montagu, 1965:227, 1977:305–6.

[27]Brace and Hunt, 1990; Brace, in press (c).

[28]Eldredge and Tattersall, 1982; Groves, 1989; Rightmire, 1990; Kimbel, 1991; Howells, 1993; Stringer and Gamble, 1993; Wolpoff, in press.

chapter ten

The Australopithecine Stage

HOMINID CHARACTERISTICS

Africa, which has provided us with the earliest archaeological evidence for human existence, has also yielded the earliest hominid skeletal remains. The term "hominid" is a colloquial version of the technical term Hominidae, the taxonomic family to which human beings belong. The closest human relatives within the order Primates are the living anthropoid apes. These belong in the family Pongidae. Together with the Hominidae, they are traditionally included within the superfamily Hominoidea.[1] To simplify matters of reference, the term "pongid" is generally used to designate anything that is more apelike than manlike, while the term "hominid" is generally used to mean "taxonomically included within the family which harbors human beings proper."[2]

Raymond Dart's initial specimen, *Australopithecus africanus,* has given its name to a whole group of what has been variously called "ape-men," "man-apes," "near-men," or even "primitive men."[3] We can avoid the implications of such terms by referring to them simply as early hominids. These include the South African finds by Dart, Broom, Robinson, and others. The category can also be extended to include "Zinj" and other specimens from Bed I at Olduvai; many of Richard Leakey's discoveries near Lake Turkana in northern Kenya; material from the Omo River Valley in southern Ethiopia; and the Pliocene finds of more than 3 million years antiquity made by Don Johanson in the Afar depression of Central Ethiopia and by Mary Leakey at Laetoli, 25 miles south of Olduvai in Tanzania. Broom and others have attempted to elevate these to subfamilial status within family Hominidae and call them "Australopithecinae."[4] This would allow the retention of all the separate generic names as valid taxonomic units, but despite the recent enthusiastic resurgence of a new generation of splitters, in terms of the present analysis this course of action seems untenable. It is still useful to refer to the group as Australopithecines, and, as will be seen, they can properly be regarded as the first stage in human evolution.

The differences of opinion concerning Australopithecine taxonomy revolve around the criteria that are considered important for purposes of classification. For those scholars who do not approach these issues from the perspective of evolutionary theory—and this includes Broom, Robinson, and the recent school of cladistic splitters—the enumeration of visually perceived differences and similarities is of prime importance, with taxonomic status depending on how many there are of each regardless of their importance.[5] Thus, the Australopithecines are apelike in the possession of small brain cases, big molar teeth, facial projection, and a number of other features, but they differ from the apes in that they lack projecting canines, have a downward instead of a backward facing *foramen magnum* (hole at the base of the skull where the spinal chord enters), and have a shortened and expanded *ilium* (hip bone) and other related characters. In this latter regard, they resemble humans more than apes. Broom and Robinson (and others) consider that this balance of human and pongid features justifies a taxonomic position distinct from the one occupied by modern humanity, and of greater importance than merely either a specific or generic distinction. It is a position that has to be given thoughtful consideration even if we do not accept it at the formal level. Note, however, that the Australopithecines can still be formally considered within the family Hominidae, and hence they are called hominids. (Figure 10–1 offers an artist's conception of the Australopithecine.)

Without denying that the balance of Australopithecine characteristics lands somewhere between the pongid and hominid categories, it is worth pointing out that not all characteristics are of equal importance to the survival of the organism. It would seem that those characteristics which have the greatest adaptive significance should be the ones to determine the major taxonomic name used to indicate adaptive evolutionary change.[6] In the case of the Australopithecines, two characteristics outweigh all others, but it is not so much the characteristics themselves as it is what they signify. The first is the nonprojecting canine, and the second is bipedal locomotion.

Figure 10–1.
Artist's conception of an Australopithecine. Note the simple look on his face and the presence of fur. This is sheer fancy, since there is no way of telling facial expression or other aspects of the soft parts of the body from the fossil record.

CANINE TEETH

To take up the first of these, it is most suggestive that the Australopithecines and subsequent human beings, alone of all the terrestrial primates, do not have projecting canine teeth. Figure 10–2 provides an example. Typically, terrestrial primates have greatly enlarged canine teeth (witness the baboons), since, as small, relatively slow creatures, they could not survive the depradations of a variety of carnivores without some effective means of defense. At the same time, it has recently become apparent that the extraordinary enlargement of *male* canine teeth in many primates is due more to competition between males for access to females than it is a response to the threat of predation.[7] Even so, female baboon canines project well beyond the level of the rest of the teeth in the dental arch, and it can be painful indeed to be bitten by a female baboon. In human beings, however, canine teeth do not project beyond the level of the other teeth and consequently play no role either in defense against predation or in competition with other males in gaining access to available females. In the human case, the lack of canine projection is clearly compensated for by the use of hand-held tools employed for a variety

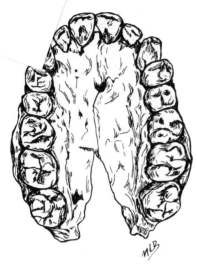

Figure 10–2.
The palate AL 200 from the Hadar site in the Afar Depression in north central Ethiopia, approximately 3 myrs. ago. All of the teeth are large and robust, and there is an ape-like gap, or *diastema,* between the lateral incisor and the canine. The canine, while large, does not project in a functional fashion above the occlusal level of the rest of the teeth. The apparent projection of the right upper canine resulted because it had partially extruded from its socket prior to fossilization. The normal condition is shown by the canine on the other side. Even though the canines do not project, the form of this palate and these teeth is almost more pongid than hominid. All told, it is sufficiently intermediate that a decision as to which it should be called cannot be made on this part of the skeleton alone. Although these features have been recognized for years—in fact, they have largely contributed to the inclusion of the Australopithecines within the category hominid—their full significance has often been misperceived, and arguments about interpretation continue among the experts.

of purposes, including defense and aggression, and it is difficult to interpret the Australopithecines in any other light. Furthermore, this applies to the robust as well as the gracile Australopithecines.

BIPEDALISM

The other point to consider is the fact that the Australopithecines were bipeds, as can be seen from the anatomy of the pelvis and leg, and as is evident from the placement of the skull. To be sure, some recent studies have shown that a number of features visible in the finger and toe bones, as well as in the arms, shoulders, and chests, suggest that the Australopithecines retained climbing capabilities of a far more specific nature than is true for the odd tree-climbing modern human.[8] And in the two instances where arm and leg bones of the same individual have been found, it appears that the arms are larger in proportion to leg size than is true for the more recent specimens included in the genus *Homo.*[9]

Figure 10–3 shows a reconstruction of the trunk skeleton of Lucy flanked by a chimpanzee on the right and a human on the left.[10] Kevin Hunt, of Indiana University, has demonstrated that the somewhat pyramidal shape of the rib cage in the chimpanzee is an adaptation to arm-hanging, one of its important feeding postures.[11] The shortening of the lumbar portion of the spinal column and the expansion of the blades of the ilium up towards the bottom of the rib cage is a part of this whole complex. In Lucy, the ribs still display a pyramidal configuration, but the pelvis does not approach

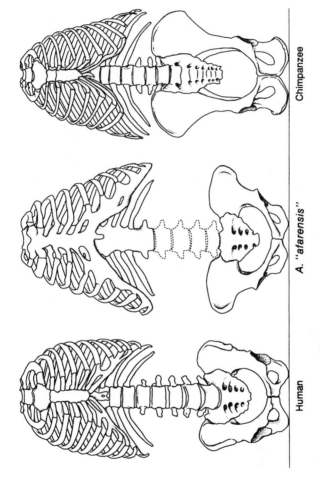

| Human | A. "afarensis" | Chimpanzee |

Figure 10–3. The trunk skeleton of the most complete known Australopithecine, Lucy, in the center, compared with a modern human on the left and a chimpanzee on the right. (Courtesy of Kevin D. Hunt.)

123

them so closely and, although the evidence has had to come from other individuals, the lumbar region evidently was not so compressed as it is in a chimpanzee.

Figure 10–4 shows the shape of the pelvis of Lucy flanked by that of a human and a chimpanzee, all viewed from the top.[12] In the human, it is obvious that the blade of the ilium curves around the pelvic inlet and provides a broad area for the attachments of the muscles that control the position of the trunk as it rises above the point of articulation at the hip socket. In the chimpanzee, the restriction of the plane of orientation of the iliac blades implies a limitation in the capacity to exercise that kind of muscular control. Lucy, once more, displays an intermediate condition. Other Australopithecines simply reinforce the picture presented by Lucy and confirm the suspicion that an arm-hanging feeding posture was an important adaptation in the immediate predecessors of the hominids.[13]

Because of this, it has been suggested that the Australopithecines may well have continued to use trees as places of refuge. This is perfectly plausible and even likely, but it does not change the fact that their lower appendages, even while retaining a number of pongid and transitional aspects, were those

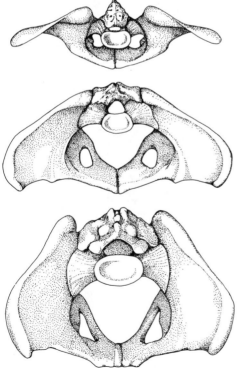

Figure 10–4.
The reconstructed pelvis of Lucy, in the middle, compared with a chimpanzee on the top and a modern human on the bottom. (Courtesy of C. Owen Lovejoy.)

of terrestrial bipeds whose style of locomotion on the ground was far more like that of ourselves than it was like that of chimpanzees or gorillas.

Even though they were indeed bipeds, this has been sometimes taken to imply more than could be justified by the evidence. It was fashionable a generation ago to envision the Paleolithic hunter bounding across the grassland on his long, straight legs, as though bipedalism were somehow the most efficient, speediest, and "best" possible way of getting around. There are even some artists' depictions of Australopithecines sprinting across the savannas in hot and threatening pursuit of herds of antelope.[14] To any who may still harbor the lingering residue of such an illusion, I suggest that you seriously consider the vision summoned by an irate adult *Homo sapiens* in hot pursuit of a thoroughly frightened *Felis domesticus* (house cat). As anyone who has ever engaged in this exercise in futility knows, the point is obvious: as a mechanism for high-speed locomotor efficiency, hominid bipedalism is ludicrous. Obviously a creature who cannot even catch a small cat has a proportionately smaller chance of escaping from a large one, and it is certain that such felines as leopards and lions, as well as a variety of pack-hunting canines, must have posed a constant threat to the survival of any savanna-dwelling primate during the Plio/Pleistocene.

The only possible excuse for the development of hominid bipedalism is that it allowed for the development of compensating features (but clearly not formidable canines). Because the main functional correlate of bipedalism is that the hands are freed from any involvement in the locomotor process, it would seem that the hands must have been used in wielding a nonanatomical defensive mechanism.[15] Given a creature lacking in dental defenses and pathetically slow of foot, we could postulate the existence of culture even *without* any direct evidence. Culture, in the form of rudimentary but recognizable stone tools, does exist right back into the Pliocene, around 2.5 million years ago, and it is evidently ancestral to the subsequent traditions of the Lower, Middle, and Upper Pleistocene where it is clearly the manufactured product of our own forebears. Furthermore, the hominids at that time were all recognizable as Australopithecines.

Not very many years ago, we could feel a sense of gratification in the association of the earliest demonstrable evidence for culture with hominids whose anatomy indicates that they could not have survived without it. As we have since discovered, however, things are not quite so simple. On the one hand, in the Hadar and Maka regions of the Afar depression in North-Central Ethiopia and at Laetoli, just south of Olduvai Gorge in Tanzania, there are abundant remains of recently discovered Australopithecines that date back more than 3.5 million years. This is well back into the Pliocene and about a million years before the first stone tools. By the time the first identifiable tools do appear prior to the onset of the Pleistocene (about 2.5 million years ago),[16] there is clear evidence for two distinct kinds of Australopithecine.

Finally, between 1.5 and 1.4 million years ago, we find a more developed stone tool assemblage, Australopithecines, and full-fledged Pithecanthropines.[17] Given these data, we can legitimately ask, "What does it all mean?" Can we interpret it in such a way that we can get some sense of what was going on? In the current vernacular, what "scenario" does this suggest? Admittedly, there are many pieces of information not mentioned in the above sketch that can bear on the question, but many are so scrappy and incomplete that they are just as likely to confuse as to clarify. Despite that, it is indeed possible to sketch the outlines of a synthesis.

SCAVENGING AND THE ORIGIN OF HUNTING

One of the keys to our understanding is the realization of what the evidence does and what it does not tell us concerning the dimensions of the cultural ecological niche. As we have noted, the presence of manufactured tools is direct evidence for the existence of culture, and this in turn has led us to anticipate the presence of those other aspects we have come to associate with it: expanded dependence on learning, symbolic behavior, planning for the future, and the like. These are inferences, however, and the mere presence of tools per se provides no more evidence in their support than does the existence of a biped that does not have projecting canine teeth. Indeed, the American paleontologist Elwyn Simons has warned that we may have invested the Australopithecines with more of the distinguishing attributes of humanity than the evidence really warrants.[18]

On the other hand, the context and associations of the tools can tell us more than the not-so-insignificant fact that their makers depended on culture for survival. The shape of the worked stone pieces themselves, however, may prove to have been seriously misleading. The early ones are about the size of a dinner roll with a flake or two knocked off presumably to make a pointed or chisel-like business edge. As mentioned earlier, there have been growing doubts about whether the so-called pebble tools were actually utensils or merely the cores that served as the sources for what was really intended to be the working implements themselves; that is, the flakes that had been removed.[19] Not only that, but experimental efforts to duplicate the precise techniques needed to manufacture tools of that type have led to the conclusion that most of those early hominids who made them were predominantly right-handed![20]

And although no one doubts that the object in making tools had been to produce a working edge that could be employed for some important function, there has also been much uncertainty about what that function actually was. Guesses concerning tool use traditionally assumed that the cores, and not the flakes removed from them, were the tools intended, and that they may have been employed for digging roots, for shaping wooden objects, or as hand-held weapons. Artists' reconstructions variously depict Australopithecines facing marauding carnivores or even each other with pebble tools clutched in hand in daggerlike fashion, or sprinting across the African savanna in pursuit of an antelope or gazelle while wielding their supposed tools in a threatening manner.[21]

One of the problems in dealing with the events of prehistory is that we can never go back and put our interpretations to any immediate test. Instead, we have to rely on circumstantial evidence. Our conclusions, then, are tentative at best, and we can only offer them with varying degrees of probability instead of proof. With perseverance, awareness, and luck, we can identify some of the situations in which prehistoric activities took place. In most instances, the tools were lost or abandoned in areas unrelated to their use and then subject to repositioning by the weathering actions that generally reshape the landscape.

But in rare fortunate cases, they remain concentrated at the scene of their actual employment with their relationships relatively undisturbed. A number of such examples have been discovered at Olduvai Gorge and east of Lake Turkana, and perhaps the most instructive find was at Koobi Fora in East Turkana. There, a concentration of flake tools and pebble "choppers" occurs in the sediments of what had once been a river delta, distributed among the bones of an extinct hippopotamus. The scatter and positioning of the hippo bones strongly suggest that it was butchered and eaten on the site, and furthermore that the stone tools had been used to do the butchering.[22]

Careful geological analysis of similar sites in the surrounding area has enabled us to build a picture of what things were like, not only at that time, but back to more than 3 million years as well, and the picture is not much different from what can be seen in much of East Africa today. Large lakes lay along the north-south fault axes of the rift valleys, much as do Lakes Turkana, Manyara, Eyasi, and others today. These were surrounded by grassy savanna lands, which in turn were crossed by meandering watercourses that ended in deltas and swamps at the lake margins. Riverine and gallery forests were distributed along the banks of the lakes and streams. The evidence suggests that these patches of woodland were the preferred habitats of the earliest hominids, and we can guess that the availability of fruiting trees as both sources of nourishment and refuge from the threat of predators was as important to the Australopithecines as it was to baboons, then as well as now.[23]

The hippopotamus butchery site at Koobi Fora was in the delta of one such stream where it joined the Plio/Pleistocene ancestor of Lake Turkana (formerly Lake Rudolf). There, approximately 2 million years ago, a band of Australopithecines encountered a hippopotamus that had died and been washed downstream, to become mired on its side in the shallow waters of the delta. This then became the scene of an Australopithecine banquet. Hippopotamus hide, however, is pretty well impervious to even the most power-ful of modern and presumably ancient carnivores. The jaws and teeth of lions and hyenas cannot penetrate until putrefaction has proceeded to a consider-able extent, and one can surmise that the teeth and fingernails of the Aus-tralopithecines were not adequate for the task.

But modern experiments have shown that Oldowan tools, even in the much weaker hands of twentieth century *Homo sapiens,* will suffice to gain ac-cess to the meat that is beneath the toughest of animal skin. Tests made by ar-chaeologists on zoo elephants that had died of natural causes show that, although Oldowan "choppers" are essentially useless for such purposes, the flakes detached to make the pebble "tools" are themselves quite efficient in getting through the skin. These flakes become dull quite quickly, however, and new ones need to be created. This provides a satisfying explanation for the cut-marks preserved on animal bones and for the quantities of flakes sur-rounding the butchery sites of Koobi Fora, Olduvai Gorge, and elsewhere in the Plio/Pleistocene of Africa.[24]

It would seem, then, that the possession of chipped stone tools allowed the Australopithecines to scavenge on material that no other potential user could get at, and it is just possible that the early hominids were able to exploit a niche as pachyderm scavengers for at least a part of their subsistence. At the Hippopotamus Artifact Site at Koobi Fora, they evidently made their tools on the spot and feasted on the exposed upper side of the animal. The other side remained buried in the mud and silt, which preserved it down to the smallest toe bones until both it and the scatter of stone tools were excavated by Richard Leakey's team some 2 million years later.

At Olduvai Gorge, the careful analysis by Mary Leakey, Richard's mother, has shown that Australopithecine tools were associated with faunal remains from mice on up to elephants, although the most common bones are those of antelopes and smaller mammals. An analysis of the surface of many of the bones with the use of a scanning electron microscope, compar-ing the scratch marks with experimentally treated samples, has provided con-clusive evidence that stone tools were being used to butcher a good number of the animals whose bones have been recovered.[25]

Modern chimpanzees and baboons will kill and eat young gazelles, bush pigs, monkeys, and other animals when the occasion arises, but it is principally an opportunistic and relatively uncommon adjunct to their nor-mal way of life.[26] Some Plio/Pleistocene Australopithecines, however, were evidently more systematic in their use of animals as dietary resources. We can guess that they started from a kind of chimpanzee-like opportunism, preying on the relatively helpless newborn. Gradually they extended their pursuit to just slightly older juveniles, and eventually they developed the skills and capa-bilities that transformed them into full-scale hunters and proper members of the genus *Homo.*

The archaeological sequence from Bed I to the overlying Bed II at Olduvai provides the best evidence we have for that transformation.[27] The tools at the lower levels of Bed I are crude, and the treatment of the animal bones with which they are associated suggests that the hominids were concentrating on scavenging. By the middle of Bed II, however, tool categories display regular differentiation, and it is clear that the adults of large-sized game animals were being regularly hunted. What we can see there, apparently, is the record of the transformation of a precocious bipedal ape who was an opportunistic hunter of juveniles and a scavenger of large animal carcases into a full-fledged hunting hominid. The arguments about how much hunting and how much scavenging they did continue unabated, but certainly by Bed II times at Olduvai, the early hominids were pursuing a life-way that was radically different from that of any other primate known. It is tempting to associate this change in life-way with the development of those traits in which modern humans are most different from their closest nonhuman relatives.

GATHERING AND HUNTING

The life-way pursued by Pleistocene and Recent hominids, prior to the development of agriculture, has been commonly called a "hunting-and-gathering" means of subsistence. In our focus on the origins of the hunting part of that hunting-and-gathering complex, we run the risk of failing to give adequate credit to the importance played by the gathering component. Studies of those hunter-gatherers who have continued to pursue this mode of subsistence right up to the present show that gathering activities can be responsible for as much as eighty percent of the food used. This is true, for example, for the hunter-gatherers of the Kalahari desert in South Africa, the San (often called by the derogatory term, "Bushmen").[28]

Among the Eskimo in the Arctic, however, the proportions are effectively reversed. For much of the year, the products of the chase are the only things available. Although gathered berries and vegetable products are highly valued, they are available only in small amounts and for brief parts of the year.[29] Those who have assessed the case of the Eskimo have pointed out that they are very far from representing a classic Pleistocene way of life. Their technology is highly specialized, and the whole phenomenon of arctic hunting that they represent is something that has developed only within the last 5,000 years.[30]

If one looks at the San of the Kalahari a bit more closely, however, the same objection also holds true. The use of the bow and poisoned arrows is a technical refinement not present back in the Pleistocene, and the mortars and pestles they use to process the seeds and nuts that are such an important part of their food supply also were not available to Pleistocene hunter-gatherers.

Even the Australian aborigines, sometimes assumed to have preserved a Pleistocene form of hunting and gathering up to the twentieth century, possess a sophisticated post-Pleistocene food-processing technology.[31] None of the surviving hunting-and-gathering people in the world can give us an unmodified picture of what life in the Pleistocene was really like.

We can guess from the various surviving components that gathering of vegetable foods was at least as important as the meat brought back by the hunters for basic subsistence. On the other hand, the grain foods that are so important to the modern hunting-and-gathering societies were not available as potential foods until the development of the grinding and cooking techniques at the end of the Pleistocene. The same thing is true for many vegetables that require specific routines of preparation and cooking before they can become a source of nourishment for human beings.

Our best guess, then, is that there was a balance between the importance of the products of the chase and the collecting efforts of the women and children. There are some ingenious chemical tests that can be made on the bones of prehistoric individuals to find out what proportions of meat and vegetable matter had been in the diet of the specimens tested, but these studies are in their infancy as yet. The preliminary results do suggest that, up until near the end of the Pleistocene, hunting provided a larger proportion of the diet than is true for the San in the Kalahari, but not so large as that found in the Eskimo.[32] Such a balance is reasonable to expect, but much remains to be done before we can make any definitive statements.

THE EARLIER ORIGIN OF TOOL USE

It is abundantly clear that the bipedalism and related dependence upon hand-held tools of the early Australopithecines preceded the focus on hunting behavior by at least a million years. And, obviously, the tools being used at the earlier stages were made of perishable materials. While we can never "know" this, we can guess that the wielding of a pointed stick was the crucial element that led to the change in selective forces that produced a tool-dependent biped in the first place. As the American anthropologist S. L. Washburn has pointed out, the addition of a simple digging stick to the behavioral repertoire of a baboon could nearly double its food-getting efficiency. This, then, may very well have been the key that allowed the Australopithecines to compete successfully with baboons and wart hogs for the roots and tubers that constitute some of the basic items of subsistence available on the savannas.[33]

To this we could add the suggestion that the digging stick redirected is a more effective defensive weapon than even the formidable canine teeth of the average male baboon. After all, to bring canine teeth into effective use, the baboon literally has to come to grips with its adversary, and if that happens to be 200 pounds of hungry leopard, the chances are poor that even the most powerful baboon can get away unscathed. If the leopard is fended off by a five foot length of stout, pointed stick, however, the survival chances are slightly better.[34] And if the leopard should throw caution to the winds and charge, the butt of the stick can be planted on the ground with the point directed towards the oncoming predator, which would literally impale itself. This is a technique that modern Masai warriors use in dealing with charging lions, and it is possible that such a form of usage goes all the way back to the Pliocene.

As a dual-purpose defensive weapon and food-getting device, the digging stick would have given the earliest hominids a good competetive edge over the baboons, with whom they shared the Pliocene savannas of East Africa. It is certainly plausible to suggest that these were the circumstances that led to the shaping of the ingrained tool-dependence which is the closest thing to instinctive behavior that we possess. Along with this, we would expect the development of a mode of locomotion that freed the hands for a tool-

Figure 10–5. Australopithecine sexual dimorphism, as illustrated by a large (SK 12) and a small (SK 74a) mandible from Swartkrans in the Transvaal region of South Africa. The difference in robustness greatly exceeds the greatest male-female difference one would normally encounter in a modern human population. (I am grateful to Dr. C.K Brain for allowing me to photograph these samples from the collections of the Transvaal Museum in Pretoria.)

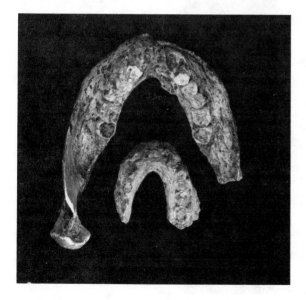

wielding role. Indeed, the essentials of hominid bipedalism were already visible in Lucy over 3 million years ago at Hadar.

We could raise the objection that even wielding a stout, pointed stick, a three to three-and-a-half foot tall Australopithecine would be quickly tumbled by a smack or two from a leopard's paw. But Lucy was female, and if the males of her group were double her size and robustness, then the scenario becomes more plausible. Although no skeleton of that date is anywhere near so complete as that of Lucy, skeletal pieces at Hadar and Maka (Afar) and at Laetoli show that sexual dimorphism was quite as marked as it is in the other terrestrial primates.[35] Even the canines and lower first premolars show an elongation that suggests a pongid condition in their not-too-distant past.[36]

If the earliest Australopithecines were tool-using bipeds, there is not much reason to expect that their other adaptations were much different from those of nonhuman terrestrial primates. With molar teeth closer to gorilloid than chimpanzee size, they obviously depended for their nourishment on the tough seeds, nuts, roots, fruits, and vegetables that could be gleaned

Figure 10–6.   The skull of Broom's "Mrs. Ples," Sts 5, from Sterkfontein, with the jaw of SK 23 from Swartkrans. Individuals from these two sites in the Transvaal of South Africa have been considered specifically, or even generically distinct, but it is clear that if Mrs. Ples had not lost her teeth, she would have required a mandible of almost exactly the size represented by SK 23. The supposedly robust and gracile South African Australopithecines are very much closer in size than is commonly reported. (Dr. C. K. Brain/Collections of the Transvaal Museum in Pretoria.)

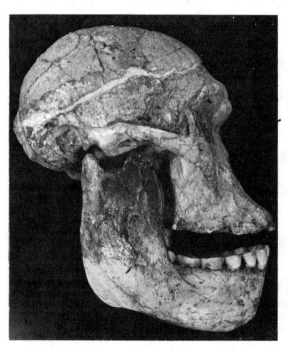

from the savanna and its riverine forests.[37] The yearly round of events and their dietary elements must have been quite similar to those aspects of the life of the baboons with whom they shared the area. For that reason, we can suspect that many aspects of their behavior may have been more like that of baboons than what we think of as characteristically human. We can guess that adult males maintained a dominance hierarchy that helped to promote group cohesion and group defense and which included the sexual control of many females by one or a few males. There is no reason to suggest that there was a prolonged male-female bond approaching our concept of monogamy, nor is there any reason to suspect that sexual activity had become a year-round rather than a seasonal enterprise.[38] There is also no reason to believe that they had yet lost the normal primate fur coat.

Finally, Dr. B. H. Smith of the University of Michigan has demonstrated in elegant fashion that the sequence of tooth root formation and dental crown completion and eruption in the immature gracile Australopithecines of South Africa follows a chimpanzee rather than a human pattern (see Figure 10–7).[39] Further work by Chris Dean at the University of London and Tim Bromage at the City University of New York has shown from the details of enamel structure that dental calcification in these Australopithecines proceeded at a pongid rather than a hominid rate of growth and maturation.[40] The American paleontologist, Elwyn Simons, had

Figure 10–7. A late Australopithecine of the robust South African type from Swartkrans in the Transvaal. (Courtesy of the American Museum of Natural History.)

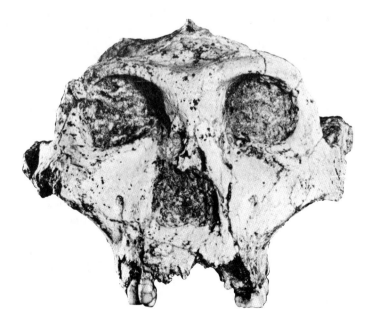

warned us some years ago that in the effort to show that the Australopithecines were more than "just another ape," as their earlier detractors
had claimed, we may have gone too far in assigning Modern attributes to
them.[41] All told, this new work suggests that the earliest hominids might
strike us as more apelike than human, despite their tools and their gait. It is
this realization that has led most scholars to grant them generic distinction
from true human beings.[42]

Backing off from the position I took in the first edition of this book in
1967, it seems most in line with the evidence to recognize the initial hominids as belonging to genus *Australopithecus* as Dart proposed in 1925. Although a number of differing suggestions have been offered, the case has yet
to be made that the first hominids are specifically distinct from Dart's *Australopithecus africanus*. Of course, further clarifying discoveries could cast
things in quite a different perspective. As it stands, the modern representatives of the medieval philosophical outlook, the cladists and splitters, look at
the same evidence but come to totally different conclusions. More evidence
may help, and it is eagerly sought for by all interested parties, but it is obvious
that evidence alone will not clear up the longstanding differences of opinion
concerning the nature and the naming of the earliest hominids. These continuing disagreements demonstrate how theory can shape the meaning conveyed by a given set of data.

AUSTRALOPITHECINE ORIGINS

Although a hominid arm bone fragment from Kanapoi to the west of Lake
Turkana (formerly Lake Rudolf) in northern Kenya dates to some 4 million
years ago, and an Australopithecine mandible from Lothagam Hill some 35
miles to the north may go back as much as 6.5 million years,[43] the oldest us-
able sample of Australopithecine remains is that found by Mary Leakey and
her coworkers at Laetoli just over 25 miles south of Olduvai in Tanzania.
Fragments of skulls, jaws, and teeth have been found in deposits that can be
dated to between 3.5 and 3.8 myrs. ago. These clearly are Australopithecines,
but there are continuing arguments over just what kind of Australopithecines
they were.[44]

One of the most dramatic glimpses of life in the past was provided at
Laetoli by the discovery of literally thousands of animal footprints, preserved
in a volcanic tuff. Among the prints are those of rhinoceros, giraffes, os-
triches, guinea fowl, antelopes, chalicotheres (an extinct clawed herbivore),
saber-toothed cats, *Hipparion* (an extinct primitive horse), hyenas, baboons,
and, most surprising of all, hominids! Two hominid footprint trails can be
traced for more than 30 feet as they walked side by side over a layer of volcanic ash that had been dampened to the consistency of moist beach sand.
Shortly after that, another airborne ash fall sealed them in. The accumula-

Figure 10–8. Location of a number of Australopithecine sites: 1. Taung. 2. Sterkfontein. 3. Swartkrans. 4. Kromdraai. 5. Makapansgat. 6. Laetoli. 7. Olduvai Gorge. 8. East Turkana. 9. Omo. 10. Hadar (Afar Depression).

tion of further sediments and the passage of time converted the deposits into the kind of rock geologists call tuff, and only now has erosion brought to light this picture of a moment in time in East Africa 3.5 million years ago.[45]

By measuring the length of the stride and the size of the footprints themselves, we know that the hominids who made them stood, respectively, about 4 feet, and 4 feet 8 inches tall, and they moved much as modern humans do. This, of course, is confirmed by the size and morphology of the nearly contemporary skeleton, AL 288–1, from Hadar in Ethiopia—Lucy.[46]

There are many more specimens from Hadar than from Laetoli, and many are less fragmentary and incomplete. Dated to somewhere between 3.1 and 3.5 myrs., they are slightly younger then the remains from Laetoli, which is over a thousand miles to the south. When Don Johanson and his colleagues described the original Hadar discoveries, they compared them to the evidence from Laetoli and used the latter to define yet another Australopithecine species—*Australopithecus "afarensis."* However, it is not at all obvious that the specimens from the two localities belong to the same species.[47] More than one specialist has noted that there are features in the Hadar Australopithecines that continue in the robust Australopithecines up to 2 million years later. These same traits, however, have not been found at Laetoli, but this might just be because of the very fragmentary and skimpy nature of the Laetoli specimens.

At the moment, the Hadar material gives us our best picture of what the early Australopithecines looked like, and we are tempted to regard them as the stem from which all subsequent hominids arose—including ourselves. Because of the problems associated with their naming, we can only note for now that they can legitimately be identified as genus *Australopithecus.* The species designation "*afarensis*" was proposed amidst much confusion and contradiction,[48] and it has never been made clear by adequate comparative study that there is any significant specific distinction between the collection from Hadar and *A. africanus.*[49] For the moment, the species designation will have to remain disputed and uncertain.

The continuity of the lineage of robust Australopithecines is clearly shown by the "Black Skull," WT 17000, found at Lomekwi *west* of Lake Turkana in 1985 as a result of fieldwork led by Alan Walker of Johns Hopkins University and by Richard Leakey.[50] Mercifully they have refrained from creating yet another new name and have referred to it as *Australopithecus boisei.* They note that it provides a fine link between the characteristics shown in the Hadar specimens in Ethiopia and the robust Australopithecines in both East and South Africa at 1.7 to 1.0 myrs. With a date of 2.5 myrs. the robust specimen from West Turkana is in the middle, timewise, as well. Unfortunately, the splitters are at it again, and, as a result of some curious juggling, they are promoting the designation of *Australopithecus* "*aethiopicus.*"[51]

AUSTRALOPITHECUS TO *HOMO*: THE ROLE OF THE BRAIN DRAIN

At the same time that the Black Skull from West Turkana was indicating the direction in which the later robust Australopithecines were to develop, the form of its contemporaries at Sterkfontein in South Africa was clearly taking a different path. Australopithecine brain size, while in the same range of absolute volume as the pongids, was actually somewhat larger in proportion to body size.[52] Furthermore, the specimens of *Australopithecus africanus* at Sterkfontein showed the first occurrence of some of the features that are found later in *Homo.*

The business of holding the head distinctly above the body creates problems in the area of arterial and venous blood flow that are significantly different from those that are faced by most quadrupeds. Although it is a quadruped, the case of the giraffe is the most celebrated of those involving the circulatory mechanics associated with an elevated head. But the hominid bipedal stance produces a minor version as well. In modern human beings, most of the blood supply for the head is provided by the carotid artery, and the same is true for other animals. The return of the blood to the general circulation, however, is not primarily by the jugular vein system, as it is in other primates and most other mammals, but by the vertebral plexus deep in the back of the neck. From the markings on the insides of Australopithecine cranial bones, Dean Falk, at SUNY Albany, has suggested that the vertebral plexus route of venous blood return was present in the early hominids as a correlate of their bipedal stance. However, the internal route from the brain to the vertebral plexus differs between the robust and the gracile Australopithecines.

In the robust Australopithecines, the route is by the occipital-mastoid sinus pathway. This is true for the South African robust specimens, for *A. boisei* (including WT 17000) in East Africa, and for the *"afarensis"* group at Hadar over 3 million years ago. This, however, was not the case for the preserved Laetoli individuals.[53]

In the *Australopithecus africanus* specimens at Sterkfontein in South Africa, the route by which blood flows to the vertebral plexus involves a series of cranial emissary veins as well as smaller contributions from the occipital-mastoid sinus system. These small emissary veins include the posterior condyloid, mastoid, occipital, and parietal emissary veins. This is the pattern that is found in modern *Homo sapiens,* and Falk has demonstrated that, from a count of the tiny foramina associated with its manifestation, it became more clearly developed through time as *Australopithecus africanus* was followed by *Homo erectus* and ultimately by *H. sapiens.*

Both routes of returning blood to the general circulation are equally effective. However, the pattern that made its appearance at Sterkfontein 2.5 million years ago is the one that has been elaborated to characterize the modern human condition and may reveal something about the course of ancestral-descendant relationships. If both routes are equally effective at returning blood to the general circulation, the one that uses the cranial emissary veins does something that the other does not. It brings blood from the interior of the brain out to the surface before channelling it back inside and thence to the vertebral plexus. At the surface of the head and neck, evaporation of sweat can cause a dissipation of heat and a cooling down of the blood before it is returned to the interior. In effect, the cranial emissary veins can serve as a radiator for the brain and prevent the problems associated with heat build-up.

This is of particular significance for two critical situations. First, the brain is a very energy-costly organ,[54] and some kind of heat dissipating mechanism is essential before an even larger brain can be developed. In a lineage where relative brain enlargement is visible through time, it is interesting to note that this is accompanied by an increase of the foramina, visible on the skull, associated with the cranial emissary vein route of cerebral blood return—the radiator has to expand as the size of the mental engine increases.

Second, the heat build-up associated with diurnal hunting activities would lead to problems in maintaining adequate brain functioning if there were no effective cooling system. Modern humans do surprisingly well under conditions of heat and exercise when they are compared to the rest of the mammalian world.[55] A good case can be made that the rise in frequency of the number of cranial emissary veins visible in the gracile Australopithecines at Sterkfontein was in response to selective pressures generated by an increase in the focus on diurnal hunting activities.

If the "brain drain" pathway can give us some clues about the nature of the selective forces that shaped the development of our lineage, we can also get some information from indications concerning the actual organization of the brain itself. These are provided by one of the most important discoveries made by Richard Leakey's field team, the famous ER 1470 skull found at Koobi Fora east of Lake Turkana in August of 1972.[56] Although it was broken into many pieces and there was more than a little confusion about the date of the deposits, these problems have been overcome and the specimen can provide us with a key glimpse of *Australopithecus* on its way to developing into *Homo*.

The date of ER 1470 is just under 2 million years, which puts it in the period when the use of stone tools for the process of butchering large animals was a regular occurrence, but just before the time when the evidence suggests that systematic big game hunting was being practiced.[57] Repeated efforts at measuring the size of the brain agree that it had a capacity of near 750 cc., which is larger than anything that could be called *Australopithecus* and smaller than anything classified as *Homo*.[58] No teeth were present, but the sockets for the tooth roots in the upper jaw and the shape of the face as a whole suggest that it had a dentition that was more in the Australopithecine range than that of later humans. But of crucial interest, the traces of the fissures and sulci that outline the convolutions of the brain itself, preserved on the inner surface of the cranial bones, show that the brain was characterized by the "oldest human-like sulcal pattern to date in the hominid fossil record," to use the words of Dean Falk, one of our acknowledged experts on the anatomy of the early hominid brain.[59]

Here, then, is the best evidence that has been discovered so far for the pathway by which an Australopithecine became transformed into an early member of our own genus. Unfortunately, the urge to recognize anything that could serve as "ancient true man" struck again, and it was referred to that Leakey grab bag, "*Homo habilis*." ER 1470 has been put in there along with specimens that are probably *Australopithecus* and others that are certainly *Homo erectus*. But this cannot change the fact that it comes from that crucial time when a major development was occurring in the evolving hominid line, and that it shows just how that development was taking place.

HUNTING AND NICHE DIVERGENCE

If systematic hunting was not a significant aspect of early hominid behavior for at least a million years that we know of (and possibly more for which we have no evidence as yet), it eventually became so, as the archaeological record in Olduvai Gorge graphically shows in the cultural developments between Bed I and the middle of Bed II. But also at Olduvai and even more clearly at East Turkana, it is apparent that not all Australopithecines added a hunting component to their subsistence behavior.

The record shows butchering technology growing in sophistication through time, paralleled by increasing evidence for the successful hunting of large game animals. The record also shows that brain size was increasing and molar tooth size was reducing in one hominid line. But further evidence shows that brain size did not increase in another hominid line while molar tooth size did. The Leakeys' famous "Zinj" find of 1959 has molar teeth of fully gorilloid size. Its brain is also of gorilloid size, which is to say that it is only half Pithecanthropine size and merely one-third that of the modern average.[60]

"Zinj" at 1.75 million years is very nearly duplicated by the ER 406 skull from Ileret, east of Lake Turkana half a million years more recently, by which time there is also evidence for a fully emerged Pithecanthropine—for example, ER 3733 from Koobi Fora.[61] We are constrained to accept a relationship between the evidence for increasingly successful hunting and cerebral expansion, and if that is the case, then the Australopithecines that continued on through the Lower Pleistocene *without* showing an increase in brain size were probably not engaged in systematic hunting activity. The increase in molar size to a fully gorilloid level suggests a concentration on plant food.

It would appear, then, that starting with the evidence for the first stone tools at the Plio/Pleistocene boundary, a division arose in hominid subsistence strategies between those that concentrated more on hunting and those that focused on the products of the plant kingdom. The former became transformed into what we recognize as belonging in genus *Homo,* while the latter remained as members of genus *Australopithecus.* Since the clearest and best described example of the surviving line of robust Australopithecines was the Leakeys' *"Zinjanthropus" boisei,* and since most feel that the generic designation is unwarranted, there is a tentative feeling that the robust East African lineage can be identified as *Australopithecus boisei.*

At the moment we have no idea how the separation between the robust line and the lineage that evolved into *Homo* took place. Presumably some kind of ecological event isolated one group from the other, during which time speciation occurred. This has happened often enough to have produced specific distinctions between many related groups of African monkeys, and there is no reason why it could not have occurred in the hominids at least once. Since the Australopithecines were all essentially savanna dwellers, the crucial separation could have occurred during one of the damper periods when the African rain forest extended from the Congo basin all the way across East Africa to join with the rain forest on the east coast, thus separating the savanna into isolated northern and southern regions.[62]

Did the northern Australopithecines develop the rudiments of hunting during that separation and take the first step that propelled them towards becoming *Homo*? Or was it the southern group that did so? Or was it some other sequence of events? We simply have no evidence as yet. All we know is that the hunter was the only one left by the end of the Lower Pleistocene. Did the hunters do in their vegetarian cousins? Or did they, as some have recently suggested, simply out-compete them for the resources necessary for survival? Certainly these are all possibilities. And if this is a form of catastrophism, we cannot deny that such things have happened frequently enough in the fossil record. Extinctions are commoner than survivals, and it is no denial of the principles of evolution to show how the successful development of one group spells doom for another.[63]

Given the various phylogenetic schemes suggested, the relatively small number of individuals and sites, and the long periods of time involved, no one summary scheme can hope to be correct as things stand now. Certainly each specialist in the field will vigorously defend various different ones. In spite of this, we offer a version of one such scheme that others have tentatively suggested. Hadar stands at the root and gives rise to the robust Australopithecine branch on the one hand and the gracile Australopithecine-to-*Homo* branch on the other hand.

AUSTRALOPITHECINE DISTRIBUTION

So far, the Australopithecines have been treated solely as an African phenomenon, starting in the Pliocene as an outgrowth of the preceding Miocene "proto-apes." In that sense, they are part of a uniquely African savanna-dwelling fauna that included a variety of other forms such as Cape buffalo, gazelles, hyenas, lions, and elephants.[64] The continent of Africa had been moving slowly northwards during the Oligocene and had made contact with portions of the Eurasian land mass by the middle of the Miocene at least 17 million years ago.[65] At that point, the Miocene proto-apes spread throughout the Eurasian tropical and temperate forests to enjoy a distribution that was continuous from the Atlantic edge of Europe to the Pacific margins of Asia, and their descendants survive as a few patches of orangs in Borneo and Sumatra.

In principle, there is no reason why their Pliocene hominid descendants in Africa could not also have spread in similar fashion throughout the savannas of Eurasia. Clearly, the elephants, who arose in Africa early in the Pliocene, did exactly that.[66] The horse group, on the other hand, had originally formed in the western hemisphere and moved across Asia to the point where they could enter Africa from the northeast corner at the same time that the elephants were going the other way. The contact between Africa and Eurasia remained in the form of a narrow corridor through Israel and Egypt, since the Arabian peninsula, which had originally been part of the African block, split off by the formation of a rift that opened to produce the Red Sea at the end of the Miocene or early in the Pliocene.[67]

That Africa-Eurasia contact point between Israel and Egypt constituted something of a bottleneck. Although some animals apparently moved back and forth with evident ease, others did so only occasionally or not at all. As is obvious to us from our knowledge of the world today, the African Plio/Pleistocene hominids evidently produced descendants who not only made it past that bottleneck but succeeded in the effort to the extent that they now are the most widely distributed mammal in the world—*Homo sapiens*. But whether it was just a single dispersal or a repeated phenomenon is a matter of a great deal of current paleoanthropological dispute. The view that I defend in this book is that there was just one major movement early in the Pleistocene, and that gene flow subsequently maintained specific unity throughout the whole occupied extent of the Old World.

From this perspective, change from the earlier to the later forms of that species took place, effective simultaneously throughout that whole occupied area. The school of thought that remains in the grip of the pre-Darwinian paradigm regards such a view as inherently unlikely.[68] However, when we take into account the nature of the major selective forces produced by the emerging cultural ecological niche and how these get distributed, it becomes increasingly clear that cultural developments in one part of the world diffuse rapidly enough to the inhabitants of other places so that local isolation and consequent speciation just was not allowed to take place.

The question of just when that spread from the original African homeland took place is still somewhat hard to pin down with certainty. Clearly the African Australopithecines were a savanna-adapted form, and this includes the several varieties—species—that lived simultaneously in East and South Africa. Our knowledge of these is confined to the skeletal scraps that have been mentioned earlier in this chapter, but we know a good deal more about the distribution of the form that was to evolve into the genus *Homo*. This is because they left their tools behind, and stone tools endure indefinitely whereas the actual bones are preserved only under rare and fortunate circumstances. Using these tools as a basis, then, the area inhabited by the Australopithecine ancestors of later full human beings is shown in Figure 10–9.[69]

As can be seen in this map, there is an apparent spillover out of Africa both at the eastern and western ends of the Mediterranean. At the western

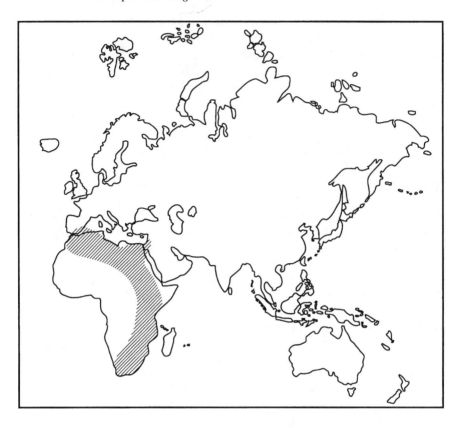

Figure 10–9. The area of Australopithecine habitation as indicated largely by the distribution of Oldowan tools.

end, there are reports of Oldowan-like tools at dates of more than 2 million years in France in the Massif-Central and in the southeast,[70] and of similar tools, African mammals, and fragments of hominids in eastern Spain at perhaps slightly less ancient time levels.[71] The Mediterranean had repeatedly dried up late in the Miocene starting six million years ago,[72] but that was long before there were any tool-making hominids. With the onset of the Pliocene about 5.5 million years ago, the Strait of Gibraltar opened, allowing the Atlantic to pour into the dessicated Mediterranean Basin and presumably preventing movements of African forms across into southwest Europe.[73] At the moment, the candidates for Oldowan tools and the early hominid fragments are tantalizing but unsubstantiated clues.

The evidence for the spillover at the eastern end of the Mediterranean is much better substantiated although not quite so old. At the site of 'Ubeidiya, 1.4 million-year-old tools have been found that show a "striking similarity" to the tools in Bed II of Olduvai Gorge that also have a date of 1.5 million

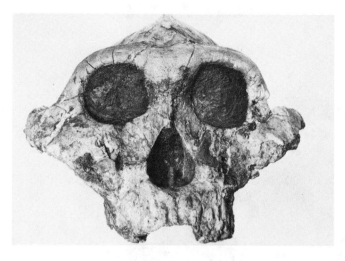

Figure 10–10. A late robust Australopithecine, ER 406 above, and a Pithecanthropine, ER 3733 on page 144, both from the area east of Lake Turkana at about 1.5 myrs. ago. Note the expanded cheek bones for chewing muscle attachment in the Australopithecine, and the higher and broader braincase in the Pithecanthropine. (Courtesy of the National Museum of Kenya.)

years.[74] 'Ubeidiya has been called "the earliest well-researched and dated stone tool locality outside Africa" by Desmond Clark, Professor emeritus from the University of California at Berkeley and one of the most experienced and respected archaeologists in the world.[75] By 1.5 million years ago at Olduvai, however, the hominid involved was no longer an Australopithecine but a member of the succeeding stage of human evolution. While tools of

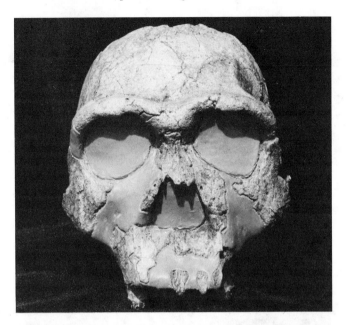

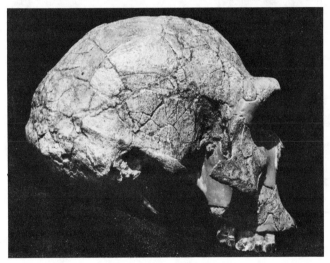

Figure 10–10. *(continued)*

Oldowan-like appearance continued to be used, they were also joined by more carefully produced, shaped forms referred to as "bifaces," or "hand-axes."

The site at 'Ubeidiya, just south of the Sea of Galilee in Israel, may represent the first clear suggestion of the expansion of members of our own

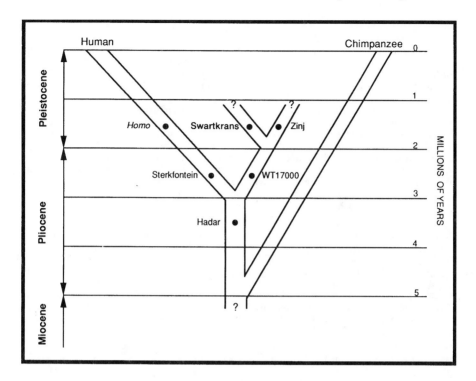

Figure 10–11. A provisional scheme depicting hominid ancestry and descent.

genus—*Homo*—out of Africa and on their way to spread throughout the tropics of the Old World.

CHAPTER TEN NOTES

[1]The tradition referred to is the one used by such figures as the paleontologist/systematist/evolutionary theorist, George Gaylord Simpson (1902–1984) (Simpson, 1961), and the primate paleontologist, Elwyn L. Simons (Simons, 1972).

[2]Darwin was the first to recognize the fact that the most useful system of classification is based on the fact that the ties "between any two or more species are those which have been inherited from a common parent," and that, therefore, "all true classification is genealogical" (Darwin, 1859:420). Darwin set the standard for virtually all subsequent systematists with his conclusion that "classifications will come to be, as far as they can be made so, genealogies" (1859:486). While one can quantify the criteria for making distinctions at the specific level, "there would seem to be no objective criterion for deciding what degree of modification justifies an increase in rank" (Ghiselin, 1969:84). Rankings at the level of genus or family, then, have an inevitable element of the subjective in them. In an attempt to make classifications correspond strictly to ge-

nealogical relationships, the case has been made that the African apes, the gorilla and the chimp, are closer to humans than they are to the orangs of Southeast Asia (see Marks, 1993), and that we all belong in the same family, Hominidae (Goodman, 1975, 1989; Gould, 1992:20). Pongidae as a separate family would disappear, and the subfamily Ponginae would be retained for the orang only. Such assessments are based on a strict accounting of molecular similarities and differences, and major adaptive differences are simply left out. When the "adaptive component of evolution" is taken into consideration (Mayr, 1974:107) and used in the recognition of taxonomic categories such as families, there should be sufficient justification for regarding the adaptive similarities of orangs, gorillas, and chimpanzees as qualifying them for membership in the same family, Pongidae, and recognizing the evolutionary if not genealogical distinction of human beings and their bipedal ancestors as what is meant by the term Hominidae. This is consistent with Darwin's recognition that the arrangement within each taxonomic class should be "strictly genealogical," but that the "*amount* of difference" in related branches is expressed in "different genera, families, sections, or orders" (Darwin, 1859:420). Finally, this is also consistent with the recognition of the adaptive developments in human evolution as constituting a series of gradelike "Stages" (see Chapter 1, note 15).

[3]Clark, 1967.

[4]Broom, 1950c. Actually, Broom only meant the subfamily "Australopithecinae" to include *Australopithecus africanus* and what he had distinguished as *"Plesianthropus transvaalensis"* (Broom, 1939, 1947). The species he recognized in genus *Paranthropus* were included in yet another subfamily—"Paranthropinae" (1950b:12). In this, most recent students feel he went too far in his enthusiasm for splitting. The term "Australopithecinae" had initially been used to rank the South African discoveries as a subfamily within the Pongidae (Gregory and Hellman, 1938), and, whether one accepts it as a proper subfamily or not, the term has proven to be a useful way to refer to the bipedal hominids of the Pliocene and early Pleistocene before brain size increased to put them out of the anthropoid ape range.

[5]Grine, 1988a, b; Groves, 1989; Kimbel, 1991; Kimbel and Martin, 1993.

[6]Where classification simply reflects relationship or genealogy, Darwin observed that "it may be given as a general rule, that the less any part of the organisation is concerned with special habits, the more important it becomes for classification" (1859:414). Adaptive traits, on the other hand, however valuable they may be for the organism in question, "are almost valueless to the systematist" (Darwin, 1859:427) unless it can be shown that those organisms that share them do so because of recent common descent.

[7]Harvey et al., 1978.

[8]Ricklan, 1987; Stern and Sussman, 1983; Hunt, 1989.

[9]Jungers, 1982; Johanson et al., 1982, 1987.

[10]"Lucy" is one of the most complete Australopithecine skeletons found. The discovery was made on November 24, 1974, at Afar Locality 288-1 (AL 288-1) in the valley of the Hadar River in the badlands of central Ethiopia. The Beatles' song, "Lucy in the Sky With Diamonds," was playing on the tape recorder in camp that evening, and that is how she came to be given a name that is somewhat more memorable than AL 288-1 (Johanson, 1976:793; Johanson and Taieb, 1976:996; Johanson and Edey, 1981:18).

[11]Hunt, 1989, 1991a, b, 1992.

[12]Lovejoy, 1988:123.

[13]McHenry, 1975a; McHenry and Corruccini, 1978.

[14]For example, Plate 2 of Carrington, 1963.

[15]The first scholar to have made this point with full and incisive clarity was none other than Charles Darwin in his *Descent of Man* (1871 I:138). At that time, of course, there was absolutely no hominid fossil and archaeological material to put this to the test, but, now that there is, the same insights have been repeated with a splendid boost from the increasing roster of Plio/Pleistocene discoveries (McHenry, 1986a).

[16]Harris, 1983:26.

[17]Klein, 1983, 1988; Blumenschine and Cavallo, 1992.

[18]Simons, 1989.

[19]Toth and Schick, 1983.

[20]Toth, 1985.

[21]Howell, 1965:74–75.

[22]Isaac, 1978:94–95; Leakey, 1981:78.

[23]Behrensmeyer, 1976; Toth, 1987b; Vrba, 1988, 1993.

[24]Clark and Haynes, 1970; Stanford et al., 1981; Shipman and Rose, 1983; Toth and Schick, 1983; Shipman, 1986; Stanford, 1987; Toth, 1987a, b.

[25]L. Leakey, 1951, 1965; M. Leakey, 1966, 1971; Bunn and Kroll, 1986.

[26]Goodall, 1963, 1986; Boesch and Boesch, 1989; McGrew, 1992:99 ff.

[27]Leakey, 1951.

[28]Lee and DeVore (eds.), 1976; Yellen, 1990.

[29]Brody, 1990.

[30]Dumond, 1980, 1987.

[31]McCarthy, 1940, 1970.

[32]Schoeninger, 1980, 1982.

[33]Washburn, 1959, 1960:63.

[34]Occasional effective stick wielding by savanna chimpanzees and the potential advantages for Australopithecines is vividly discussed by Kortlandt (1980).

[35]McHenry, 1986b, 1991; White et al., 1993; Kimbel et al., 1994.

[36]Robinson, 1954, 1956; Wolpoff, 1979.

[37]Ryan, 1980; Ryan and Johanson, 1989; Kay and Grine, 1988.

[38]Actually, there was a lovely little scenario of "true love," Australopithecine style, presented some years ago with an argument for permanent pair bonding and male provisioning of females and infants (Lovejoy, 1981), but it seems more like wishful thinking projected into the past than anything that could be derived from the comparative primate studies that are the points of departure for our most defensible speculations.

[39]Smith, 1986, 1991a, b, 1992.

[40]Bromage and Dean, 1985; Dean, 1985a, b, 1987, 1988; Dean et al., 1993. There has been an attempt at a naysaying rebuttal, which declares that none of the techniques used can tell us anything about rates of maturation (Mann et al., 1990, 1991). The users of the various approaches have not been able to get permission to apply their techniques to the sample used to support those denials, and the evidence continues to mount that the Australopithecines had a maturation pattern much more like that of anthropoid apes than of living humans.

[41]Simons, 1989.

[42]Mayr (1951) initially suggested that the Australopithecines could all be put into the genus *Homo,* and I was among those who followed with more enthusiasm than reflection. Mayr subsequently retracted (1963), and, like most others, I have followed suit.

[43]Patterson and Howells, 1967; Patterson et al., 1970; Maglio, 1973:69; Kramer, 1986.

[44]M. Leakey et al., 1976; White, 1980, 1981; Johanson and Edey, 1981; Drake and Curtis, 1987; Johanson and Shreeve, 1989; M. Leakey and Harris (eds.), 1987; Falk, 1988.

[45]The account of how the footprints were actually discovered is something that one can never find in sober scientific reports. On September 15, 1976, while enjoying a break, some of the paleontologists were lightheartedly heaving lumps of dried elephant dung at each other. One of them fell down, while trying to evade one such missile, and there, in front of his nose, noticed the fossilized animal tracks in an exposed section of tuff. In time, more than 18,000 individual prints were found, eventually including the hominid ones (M. Leakey, 1979a; 1984:173; 1987:7).

[46]M. Leakey, 1979a; Hay and Leakey, 1982; White and Suwa, 1987.

[47]Olson, 1981, 1985; Coppens, 1983; Falk, 1988.

[48]Johanson et al., 1978: Johanson and White, 1979; Leakey and Walker, 1980.

[49]Tobias, 1980; McHenry, 1983. Work begun over a decade ago (White, 1984) and interrupted by the occasionally lethal political instability of the area has resulted in the recovery in 1990 of the first major addition to the fossil record of the earliest hominids since the 1970s (Wilford,

1993c). Some fifty miles downstream of Hadar in the Middle Awash drainage region in Ethiopia, the Maka area has now yielded some important new Australopithecine remains. Tim White of the University of California at Berkeley has shown that sexual dimorphism in the Maka Australopithecines of 3.4 million years ago was of positively baboonlike proportions (White et al., 1993). The dental profile puts Maka mandibular tooth size right in the range of the Laetoli specimens, but it also does not differentiate them from the South African *Australopithecus africanus* dental dimensions (Brace, 1973). Finally, the sexually dimorphic nature of the Australopithecines has been confirmed by the discovery at Hadar of a complete male skull—AL 442-2—along with other skeletal elements that are markedly more robust than Lucy (Kimbel et al., 1994).

[50]Leakey and Walker, 1985; Walker et al., 1986.

[51]Johanson, 1986; Kimbel et al., 1988.

[52]Holloway, 1981.

[53]Falk, 1988, 1990, 1992.

[54]Martin, 1983:5.

[55]Carrier, 1984; Bortz, 1985.

[56]R. Leakey, 1973.

[57]The story of the disagreements associated with establishing the now-accepted date—1.8 million years—is a classic little paleoanthropological soap opera. Richard Leakey, like his father before him, has been convinced that some sort of "true man" was back there "in the beginning," and no benighted Australopithecine or *erectus* form should be associated with the human family tree. Consequently, he supported the flawed 2.6 million year date first calculated for the stratum immediately overlying ER 1470. (Fitch and Miller, 1969; Fitch et al., 1974). When the paleontologists—including the distinguished Basil Cooke, who had been a longtime friend and colleague of Richard's parents—tried to indicate that the well-dated fossil pigs in East Africa indicated quite a different age for ER 1470, Richard refused to listen. Cooke eventually published his evidence (Cooke, 1978a, b), and further radiometric dating demonstrated that he was absolutely right (Curtis et al., 1975; Cerling et al., 1979). The extent of Richard Leakey's intransigence is told in engaging fashion in *Lucy: The Beginnings of Mankind* (Johanson and Edey, 1981:238–39). Richard Leakey provides unintended corroboration of the general outlines of the story in his own autobiography, *One Life* (1984:168). Evidently there is something about paleoanthropology that tends to produce symptoms of an overweening arrogance in its practitioners that is often manifested by an expansion of ego in inverse proportions to evidences for intelligence.

[58]Holloway, 1975.

[59]Falk, 1983:1073.

[60]Tobias, 1967.

[61]R. Leakey and Walker, 1976; White and Harris, 1977.

[62]Vrba (1993) has discussed the effects of the changing African climate on the distribution of the plants and animals of the Pliocene and on into the Pleistocene, and she has done this with a clear eye to the influence these correlated changes must have had on the conditions for hominid survival.

[63]Nitecki (ed.), 1984; Walker, 1984; Larwood (ed.), 1988.

[64]Maglio, 1973; Vrba, 1993.

[65]Andrews and VanCouvering, 1975:65,85.

[66]Maglio, 1970:328, 1973:67.

[67]Girdler and Styles, 1974:9; Clark, 1975:180; Pilbeam, 1984:91; Groves, 1989:318.

[68]Keith, 1915; Boule and Vallois, 1957; Eldredge and Tattersall, 1982; Foley, 1987; Groves, 1989; Howells, 1993; Stringer and Gamble, 1993.

[69]The documented distribution of Oldowan tools runs from Morocco (Neuville and Ruhlmann, 1941) and Algeria (Balout, 1955) via Ethiopia (Chavaillon and Chavaillon, 1969) and Olduvai Gorge (M. Leakey 1966, 1971) through Malawi and down into South Africa (Clark, 1950, 1959, 1993).

[70]Bonifay, 1991.

[71]Gibert et al., 1991, 1992; Gibert, 1992.

[72]Hsü, 1972, 1983:94, 171.

[73]See note 72.

[74]Tchernov, 1992:153.

[75]Clark, 1993:149.

chapter eleven

The Pithecanthropine Stage

THE CONSEQUENCES OF HUNTING

The obvious skeletal changes that convert an ape into an Australopithecine are the shortening and spreading of the pelvis, accompanied by the modification of the feet for support rather than grasping, and the reduction of the formerly projecting canine teeth. These are related to the adoption of a bipedal mode of locomotion and hand-held weapons as a means of defense.[1] They are very ancient and fundamental developments and are united in a biobehavioral complex that provides a necessary base for the later development of those largely behavioral traits that we have come to regard as constituting the essentials of human nature.

The obvious anatomical changes that convert an Australopithecine into a Pithecanthropine are even simpler, but the implications are at least as profound (See Figure 11–1). The key element signalling that conversion is the increase in brain size. Australopithecine brain size was approximately 500 cc., which is about average for the larger of the Anthropoid apes.[2] The Pithecanthropine average is roughly twice that, which puts it well within the lower part of the normal range of variation of modern humanity. Surely this must be related to the development of that constellation of behavioral capacities that is distinctly human. Just as surely, it was the selective forces of the non-pongid

FIGURE 11–1.
The Pithecanthropine Stage. Note the artist's conception of early man as brutish and flea-bitten, clutching his "hand-axe."

subsistence strategy adopted by the emerging Pithecanthropines which led to that cerebral expansion and its implied behavioral correlates. A large brain is an energy-expensive organ and can only be supported by a reliance on high quality foods.[3] The dramatic expansion of hominid brain size suggests that, among other things, a significant dietary change had occurred.

The crucial factor, as a number of observers have noted, was the addition of a major hunting component to their foraging life-way. In spite of the casual examples of baboon and chimpanzee predatory activity, the systematic pursuit of animals for food is a profoundly un-primate kind of activity. One could guess, then, that most of those features that make humans unique among the primates—except bipedalism and its correlates—are the results of the retooling that occurred when the genus *Homo* emerged as a major predator early in the Pleistocene.[4] Because this remodelling involved only relatively minor visible changes from the neck on down, our focus on the importance of the changes in brain size and form would seem to be justified.

In fact, the one post-cranial change that is noticeable, if minor, appears to be more a direct correlate with brain size than with any change in bodily usage. The major changes associated with bipedal locomotion had been accomplished during the Australopithecine stage, although there were minor

the pelvis and the upper end of the femur differed from mod-
mechanical analysis has shown that the greater iliac flare and
al neck of the Australopithecines were actually more efficient
..an the modern condition and required less muscular effort than their
modern counterparts.[5] The modern configuration appears to have developed during the Pithecanthropine stage. It has been suggested that it was
created by the development of the wider birth canal that was necessary to
bear the larger-brained infants of the genus *Homo*.

Another correlate with brain size increase is a decrease in the male-
female body size difference. Sexual dimorphism remained marked in the
Pithecanthropines, but it had reduced from its Australopithecine extreme.
The reduction in dimorphism was not caused by a decrease in male size and
robustness, but rather by an increase in female size. Again, we can suspect
that the selective forces that led to this were those related to the bearing of a
large-brained infant. Not only that, but carrying an infant for a full nine-
month term of pregnancy, rather than the shorter pongid term, is more easily accomplished when maternal body size is larger than it had previously
been.[6]

Larger brains imply greater intellectual capabilities, and surely that was
the key to the successful adoption of hunting as a subsistence strategy by early
members of the genus *Homo*. Not only is the brain larger, but an appraisal of
the sulcal pattern from the evidence left on the inside of the cranial bones
shows that the configuration in the area that controls articulate speech in
Modern humans is now more Modern than pongid.[7] But unlike brain size
and conformation, intelligence is not a simple product of heredity. Realized
intellectual capacity only occurs after years of trial and experience. Human
intellectual achievement is vastly greater than that possible for even the
brightest of our pongid relatives, but its mature manifestation is made possible only by a prolonged period of infant and juvenile dependence during
which the young are nurtured, protected, and given the benefits of the experience previously acquired by their elders. This period of prolonged dependence is only made possible by an equally long period of parental responsibility. And in a situation where hunting activities take males away from the
group for days at a time, the role of instructor and protector is better played
by females who are considerably larger than the three-and-a-half foot early
Australopithecine females.

Although sexual dimorphism was therefore less pronounced than it
had been during the Australopithecine stage, it was still maintained to a
greater extent than we currently see in Modern human populations. The
stress put on the male physique during hunting activities was such that muscularity, joint reinforcements, and general skeletal robustness were all developed to a degree not now encountered (See Figure 11–2). However much
stealth and cunning were used in tracking and stalking, the moment inevitably came when the hand-held spear was thrust into the intended victim.
The chances that a ton or so of Pleistocene buffalo will quietly and obligingly

FIGURE 11–2. Pithecanthropine sexual dimorphism shown between a female (OH 13) and a male (OH 9) from the middle of Bed II at Olduvai George, Tanzania. The broad base of the male skull provided an attachment for the muscles of a neck that was very much stouter than that of the female.

expire at the first jab of a hunter's spear are small indeed. In the twitching and thrashing of wounded prey, it is certain that, during the Early and Middle Pleistocene, the hunters regularly got banged around a bit. Torn knee ligaments, broken bones, dislocations, or cracked skulls could easily have had fatal consequences.

Recently some doubts have been expressed about whether large game hunting was in fact being pursued by the Middle Pleistocene hominids,[8] but as the sportsmen of the Middle Ages and more recently were well aware, even a wild boar can be a formidable adversary.[9] Even if "large" game was not the focus of the Pleistocene hunters, pork was definitely on the menu, and the bacon was brought home with a far more rudimentary weaponry even than that of the medieval boar chasers. Not surprisingly, we see the development of bony and muscular reinforcements in the skeletons of the male hunting hominids. Skull walls and long bone shafts are thicker than before or since, joints are expanded and reinforced, and the muscle markings suggest great bodily strength.[10]

Actually, we are more than a little shy of good evidence for the nature of the post-cranial skeleton of the Pithecanthropines, but a recent if immature find from West Turkana in 1984 has given us just a bit more to go on. This specimen, WT 15000, was discovered by Kimoya Kimeu, one of the most successful fieldworkers associated with the Leakey family enterprises, late in the field season of 1984[11] (see Figure 11-3). The discovery was that of a nearly complete skeleton of a boy on the threshold of adolescence, equivalent in development if not in actual age to a Modern eleven-year-old, in strata that can be dated to 1.6 myrs. ago. Brain size is 900 cc., which is just what we would expect for a Pithecanthropine. Stature was 1.68 meters, which is just over 5 feet 5 inches, and the indications are that, had he grown to adulthood, he might have exceeded a good 6 feet.[12]

WT 15000— "Strapping Youth" —was found by the course of an intermittent and often dry "river," the Nariokotome (remember, rhymes with "frontal lobotomy"), and, as the most complete single Pithecanthropine skeleton found so far, he has generated a great deal of interest among scholars and the public at large. The lower legs and forearms are relatively long in proportion to their upper members, as is true for all tropical people today. This suggests that subsistence activities were actively pursued during the heat of the day since it is those elongated distal portions of the arms and legs that are particularly effective in dissipating the heat generated by vigorous exercise. The pelvic opening where the birth canal would be if he were female is relatively narrow, but then Pithecanthropine brain size was still only two-thirds that of recent *Homo sapiens.*

A detailed study of the formation and calcification of the tooth roots and crowns in conjunction with details of the growth of the long bones has led to the conclusion that the course of growth and development was intermediate between that of living modern anthropoid apes and human beings. In other words, he was slated to reach maturity more slowly than an ape like a chimpanzee, but not quite so slowly as is characteristic for modern human beings.[13] Likewise, maximum lifespan would have been longer than that of a chimpanzee, but not so long as that of living human beings. But again, that is just what we should expect for an early member of genus *Homo* who was more than an Australopithecine but not yet *sapiens.*

FIGURE 11–3.
"Strapping Youth," an adolescent Pithecanthropine from Nariokotome (KNM-WT 15000) from northwest Kenya, Africa. (Drawn by Kay Clahassey after Walker and Leakey, 1993.)

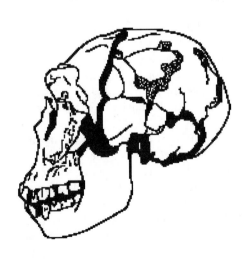

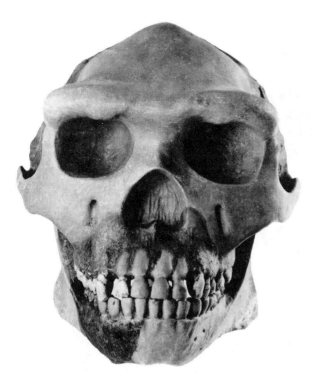

FIGURE 11–4. "Pithecanthropus IV," as reconstructed by Dr. Franz Weidenreich. The dark parts are original; the light, reconstruction. The whole back part (not visible) was preserved. Subsequent finds in Java, China, Africa, and Europe have confirmed the accuracy of Weidenreich's reconstruction. The individual was probably a male. (Courtesy of the American Museum of Natural History.)

Until the discovery of "Strapping Youth" west of Lake Turkana, the most complete picture of the Pithecanthropine Stage was based upon the fragments excavated from Zhoukoudian (Choukoutien), just southwest of Beijing (Peking), China, between the late 1920s and the beginning of World War II in the Far East.[14] A composite reconstruction based on the Pithecanthropine fragments is shown in Figure 11–5. In terms of the Pleistocene glacial sequence, these date to an interglacial time somewhere around 300,000 years ago. They are somewhat more recent than the remains that Dubois, and later von Koenigswald, discovered in Java, but they are clearly the same sort of thing.[15]

Aside from the expansion of the brain, the other major contrast between the Australopithecines and the Pithecanthropines was in the dentition and its supporting facial skeleton. Pithecanthropine front teeth were slightly larger, but the molars had reduced to the point where they were within the upper limits of the modern range of variation.[16] A selection of the tools that allowed the Pithecanthropines to pursue their hunting activities is shown in Figure 11–6.

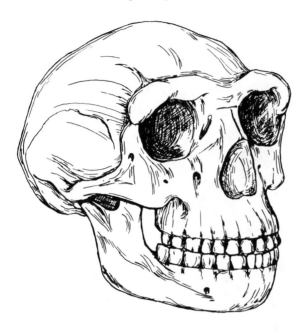

FIGURE 11–5. A composite reconstruction made under the direction of Franz Weidenreich and based upon the Pithecanthropine fragments found at Zhoukoudian (Choukoutien), near Beijing (Pekin). The specimen was originally called *"Sinanthropus pekinensis."* The individual on which this was based was almost certainly female.

With a significant quantity of meat as a regular part of the diet, the amount of chewing formerly necessary was considerably diminished. The amount of mastication necessary to reduce animal protein to digestible form is far less than is true for vegetable products. Ruminants are forced to chew, chew, and rechew their food so that a thorough mixture with salivary enzymes will assure its digestibility.[17] A quick look at the molars of a cat, however, will demonstrate that shearing rather than crushing is their main function. For a carnivore, the main purpose of the molars is to slice food chunks to swallowable size since animal protein does not require extensive salivary enzyme action before it can start to be digested in the stomach.

If Pithecanthropines were eating significantly greater quantities of meat than their Australopithecine ancestors, then they should have had less need for the greater crushing molars of the hominids at the Plio/Pleistocene boundary. With molar size free to vary, the probable mutation effect could do its work. The consequence was that reduction took place as the result of mutations accumulating under conditions of relaxed selection. Of course, since tools were being used to do the slicing and since a significant amount of raw vegetable matter continued to be an important part of the diet of the omnivorous Pithecanthropines, their molars retained a substantial measure

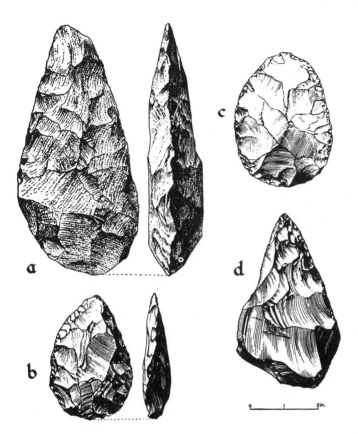

FIGURE 11–6. Lower Paleolithic tools. While most of the tools of the Lower Paleolithic are less regularly shaped flakes, picks, cores, and fragments, most assemblages include an occasional representative of the "hand axe" type first recognized by Boucher de Perthes at St. Acheul. Variants on that theme are depicted here: (a) Lava biface (hand axe) from Ol Orgesailie, Kenya; (b) Biface from St. Acheul, northwestern France; (c) Ovate biface from Israel; (d) Late Lower Paleolithic biface from Suffolk, England. (Reprinted from Oakley 1950, by permission of the British Museum of Natural History.)

of crushing surface and never took on the shearing characteristics seen in the molar teeth of the Carnivora proper.

So far we have mentioned the use of cunning and stealth in hunting, but it seems likely that another basic approach was also used. The human adaptation to long-distance locomotion is actually fairly remarkable in its own right. As an example of the potential capability of a well-conditioned human being, we can cite the mode of hunting practiced even today by certain peoples. This involves literally walking one's quarry into the ground.

South African San ("Bushmen"), American Indians, and Australian Aborigines are noted for this simple, if rather exhausting, technique.[18] The hunter takes up the trail of a large herbivore and sets out after it at a persis-

FIGURE 11–7. Sites of major Pithecanthropine discoveries. 1. Java. 2. Zhoukoudian. 3. Lantian. 4. Vertesszöllös (Hungary). 5. Heidelberg. 6. Arago (France). 7. Rabat (Morocco). 8. Ternifine (Algiers). 9. Bodo (Ethiopia). 10. East Turkana. 11. Olduvai Gorge. 12. Swartkrans.

tent trot and keeps it moving until, out of sheer fatigue, it can go no farther, at which point the hunter moves in and dispatches it. Because the process may actually drag out over a number of days, it involves a skill in tracking and a degree of patience and endurance difficult for members of this mechanized age to imagine. This has been labelled "persistence hunting,"[19] and we have already noted that it may well have had its origins in the pursuit of newborn, juvenile, and increasingly older animals by the Australopithecine ancestors of the Pithecanthropines.

Two physiological facets aid the hunter in this form of activity. First, a large herbivore depends upon the ingestion of great quantities of food of relatively low nutritive value, which means that it has to spend a considerable portion of its lifetime eating. The hunter, on the other hand, fortified by occasional nibbles of concentrated nourishment in the form of dried meat products, nuts, and other high-quality edibles, can keep pushing on without stopping, prodding his quarry along just fast enough so that it does not have an adequate chance to stop and replenish itself. In a couple of days, his patience is rewarded.

An interesting comment can also be made at this point. Human digestive physiology is quite different from that of the average nonhuman primate. The normal primate eating pattern is that of the nearly nonstop snack, which is paralleled by nearly nonstop elimination. Humans, in contrast, have entered the realm of "intermittent eaters and digesters."[20] Admittedly the fast-food industry in the Western world has shown how easy it is to reintroduce the old primate eating habits, but fortunately this has not been accompanied by a resumption of nonstop feces production. It would seem that the retooling job that made a primate into a hunter by the Middle Pleistocene successfully accomplished a permanent change in the digestive physiology.

The second physiological fact involves the human ability to dissipate metabolically generated heat. The hairless human skin has more sweat glands in proportion to surface area and human beings sweat more than any other animal.[21] This, and the brain-cooling capacity indicated by the focus on the cranial emissary-to-vertebral plexus brain drain pathway, means that humans exhibit a remarkable capacity to eliminate the excess body heat built up during the course of physical exertion. The elongation of the distal segments of the arms and legs of Strapping Youth is fully compatible with this. Consequently, human beings can continue to function effectively throughout the heat of the day. The San ("Bushmen") of South Africa capitalize on this fact by running down large quadrupeds in the middle of the day when the animals are prone to develop heat exhaustion if they attempt any continued rapid locomotion. In the tropics, mammalian life usually reposes in the shade during the hot part of the day. It is not without significance that all of the predatory carnivores that survive as the result of active pursuit of prey engage in their maximum expenditure of energy in the relative coolness of the early morning or late afternoon and evening.[22]

The relative night blindness which humans have inherited from their diurnal primate ancestors means that they could not even begin to mount an effective challenge to the established predators at the time when they are most active. But there was no competition at all for the role of a diurnal predator, and this was the niche that was adopted by the early members of the genus *Homo*. Except for mad dogs, man alone goes out in the noonday sun—nor is this a peculiarity of the English either. It would appear that the development of human predation long ago capitalized on the limitations a coat of fur has placed upon mammalian activity during the heat of the tropical day, and one can suspect that the perfection of the hominid pelvis for long-distance walking was accompanied by the the effective loss of body hair.

At the same time, the intensity of the ultraviolet component of equatorial sunlight poses something of a problem to the hairless tropic-dweller, since it greatly increases the chances of developing skin cancer. The solution is the development of a concentration of the protective pigment melanin.[23] It is possible to postulate, too, that with the development of effective hunting techniques, somewhere in between the Australopithecine and the Pithecanthropine stages, people became hairless and "black." Later we will account for the depigmentation which occurred in the background of some of the world's peoples, but at present it is sufficient to suggest that all of humankind passed through a heavily pigmented stage.

FIGURE 11–8.   Pithecanthropine skullcap from site LLK in Bed II of Olduvai Gorge, Tanzania. (Photo by the late Dr. L. S. B. Leakey; copyright National Geographic Society.)

PITHECANTHROPINE CLASSIFICATION

Yet to be considered is the formal taxonomic designation of the Pithecanthropines and their geographic distribution. The controversy that raged over the status of the original *"Pithecanthropus"* around the turn of the century now belongs to history, although there is a growing number of scholars who would like to turn the clock back and treat the fossils of which that taxon was constituted as representatives of a sideline that became extinct without issue.[24] If a great many anthropologists balk at accepting the Australopithecines for one reason or another, many are willing to regard the Pithecanthropines as genuine human beings who were ancestral to all later forms of humanity. Some would still prefer to posit an ancient form of "true man,"[25] as yet unfound, but there is little doubt that the Pithecanthropines, with their obvious dependence on tools for survival, can be considered genuine, if primitive, human beings.[26] As a result, the validity of the term *"Pithecanthropus"* as a formal generic designation has been questioned, and most authorities now regard them as belonging within genus *Homo.*

But if they can be considered genus *Homo,* there is good reason to grant them separate specific status. Brain size, on the average, is just halfway between that of the Australopithecines and *Homo sapiens,* and since this has major adaptive implications, it should be of decisive significance in justifying specific designation. Furthermore, in her analysis of the details of tooth eruption and crown and root formation, Dr. B. Holly Smith has noted that, whereas the Australopithecines display a timing in their patterns of growth and development that is much closer to the pongid than to the Modern human situation, the Pithecanthropines that she has studied fall somewhere between the pongid and the modern human condition.

As with brain size, the timing of bodily growth and maturation is halfway in between the situation typical for anthropoid apes and that characteristic of Modern human beings. This would seem to be ample grounds for recognizing them as a separate species within the genus *Homo,* and, since the original specific designation was *erectus,* many workers are happy to retain that and recognize the Pithecanthropines, formally, as *Homo erectus.*[27]

It is the view that I have adopted in developing the account that I am presenting in this book, but, although this derives from applying the principles of modern evolutionary biology to the analysis of the available fossil record, ironically it is not the view that is accepted by the majority of the paleoanthropologists actually involved in the study of the specimens in question. Indeed, in the single most exhaustive attempt to deal with the relevant material, *The Evolution of **Homo erectus,*** Professor G. Philip Rightmire of the State University of New York at Binghamton has adopted the stance that *Homo erectus* was a stable entity from beginning to end, arising in some unknown fashion, and becoming extinct without giving rise to anything else.[28]

The principal reason for our difference in outlook is a basic difference in what is accepted as a species. Paleoanthropology has traditionally held a view of species that derives straight from the categories of logic employed by medieval scholastics where a "species" is a fixed and finite entity of invariant nature, and each species has the same status as an entity as each other species.[29] It is an approach that has been referred to as "typological essentialism," and it was the particular outlook of the Aristotelian logicians in the medieval Christian church. In this view, individuals are imperfect reflections of the true underlying reality that represents the species in question. In the traditional Christian outlook, that underlying "reality" was what God intended, and deviations from it only signified the imperfections of the tangible world.[30]

Some of the famous levels of contentiousness associated with medieval disputation were generated when the "nominalists" complained that the "essentialists" were taking it upon themselves to identify the categories of God's creation and, in assigning names to those categories, imposing a picture of the world that was more for their own convenience than it was an effort to see God's world as it really is.[31] It was Darwin's role to establish a solid biological basis for the nominalist critique of species as timeless and unchanging essences, but Darwinian thinking is still alien to many paleoanthropologists who continue to assume that science is confined to giving things the right name.[32]

As a consequence, a level of confusion has arisen that threatens to paralyze the field—to say nothing of dismaying the poor student—for the foreseeable future. For example, at the earlier portion of the Pithecanthropine time span, one of the splendid mandibles from east of Lake Turkana (ER 992) has been considered to be the type specimen of *Homo "ergaster."*[33] Meave and Richard Leakey, on the other hand, have assigned it with a skull and upper jaw (ER 1813) from another site to *Australopithecus africanus,*[34] although neither account made any attempt to compare the details and measurements with representative samples of either *Homo* or *Australopithecus.*

Compounding the confusion, the late Valerii Alexeev added ER 1813 to a group containing the specimen ER 1470 from another East Rudolf site, a specimen equated with *Homo "habilis"* by many authors, and has rechristened them *"Pithecanthropus rudolfensis."*[35] But since *"Pithecanthropus"* is regarded as a suspect genus, that boils down to *Homo "rudolfensis,"* which is regarded as having replaced *Homo "aethiopicus."*[36] Depending on which author one follows, ER 1813 has been regarded as *Australopithecus africanus, Homo "habilis," "rudolfensis," "ergaster,"* and *erectus.* The presumed species *"ergaster"* has been said to replace *"rudolfensis"* with the omission of ER 1813 but with the addition of a skull from another East Turkana site, ER 3733.[37] In none of these accounts, however, is there any recognition of the fact that the mandible that started this all—ER 992—cannot be distinguished from a typical specimen of *Homo erectus.*[38]

Not to be outdone, the scholars who have treated specimens from near the end of the Pithecanthropine time period have engaged in a similar game of mix and match. The first European specimen that could qualify was the Mauer mandible found near Heidelberg in 1907. Its first describer referred to it as *Homo "heidelbergensis"*[39] although, until recently, few have ever thought of it as constituting sufficient evidence upon which to erect a complete, new species. On the contrary, there have been repeated efforts to show that it was not beyond the range of expectations for "modern" humans.[40] However, since Schoetensack, its original describer, published the measurements of all of the teeth, it is possible to demonstrate that they are basically indistinguishable from the teeth of the extensive Middle Pleistocene *Homo erectus* sample from Zhoukoudian in China.[41]

With the recently emergent enthusiasm for multiplying specific names, however, factual matters such as that are generally ignored. Instead, it has been noted that robust Middle Pleistocene skulls such as Bodo and Kabwe from Africa and Petralona from Greece lack mandibles, but the Heidelberg specimen is about the same size that their own missing jaws must have been. Therefore, a composite has been duly constructed, labelled *Homo "heidelbergensis"* with African cranial characteristics and a European mandible.[42] However, there is no diagnostic distinction between any one of them and the accepted spectrum of crucial traits that are encompassed by *Homo erectus.*[43]

If we think of *Homo erectus* in a more Darwinian sense, we have to consider the circumstances associated with population relationships of a species that had embarked upon a most un-primate-like way of life. As a new member of the "large carnivore guild,"[44] *H. erectus* soon achieved a distribution throughout the tropics of the Old World that rivaled the distribution of the wolf in the arctic and temperate portions of the northern hemisphere. Throughout that whole tropical expanse, the widespread distribution of stone tools, all made basically in the same pattern, suggests that behavioral continuity was unbroken.[45] With wide-ranging and mobile popu-

lations continually coming in contact with each other, the probability of local isolation and speciation was greatly reduced. Instead of small amounts
of variation associated with species difference, as is the case of forest-
dwelling birds and primates,[46] we should expect species continuity throughout the entire area occupied in spite of local differences of adaptively
unimportant traits. (For example, consider the baboons of Africa,[47] or the
wolves spread across the arctic and temperate zones of both the eastern and
western hemispheres.[48])

THE PITHECANTHROPINE SPREAD

A generation or two ago, when the Pithecanthropines were unchallenged as
the oldest hominids known, and when they were recognized only in Java and
China, there was a general feeling that Asia had been "the chief cradle of the
human race."[49] Now, however, with Africa possessing the strongest claims of
being the initial human homeland, there is much more willingness to view
the Pithecanthropines as having spread throughout the area that the archaeological remains indicate was inhabited, rather than to regard them as having
been restricted to one small province.

New finds and the reappraisal of some old ones confirm this suspicion.
For example, Robinson reappraised the Swartkrans specimen, which he and
Broom originally called *"Telanthropus,"* and demonstrated that it could be
considered a proper Pithecanthropine.[50] This was the first evidence discovered that showed the contemporaneity of an Australopithecine with an early
Pithecanthropine. Additional evidence, although tantalizingly skimpy, has
been found at Olduvai Gorge, and it has finally been clearly and dramatically
confirmed by the spectacular East Turkana finds made during the last twenty
years.[51]

One problem with trying to identify possible Pithecanthropines on the
basis of jaws and teeth and not much more is that they are indistinguishable
from Neanderthal jaws and teeth.[52] With no more skeletal evidence available,
the nod as to which stage gets assigned is determined by dating. If the specimen is Middle Pleistocene in age, jaws and teeth of Pithecanthropine size can
be comfortably referred to the Pithecanthropine Stage. An example is the famous Heidelberg mandible of 1907.[53] The teeth correspond quite nicely to
those discovered at Zhoukoudian in China,[54] and, because the dating can be
shown to be approximately the same,[55] it is reasonable to infer that Heidelberg represents the northwesternmost extreme of the Pithecanthropine
range, just as *"Telanthropus"* may represent the southwesternmost extreme.

Joining Heidelberg as European representatives of the Pithecan-
thropine stage are specimens from Germany (Bilzingsleben),[56] France
(Arago),[57] and possibly Greece (Petralona).[58] In Africa—except for the Kabwe
("Rhodesian") skull from Zambia[59]—the Saldanha skull from near the Cape

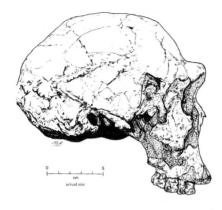

FIGURE 11–9.
A Pithecanthropine (ER-3733) from east of Lake Turkana in northern Kenya, found in 1975 by Bernard Ngeneo, one of the associates of Richard Leakey. (Drawn by M. L. Brace, in Brace et al. 1979.)

of Good Hope,[60] and Bodo from Ethiopia[61] as well as Ternifine from Algeria[62] show the form as well as the distribution of the African Pithecanthropines.[63]

The Pithecanthropines at Olduvai and in the East Turkana area not only can be associated with a tool-making tradition that had developed straight out of the earlier Oldowan, they also occur in deposits that can be dated by radiometric means. At about 1.6 million years old,[64] they are older than most of the other Pithecanthropine remains. There have been claims for a comparable degree of antiquity in Java, and many observers now feel that the Pithecanthropines in Southeast Asia may go back at least that far.[65] All of the more northern representatives, including the North Chinese (Zhoukoudian and the 1989–1990 Yun County specimens from Hubei Province)[66] and the increasing number of European discoveries, are no more than half that age, belonging in the Middle Pleistocene which began only 700,000 years ago.

According to all of the available evidence, the Australopithecines were confined to the continent of Africa. Presumably the Pithecanthropines evolved from these Australopithecines and only later spread out of their continent of origin. If the Javanese dates can be trusted, the spread to the East occurred more rapidly at an equatorial latitude, but the spread to the North, whether Northwest (Europe) or Northeast (China) took much longer to accomplish. Lower Paleolithic tools occur in a continuous distribution from Africa through India to Southeast Asia during the Middle Pleistocene, and wherever human skeletal remains are found with them, these are of Pithecanthropine form. Figure 11–12 suggests the course by which the Pithecanthropines of African origin spread throughout the tropics of the Old World just after about 2 million years ago.

Physiologically, people are still tropical mammals, and that must have been no less true for the early Pithecanthropines. Presumably after their subsistence pattern was developed in Africa, they were easily able to fill the diurnal hunting niche all the way across the tropics of the Old World. The spread North into what we curiously refer to as the "temperate" zone must have been a tentative and impermanent thing for some time after that initial exo-

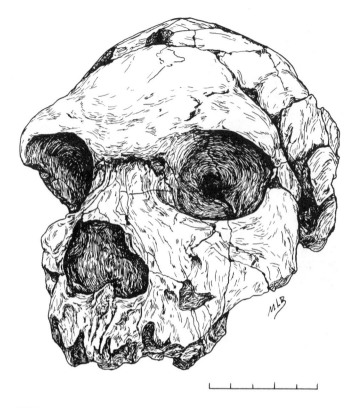

FIGURE 11–10.　Bodo, an *erectus* skull from Ethiopia. (Drawn from a cast by M. L. Brace, courtesy of Prof. T. D. White, University of California, Berkeley.)

dus from Africa. (Figure 11–13 illustrates the various routes followed.) With the onset of each glacial stage, the inhabitants of the latitudes of Europe and China must have dwindled and disappeared. They would scarcely have been welcomed back into the tropics by the people who lived there and thought of it as home, and it seems likely that they simply failed to leave descendants to perpetuate a Pithecanthropine presence in the North.

Permanent residence in the North became possible only with the development of cultural adaptations that could compensate for the physiological limitations imposed by the tropical primate heritage. The development of clothing, of course, is one such compensation. So is fire, and there has been some tentative suggestion that Pithecanthropines in both Europe and China were found with traces of charcoal.[67] But there is serious doubt about whether that was the product of human activity, or simply the result of naturally occurring brush fires.[68] Human beings eventually did control the use of fire, and it is tempting to suggest that this is what finally allowed the permanent settlement of the northern areas of habitation in the Old World at the end of the Middle Pleistocene. We shall return to this matter later on.

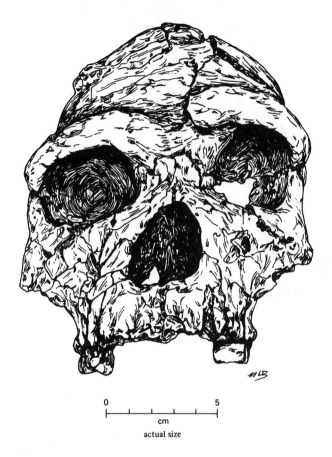

0   5
cm
actual size

FIGURE 11–11.   Arago XXI. (Drawn by M. L. Brace from a photograph taken with the permission of Drs. Henry and Marie-Antoinette de Lumley.)

The initial occupation of previously uninhabited areas, whether the tropics of the Old World, or, later, the Temperate Zone, was obviously in the nature of an actual movement of people—even if this only involved the excess population of locally established groups budding off and inhabiting the next territory just a few miles away. However, once the habitable world was occupied, development from the Pithecanthropine Stage to the succeeding ones was something that probably occurred gradually and simultaneously throughout the entire occupied world.

This expectation, however, assumes that human form, like that of any other animal, is shaped by the kinds of evolutionary forces and constraints we have considered in previous chapters. Many who deal with interpretations of human origins, however, are not comfortable with such an approach and maintain an outlook that is more compatible with traditional pre-Darwinian world views. The idea that one or another hominid category—whether the

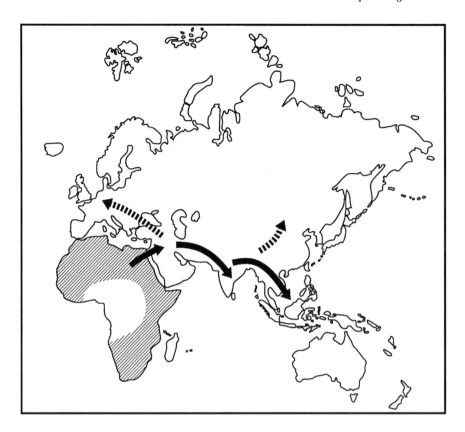

FIGURE 11–12.   The route by which the Pithecanthropines—*Homo erectus*—spread from Africa throughout the tropics of the Old World starting about 2 million years ago. Taken from Brace (in press [d]).

Australopithecines, Pithecanthropines, Moderns as a whole, or one or another "race" of humans—arose in sudden and almost miraculous fashion has been referred to as "the 'Garden of Eden' school of thought."[69] This view has enjoyed a recent resurgence of popularity, and it is currently being used by some to account for the sudden emergence of Modern human form—"out of Africa"—during the latter part of the Pleistocene.[70] This is treated in greater detail in the chapters on the Neanderthal and the Modern Stages.

Those who maintain this traditional outlook have tended to assume that the Pithecanthropines arose at a single point, after which they would presumably have spread by extinguishing the conservative local inhabitants, wherever they might be. In turn, Modern human form is also assumed to have had a point origin from which it spread by extinguishing the Pithecanthropines.[71] But since the circumstances that led to the development of each Stage from its predecessor were widely distributed, it seems more in line with evolutionary mechanics to expect the emergent new Stage to have arisen throughout the broad zone of hominid habitation rather than at any one re-

FIGURE 11–13. The routes of temporary interglacial penetration into the temperate zone by Pithecanthropines spreading from the tropics. The shaded areas indicate the zones of permanent habitation. Taken from Brace (in press [d]).

stricted spot.[72] Subsequent migration to previously uninhabited areas would be the next expectable step. After the initial Pithecanthropine spread, invasions of any note probably did not occur until the Modern spread across the Bering land bridge from Asia into North America just before the end of the Pleistocene, and subsequently at the time of the great population imbalances and technological disparities that grew out of the food-producing revolution within the last 10,000 years.[73]

The reason for this view can be seen in appraising the nature of the cultural adaptive mechanism. Cultural adaptations can and do diffuse with ease across the boundaries of specific cultures. The bow and arrow, for instance, diffused to most corners of the globe in a relatively short period of time,[74] and the documented spread of the use of tobacco indicates a rate of diffusion and a disregard for cultural boundaries, which is nothing less than phenomenal.[75] With the high degree of mobility and relative cultural uniformity functionally characteristic of the Lower Paleolithic hunters, any significant advance in hunting technique, food preservation process, or the like must have diffused quite rapidly throughout the inhabited world—accompanied by the inevitable if not large leakage of genes across population boundaries as well. With the major forces shaping human evolution heavily influenced by major cultural adaptations, and with the latter effectively diffused, whatever their local origins, one can postulate relative similarity in the selective forces operating on human form throughout the Lower Paleolithic. Similar forces would have produced similar evolutionary consequences in widely separate areas, even without an accompanying slow genetic interchange, although this must have occurred as well.

Starting with the Pithecanthropines, it is just possible that the diffusion of the cultural reasons for the specific physical changes which characterize the succeeding Stages of human evolution were rapid enough so that the unity of the human species was maintained at any one time. Development from one Stage to the next, then, would have proceeded at approximately the same time and at roughly the same rate throughout the inhabited world. The probability that a given population will be genetically more like its precursors in the same locality is, of course, greater than the probability that it will be genetically closer to groups in adjacent areas, and this allows for the development of regional peculiarities; however, at the same time, genetic material is continually being exchanged with adjacent areas.[76] The result is that no human population has ever become different enough from its contemporaries to warrant formal taxonomic recognition.

Once again, observations on contemporary representatives of a hunting-and-gathering form of subsistence economy provide evidence that reinforces this suspicion. Among these people, exogamy—seeking mates from other unrelated groups—rather than endogamy—inbreeding—is a virtually universal phenomenon.[77] This greatly increases the possibilities not only for gene flow from group to group but also for information transfer as well. Not until local populations became sedentary, following the development of a food-producing subsistence economy, did group endogamy become a phenomenon to be reckoned with.

CHAPTER ELEVEN NOTES

[1]Darwin, 1871:I:132ff: Bartholomew and Birdsell, 1953:482; Washburn, 1959:23; McHenry, 1986a:178;

[2] Holloway 1970:967; Martin, 1983:46. Actually, when body size is taken into account for *Australopithecus africanus*, brain size is some thirty percent larger than would be expected of a similarly sized modern great ape (Martin, 1983:44), and "about half of what one would expect in a modern human brain" (Radinsky, 1979:21).

[3]Martin, 1981, 1983; Armstrong, 1983.

[4]Washburn and Lancaster, 1968; Walker, 1984. Others have resurrected the idea that early members of the genus *Homo* were innately too dim of wit to have been able to plan successful hunts (Binford, 1987; Trinkaus 1987). Those arguments are less convincing than the ones that have noted how the hominids became part of the "large carnivore guild" over a million years ago

(Walker, 1984:144) and what the consequences were for the course of subsequent human evolution (Brace, in press [d]).

[5]Lovejoy et al., 1973; Lovejoy, 1974, 1978, 1988; McHenry, 1975a; Zihlman and Brunker, 1979.

[6]Brace, 1979a.

[7]Tobias, 1981, 1987:741; Falk, 1983, 1992:48–49. Holloway, 1982:226.

[8]See note 4 above.

[9]Baden-Powell, 1924. And yes, the author is none other than the founder of the Boy Scouts.

[10]Jacob, 1973, 1975; Tappen, 1979; Day, 1984; Kennedy, 1985, 1991, 1992:214–15; Ruff et al., 1993.

[11]Brown et al., 1985.

[12]Walker, 1986. The most complete listing of what was found, when and where, had been the fourth edition of Michael Day's *Guide to Fossil Man* (Day, 1986:234–39), but Alan Walker and Richard Leakey have just edited a volume that presents a series of detailed studies of particular aspects of WT 15000. Stature and limb proportion information has been reported by Ruff (1993:56), who has collaborated with Alan Walker to produce a chapter on that subject for the same volume (Ruff and Walker, 1993).

[13]Smith, 1990, 1992. I am much indebted to Dr. B. Holly Smith for letting me measure the cast of the dentition of WT 15000 and for recounting to me the results of her analysis of the crown and root formation sequence prior to the publication of her contribution to that volume edited by Alan Walker and Richard Leakey (Smith, 1993).

[14]The masterful treatment of the Zhoukoudian material by the late Franz Weidenreich (1943) remains as a model for the treatment of an important collection of prehistoric human remains. A much more "popular" account of the finding of those crucial specimens is given by von Koenigswald (1956).

[15]Summarizing what has been done since the end of World War II in China (where the war is referred to as the Sino-Japanese War) is the volume edited by Wu Rukang and John Olsen (1985) in which there are reports of the application of the latest and most sophisticated dating techniques.

[16]Brace, 1979a, b.

[17]Vonk and Western, 1984:451–53; Magee and Dalley, 1986:26.

[18]Eyre, 1845, II:276; Dornan, 1925:100, 110; Bennett and Zingg, 1935:113; Carrier, 1984; Bortz, 1985:149.

[19]Carrier, 1984.

[20]Magee and Dalley, 1986:131.

[21]Macfarlane, 1973, 1976:185; Falk, 1990, 1992: 161.

[22]Gittleman (ed.), 1989.

[23]Robins, 1991.

[24]L. Leakey and Goodall, 1969:184; Wood, 1984; Bilsborough and Wood, 1988:84; Stringer and Gamble, 1993:72.

[25]For example, Richard Leakey's "hunch" that *Homo* had a separate origin somewhere around 6 million years ago (as reported to Helen Fisher, 1983:104).

[26]Lancaster, 1968:64; Isaac, 1972:401; Clark, 1993:149.

[27]At the other end of the extreme, there is the view that all this treatment of *Homo erectus* as a special species has gone too far, and that we should best regard them as an early form of *Homo sapiens*—such crucially important things such as lesser brain size, lack of language, and non-Modern rates of growth and maturation notwithstanding (Jelínek, 1978; Wolpoff, in press).

[28]Rightmire, 1990. And these views are essentially the same as those held by the head of the Human Origins Project at the British Museum (Natural History) in London, Christopher Stringer (Stringer 1984, 1988; Stringer et al., 1979; Stringer and Gamble, 1993:72).

[29]Brace, 1988, 1989, in press (a).

[30]Ghiselin, 1969:52; Mayr, 1982:27.

[31]Moody, 1935.

[32]This is exemplified by the majority of the essays in Kimbel and Martin (1993), and the convoluted, jargon-ridden disputatiousness of many of them is startlingly similar to that found in medieval theological writings.

[33]Groves and Mazák, 1975:243; Groves, 1989:318.

[34]M. Leakey and R. Leakey, 1978:89.

[35]Alexeev, 1986:93

[36]Groves, 1989:318.

[37]Ibid.

[38]Lieberman et al., 1988:510.

[39]Schoetensack, 1908.

[40]Van den Broek, 1932; Day, 1977:57, 1986:74.

[41]Schoetensack, 1908:49–53; Weidenreich, 1937; Brace et al., 1973.

[42]Rightmire, 1990:86,224.

[43]The French skull from Arago, the German fragments from Bilzingsleben, an East African specimen from Ndutu at the head of Olduvai Gorge, and possibly the Saldanha skull cap from Elandsfontein near Hopefield (not far from the Cape of Good Hope in South Africa) have all been tentatively lumped into this dubious taxon (Rightmire, 1990). At this point, the beleaguered student has a right to query in exasperation, "aren't there any rules in this business?" There are indeed, but the guiding document, *The International Code of Zoological Nomenclature*, in all its editions, is silent in regard to the usefulness or even the competence of what is proposed by the taxonomists. The principal role played by that august document is in insisting that the first name bestowed upon an organic entity is the one by which it is forever more to be known. The distinguished scientist/journalist, Stephen Jay Gould, quotes an entomologist who noted: "In other sciences the work of incompetents is merely ignored; in taxonomy, because of priority, it is preserved" (Gould, 1990:18). One could modify Henry Higgins comment on "The French" in *My Fair Lady* to read "paleoanthropologists never care about the evolutionary meaning of the taxa they create so long as they name them properly" (and see the original in Loewe and Lerner, 1956:22). I cannot escape the feeling that paleoanthropology is doing its best to generate a fossil version of the Weird Sisters concoction in Act 4 of Macbeth:

> Double, double, toil and trouble,
> Mix the fragments from the rubble;
> A bit of this, a piece of that,
> Jaw that's chinless, skull that's flat,
> Orphan tooth and rib that's broken,
> Scrap of femur as a token,
> Some from here, some from there,
> Another chunk from God knows where;
> Assembled in a dreamer's bubble,
> Named a species: Endless trouble.
> *(with abject apologies to William Shakespeare)*

[44]Walker, 1984:144.

[45]Isaac, 1972; Clark, 1993.

[46]Brace and Brace, 1976; Tattersall, 1993.

[47]Tropical Psittacines—parrotlike birds—and arboreal monkeys are restricted to tropical forests, and these expand and then contract into patches in rhythm with the contraction and expansion of Pleistocene glaciations (Moreau, 1963, 1966; Fisher, 1970; Grubb, 1982). Those circumstances have produced repeated periods of isolation of related populations, and these often changed to a sufficient extent that they had become specifically distinct by the time the forest patches re-coalesced during the next period of increased rainfall. Similarly adapted forest species, then, will show little skeletal difference between related but distinct species (Tattersall, 1993), while wide-ranging grassland species may show more skeletal than specific difference (Jablonski, 1993; Jolly, 1993). *Homo erectus*, being a widespread savanna species, should approximate Jolly's baboon model more than Tattersall's lemur-based expectations.

[48]See the papers in Fox (ed.), 1975, and especially Mech (1970, 1972, 1975).

[49]Osborn, 1926:107.

[50]Robinson, 1961.

[51]Leakey and Walker, 1976.

[52]Brace, 1979b; Brace et al., 1987, 1991.

[53]Schoetensack, 1908.

[54]Weidenreich, 1937.

[55]Day, 1986:76.

[56]Mania andVlček, 1987.

[57]de Lumley and de Lumley, 1971.

[58]Poulianos, 1967; although, see Chapter 12.

[59]Woodward, 1921; and, again, see Chapter 12.

[60]Drennan, 1953.

[61]Conroy et al., 1978.

[62]Arambourg, 1954.

[63]Curiously enough, the professionals involved in their analysis have been hard at work denying that the specimens enumerated have anything to do with *Homo erectus*. Both Stringer et al. (1979) and Rightmire (1990:29) have stressed minute details of their skulls that are also found in more recent humans and concluded that this must make them proper *Homo sapiens!* In their concept of classification, however, the adaptive significance of the pieces of morphology referred to is never mentioned. Since they have accepted it as a given that relationship through time must indicate specific identity because species are by definition fixed and timeless entities incapable of evolving, it follows that if traits found in living humans are also present in fossils they must all be the same species. The fact that brain size is distinctly below the modern average, that robustness is vastly greater, and that the behavioral record indicates that they were incapable of language as we know it are not figured into the assessment at all. From the point of view of evolutionary biology, however, those crucial points suggest that it would be ludicrous to include those specimens in the species *sapiens*. They do share a number of adaptively trivial traits with later demonstrable *sapiens*, but that is just what one would expect if they were indeed members of a previous evolutionary grade that gave rise to subsequent *Homo sapiens* by relatively simple and predictable steps of transformation. As far as the traits that indicate major adaptive status are concerned, they share these with the specimens that all agree belong in *Homo erectus*. Since they also were members of the same manifestation of the cultural ecological niche, it seems much more sensible to regard them all as representatives of *Homo erectus* prior to the evolution of what we could designate *Homo sapiens*.

[64]Curtis et al., 1975.

[65]Eijgenraam, 1993; Swisher et al., 1994.

[66]Li and Etler, 1992.

[67]de Lumley, 1969:43; Christen, 1979:44.

[68]Binford and Ho, 1985.

[69]Sarich, 1971:188; Brace, 1979b:539.

[70]Howells, 1993:219; Stringer and Gamble, 1993:132.

[71]Just why Modern form should have had a point origin is never considered. In fact, why Modern form should have arisen at all is never mentioned. A discussion of the mechanisms for Modern emergence is presented in Chapters 13 and 14.

[72]Actually, Modern form did not emerge all-of-a-piece, as it were. The technological innovations that led to the different manifestations of Modern form appeared in different parts of the world to start out with, and the morphological consequences appeared in those separate regions first. As the technologies spread, the people who adopted them then underwent changes as a consequence and took on their subsequent Modern appearance. It was the spread of the aspects of technology that led to the emergence of Modern form, and not the spread of the genes for that Modern form from any one source (Brace, in press [d]).

[73]Brace and Tracer, 1992.

[74]Kehoe, 1978:2;Klein, 1983:43.

[75]Kroeber, 1948:417–18, 478–80.

[76]Brace, in press (c).

[77]Birdsell, 1979:36.

chapter twelve

The Pithecanthropine
to Neanderthal Transition

REGIONAL CONTINUITY

If the most important factors that conditioned human evolutionary change during the greater part of the Pleistocene were in the extent to which innovations in the cultural realm altered environmentally imposed aspects of selection, then we ought to be able to equate regional cultural differences with significant differences in human physical form in the various inhabited parts of the world. But when archaeologists appraise the Lower-to-Middle Pleistocene, they invariably conclude that there is no evidence for a degree of regional cultural differentiation equivalent to that which has arisen within the last 100,000 years.[1] Significant cultural innovations, insofar as they can be inferred, were diffused from one area to another and became the property of all extant populations before any kind of differential regional biological response was able to occur.

Of course, genetic continuity in each region meant that ancestor-descendant sharing of trivial inherited characteristics would have made for a picture of continuity of minor regional distinction.[2] But where the response to major selective forces was concerned, the fact that people in all the major inhabited geographic regions of the world were living essentially the same kind of life meant that, starting with the Pithecanthropine Stage, no major change in Stage was likely to occur in one particular area that would not be shared by all others soon enough so that, from the perspective of evolutionary time, all would be perceived as essentially contemporaneous. This would have been particularly the case if specific cultural developments were what had changed the nature of selection, thereby inducing a consequent change in Stage. As we shall see, that is probably exactly what happened.

Humans, in hunting-and-gathering bands, maintained population densities and areas of control and exploitation that were remarkably similar in extent to those canine hunters—the wolves[3]—that have maintained specific unity throughout the temperate and arctic portions of the world since the end of the Pliocene—much as the hominids did in the tropics. Gene flow between adjacent populations was sufficient so that specific unity was maintained through time as well.[4] For these reasons, we would expect that the hominid fossil record should show that the major changes in Stage should have occurred essentially simultaneously in all human populations starting at the beginning of the Middle Pleistocene, but that there should be evidence for continuity in adaptively trivial traits that link the earlier with the later inhabitants of each of the major geographic regions inhabited.

The idea that we should expect to see continuity between the prehistoric and recent populations of the various inhabited regions of the world was first articulated by the describer of the extensive *erectus* material found in China over half a century ago, Franz Weidenreich. It was his idea that the human inhabitants of the various regions of the world evolved through a series of "phases" or "stages" in more or less the same fashion at more or less the same time in each area.[5] Opponents of such a view have regarded it as incredible that the various regionally separate human groups should have independently followed the same course of development and independently arrived at the same "Modern" end point.[6] Actually it is a serious misrepresentation to portray Weidenreich's position in this manner,[7] since he stressed the fact that human populations always maintained reproductive continuity with each other at the borders, and that they could never have been characterized as proceeding in isolation from each other.[8]

Weidenreich's view of separate regional populations proceeding in the same direction has been caricatured as the "Polyphyletic or Candelabra School,"[9] and, although the elimination of the connections between the regional populations envisioned by Weidenreich is a major weakness in the critique, there is a real point to be made. That is the fact that there is no credible mechanism cited that would drive the various regional human populations on a similar course of change. Weidenreich had rejected natural selection operating on randomly occurring mutations as the driving force for evolution,[10] and embraced a fuzzy sort of "orthogenesis"[11] with a clear sympathy for a neo-Lamarckian kind of inheritance of acquired characteristics.[12]

Specifically, Weidenreich felt that, as the source of "self-differentiation," the human brain was responsible for generating the changes that were most important in the course of human evolution.[13] The brain did this by some sort of inner momentum somehow related to erect posture, and changes in the face, jaws, and teeth simply followed as a natural consequence. Although the first three Stages of human evolution portrayed in this book stress the importance of major differences in brain size, the approach taken here differs fundamentally from that of Weidenreich in that it does not assume that brain expansion was driven by a kind of *sui generis* momentum. Instead, the expansion is seen as having been a direct result of the adaptive value of having a larger brain for a creature in which learned behavior plays an ever more important role in assuring survival. Changes in faces, jaws, and teeth, on the other hand, follow a separate evolutionary course constrained by factors that have nothing directly to do with the circumstances that led to the increases in brain size.

EVOLUTIONARY DYNAMICS: GENE FLOW, SELECTION, AND MUTATION

One of the recent efforts to delineate what constitutes a species has suggested that recognition of breeding partners is a crucial factor.[14] After all, if a member of another population is not perceived as a desirable "sex object," reproductive behavior will not occur and no offspring will be produced.[15] However, where living humans are concerned, differences in color, shape, language, and culture seem to have no effect whatsoever in limiting sexual behavior when people from one area encounter those from another.

At population boundaries, genetic material that originated in one population regularly enters into the other and vice versa. The movement of genes across population boundaries is referred to as "gene flow," and it has proceeded at low but constant levels between human groups to such a continual extent that genetic compatibility has been maintained throughout the whole geographical extent of *Homo sapiens*. Not only has it maintained us as a single diverse "breeding population," but it has ensured that the occurrence of a favorable genetic mutation in one or another part of the world will eventually become the property of all.

Although he did not use the words, Weidenreich clearly recognized the importance of gene flow. Recently gene flow has been proposed as a "driving mechanism" for human evolution.[16] Important as it is, however, gene flow is not a driving mechanism for anything. All it can do is to redistribute what is already there. The normal driving mechanism is natural selection operating on the genes that are shared as a result of gene flow, or, if natural selection is relaxed in particular instances, the driving mechanism will be in the mutation process itself.

Throughout the time span of *Homo erectus* from over 1.5 million years ago until it actually becomes an archaic form of *Homo sapiens* towards the end of the Middle Pleistocene, there is a slow increase in brain size.[17] Moreover, the picture of that increase is not restricted to just one part of the inhabited world, but seems to be shared by all the diverse regional Pithecanthropine populations. Obviously the selective force circumstances that led to that increase were equally distributed throughout the area inhabited despite the differences in local ecological circumstances. There is one other thing distributed in nearly uniform fashion, and that is the cultural evidence (the form of the tools used).

These tools indicate that a similar life-way was being pursued over the entire geographic extent of the Pithecanthropines, and this suggests that the selective pressures generated by the cultural ecological niche itself were of paramount importance for survival. Because a premium was placed on learning itself and not the different kinds of things learned in different areas, the selective pressures associated with entry into the cultural ecological niche were essentially the same throughout its whole extent. The tools that demonstrate the extent of the cultural ecological niche showed little in the way of regional differences in the style of their manufacture. This allows us to guess that their makers did not yet have the use of language as we know it.

LANGUAGE

Language, of course, gives its possessors a profound edge over any potential competitors who do not possess it. But language did not arise instantly like "the flick of a switch."[18] It was not simply a matter of a sufficient quantity of brain serving as a threshold above which linguistic behavior is possible and below which it is not.[19] There were some profound neurological changes necessary before our predecessors could exert voluntary control over the nature of the sounds they uttered.

In Modern humans, vocal control is under the supervision of the neocortex of the brain and therefore can be regulated by deliberate intent, whereas, in the rest of the primates and all other mammals, control is involuntary since it is exerted by the limbic system.[20] A dog or a monkey, then, will have just as much trouble shaping vocalizations at will as we would in willing the production of adrenalin or sex hormones or digestive enzymes. Some scholars have suggested that the shape of our jaws and our oral cavities have influenced the capacity to speak,[21] but there is extensive clinical evidence to show that "it is the brain, not the vocal cords, that matter most."[22]

Prior to the end of the Middle Pleistocene, somewhere between 200,000 and 130,000 years ago, change in human form had proceeded in the same fashion throughout the Pithecanthropine world. Since the appearance of the genus *Homo* over 1.5 million years ago, that change was principally characterized by a slow, gradual increase in brain size. Differences between the various regional populations of the Pithecanthropines were confined to trivial little details of suture configurations on the skull, nuances of cranial morphology, details of the jaw joint, and other minor matters that were only representations of genetic continuity in given regions and of no adaptive or evolutionary significance. It seems pretty clear that the main constraints on human survival were much the same from one end of the inhabited world to the other, and that a relatively undifferentiated cultural ecological niche was basically shared by all.

Well before brain size had reached its modern levels as the Late Pleistocene began 130,000 years ago,[23] we begin to see regional differences in the manufacture of stone tools and in other cultural dimensions. This is treated in greater detail in Chapters 13 and 14, and the implications for a growing picture of human biological differentiation are tied in. At this point, we can suspect that the rudiments of linguistic behavior as we know it were being established. Brain size had ceased to expand, but, with the emergence of stylistic differences in regional traditions of tool manufacture, we begin to see areas of stylistic similarity that come to bear an eery resemblance to the kind of areas characterized by the extent of known language families.

At the same time, the pace of technical innovation begins to quicken. Surely the intellectual developments that this symbolizes also include an increase in linguistic capability. Even though there is an increase in regional cultural differentiation, there is no evidence that the overall selective forces exerted within the various manifestations of the cultural ecological niche were significantly different in one area as compared with another. The pressure to master verbal skills was just as intense on northern as it was on southern populations and on eastern as on western ones.

Today, all human populations have the same linguistic capabilities. Children everywhere learn to speak at the same age and develop linguistic skills that are no different from one end of the world to another. All languages are equally complex—there are no "primitive" or simple languages[24]—and it takes the same level of ability to learn to use each. If we look at traits where there are differences that reflect over 100,000 years of the differential application of selective forces—tooth size and skin color, for example—their possessors show no difference in their essential linguistic skills. The regional continuity in the common human intellectual heritage evidently has proceeded unbroken from its Middle Pleistocene roots, even while other aspects of human form have been diverging.

Now it only remains to consider some of the fossil representatives of those Middle Pleistocene populations that ultimately gave rise to the living peoples of the world. The remainder of this chapter is given over to describing a series of these specimens.

AFRICA: THE KABWE OR "RHODESIAN" FIND

If the Neanderthals were characterized by having a Modern-sized brain in a creature that still had a Middle Pleistocene body and face, then their predecessors late in the middle part of the Pleistocene ought to show signs that final expansion of the brain was taking place. This indeed is exactly what we find. The first of these late Middle Pleistocene finds to be recognized was the famous "Rhodesian" skull, discovered in 1921 deep in a mine shaft in Kabwe (then Broken Hill) in Zambia (then northern Rhodesia).[25] (The Rhodesian skull is illustrated in Figure 12–1.) Brain size, at just over 1,250 cc., is well above the Pithecanthropine average of 1,000 cc., but below the modern male mean of 1,450 cc., although well within the normal modern range of variation. The face is a good, unreduced Middle Pleistocene representative, capped by a stupendous brow ridge. The neck muscle attachments likewise indicate that the head was set upon the body of a powerfully constructed Middle Pleistocene male.[26]

The date of the Rhodesian skull has been a matter for debate ever since it was found. Recently, a new technique based upon the racemization of aspartic acid has been applied, and this yields a date of 120,000 years, which would be at the very end of the Middle Pleistocene.[27] But there are many doubts and questions about the use of such techniques to assess the antiquity of terrestrial as opposed to oceanic material, so there is still no final word on the date of the Rhodesian specimen. Perhaps the best assessment is its cautious attribution to the latter part of the Middle Pleistocene between 250,000

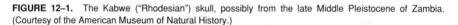

FIGURE 12–1. The Kabwe ("Rhodesian") skull, possibly from the late Middle Pleistocene of Zambia. (Courtesy of the American Museum of Natural History.)

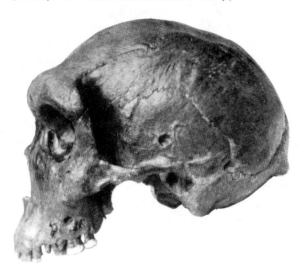

and 130,000 years ago.[28] Morphologically, it certainly appears to be on the boundary between Pithecanthropine and Neanderthal form.[29]

AFRICA: SALDANHA

In 1953, a similar skull vault, lacking the face, was found at Saldanha Bay near Hopefield, a scant hundred miles north of the Cape of Good Hope in South Africa. The name of the actual site is Elandsfontein, and various specialists refer to the specimen by one or another of these names—Hopefield, Elandsfontein, or Saldanha—without telling the reader that they all refer to one and the same specimen.[30]

In the details of its form, it is strikingly similar to the Rhodesian skull, although, since it was completely missing its lower half, there is no way of making an accurate estimate of its capacity.[31] It was found associated with faunal remains of characteristic Middle Pleistocene forms and also with artifacts recognized as final Acheulean, which suggest a late Middle Pleistocene date.[32] All of this is consistent with an interpretation that would regard this specimen as evidence for the transition from *erectus* to *sapiens*. As one might expect, then, there has been continuing disagreement about just what taxon the specimen belongs to, and this could very well be the reason why it cannot be precisely placed. The late Carleton Coon (1904–1981) declared that it was "a classic example of *Homo erectus*,"[33] it has been accepted as *Homo sapiens*,[34] and it has been attributed to that headless wonder, *Homo "heidelbergensis."*[35]

INDIA: NARMADA

The Indian subcontinent—South Asia—has been yielding an abundance of Lower Paleolithic tools for many years, so it is quite clear that people were there during the Lower and Middle Pleistocene.[36] Since tools of this kind were the products of the Pithecanthropines elsewhere, it has always been assumed that they must have been the makers of the Indian tools as well. Until just over a decade ago, however, although Pleistocene animal bones have also been found in quantity, there was not a trace of the human manufacturers of the stone tools recovered.

Then, on December 5, 1982, a partial human skull was found at Hathnora near Hoshangabad in the Narmada Valley of Madhya Pradesh in central India (see Figure 12–2).[37] Fossil bones of extinct mammals and Acheulean-type stone tools were also recovered. The tools have been called "typical later Acheulian,"[38] and suggest that the date must be late in the Middle Pleistocene. This, of course, was just when the transition from *erectus* to *sapiens* was taking place in other parts of the world, and it comes as no surprise that the Nar-

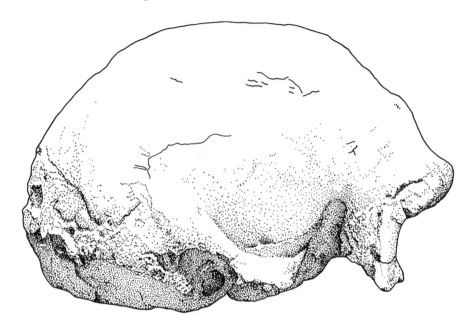

FIGURE 12–2.   Narmada, a Pithecanthropine-to-Neanderthal transitional specimen from Hathnora in Madhya Pradesh, central India. (Drawn with the help of Kay Clahassey from a photograph furnished by Professor Arun Sonakia.)

mada skull has sometimes been called one and sometimes the other. Even the most considered assessment, which removes it from *erectus,* grants it *sapiens* status with reluctant caution.[39] Not only is the time span in between the Pithecanthropine and more recent stages, but the form is intermediate as well.

INDONESIA: SOLO

The tropics in the Far East have also obligingly yielded some crucial fossils. As with the initial discovery and the confirmation of the Pithecanthropine stage, Java has played the central role. Starting in 1931, eleven broken and faceless skulls were unearthed on the banks of the Solo River, not far from the town of Ngandong (see Figure 12–3).[40] This has led to a confusion in names, which continues to the present day. Some authors refer to them as the "Solo" finds, as I have done here following the original usage, but others refer to them as the "Ngandong" finds (without indicating that they are the same). The specimens recall the Pithecanthropines on the one hand and the Neanderthals on the other. The bones of the cranial vault are thick, the brow ridges and muscle markings are heavy, and the keeling along the midline, together with other details, looks more than faintly Pithecanthropine.[41]

FIGURE 12–3.   One of the Solo skulls, a Javanese representative of the transition between the Pithecanthropine and the Neanderthal Stages. (Courtesy of the American Museum of Natural History, New York.)

However, the cranial capacity is half way between Pithecanthropine and Neanderthal/Modern levels,[42] and the date is considered to be from just before the beginning of the Upper Pleistocene.[43] All told, the Solo skulls appear to represent an evolutionary transition from the Pithecanthropine to the Neanderthal Stage in the Far East. Together with more recent skeletal remains, the evidence is most suggestive that, after the Pithecanthropine Stage had been reached, Stage-to-Stage evolution occurred approximately simultaneously in all parts of the inhabited world: Europe, Africa, Asia, and, by inference, the areas in between.

CHINA: DALI

The one specimen from the appropriate time level in China also shows all the characteristics of being intermediate between the Pithecanthropine and the Neanderthal Stages. A skull was found in river gravels in 1978 in Dali County, just east of the ancient Chinese capital of Xian, in Shaanxi (see Figure 12–4).[44] The date is late Middle Pleistocene,[45] and, with a capacity of 1,120 cc.,[46] it is appropriately intermediate. Dali is also interesting in that it shows, admittedly in very robust form, some of the same aspects of facial proportion that serve to distinguish the faces of modern Asians from the modern inhabitants of other parts of the world. This adds to our suspicion that modern human form emerged simultaneously in the various geographic regions of the Old World.

EUROPE: SWANSCOMBE

Europe has also yielded specimens from the same time period, and it would seem that there is plenty of evidence to support the uncomplicated view that Neanderthal form emerged gradually from that of the preceding Pithecan-

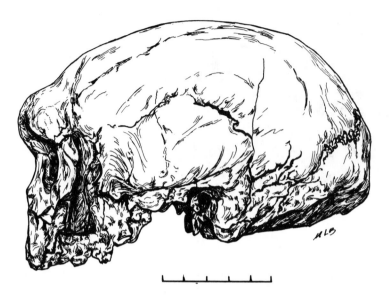

FIGURE 12–4.   The Dali skull, a Pithecanthropine/Neanderthal transition from China. (Drawn by M. L. Brace from a photograph; courtesy of Professor Wu Rukang.)

thropines. But this is not the way the majority of analysts prefer to look at things, so we should consider the evidence and what is said about it to produce the confusions that pass for current orthodoxy. Three European finds are frequently cited as contradicting this apparently straightforward scheme. These are, in order of their discovery, the specimens from Steinheim in western Germany, Swanscombe in England, and Petralona in Greece.

The geologically oldest of these "skulls" is the Swanscombe skull (see Figure 12–5). Although there are continuing arguments about just how old it is, it is certainly Middle Pleistocene and possibly in the latter part of the Middle Pleistocene.[47] The pieces of this skull were discovered in a gravel pit by the lower Thames River in southeastern England; the three major fragments constituting the rear of the cranial vault being unearthed in 1935, 1936, and, by an almost impossibly rare piece of good fortune, in 1955.[48]

At the time when the initial pieces were found, British anthropologists, because of their longstanding lack of enthusiasm for facing the possibility that modern humanity may have had a Neanderthal ancestor, were desperately eager to find evidence for the existence of "men" of modern form at an earlier time level than that attributable to the Neanderthals. As a result, modern features were stressed whenever possible.[49] Because the all-important facial parts of Swanscombe were missing, opinions concerning its status could be promoted without much risk of encountering solid objections from any quarter whatsoever. By default, then, Swanscombe has been regarded as "Modern" ever since.

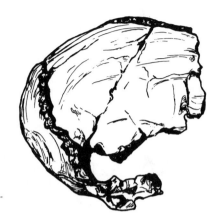

FIGURE 12–5.
The Swanscombe skull. (Drawn from a cast by M. L.
Brace.)

Even though the back end of the skull is relatively nondiagnostic in the assessment of the major distinguishing characteristics of evolutionary Stage, there are some features that generally accompany those of diagnostic significance, and it is not without interest to discover some of these on the Swanscombe skull. For instance, the greatest width is far back and low down on the skull, and skull height is remarkably low in proportion to width. The width across the occipital bone alone is greater than 99.0 percent of comparable modern skulls, and the bones are remarkably thick.[50] Other indications as well locate the Swanscombe skull right in the middle of the characteristic Middle Pleistocene range of variation,[51] but, lacking the crucial frontal bone and attached facial parts, we are not at liberty to do more than suspect that those parts may well have agreed with the indications of the vault. Unequivocal interpretation of Swanscombe is not possible, but, in marked contrast to the majority of the claims put forward on its behalf, it most certainly provides no evidence whatsoever for the existence of Modern human form in the Middle Pleistocene.

EUROPE: STEINHEIM

The Steinheim skull, found two years earlier in a gravel pit near Schiller's birthplace, not far from Stuttgart in West Germany,[52] would at first consideration seem to be a more promising subject for interpretation than the Swanscombe skull. (The Steinheim skull is illustrated in Figure 12–6.) Steinheim is of about the same antiquity, and it is relatively complete with much of the face preserved. Yet the arguments surrounding the attempt to establish its significance show no signs of diminishing. The skull is small and low, and it has a cranial capacity of approximately the Pithecanthropine average. The brow ridge is a formidable bony bar, but the back is rounded and smooth,

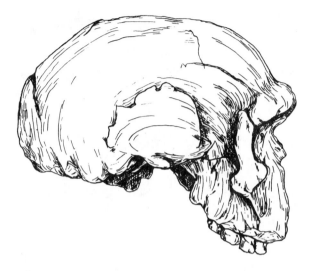

FIGURE 12–6.   The Steinheim skull. (Drawn from a cast by M. L. Brace.)

suggesting modern form, and the third molar is markedly reduced. Although the modern form of some of the other parts of the face has also been stressed, there are two principal difficulties in the way of definitive interpretations. First, the whole lower front part of the face is missing, leaving only the molars and one premolar at the rear of the dental arch. This is particularly regrettable since the most crucial features distinguishing Modern from Middle Pleistocene morphology are those centered upon the forward end of the dental arch. The second difficulty lies in the distortion that the skull has undergone. The whole left side of the skull is crushed towards the midline, reducing the width of the base to less than that ever recorded for a normal modern individual (in whom the width of the base tends to be less than for Middle Pleistocene individuals in the first place). The palate has been reduced in width, and the whole of the facial skeleton has been pushed slightly back underneath the skull. As a result of the missing and distorted aspects, it is evident that no unequivocal judgment can be made. Yet, with its small cranial capacity and heavy brow ridge, it can tentatively be regarded as belonging somewhere in between the Pithecanthropines and the Neanderthals.[53]

In the case of both Swanscombe and Steinheim, there is another matter that has rarely been given due consideration. Both individuals were female and therefore lacked the bony reinforcements and evidences for heavy muscle attachments that are so prominent on Middle Pleistocene male skulls. In a population where sexual dimorphism was pronounced, as it was during the middle of the Pleistocene, the choice of any single skull to characterize the appearance of the group as a whole is bound to be misleading. Such would seem to be the case for those who have taken the female form of Steinheim and Swanscombe to show that Modern "man" existed before the Neanderthals.

EUROPE: PETRALONA

A near duplicate of the Rhodesian skull was found by a group of cave explorers near the village of Petralona in northern Greece in 1959.[54] The face and brow ridges suggest Pithecanthropine affinities. The cranial capacity, at 1,220 cc.,[55] is half way between the Pithecanthropine and the Neanderthal levels, but, until recently, this was only suggestive until there was a means of assigning an absolute date. The calcite in the cave was similar to that encrusting the skull and could be used for running ESR, TL, and Uranium series dates. The spectrum of 160,000 to over 350,000 years ago can hardly be called pinpoint accuracy,[56] but it is a good estimate for what on faunal and morphological grounds would seem to be a late Middle Pleistocene hominid.

The Petralona skull (Figure 12–7), like many of the other African and European Pithecanthropines and *erectus-sapiens* intermediates, has been labelled *"Homo sapiens"* by a number of anthropologists who have abandoned evolutionary theory for a cladistic outlook.[57] They have correctly noted that there are a number of details in the construction of these crania that continue to be visible in more recent populations of genuine *Homo sapiens*. But since cladistics takes it as a Platonic given that no species can be transformed gradually into another one, its proponents justify the classification of these various specimens as *sapiens* even though they lack the one adaptively crucial criterion for *sapiens* inclusion, namely fully modern brain size. Obviously that is not the interpretation we are advancing here. The morphology is just what we would expect for a Pithecanthropine/Neanderthal transition,[58] and it comes from just that stretch of time when the transition was taking place wherever we have evidence for human form.

SETTING THE STAGE FOR REGIONAL DIFFERENTIATION

Towards the end of the Middle Pleistocene, maybe somewhat over 200,000 years ago, the actors were all in place, and a sampling of these has been sketched above in the body of this chapter. Obviously the ones mentioned simply serve as representatives of the populations that inhabited the areas in which they were found. Human habitation was continuous throughout the tropics of the Old World, and it was tentatively and temporarily extended into the realm of the Temperate Zone. The cultural evidence available shows

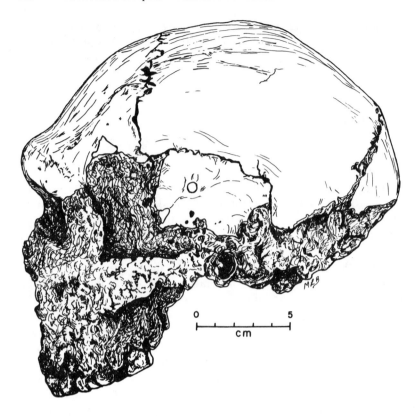

FIGURE 12–7. Petralona, a candidate for a Pithecanthopine/Neanderthal transitional skull from Greece. (Drawn by M. L. Brace from a photograph by P. Kokkoros and A. Kannelis published in *L'Anthropologie,* 1960, and reproduced courtesy of Masson & Cie., Paris.)

that there was no significant difference in way of life from one end of human habitation to the other, but that was soon to change.

Previously the pace of cultural innovation had been so slow that, when something advantageous arose in one area, the spread throughout the whole human world was fully accomplished long before another such innovation could occur. Humans everywhere, then, were the eventual beneficiaries of developments that originally were associated with one particular location. Those benefits endured as the common human heritage long enough so that they did not encourage localized differential responses to the advantages that they conveyed.

Starting somewhere around 200,000 years ago, however, significant technological innovations began to occur in given areas that made such a difference in the life-way of the inventors that it led to significant changes in their appearance. These changes began to become apparent before those particular aspects of technology had spread to the other inhabitants of the world. Some of the differences in appearance of living human populations are the consequence of that delayed spread and have their roots in innovations that occurred some 200,000 years ago.

What symbolizes the end of the Pithecanthropine-Neanderthal—or, as I would suggest, the *erectus-sapiens*—transition was the attainment of Modern levels of relative brain size. After that had been accomplished, virtually all of the other morphological changes that occurred in human evolution were in the nature of reductions from the levels of robustness that had characterized our Lower and Middle Pleistocene ancestors. Those reductions, in turn, can all be tied to cultural innovations, which themselves were the products of that Modern-sized brain. There may very well have been intense pressures to alter the neurological organization of aspects of that brain, but these we cannot see. The available evidence simply shows that brain size stopped growing, but the products of human ingenuity began a trajectory of acceleration that has showed no signs of slowing down.

The selective pressures maintaining the ability to participate in and benefit from that ingenuity surely continued to maintain the collective human intellect at levels approached by no other creature, but the reductions in the other aspects of the human physique cannot be explained by invoking positive selection in a similar manner. All those reductions follow the relaxation of selection that ensued when particular aspects of technology took the burden off the unaided human physique. The driving force was the action of mutations alone occurring under conditions of relaxed selection—the consequences of the probable mutation effect discussed in Chapter 7.

Ironically, it was some of the cultural innovations of the Neanderthal stage—the products of their Mousterian culture—that were particularly important in leading to some of the changes that were to occur in their descendants. These innovations, differentially applied, also account for some of the visible differences among the living peoples of the world today.[59] But it is the task of the next chapter to develop that theme and to show how it worked in specific instances.

CHAPTER TWELVE NOTES

[1]Clark, 1975, 1988, 1993; Klein, 1989b:212.

[2]Regional distinctions in living human populations have traditionally been called "racial," but it can be shown that adaptively significant biological variation is only found in traits that follow selective-force gradients across population boundaries as clines. Groups that link together to form regionally identifiable clusters do so by virtue of sharing traits that are adaptively unimportant and only reflect a large-scale version of family resemblance. For that reason, to describe human biological variation in terms of "race" simply prevents us from understanding the evolutionary significance of the dimensions of human difference (Brace and Hunt, 1990; Brace in press [c]). If the concept of "race" prevents us from understanding the significance of biological variation in living human populations, the same is certainly true for our efforts to understand the nature of biological variation in the past.

[3]Mech, 1970, 1972, 1988.

[4]It was this realization that led Dobzhansky to refer to humans at any time, past and present, as a "single polytypic species" held together by "gene flow" (1944:254, 265). While I have generally accepted this view, I have rejected the typological assumptions behind his faith that regionally related human populations share in an essence that can be called "racial" (Brace and Hunt, 1990; Brace in press [c], and see note 3 above). The idea that the various human populations have long acted as "genetically a single system" (Dobzhansky, 1944:263) has recently been reaffirmed as a result of a careful appraisal of the information available from mitochondrial DNA (mtDNA) (Templeton, 1993, 1994). On the other hand, the levels of gene flow across population borders never led to the condition where all human beings could be regarded as "one panmictic population" (Frayer et al., 1993:16).

[5]Weidenreich, 1928:29, 1936a:288, 1936b:46, 1939:85, 1940:382, 1946:30, 1947a:201.

[6]Howells, 1959:235–36.

[7]Brace, 1964:15, 1981a:423.

[8]Geneticists would use the term "gene flow" to characterize the kind of situation Weidenreich described. Although Weidenreich did not use that term, it is clear that his understanding of the mechanism for mainaining specific unity was essentially the same as that indicated when other biologists use the genetic terminology. This is implicit in the sympathy expressed for Weidenreich's scheme by the late Theodosius Dobzhansky (1944:260). I had suspected this, but I had the privilege of being able to ask Dobzhansky about it myself, and he confirmed it by saying that he and Weidenreich had discussed such matters often at the American Museum of Natural History in New York where Weidenreich spent the last years of his life (personal information from Th. Dobzhansky, 63rd annual meeting of the Anthropological Association, Detroit, Michigan, November, 1964).

[9]Howells, 1959:236, 1993:124. That caricature also was meant to apply to Coon (1962), who actually deserved it, and to the position I had defended in 1964 and, from 1967 to the present, in the previous editions of this book. It has been taken up with vigor and rechristened "multi-regional continuity" (Wolpoff et al., 1984:450; Frayer et al., 1993).

[10]Weidenreich, 1939:92, 1947b:235.

[11]Weidenreich, 1939:85, 1941:435, 1947b:234.

[12]Weidenreich, 1930:369, 1932; and see the account by Curt Stern in Mayr, 1980:428. In the discussion following presentations at the session, "Franz Weidenreich: His Contribution to Paleoanthropology," on August 25, 1992, at the 3rd International Congress on Human Paleontology in Jerusalem, I raised the point that one really needed to take Weidenreich's orthogenesis and Lamarckianism into account in order to understand why, for all his insights into human phylogeny, he had produced no defensible scheme of why it had occurred. My view was vigorously contradicted by Milford Wolpoff, who vehemently denied the Lamarckian element in Weidenreich's thinking, and said that anyone who did not understand the importance of *"Bauplan"* in his views needed "a refresher course in the history of science." *Bauplan*, however, was the Germanic equivalent of the "Archetype" or Platonic Ideal that underlay the outlook of *Naturphilosophie* in the early nineteenth century, and its adherents were fundamentally opposed to the possibility of organic evolution (Ghiselin, 1969:81; Appel, 1987:229). This had largely run its course by the middle of the nineteenth century (Mayr, 1982:668), and gave way in Germany to the romantic evolutionism of Ernst Haeckel (1834–1919) who treated "evolution" not as a description of what had happened in nature but as a kind of "cosmic force" in itself (Gasman, 1971:15–16). This manifestation of romantic evolutionism had its parallels in the *"élan vital"* of Henri Bergson in France (Bergson, 1907; Lovejoy, 1936:317; Brace, 1981:414). Weidenreich evidently was influenced both by the romantic evolutionism and also by the neo-Lamarckianism of the late nineteenth and early twentieth centuries (Aldrich, 1974:210–11; Limoges, 1980:322–23; Mayr, 1980:428, 1982:882). Unlike the earlier *Naturphilosophen*, Weidenreich was a genuine evolutionist. His concept of mechanism, however, was not compatible with the Darwinian approach that characterizes the mainstream of twentieth century evolutionary biology.

[13]Weidenreich, 1939:84, 1941:421.

[14]Paterson, 1980, 1985. As has been pointed out, however, there is virtually no way that we can determine whether one kind of fossil population would or would not have recognized desirable sex partners in another related fossil population (Jolly, 1993:98).

[15]There is reason to suspect that it is actual lack of mutual fertility and not failure to recognize sex partners that has determined specific hominid boundaries in the past. From the information provided by the most recognized expert on orang-utan behavior today, Dr. Biruté Galdikas, male orangs on occasion will actually rape human females (Maugh, 1992).

[16]Frayer et al., 1993:17. This treatment also suggests that Weidenreich emphasized "genic exchange to the exclusion of geographic variation" (1993:16) in proposing his "stages of human evolution," but it is clear that Weidenreich was defending a view that was far closer to that of Dobzhansky than the one attributed to him by his critics.

[17]The abstract of the term paper in which this was developed was published by Allen (1982). This was then rewritten by Wolpoff (1984). Some of the acknowledged experts on Pithecanthropine form have not recognized that increase in brain size, but they do this by denying Pithecanthropine status to the earlier, small-brained representatives, and they put the later and larger-brained ones into *Homo sapiens,* even though brain size is not yet quite up to average modern levels and other aspects of robustness absolutely dwarf the modern condition (Rightmire, 1990; Stringer and Gamble, 1993).

[18]Stringer and Gamble, 1993:204.

[19]Although the idea was not original with him, Sir Arthur Keith suggested that the figure of 650 cc. for brain size represented a cerebral "Rubicon"—a decisive boundary separating the human from the apish condition (Keith, 1949:206).

[20]Hockett, 1978:255; Holden, 1979:1066; Schiller, 1979:249.

[21]Lieberman and Crelin, 1971; Lieberman, 1975; Lieberman et al., 1992. The anatomical gaffes of those claiming that the Neanderthal larynx would have prevented the use of articulate speech have been repeatedly demonstrated (Falk, 1975; Houghton, 1993). The denials by Lieberman and colleagues that Neanderthals were anatomically capable of producing the requisite sounds were all based on their attempts to model the vocal tract of a "typical" Neanderthal by using the reconstruction of the La Chapelle-aux-Saints skull made by Boule early in the century. However, Jean-Louis Heim at the Musée de l'Homme has recently shown that Boule made a series of errors in his reconstruction that significantly distorted the shape of the base of the skull (Heim, 1989). Boule had put a cork in the foramen magnum that was too large, and then filled in some of the spread parts with wax. As a consequence, the skull was lowered and elongated, the face projected forwards, and the base was flattened (Heim, 1993:27). When the wax was removed and the skull properly restored, it had a basicranial flexion that was within the modern human range (Heim, 1989:105). Equally as effective, however, has been the demonstration that there is at least one modern language that uses only those vowel sounds to which the Neanderthals were supposedly limited, and the speakers have no trouble expressing anything that they wish (Hockett, 1978:295). At the fifty-first annual meetings of the American Association of Physical Anthropologists in Eugene, Oregon, at the beginning of April, 1982, I tried to explain to Philip Lieberman that I had heard chimpanzees making the full gamut of human vowel sounds. His reply was that, if he had an oscilloscope, he could prove to me that they were not exactly like the vowel sounds humans make. The obvious answer is that if the imitation is good enough so humans think those are the sounds being made, then they are surely good enough to convey the meanings for which humans use them. The problem for chimpanzees, however, is not that they cannot make a requisite roster of sounds, they just cannot do so as an act of will.

[22]Donald, 1991:39.

[23]Mellars et al., 1993:8.

[24]Hymes, 1964:104; Swadesh, 1971:1; Hockett, 1978.

[25]Woodward, 1921; Hrdlička, 1926.

[26]Singer, 1958.

[27]Clark, 1976:528.

[28]Partridge, 1982.

[29]Beset by the compulsion to classify, traditional anthropolgists have obviously had their problems with specimens that are right between well-established categories. The Kabwe specimen has been called *Homo "rhodesiensis"* (Woodward, 1921), *"Cyphanthropus"* (Pycraft, 1928), *Homo erectus* (Coon, 1962:337—actually Coon was inconsistent in his designation, see p. 625ff.), *Homo sapiens rhodesiensis* (Rightmire, 1984), and most recently, it has been invested with the attributes of the

nonexistent Mauer skull and called *Homo "heidelbergensis"* (Rightmire, 1990:229). I must admit that, in the first edition of this book, I called it "an African Neanderthal" (1967:94), which would have made it *Homo sapiens*. But there it is: more than a Pithecanthropine, certainly not Modern, but just not well-enough endowed with brains and evidence for cultural development to warrant inclusion with the archaic manifestations of *sapiens*. Like other specimens from the same stretch of time, it represents a transition in the course of taking place.

[30]Drennan, 1953, 1955.

[31]Singer, 1958.

[32]Singer and Wymer, 1968.

[33]Coon, 1962:620.

[34]Klein, 1988:500.

[35]Rightmire, 1988:252–53.

[36]Khatri, 1963.

[37]Sonakia, 1985.

[38]Clark, 1993:150.

[39]Sonakia (1985) called it *erectus* in his first description, but ceded to his co-authors and allowed it to be called an archaic form of *sapiens* in a more recent study (Kennedy et al., 1991). Of course, "archaic" *Homo sapiens* is just what a Neanderthal is, and this just might qualify as an Indian Neanderthal. The specimen is simply too incomplete to make a decision.

[40]Oppenoorth, 1932.

[41]The lack of properly trained scholars in Southeast Asia during the 1930s and the outbreak of war delayed the description of the Solo material for some time. One specimen was even taken back to Kyoto by the invading Japanese, where it was found among the imperial possessions after the war ended in 1945. From there, it was sent to the American Museum of Natural History in New York to be reunited with the rest of the collection that was being worked up by Franz Weidenreich—himself doubly a refugee: first from Hitler's Germany in the early 1930s and later from Beijing in 1941 when the Japanese invaded China. Weidenreich was well into his usual splendid comparative treatment when he died suddenly, literally as he was in the middle of a sentence (from the Introduction by G. H. R. von Koenigswald, pp. 211–14, and the Foreword by Harry L. Shapiro, pp. 205–6, to Weidenreich, 1951). Weidenreich's monograph was published as he had left it, incomplete sentence and all. He had not written the major interpretive section, which means that this has been left to more recent but less perceptive students, for example, Santa Luca (1980).

[42]Although the skulls are great robust and reinforced phenomena, the average brain size is 1,151 cc. (Holloway, 1982) compared to a size of just over 1,000 cc. for late *erectus* (calculated from Weidenreich, 1943) and just under 1,350 cc. as an average for the living populations of *Homo sapiens* (Tobias, 1971:43).

[43]There continues to be a great deal of confusion and indecision over Pleistocene dates in Java, and a systematic investigation is badly in need (see a report of some of the recent disagreements noted in Eijgenraam, 1993).

[44]Wu and Wu, 1985:91.

[45]Wu and Wang, 1985:41; Wu and Wu, 1985:94.

[46]Frayer et al., 1993:25.

[47]Day cites a thermoluminescence date of 225,000 years (1986:20).

[48]Ovey (ed.), 1964; Day, 1986:19–25.

[49]Just for example: Howells, 1959:201; Montagu, 1960:232; Howell, 1965:107; Campbell, 1966:348.

[50]Brace, 1964:10–11, 34–35.

[51]Sergi, 1953:67; Weiner and Campbell, 1964:193.

[52]Berckhemer, 1933; Weinert, 1936.

[53]Wolpoff, 1980:348; Adam, 1985:275.

[54]Kokkoros and Kanellis, 1960; Poulianos, 1967. The small cavern in the main cave has been called, appropriately enough, the "Mausoleum" (Latham and Schwarcz, 1992:135).

[55]Kokkoros and Kanellis, 1960:445.

[56]Hennig et al., 1981; Stringer, 1988; Latham and Schwarcz, 1992:140.

[57]Stringer et al., 1979; Rightmire, 1990:216, 224, 227.

[58]Murrill, 1981. Recently, the use of a sophisticated morphometric approach plotting the thin-plate spline transformations of Petralona and Kabwe cranial outlines into a mean Neanderthal outline has shown that the key change is in the enlargement of the braincase (Yaroch, 1994). Both in mean shape decomposition and comparison of the geometrically independent partial warps, Petralona and Kabwe are significantly farther removed from modern form than are mean Neanderthals. This should have been obvious just using linear measures, but it is particularly convincing when demonstrated by the computation of Cartesian deformation.

[59]Brace, 1992, in press (d). These general expectations are right in line with the latest attempt to synthesize the approach of population genetics and the indications from the available mtDNA evidence, although there is still a possible discrepancy in the dates suggested. In any case, "The suggestion is that Culture rather than biology drove the burst of growth of our ancestors" (Harpending et al., 1993:495.

chapter thirteen

The Neanderthal Stage

FINDING AND DATING THE NEANDERTHALS

Of all human fossils known, Neanderthals have generated the most public interest, serving as the prototype of the cartoon "cave man." Figure 13–1 illustrates this image. Somewhat ironically, now that the reading public has finally gotten to the point where it is willing to accept the hominid record as indicative of the course of human evolution, it is the professional anthropologists who have tended to become uneasy at the possibility of discovering a Neanderthal skeleton in the *sapiens* closet.[1] However, if one accepts the Pithecanthropines as being a Stage of human evolution,[2] it is difficult to get from there to Modern form without going by way of something that must be regarded as Neanderthal.[3] Add to this the occurrence of Neanderthals in some quantities in the time immediately prior to the earliest reliably dated appearance of humans of Modern form, then the probability that Neanderthals were our ancestors is greatly increased (see Figure 13–2).

Prehistoric research has been going on longer in western Europe than anywhere else, so it is no surprise to find that evidence for the evolutionary stage immediately prior to ourselves was first discovered and named in Europe and that more Neanderthal remains have been discovered there than anywhere else—starting with the first recognized specimen in 1856, which

FIGURE 13–1.
This is an attempt to depict the mental image held by most professional paleoanthropologists of a "typical" Neanderthal, the classic "cave man"—leopard skin, club, and all—dimly peering at a world that is largely beyond his comprehension. In fact, the Neanderthals almost certainly had more effective weapons and clothing, and there is reason to believe that they were at least as intelligent as modern humans, if not more so.

gave its name to the whole Stage. One of the consequences of this is that the accepted stereotype of Neanderthal form is dominated almost entirely by European Neanderthals.[4] If there is any truth to our expectation that the course of human change through time has been one of regional continuity, then it would be most unrealistic to expect that the pre-Modern ancestors of the Chinese, Africans, Australians and so forth should look like European Neanderthals. A Chinese Neanderthal should show characteristics that foretell the Modern inhabitants of China, which is indeed the case for the two specimens available,[5] and an African Neanderthal should foretell Modern African form[6]—each, of course, with the appropriate manifestations of surviving Middle Pleistocene robustness.

It has taken the better part of a century for the various areas of interest that constitute the science of prehistory to mature. In the meantime, many discoveries have been made that could not be treated adequately because of the limitations of the times: stratigraphy was not controlled; faunal or cultural associations were not recorded; absolute dates could not be determined; and so on. Consequently, despite the quantity of Neanderthals from Europe, virtually none of the major specimens had been precisely placed in time. The best that could be done was to associate them with the Mousterian tool-making tradition. Now, however, these can be dated by using modern techniques to a time span ranging from approximately 35,000 years ago back

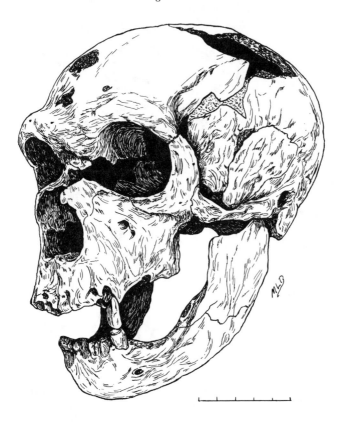

FIGURE 13–2.   La Chapelle-aux-Saints, one of the most frequently depicted Neanderthal skulls. It is a very large and robust male specimen, and, as such, an extreme rather than a typical representative of "classic" Neanderthal form. (Drawn by M. L. Brace in the Musée de l'Homme, Paris, from the new reconstruction of J-L. Heim.)

beyond the last interglacial and into the next-to-last glaciation some 250,000+ years ago.[7]

Mousterian hearths at the southwestern French site of Pech de l'Azé have been dated to over 250,000 years ago.[8] Mammal teeth from the famous site of La Chapelle-aux-Saints, presumed to be at the same level as the human burial, have yielded an ESR date of over 55,000 years ago.[9] Carbon dates for the late "Neanderthal" site of Hortus just north of Montpellier in southeastern France range from 35,000 to 39,000 years ago,[10] although the only reason the specimens were called "Neanderthal" was because they were found in a Mousterian context—the dentition cannot be distinguished from early Upper Paleolithic "Moderns" either in size or morphology.[11]

Finally, the most recent "Neanderthal" from western Europe is the 1979 discovery of a female skeleton from Saint-Césaire in the Charente-Maritime of southwestern France.[12] The skeletal remains were found in a Châtelperronian cultural layer—an early Upper Paleolithic tool-making tradition that had evolved out of the late Mousterian[13]—and they have yielded a TL date of 36,000 years ago.[14] Although it has been referred to as "a Neanderthal through and through" and "not a transitional form nor with any signs of mixture",[15] this would seem to be more of an expression of wishful thinking than anything generated from an examination of the specimen itself.

Here I am including a tooth-size profile graph comparing the dental dimensions of early Neanderthals, the "classic" Neanderthals of 50,000 years ago, Saint-Césaire, early Upper Paleolithic and Modern Europeans to show that Saint-Césaire is dentally indistinguishable from the "Moderns" of the early Upper Paleolithic and obviously reduced from full Neanderthal status (see Figure 13–3). An assessment of the details of dental morphology leads to the same conclusions.[16] In fact, as with the Hortus material, if the jaws and teeth had been found in an Aurignacian context, they would have been considered early "Modern" without a second thought. Only the swelling at the center of the brow has led people to assume that Saint-Césaire was a Neanderthal, and that in itself is not out of the Modern range of variation, although, admittedly, Moderns who have brow ridges that large are almost always males (see Figure 13–4). But then, that is just the consequence of the reductions in both male and female robustness that have taken place during the last 35,000 years.

FIGURE 13–3.   Tooth-size profiles of early Neanderthals, "classic" Neanderthals, Saint-Césaire, early Upper Paleolithic, and Modern European (French) samples.

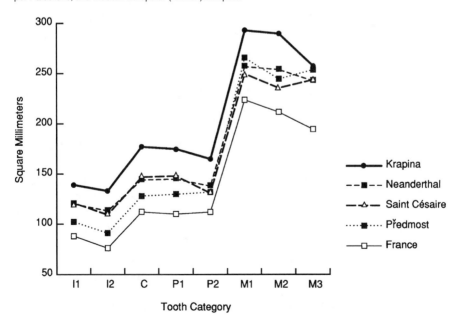

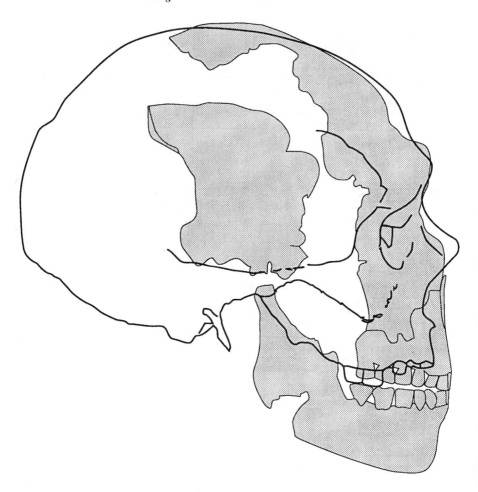

FIGURE 13–4. Cranoifacial outline of a medieval Norwegian male compared with Saint-Césaire adjusted so that facial height is the same.

Absolute dating of Neanderthal skeletal material has also been made at sites in the Middle East, several in Israel (including Tabūn and Kebara) and one in Iraq (Shanidar). On the basis of ¹⁴C determinations, Shanidar (Figure 13–5) can be dated to somewhere between 40,000 to 60,000 years ago.[17] The surprise has come from recently run dates for Tabūn. Previous efforts, based on the use of ¹⁴C, tended to put it into the 50,000 year range.[18] This would be comfortably similar to the dates for "classic" Neanderthals in Europe, but newer attempts to date the sediments from the cave by using ESR and TL have upped the antiquity by orders of magnitude. The strata now can be shown to extend from somewhat less than 100,000 back to more than 350,000 years ago.[19] The problem now is that there is no way to go back and pinpoint

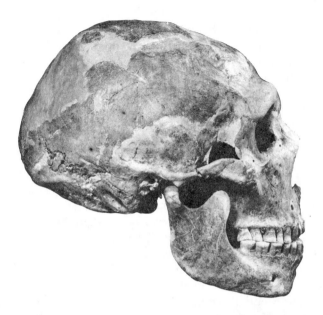

FIGURE 13–5.   The skull of Shanidar I, a classic Neanderthal from Iraq. (Courtesy of the Iraq Museum, Baghdad.)

just where in that span the crucial Tabūn Neanderthal skeleton was located, although there is some feeling that it belongs in the 110,000 year range.[20]

At Kebara, there is a TL date of 48,000 to 60,000 years.[21] Some of the classic European sites have been dated recently using the TL technique, and, as a result, some of the old assumptions about cultural relationships and sequence during the Mousterian have had to be revised. The original site of Le Moustier itself has been shown to extend from 40,000 years ago back to 55,000 years ago,[22] but another site not far away and long thought to be contemporary, Combe Grenal, has been said to be between 55,000 and 115,000 years ago.[23] This has cast doubt on some of the traditional assertions of contemporaneity and temporal relationships based solely on the traditional assessment of artifact types. At the moment, more than a little uncertainty remains, but it is being cleared up with the application of the new dating techniques to the rest of the tool assemblages that we once thought we knew so well.

NEANDERTHAL OR "NEANDERTAL"?

Before we go on to deal with the substantive issues of Neanderthal form, we should take a moment to consider the matter of how to spell the name. It may seem like a relatively trivial matter, but the paleoanthropologists who are actually involved with the study and interpretation of the skeletal evidence are a thin-skinned lot who are quick to take offense at differing opinions and ever on the lookout to seize a point, however minor, on which to register disapproval of a perceived rival. One such situation concerns the spelling of Neanderthal. The word actually means "Neander's valley" where "Neander" was the name of a seventeenth century German preacher and hymn writer,[24] and "Thal" was the German word for valley. So far, so good. Now, written German, like the even worse case of written English, is afflicted with a plethora of letters that are not pronounced. One of these is the "h" in "Thal." English is the only European language in which "th" actually has a pronunciation that differs from "t." In both German and French, for example, "Thal" is pronounced as "Tal" where the "al" portion is sounded as it is in Allah.

In 1901, there was a formal revision of German orthography, and, among the changes, it was decreed that henceforth "Thal" would be spelled "Tal" (the initial letter in all German nouns is capitalized).[25] This has been done, more or less, although many a locality has retained the former spelling, and German road signs today are equally split.[26]

At the midpoint of the twentieth century, Marcellin Boule's protégé and successor in Paris, Henri V. Vallois, urged that paleoanthropology follow suit and discard the "h" in Neanderthal, rendering it "Neandertal."[27] Many anthropologists have adopted his recommendation. Of course, where the name is part of a formal Latin taxonomic designation such as *Homo sapiens neanderthalensis* or even, as the resurgent splitters prefer, *Homo* "*neanderthalensis,*" the first spelling would have to be retained under the rules of the International Code of Zoological Nomenclature.

There is no formal rule of taxonomy that governs colloquial usage, so there is nothing incorrect about spelling the fossil "Neandertal." But it was "Neanderthal" when it was discovered, and, analogous to the formal taxonomic situation, I simply prefer to continue using Neanderthal today.[28] Besides, it has a nice archaic appearance in print.

NEANDERTHALS AS THE "ARCHAIC" ANCESTORS OF MODERN *HOMO SAPIENS*

Although many anthropologists deny that anything so "primitive" as a Neanderthal could be ancestral to Modern form,[29] they feel constrained to recognize an ancestral situation that shows features that are less than fully Modern. This is often termed "Archaic *Homo sapiens.*" In the course of time, this—dare one call it "Stage"?—gave rise to "Anatomically Modern *Homo sapiens*" (some authors prefer to call the latter, "Morphologically Modern *H.s.*"),[30] although the processes and dynamics by which this change took place are never considered. Then, since many scholars have allowed Neanderthals to be classified as *Homo sapiens,* and furthermore because of the retention of Middle

Pleistocene levels of skeletomuscular robustness, they conclude that fossils identifiable as Neanderthals can be called archaic *Homo sapiens*.

At this point, however, the syllogism collapses. Although they accept the idea that the ancestors of anatomically Modern *Homo sapiens* were archaic *Homo sapiens,* they simply cannot bring themselves to allow that Neanderthals, even though they are good card-carrying members of Archaic *Homo sapiens,* could in fact be ancestral to anatomically Modern *Homo sapiens.* The classic syllogism of deductive logic goes like this: all crows are black; Felix is a crow; ergo, Felix is black. Somehow, however, the modern representatives of hominid catastrophism, even though they are the heirs to the deductive essentialism of medieval neoplatonism, just cannot bring themselves to accept the simple logic of the parallel fossil hominid syllogism: ancestors of anatomically Modern *Homo sapiens* were archaic *Homo sapiens;* Neanderthals were archaic *Homo sapiens;* ergo, Neanderthals represent ancestors of anatomically modern *Homo sapiens.*

The very name "Neanderthal" seems to strike a kind of reflexive fear in their hearts, attaining the status of a veritable bogeyman. Modern ancestors were archaic; Neanderthals were archaic, too, but somehow just a bit too archaic.[31] The arguments are usually couched in terms of summary generalizations and rarely, if ever, get down to the business of dealing with the actual quantified evidence when Neanderthal vis-à-vis Modern form is dealt with.

We have actually tried to do some of this. From an analysis of two dozen craniofacial measurements on over 5,000 human skulls from all over the world, we can see that there are eight regionally identifiable clusters of Modern human populations (see Figure 13–6).[32] If we take representatives of each of these and plot their major cranial dimensions on a graph along with the known Neanderthal specimens, we can see that the cranial proportions of Modern northwest Europeans are closer to the northwest European Neanderthal cranial proportions than to any of the other living representatives of Modern *Homo sapiens.* The Cro-Magnon figure falls right in between the Neanderthal and the northwest European ones.[33] This fits nicely with our expectations of regional continuity.

Then if we generate a cladogram using European Neanderthals, Modern northwest Europeans, and representatives of other major regional populations of Modern *Homo sapiens,* we see essentially the same picture. Eleven character states were used as basic data, and the cladogram was generated by using a computer program entitled Phylogenetic Analysis Using Parsimony (PAUP).[34] The choice of the character states and the weighting assigned is more than a bit subjective, as is always the case for cladistic analysis, but the results are remarkably similar to those that are based on the quantitative analysis of craniofacial measurements: Modern northwestern Europeans and the Cro-Magnon skull fall closer to classic Neanderthal form than to Moderns from Asia and Australia (see Figure 13–7).[35] We suspect that if we actually had Neanderthal representatives from the other parts of the world, they

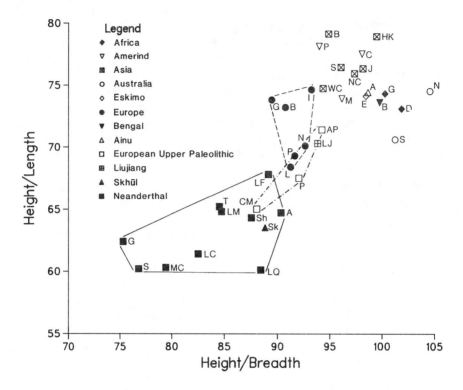

FIGURE 13–6. Cranial height/length and height/breadth proportions in a series of Neanderthal specimens compared to the averages in a series of Modern and Upper Paleolithic populations. Africa: G=Gabon, D=Dahomey; Amerind: C=California, M=Michigan, P=Peru; Asia: B=Burma, HK=Hong Kong, J=Japan, NC=North China, S=Shanghai, WC=West China; Australia: N=North, S=South; Eskimo; Europe: B=Breton, G=Germany, I=Italy, L=London, N=Norway, P=Paris; India; Jōmon-Pacific: A=Ainu; India; European Upper Paleolithic: AP=Abri Pataud, P=Předmost, CM=Cro-Magnon; Chinese Upper Paleolithic: LJ=Jiujiang; Neanderthaloid: Sk= Skhūl; Neanderthal: A=Amud, G=Gibraltar, LC=La; Chapelle-aux-Saints: LF=La Ferrassie, LM=Le Moustier, MC=Monte Circeo, S=Saccopastore, Sh=Shanidar, T= Tabūn. (Brace, 1991.)

would show continuity with the Modern inhabitants in each of the relevant areas to a greater extent than with Moderns from Europe.

NEANDERTHAL FORM: BELOW THE NECK

To consider the form of the Neanderthals, one must start by dispensing with the hairy, slouching beast, tramping through the Ice Age snow drifts clad only in a loincloth, and not quite able to stand erect. Although there are minor differences between the pelves of the known Neanderthals and those of modern humans, there is no evidence to indicate that their posture was any less erect than that of ourselves. The human line has stood upright since the Australopithecine Stage, and any attempt to inflict the Neanderthals with a "bent-knee

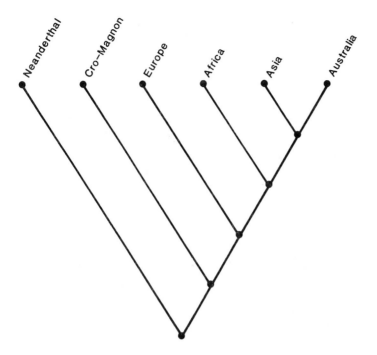

FIGURE 13–7.   A cladogram showing the relationship of Neanderthal, Cro-Magnon, and various regionally located modern crania, constructed from the character states indicated in the table and generated by the PAUP program. (Brace, 1991.)

gait" is simply a survival of the efforts on the part of early interpreters to view all aspects of Neanderthal anatomy as being "primitive" or apelike. (This also involved the incorrect assumption that apes cannot straighten their legs at the knee).[36] From the neck down, the main difference between Neanderthal and Modern form is in the indications of generally greater ruggedness in Neanderthal joints and muscles.[37] As with the Pithecanthropines, the demands imposed by a Middle Pleistocene hunting way of life continued into the early part of the Late Pleistocene. This is reflected in the continued existence of a powerfully developed skeletomuscular system, particularly in the males. When one compares this to the modern situation, it is evident that this is more an average difference in degree rather than one in kind.

From an assessment of the skeletal evidence, it is evident that "all regions and most bones" display "a most impressive aspect of . . . robusticity."[38] The ribs were rounder in cross section than the flatter and more ribbonlike Modern ribs, and the heavy torso is regularly described as having been equipped with a "barrel-shaped chest." When the lower legs were examined in regard to torsional and bending strength, it was found that they were "*twice*

TABLE 13–1 Character States for a Series of Craniofacial Features for Selected Groups of Modern and Prehistoric Human Crania

Character State	Weight	Africa	Asia	Australia	Cro-Magnon	Europe	Neanderthal
Glabella Salience	(5)	3	3	2	2	2	1
Nasal Bridge Elevation	(1)	3	2	3	1	1	1
Position of Cranial Width	(5)	2	3	3	1	1	1
Cranial Height/Length	(5)	2	3	3	1	1	1
Cranial Height/Width	(5)	2	3	3	1	1	1
Mastoid Size	(4)	2	3	2	1	1	1
Mastoid Inward Slope	(5)	2	3	2	1	1	1
Occipital Bun	(5)	2	3	3	2	2	1
Nuchal Attachment	(2)	2	3	3	2	2	1
Incisor/Molar Size	(3)	3	2	3	1	1	1
Incisor Shovelling	(1)	3	1	2	1	3	1

as strong as the modern sample."[39] Examination of the arm bones with the aid of X-rays showed that the bony cortex was especially thick in proportion to the total cross-sectional area.[40] Muscle attachments in the hand, arm, and shoulder suggest that arm strength was markedly greater than in living human beings. In this particular instance, there is no categorical distinction between Neanderthal and Modern because the early Upper Paleolithic representatives of "Modern" *Homo sapiens* characteristically are more robust than living humans but less so than Neanderthals and have a configuration of shoulder-muscle attachments that is perfectly intermediate.[41]

One post-cranial detail has led to a recent round of speculation and discussion. This is the fact that, while most of the post-cranial skeleton differs from modern form simply in being more robust, the superior branch *(ramus)* of the forward part of the pelvis, the pubic bone, seems curiously elongated.[42] In the female pelvis, this has the effect of enlarging the birth canal, and it has led one otherwise respected anthropologist to the unlikely conclusion that pregnancy in Neanderthal women lasted a full year instead of the normal human nine months.[43] For this to have been the case, it would mean that the Neanderthals had departed even further than Modern humans from the developmental patterns and timing of our closest primate relatives, but all the available pieces of relevant information suggest that Neanderthal patterns of growth and development were essentially the same as those of living humans.[44] The possibility remains, however, that the elongated superior pelvic ramus was necessary to allow passage of a relatively large newborn, albeit one whose size was not necessarily the consequence of a prolonged pregnancy.

In a recent study, Karen Rosenberg of the University of Delaware has demonstrated that no such unlikely deviation from the normally expected human biological condition need be postulated to account for what can be observed, although it may indeed be related to the birth of relatively large babies. The Neanderthals were extraordinarily robust for their stature—something that we have, in fact, known for over a century—and people who are robust for their stature develop from and in turn produce relatively large newborn infants. The superior ramus of the pelvis in modern human populations in whom the robustness-to-stature ratio is especially high, such as the Eskimo, deviate from the average modern human condition in just the direction that can be seen in its extreme manifestation in the Neanderthals.[45]

This situation may be a special feature associated with life in the North since, in living human populations for example, the comparable portion of the pelvis is longer in people of European than of African ancestry. European newborns are significantly heavier than babies of African ancestry even when the mothers do not differ in comparable fashion.[46] We can guess that the heavier European neonate might reflect the continuing legacy of a northern Neanderthal heritage. Certainly a newborn baby on a cave floor in Ice Age Europe was at more than a little risk from the cold, and a bulkier infant would stand a considerably better chance of survival.

There is another aspect of post-cranial form in the Neanderthal samples that range between western Europe and the Middle East that clearly indicates an adaptive response to life in the cold. The ratio of body surface area to body bulk is even lower than it is for living Eskimos, and both are way below what is found in the elongated modern tropic-dwellers.[47] Body warmth is dissipated at the interface between the body surface and the ambient air, and a large relative surface area indicates a high capacity to rid the body of the heat generated by physical activity. This, of course, is a necessity in the tropics and has been characteristic of tropical hominids from the time of Strapping Youth at Nariokotome over 1.5 million years ago.

In the northern reaches of human habitation, the problem is not how to rid oneself of the metabolically generated heat load but how to retain as much of it as one can. This is made possible by reducing those portions of the body that emphasize surface at the expense of bulk—namely, the distal segments of the limbs. Both in Eskimos but even more markedly in Neanderthals, it is the distal segments of the limbs that are notably short.[48] Even though the early students of Neanderthal form such as Boule went overboard in trying to stress the "pithecoid" aspects of Neanderthal form, they could not ignore the fact that the arm from the elbow to the wrist and the leg from the knee to the ankle were remarkably short by Modern human standards. The Neanderthal specimens from the Middle East to western Europe are all hyper-northern in their proportions, and are clearly adapted to life in the cold.

NEANDERTHAL FORM: FROM THE NECK UP

Above the neck, however, the differences are far more marked and obvious. To be sure, the cranial measurements of some Neanderthals do not surpass those of some moderns, but other Neanderthals present an array of dimensions that cannot be matched in recently living people. These revolve around the dentition and associated facial areas where the Neanderthals do not differ functionally from the Pithecanthropines. All told, the Neanderthals are distinguished from the Pithecanthropines mainly by the possession of braincases of fully modern size, while they are distinct from Moderns in the possession of Pithecanthropine faces and teeth. In fact, the Neanderthal front teeth include the largest to be found in the whole picture of human evolution, although this may simply be due to the scarcity of specimens from the earlier stages.[49]

Discussions of the shape of the European Neanderthal skull have developed a positive mystique with a lore and vocabulary all its own. Aspects of morphology are described with the judgmental enthusiasm of the phrenologists of yesteryear and referred to as "specializations," although there is no remaining vestige of the implication of that term as it is used in evolutionary biology. The brow ridges are "heavy and brutal," the forehead is "fleeting," the skull as a whole is "low" and "primitive," and the rear is said to be characterized by a "bun-shaped" occiput with a veritable "chignon." The latter terms refer to the hair style favored by proper Victorian "ladies" who pinned their uncut tresses into a large knot at the back of the head.

The widest point of the skull was not at the level of the ear holes, as it was in the Pithecanthropines, nor up over the top of the ears, as it is supposed to be in "modern" humans, but half way up (or down) the sides giving the skull a rounded appearance—"en bombe," to use the French designation—when it is viewed from the rear. The neck muscles attached to a low double-arched ridge of bone beneath the rear looking rather like a Pleistocene predecessor of the McDonald's logo, and the mastoid processes behind and below the ear openings were small and inwardly sloping and equalled in prominence by the paramastoid eminences on the inside of the digastric grooves. Above the neck muscle attachments on the rear of the skull was a "supra-iniac depression."[50]

As observations, these are all perfectly accurate if quaintly derogatory. The problem comes with the assumption that these are "specializations" peculiar to the Neanderthals, which distinguish them from living human populations. To be sure, many of these features are slightly more extreme in Neanderthals than in Modern humans, especially if the Neanderthal used is the the most exaggerated and improperly reconstructed of the known specimens, as is the case for La Chapelle-aux-Saints, but the problem is that those who recite these Neanderthal "peculiarities" do not have the faintest familiarity with Modern human cranial form and its variations.

As it happens, that configuration, run off as a litany to Neanderthal form, also serves to describe just how the living people at the northwestern fringe of Europe today differ from virtually all of the other people in the world.[51] If this cranial form is evident in Norwegians and the English it differs significantly from what is characteristic of the French and eastwards through central and eastern Europe. It can be shown statistically that the Cro-Magnon specimen, the supposed paragon of Modern morphology, also fits somewhere between Neanderthal and English cranial form, but it is a most unlikely ancestor for the French themselves.[52]

French cranial form tends to be shorter and higher in proportion to its length. This tendency becomes more pronounced as one goes east in Europe and reaches a maximum in Czechoslovakia and Hungary. At the same time, the rear of the skull becomes markedly flattened, the shortened area for neck muscle attachment often ends in a pronounced ridge with a hooklike thickening in the middle, and the mastoid processes behind and below the ears are thickened and enlarged. With cranial configuration displaying long-term continuity, it appears that if central and eastern Europeans had Neanderthal ancestors, they were Neanderthals who looked quite different from the western Neanderthals that have been the main contributors to our ideas about "typical" Neanderthal form.

So far, there have been no complete crania from Mousterian cultural levels found in central and eastern Europe. However, I have been privately predicting that when such discoveries are eventually made, we might well discover that cranial form was shorter and higher than the form accepted for western Europe. At one time, the extensive but fragmentary Neanderthal remains from Krapina in Croatia, excavated by the remarkable paleontologist Karl Dragutin Gorjanović-Kramberger between 1899 and 1905, were represented as relatively broad-headed.[53] Subsequent efforts at reconstruction have shown that this clearly was not the case.[54]

But if that form has yet to be discovered in eastern Europe, it has recently been demonstrated in splendid fashion in southwestern Europe. In the summer of 1992, three skulls and a quantity of Pleistocene mammal remains were found in the Sima de los Huesos, a cave in the limestone hills (the Sierra de Atapuerca) near Burgos in northern Spain.[55] (See Figure 13–8.) No stone tools were found with the human remains, and the nature of the deposits does not allow the assignation of a date more accurate than the

FIGURE 13–8.   Atapuerca 5, a Spanish Neanderthal. (Drawn by Kay Clahassey after Arsuaga et al., 1993.)

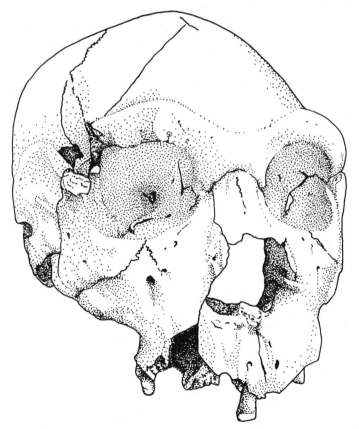

suggestion that it is somewhere in the range between 100,000 and 300,000 years ago.[56]

Dental measurements have been published, however, and these ally the human material with the later Neanderthals and not with fully Middle Pleistocene Pithecanthropines.[57] The cranial shape, however, is not long and low like the stereotypic European Neanderthals, but remarkably short and high.[58] The mastoid processes, instead of being small and inwardly sloping, are large and robust, and the ridge marking the extent of the neck muscle attachments runs straight across the rear of the skull just as it does in so many of the living people in central and eastern Europe today.

To be sure, northern Spain is not central Europe, but then expectations of regional continuity do not require that people remain rooted to one locally circumscribed area for 100,000 years or so without periodically expanding or contracting their living area. Just knowing that there was a Neanderthal population in Europe by the end of the Middle Pleistocene that had the same idiosyncratic cranial features that now characterize a major block of modern Europeans is interesting enough. Better information on dating, cultural affiliations, and population relationships and movements will come in due course.

NEANDERTHAL NOSES

Much has been made of the size of the nose in the northern Neanderthals,[59] and indeed it is the one part of the facial skeleton that shows a degree of development not present in any of the known Pithecanthropines. It is more than coincidental, however, that the Modern human populations who live in the areas once inhabited by those northern Neanderthals are distinguishable from the rest of the populations of the world by the possession of especially elevated and elongated noses. Of course, the Modern nasal aperture is not nearly so wide as that of the Neanderthals, but, as the late Carleton Coon so aptly put it, "narrowness was impossible for Neanderthals because of the size of his front teeth."[60] And, indeed, in modern humans with the largest front teeth, such as the original inhabitants of Australia, the width of the nasal aperture is especially notable.[61]

In living human populations, those whose ancestors have long inhabited the drier portions of the world are those who display the longest and most elevated nasal passages. One thinks of desert areas as being dry, and indeed the long-term inhabitants of the drier parts of East Africa and the Arabian peninsula are noted for long and elevated nasal skeletons.[62] What is sometimes overlooked, however, is the fact that the moisture carrying capacity of the atmosphere drops with temperature, and there is precious little water in the air in the colder parts of the world. Since inspired air has to reach the saturation point before oxygen and carbon dioxide can be exchanged in the lungs,[63] moisture has to be supplied to that air by the nasal epithelium and the respiratory tract. Modern human populations with a long-time association with the colder parts of the world all show elongations of that moisture producing apparatus most visibly represented by the external nose.[64]

One would expect the same thing to have been true in the past, and indeed it is. The long-term Pleistocene inhabitants of the northern portions of the Old World—the northern Neanderthals—are just those populations in whom we see the greatest elevation and elongation of the nasal skeletons. Almost perversely, however, this adaptive scenario has been rejected by one of those most familiar with the details of Neanderthal anatomy—the very person who has reinforced the view that major aspects of Neanderthal anatomy represent modifications to aid heat conservation as one might predict for those who had adapted to survive the repeated glacial influence in the northern parts of the Old World during the latter part of the Pleistocene.

According to Erik Trinkaus of the University of New Mexico, the Neanderthal nose was "a system for dissipating excess body heat, while retaining body moisture" and "not adaptation to cold."[65] Somehow the vision of "hyperactive hominids" flailing aimlessly "over the landscape" and panting like dogs to dissipate their body heat while at the same time somehow reclaiming the water whose evaporation was essential to that very heat reduction conjures up a picture that is both a hilarious caricature and a physiological impossibility.[66]

Inspired air gains moisture and heat from the airway so that it will be warm and saturated when it gets to the lungs. As it goes out, it returns much of that heat to the airways as its moisture condenses. There is some body heat lost with the expiration of water-laden air, but it amounts to just over ten percent of normal heat loss, and this reduces drastically when the individual is at stress to dissipate its heat load.[67] The only time that significant condensation occurs in the nose is when the upper respiratory tract is already cool, and of course that condensation represents retention of heat in the body and not its dissipation. This is why noses drip in the winter. It strains belief to imagine Neanderthals tilting their heads so that their runny noses dribbled down into their mouths, thereby enabling them to conserve a significant amount of body water. Or maybe that large nasal skeleton was clothed with a fleshy and pendulous proboscis that could be sucked between the lips. Science this is not, and it is even more fantasy than science fiction.

It seems most reasonable to regard the northern Neanderthal nose, like the noses of living people with long-term associations with the North, as a device for helping to warm and moisten inspired air. One would not expect African Neanderthals to have noses like their northern counterparts, and the only two available examples—Ngaloba in Tanzania (Figures 13–9 and 13–10) and Jebel Ighoud from Morocco (Figure 13–11)—indeed lack northern noses. The two extant Chinese specimens—Maba and Jinniu Shan—also lack the kind of nasal elevation and elongation of the European Neanderthals, and one could legitimately ask why, since they are essentially at the same lati-

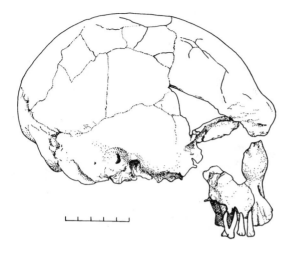

FIGURE 13–9. Ngaloba (Laetoli 18), an African Neanderthal from Tanzania. (Drawn by Kay Clahassey after Day, 1986.)

FIGURE 13–10. Omo II, "Homo Omo," an African Neanderthal from southern Ethiopia. (Drawn with the help of Kay Clahassey after Day, 1986.)

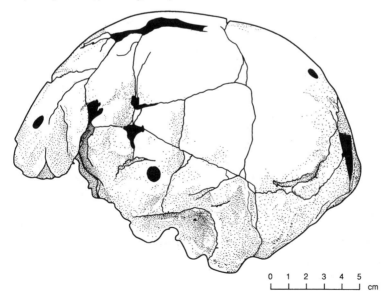

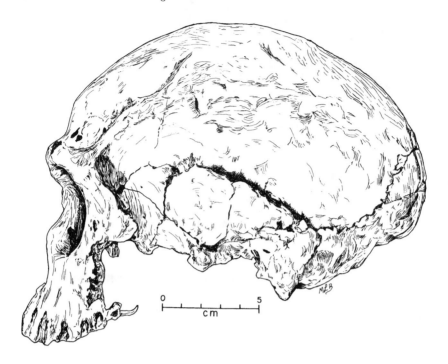

FIGURE 13–11.   Jebel Ighoud, a North African Neanderthal from Morocco. (Drawn by M. L. Brace, from Brace et al., 1979.)

tudes (see Figure 13–12). At the moment, the answer can only be something of a guess, but it is a guess worth tendering.

So far there is no archaeological evidence that inhabitants remained in the northern parts of eastern Asia throughout the intensification of cold that occurred with the penultimate glaciation. They were certainly there during the last glaciation, but not in the preceding one—at least as far as the evidence proves. The problem of negative evidence here may be partially influenced by the fact that there simply has been less attention paid to Pleistocene archaeology in China. But if we look at a couple of other indicators, we also get hints that the ancestors of the Modern inhabitants of the northeast part of the Old World have not been there for as long as has been the case for the inhabitants of Europe. The greater nasal development of Temperate Zone Europeans past and present may well be because they have had longer to respond to the selective forces characteristic of that latitude. One can add the observation that the greater extent of pigment loss in Europe and the greater relative degree of dental reduction also reflect a longer stay in place, but further investigation of this is yet to come.

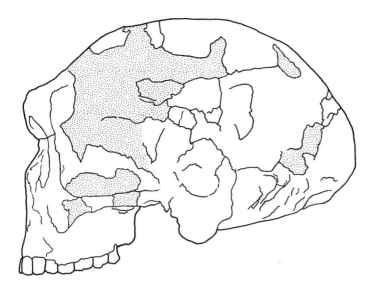

FIGURE 13–12. Jinniushan, a Chinese Neanderthal drawn by Kay Clahassey after Lü (1990).

NEANDERTHALS AND THE MOUSTERIAN

But what is a Neanderthal? In the typological mind-set of orthodox paleoanthropology, Neanderthal obviously is an essence conjured up by the contemplation of the La Chapelle-aux-Saints specimen described by Marcellin Boule. William of Occam would recognize this as a creation of the human imagination for its own purposes. This in turn brings to mind the biblical reflection on human identity, the basis for this description:

> But what is Neanderthal the We are mindful of "him"?
> and the son of Neanderthal who in fact may be ourselves?
> For We have made him little more than the bestial
> and debased him with contempt and dishonor.[68]

Some sort of agreement concerning the subject is needed; consider this as a tentative definition: "Neanderthals are the people associated with the Mousterian culture, and its temporal and technological equivalents, just before the reductions in form and size of the Middle Pleistocene skeleto-muscular system."[69] Middle Pleistocene levels of robustness and muscularity were still evident, but, because of the selective force changes that followed as a consequence of some specific aspects of that Mousterian culture, these were destined to undergo the reductions that led to the emergence of Modern form.[70] The brain, however, was already fully modern in size and, presumably, function.

Because part of the definition is in fact cultural, we next have to take a closer look at what is under consideration. The term "Mousterian" comes from the village of Le Moustier in southwestern France, where the type site is located.[71] Tools of Mousterian form are distributed throughout western and eastern Europe into southern Russia—the Crimea, the Caucasus, and Uzbekistan—and southern Europe east through the Balkans into the Middle East (see Figure 13–13). Throughout this whole area, which we could call the

FIGURE 13–13. A collection of Mousterian tools: (a,b) side-scrapers (racloirs); (c) disc-core, and (d) point, from the rock-shelter at Le Moustier near Peyzac (Dordogne); (e) small anvil or hammer-stone (pebble of ferruginous grit), Gibraltar caves; (f) hand-axe from Le Moustier; (g) hand-axe (chert), and (h) oval flake-tool (flint), from Kent's Cavern, Torquay. Items a-d are typical Mousterian; item f is a sample of Mousterian of Acheulian tradition; and items g and h are of Acheulo-Levalloisian tradition. (Courtesy of the British Museum of Natural History.)

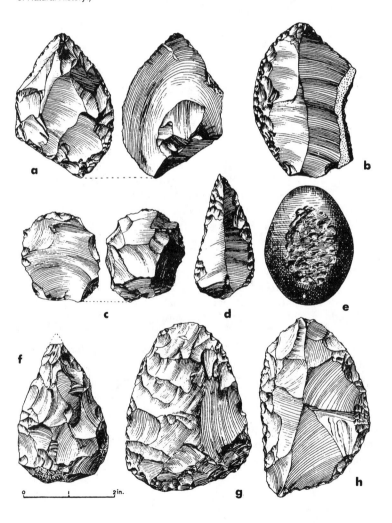

Mousterian culture area, there were a series of hunting-and-gathering bands possessing related cultures between which similar cultural elements maintained circulation.[72] Local differences in details of typology and technique of manufacture persisted, but all these subcultures possessed the same functional tool categories: scrapers, points, and knives.

Scrapers indicate a concern for the preparation of animal hides, which is reasonable for people living in a subarctic climate. It used to be thought that effective clothing was not developed until the ensuing Upper Paleolithic, with the invention and manufacture of bone needles, but there is no reason to deny the Neanderthals the use of skin clothing just because they had no needles: wrapped clothing bound on by thongs was utilized by the poorer peoples of Europe right up to historical times. Certainly the Neanderthals must have been doing something with the skins they went to so much trouble to prepare, and it is reasonable to suppose that the manufacture of clothing was one such thing. Indeed, human survival in Europe during the last glaciation without clothing would have been impossible.

The Mousterian, as it was traditionally defined, is a northern and western archaeological phenomenon, and if we postulate a general Neanderthal Stage as a predecessor of Modern human form elsewhere throughout the Old World, a brief word is in order concerning the "temporal and technological" equivalents mentioned in our definition.[73] In both Africa and India, there are tool-making traditions of the Late Pleistocene referred to as the "Middle Stone Age,"[74] and there are stone tools of similar date and sophistication in China continuing through Mongolia.[75] These are later in time than the "hand-axe" cultures of the Lower Paleolithic throughout the Old World, and they predate the equivalents of the Upper Paleolithic and Mesolithic that appear towards the end of the Late Pleistocene. In general, they suggest that their makers pursued a subsistence strategy that differed from the Mousterian in only a couple of significant respects: one of these was the much lower frequency of scrapers in their tool assemblages, and this suggests that they lacked the focus on the preparation of skins for clothing that was so important in the area of the Mousterian *sensu stricto*.

TEETH AS TOOLS

The onset of the last glaciation must have increased the problem of simple survival for the inhabitants of the northern portions of the Old World. Chances of survival obviously would be improved as people increasingly attempted to manipulate and shape the natural world confronting them. Two factors indicate an increasing concern for manipulative behavior among the Neanderthals. One is the heavy, rounded wear that appears on their front teeth. In addition, the front teeth of the northern Neanderthals reach the maximum in size and morphological complexity that they achieve during the course of human evolution, evidently in response to the selective pressures that favored the development and maintenance of that anatomical manipulating device that could serve as "vise, pliers, clamp, snippers and so on"—"the original built-in."[76]

Part of that dental "complexity" involves the elevation of the lateral margins of the incisors on the inner or "lingual" side to create what has been called "shovel-shaped" teeth. This was the name given by the Czech-born American anthropologist, Aleš Hrdlička (1869–1943), who first observed that form on Native American teeth and later noted them on the teeth of Chinese, Japanese, and Mongolians.[77] As a result of Hrdlička's observations, there has been the general feeling ever since that shovel-shaped incisors were a "racial" marker that indicated eastern Asian ancestry. Hrdlička, however, noted that the shovel shape in conjunction with an enlarged lingual tubercle, or *tuburculum dentale,* made a stronger front tooth that was more resistant to wear than the simple blade generally observed in people of European ancestry. Hrdlička also noted the extreme development of both shovelling and lingual tubercles in the Neanderthal incisors from Krapina in Croatia, and he suggested that the Modern European condition most likely arose because of a decrease in usage of the teeth through time.[78]

His suggestion was right on the mark since the shovel is still present but much less marked in the latest "Neanderthals" from Hortus and Saint-Césaire, and a distinct lingual tubercle has effectively disappeared. That same configuration is also the case for the earliest "Moderns" from Předmost in Czechoslovakia. Subsequently the shovelling decreases through time in Europe from the end of the Pleistocene right up the present day where it also has effectively disappeared.[79] Shovel-shaped incisors, then, are not just a "racial" marker or an indication of specifically Asian ancestry—they were the common human condition as the Middle Pleistocene came to an end.

The one specimen in the Far East where incisor morphology can be assessed, the Chinese Neanderthal Jinniu Shan, clearly had possessed shovel-shaped incisors.[80] The front teeth are worn half-way down the crowns, but the obvious remnants of a ridge down both margins of the lingual faces of the incisors is easily seen. Why is this not just a specifically Asian trait rather than an indicator of the general human condition? The answer is that those worn incisors were not only shovel-shaped, but they also possessed large and functional lingual tubercles, and that trait has virtually disappeared from Modern Asian populations and their descendants. Where the adaptive aspects of front tooth form are concerned, European and Chinese Neanderthal incisors are indistinguishable. However, where essentially trivial features of face form are concerned, such as whether the outer edges of the eye sockets are close to the same plane as the root of the nose, Chinese Neanderthals resemble Modern Chinese and European Neanderthals resemble Modern Europeans.

Speaking of wear, even the casual observer cannot fail to be impressed by the extensive abrasion often found on Neanderthal front teeth, which are frequently eroded to such an extent that the entire enamel crown has been ground down so that the surviving worn stumps are just what remains of the roots.[81] Moreover, a detailed examination using a scanning electron microscope has revealed that the flaking and scratch marks on the enamel of worn tooth crowns is remarkably similar to that visible in recent Eskimos who are famous for the manipulative tasks to which they put their teeth.[82] The only difference is that the Neanderthal teeth display an even more extensive amount of chipping, flaking, and scratching on their enamel.[83]

The survival value of manipulative behavior is easy enough to appreciate, and, eventually, the use of the teeth as all-purpose tools begins to give way to the employment of tools especially manufactured for particular purposes. This becomes much more obvious as the Mousterian gives way to the Upper Paleolithic with its proliferation of special tool categories—and a reduction in the extent of heavy anterior tooth wear. This increasing substitution of technology for anatomy represented a reduction in the stringency of the forces of selection that had previously maintained the size and form of the anatomical elements in question—in this case, the teeth. The situation is a classic scenario for the operation of the Probable Mutation Effect, and it is no surprise to see an ensuing reduction of both the size and the morphological complexity of the teeth.[84]

BRAIN SIZE AND THE ORIGIN OF LANGUAGE

Some people have regarded it as puzzling that the human brain should have attained full size 150,000 years ago, or possibly more, and remained the same ever since. The argument has been advanced that, if intelligence has survival value, more intelligence should have greater survival value. The question remains, however, why intelligence as symbolized by brain size should have increased in the human lineage out of all proportion to its development in other creatures.

There have been some recent efforts to suggest that the stimulus was in trying to deal with and predict the future course of actions of those most challenging members of the organic world, other human beings.[85] The basic problem with this argument is that it is essentially circular. Cleverness is selected for because it helps in dealing with other people who are clever, but the other people are clever in order to deal with the cleverness that is present in those with whom they have dealings.

While there is no reason why this could not constitute one of the aspects of selection for increase in intelligence, there is the further point that the same argument should apply to virtually all other kinds of relatively clever animals. If intelligence was of value to the evolving human lineage, why was it not of equal value for the evolving lineage of the admittedly clever chimpanzees? And if for chimpanzees, why not equally so for leopards or jackals or any other such animals that evidently depend on their wits for survival? In fact, this argument probably does serve to explain the general increase in brain size observed in the Class Mammalia since the end of the Age of Reptiles.[86] However, it does not help explain why human brain size should have undergone a relative expansion that was orders of magnitude greater than that of even our brightest primate relatives.

Darwin's contemporary, and independent co-discoverer of the principle of natural selection, Alfred Russel Wallace (1823–1913), was convinced that human beings had more intelligence than they needed to survive, and, therefore, natural selection could not have been the agency by which intelligence developed.[87] The idea that human survival under conditions of technological simplicity required less innate wit has been a continuing theme,[88] but it seriously underestimates just how much brain power is involved in making a go of it in a world where tools are few and simple and there are no reference books in which to look things up every time one has a problem. For most of human history, in fact, the reference sources are the memories of the people who experienced the unusual or life-threatening, or at least heard from those who had, at least once during a lifetime. Human survival has been aided immeasurably by the ability to share the knowledge of other people and previous generations.[89]

A classic illustration of how this works was provided by the saga of one group of aborigines in the "outback" of western Australia during the drought of 1943. As things got tough, Paralji, an old man probably in his seventies, led his group—largely kinsmen and their spouses and offspring—through a series of twenty-five water holes to reach the refuge waterhole, Karbandi, at the northwestern corner of the tribal domain. He had been there only once in his life half a century earlier when he was taken there as a part of his initiation ceremonies. When even Karbandi began to run out, he took them off again through the Western Desert through another series of over thirty water holes until they finally emerged at Mandora Station on the coast of western Australia.

The whole trek lasted more than six months and took them over a course of some 600 kilometers and across between fifty and sixty water holes, only half of which were known from personal experience by Paralji or anyone else in his group. It was not superior bushcraft that led him to find one after another in sequence, but the information he had learned from the song cycles sung at totemic ceremonies.[90] Those same "autochthonous totemic dance rituals" have been denigrated by social scientists as quaint vestiges of the kind of "mimetic" vocalizations that presumably characterized the Pithecanthropines of the Middle Pleistocene and preceded symbolic communication.[91] But if Paralji had forgotten just one water hole or gotten the sequence wrong, that would have been it for the whole group. Fortunately, the story of that remarkable trek was collected by an anthropologist who really knew and understood the nature of Australian aboriginal culture and what it took to survive in the bad seasons as well as the good in the Australian bush.

The key point here is that the primary human adaptive mechanism is culture. When culture had developed to the point where the knowledge and traditions transmitted would confer an adequate chance of survival on any who could master them, the advantage of being yet more intelligent became relatively unimportant. Although we could argue that an innovator must have more intelligence than a person who is just able to master the particular culture in which he or she is brought up, it still remains true that the dullest member of a group benefits from the innovation of the brightest to an equal extent, and that genetic endowments are passed on to the next generation with the proportions unchanged. In the face of such an explanation, it would be surprising to find an increase in cranial capacity during the last 100,000 years.

This, then, suggests that brain size should cease enlarging as soon as an effective means of passing on cultural traditions had been developed. Of course, the most effective means by which this is accomplished is the phenomenon of language as we know it. A good case can be made that this coincides with the beginning of the Neanderthal Stage.[92] Throughout the preceding Middle Pleistocene, brain size had been increasing at a slow but steady rate. Clearly the additional information storage capacity that this represented was advantageous to the possessors. Language, however, adds a completely new dimension that vastly transcends the advantages of raw storage capacity. With language, which acts in a sense the way a compiler program does for a computer, information can be processed and transferred, and comparisons and considerations can be made between all the communicating members of a group. The verbal world that we now all take for granted becomes a reality for the first time. If this required a particular biological threshold, I would argue that this had been achieved by the Neanderthals, and that the basis was now provided for all of the accelerating and accumulating cultural achievements that have subsequently taken place.[93]

NEANDERTHAL AS THE UNSPEAKABLE

Of course, Neanderthal linguistic capability is simply denied in the "normal science" that passes for the orthodox paleoanthropological view. Ever since the turn of the last century, there have been repeated attempts to deny to the Neanderthals either the physical or the intellectual capacity for articulate speech. There were early claims that their jaws lacked the indications for tongue muscles that were necessary for vocal articulation,[94] and more recently there has been a series of efforts to show that the shape of the larynx would have prevented them from making the requisite number of vowel sounds to allow the production of speech as we know it.[95] The latter claim, however, depended on a reconstruction of the missing soft parts since, with the exception of the hyoid bone or voice box, the larynx is not built from the kind of biological elements that are likely to become fossilized. Then, in the early 1980s, a complete hyoid bone was found as part of a Neanderthal burial at the Israeli site of Kebara, and it was virtually indistinguishable from a modern human hyoid.[96] Although that does not automatically prove that Neanderthals were speaking even as we do, it certainly eliminates the longtime claim that their anatomical peculiarities actually prevented them from being able to speak.[97]

This returns us to the question of the brain. The dominant interpretation was established by Marcellin Boule in his description of the skeleton from La Chapelle-aux-Saints, which he declared was "a type that represents a degree on the human scale morphologically inferior to all the levels of living humanity, and that it displays a skull clearly separate from the superior skull."[98] Boule purported to see a whole series of crudities and simplicities in the endocranial caste of La Chapelle-aux-Saints,[99] but it would appear that his conclusions were preconceived, and the most experienced of recent paleoneurologists have been unable to see any differences at all between Neanderthal and modern human brains.[100] But Boule, impressed by the "strange, bestial physiognomy,"[101] projected his judgment onto virtually everything else about the Neanderthals, and established the tradition that remains as the current orthodoxy in paleoanthropology.

When he turned his attention to the Mousterian culture associated with the Neanderthals, Boule pronounced: "There is hardly a more rudimentary or more miserable industry than that of our Mousterian man. The use of a single basic material, stone (besides wood and perhaps bone), the uniformity, the simplicity and crudity of his lithic tools, the probable absence of all traces of concerns of an esthetic order or of a moral order are well in agreement with the brutal aspect of the heavy, vigorous body, of that bony head with its robust jaws, which further affirms the predominance of the purely vegetative or bestial over cerebral functions."[102] Naturally such a vision of primitive ineptitude could only have had "rudimentary intellectual faculties" and, "without doubt, only the rudiments of an articulate language."[103]

Boule's derogatory portrait was bought with enthusiasm by an entire generation of anthropologists and an admiring public despite the fact that it contained a series of blatant errors concerning both anatomy and archaeology. The influence of the total picture lingers on, however, and the most recent considerations of the Neanderthals have continued to regard them as poor benighted brutes who "lacked complex spoken language because they did not need it."[104] The stone tool refinements that appear as the Mousterian comes to an end are regarded as "imitation rather than invention,"[105] and the huts they constructed have been denigrated more as "nests" rather than "the symbolic 'home' of the Moderns."[106]

With the Neanderthals portrayed as being more on the mental level of beavers than even wolves, it is not surprising to discover that their competence as hunters has either been denied outright,[107] or relegated to the level of "relatively unplanned opportunistic foraging."[108] They are portrayed as being "incapable of anticipating patterned animal movements,"[109] and therefore constrained to pursue their hunting activities by "irregular locomotion over the landscape" with "a high degree of minimally directed movement."[110] The skeletal reinforcements and the muscle attachments indicating resistance to laterally directed forces presumably arose as a consequence of their congenital inability to run in a straight line. All of this suggests the curious vision of dim-witted Neanderthals flailing aimlessly "over the landscape" like hyperactive inebriates.[111]

The Neanderthal brain, however, was just as large as the Modern brain, and there is no hint of evidence that this was just the result of an accumulation of endocranial fat. Whether or not there was a linguistic component associated with the expansion of the brain starting two million years ago with the *"habilis"* specimens in Africa, it still seems reasonable to suggest that "Relative brain enlargement is . . . the major fossil indicator of brain reorganization for language."[112] It has been plausibly argued that the expansion of hominid brain size during the Pleistocene was an indicator of increasing intelligence, and that the force driving this was the importance of being able to construct a cognitive map of the world for an anatomically ill-equipped entrant into the "large carnivore guild."[113] The emergence of language in the course of time was a product of this process and not of a single miraculous mutation or the flip of a symbolic "switch."[114] The driving force that led to brain expansion in the first place and then the kind of neural reorganization that accompanied the emergence of linguistic capabilities was a product of the cultural ecological niche itself and the advantages that followed from being able to make full entry into it.

If one looks at the archaeological evidence so denigrated by Boule and his followers, one perceives a most interesting change in pattern from what had been the case for the preceding million years. From the beginning of the Pithecanthropine Stage on up until towards the end of the Middle Pleistocene around 200,000 years ago, there was no evidence for regional differentiation in patterns of stone tool manufacture. Coinciding with the achievement of Modern levels of brain size, however, major regions of the world each appear to develop stylistic characteristics of their own, which set them off from other regions. That regional sharing of stylistic characteristics suggests spheres of verbal communication, and, in fact, the schematic map of their distribution looks startlingly like maps depicting major language families as we now know them (see Figure 13–14). It is tempting indeed to regard this as the best evidence we are likely to get of the actual appearance of language as we know it, and it is of more than incidental significance that this picture of regional differentiation occurs simultaneously in the occupied sections of the world.

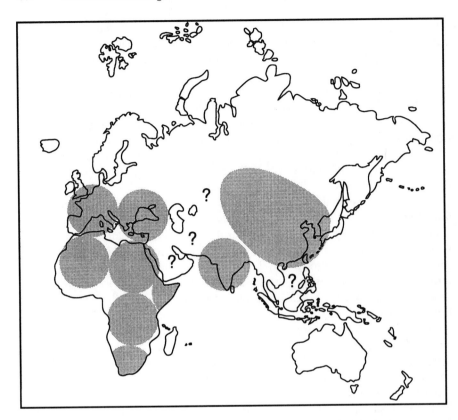

FIGURE 13–14.   A schematic depiction of the extent of areally shared stylistic elements in the Mousterian and Mousterian-related cultures of the Old World. The large extent of the Far Eastern area of shared elements is really the result of absence of information more than an indication that similar stylistic features had a wider distribution in eastern Asia than elsewhere.

SURVIVAL IN THE NORTH

Before the onset of the last (Würm) glaciation, the representatives of genus *Homo* were unable to cope with a subarctic environment. Consistent with their African area of origin, humans have remained physiologically tropical mammals to this day.[115] The ability to invade and exploit other environments is a product of specializations in the cultural adaptive mechanism. Until late in the last interglacial period, however, this cultural adaptive mechanism was not well enough developed to compensate for human physical inadequacies to the extent of allowing people to survive in a really chilly area. It is just possible that the use of fire was not controlled to a sufficient extent that it could be reliably kindled and maintained for its ability to stave off the glacial chill.[116] Also, the absence of quantities of scrapers suggests that the use of pre-pared hides as clothing against the cold had not yet been discovered.

In any case, the onset of the preceding glaciations then had repeatedly forced people out of the increasingly inhospitable parts of what had formerly been the Temperate Zone, leaving the area of continuing human occupation with approximately the same geographic dimensions as that occupied by the Pithecanthropines after they had first spread from Africa to inhabit the Trop-ics of the Old World. Climatic changes produced by the onset of glacial con-ditions were most extreme at the western end of the Old World Temperate Zone, where the Alps acted like an enormous refrigerator and cooled off the whole of Europe. Scandinavia added to this general chilling and contributed to the continental ice sheet, which moved south across the Baltic, blanketing the northern edge of continental Europe and much of the British Isles.[117] Be-cause the most extreme climatic changes in the Old World focused at the European end of the range, it is reasonable to expect that the greatest popu-lation dislocations occurred there as well.

THE CONTROL OF FIRE

Late in Middle Pleistocene, the control of fire was added to the roster of cul-tural items, and the northern extent of human habitation was considerably expanded (see Figure 13–15).[118] Because the subject of the human use of fire in prehistoric times is of some importance, it is worth exploring its implica-tions. For one thing, such evidence is a boon to the prehistorian, since it means that the difficulties involved in discovering the remains of ancient habitations are greatly reduced. With the advent of fire, caves were inhabited by humans for the first time—a fact that greatly reduces the number of places the archaeologist has to investigate before getting results. Prior to the advent of fire, caves were studiously avoided at night by prehistoric hominids since they were more in the nature of traps than shelters. Human beings, for better or worse, are strictly diurnal creatures. The keen visual sense that humans have inherited from their arboreal precursors, although remarkable among mammals for its acuity of color discernment and depth perception when light is provided, left (and still leaves) them relatively helpless in dim light, and practically disoriented in deep darkness.[119]

Fire is useful in three ways, and symbolic of a fourth phenomenon of considerable importance. It provides light, which extends the length of time during which a hominid can effectively operate. It provides nocturnal protec-tion, which can convert the limiting confines of a cave into a safe area of refuge. And it provides warmth, which can enable a fundamentally tropical mammal to extend its range into colder climates normally closed to it. The fi-nal thing—that which fire symbolizes—is related to the reuse of an agreed-

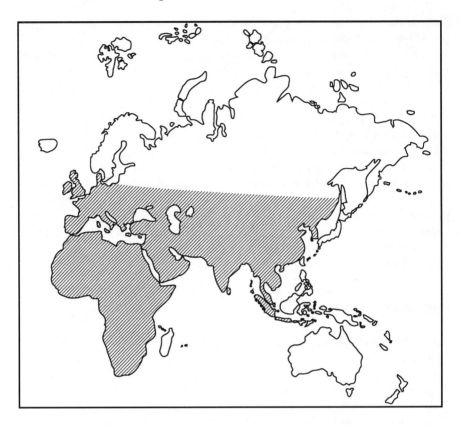

FIGURE 13–15. The area of Neanderthal occupation during the periods between Pleistocene glaciations prior to the next-to-last (penultimate) glaciation.

upon campsite.[120] Where the depth of deposition in cave sites indicates that they were intermittently used again and again, or even for a succession of days, then it is more than just likely that the users were capable of communicating time and place between each other. Given this capacity, the ability of the group to divide up and agree to meet later at the camp is also a possibility.

We must recognize in this a demonstration of the effective application of the division of labor. Because of the physiological differences between males and females—the latter being charged with the care of infants and young— the most basic form of the division of labor is inevitably by sex. The men were concerned more specifically with the chase and the women concentrated on vegetable products and slow game.[121] Even such a rudimentary division of labor as this can greatly increase the subsistence base of a foraging group, and its effectiveness is evident in the fact that it is still characteristic of the remaining hunting and gathering peoples.[122] Granting that this is rather a jump from the simple recognition of campsites via reused hearths, it nevertheless seems a legitimate interpretation to offer in regard to the activities of a creature for whom specialized hunting activities had begun to play an increasingly important role in group subsistence. Certainly at the end of the Middle and the beginning of the Upper Pleistocene, the evidence shows that there was a considerable increase in the numbers and effectiveness of the prehistoric human hunting populations.[123]

CULTURAL DIFFERENTIATION

By the time of the onset of the Würm, however, the pre-Neanderthal level of cultural attainment was just high enough so that, with some modifications, it allowed people to remain in the more northern unglaciated parts of Europe, southern Russia, and the Middle East, and to take advantage of the abundant food supply represented by the great numbers of large Pleistocene mammals that thrived there. Culturally, this represents a kind of forced adaptation that took place in the western reaches of the North Tem-

FIGURE 13–16.   The area occupied by Neanderthals during the penultimate (next-to-last) glaciation.

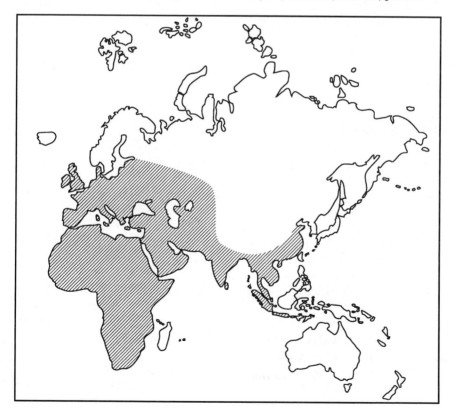

perate Zone, with the consequence that, for the first time since the Australopithecine Stage, there was a marked difference in the cultural adaptations of otherwise similar peoples in different parts of the world. This could very well indicate the start of the differential application of selective forces that produced the spectrum of variation which today is perceived under the rubric of "racial" differences.[124]

Archaeological evidence from Africa clearly shows that some of the main technological items of the Mousterian culture area were common throughout the regions to the south. In fact, there are some archaeologists who feel that there are so many elements held in common that all of the local cultures represented should be lumped under the label Mousterian.[125] This is also true in India and eastern Asia all the way to Japan, although in the latter instance, it is not clear that those items of technology go back any farther than beginning of the last glaciation between 70,000 and 100,000 years ago, if indeed they go back that far.[126]

At the same time, the "Mousterian world" began to show aspects of regional diversification that had not been visible during the preceding Acheulean and which continued at an accelerating rate during the ensuing Upper Paleolithic.[127] (Figure 13–14 illustrates the approximate local regional extexts of shared stylistic elements during this period.) Some specific elements in this regional diversity created the conditions that led to aspects of modern form and account for the fact that some of those Modern aspects are developed to different degrees in the inhabitants of different parts of the world today.

PROJECTILES

One of those Mousterian innovations that was to lead to the earlier appearance of a major aspect of Modern form earlier in one part of the world than in another was the development of the thrown spear. It has occasionally been suggested that Lower Paleolithic "hand-axes" were actually projectiles, and one recent author has compared them to "killer Frisbees" that were lobbed over herds of massed animals so that they might hit something on the way down.[128] No living hunting-and-gathering population does anything remotely like that, and, even given the great average strength of our Middle Pleistocene ancestors, it is hard to imagine them spending any time on such inherently futile efforts. Some of the larger Acheulean hand-axes weighed up to ten pounds and more, and it would have taken a mechanical catapult to hurl them hard enough for their discoidal shapes to exhibit any of their supposed aerodynamic characteristics.[129]

A spear is another matter, however, and there is evidence for the presence of hafted spear points in the latter part of the Middle Pleistocene, but only in Africa.[130] The use of the thrown spear as a major hunting device could completely change the nature of the selective forces maintaining post-cranial robustness. Prior to that time, the business of actually killing the animals hunted inevitably boiled down to a mortal tussle between the hunter and his prey. Whether the hunter accomplished his goal by strangling his victim—cutting off the victim's airway using hands or arms, as a leopard does by grabbing the throat with its jaws[131]—or by impaling it with a hand-held spear, even the business of subduing a Pleistocene pig or a medium-sized deer or antelope had to require the expenditure of a degree of physical effort that greatly transcended what was needed from the hunter who did it from a distance with the aid of a projectile.[132]

There are stone points in the Middle Stone Age of Africa—that African equivalent of the Mousterian—which show the kinds of impact fracture at the tip and microflaking at the base that are consistent with what experimental studies have produced on hafted and thrown spear points.[133] Also in the Middle Stone Age of Africa, there are barbed bone harpoon points that could only have been hafted for use as projectiles (see Figure 13–17).[134] The Middle Stone Age in Africa goes back 200,000 years, and, for a period of nearly 100,000 of those years, points used as projectiles occurred only in sub-Saharan Africa.[135] There were Mousterian "points" in the North, but experimental work has shown that they have very poor penetration power when hafted and used as projectiles.[136]

If projectiles were being used as a regular part of hunting by Africans for 100,000 years and more before that technological innovation spread to the North, then one could predict that the Africans, who were their beneficiaries, should have shown the consequences long before they appeared elsewhere. Projectiles of the sort recorded should represent a major relaxation of the selective forces maintaining Middle Pleistocene levels of robustness, and one would predict that a consequent reduction in muscle mass and skeletal robustness should occur first in Africa as a result of the operation of the Probable Mutation Effect. Since Modern form emerges simply as a consequence of reductions in those Middle Pleistocene levels of robustness, the prediction follows that Modern form from the neck on down should appear earlier in Africa than anywhere else. As we shall see when we take up the emergence of Modern form in the next chapter, that is exactly what the evidence shows.[137]

It does not follow, however, that it was the spread of Modern Africans that led to the appearance of Modern form elsewhere. What evidently happened was that the Neanderthals in the North eventually adopted those African innovations, and, in turn, the same thing happened to them that had happened to the inhabitants of Africa at an earlier time: from the neck on down they, too, in the course of time, underwent a reduction of muscularity and robustness and eventually reached what we call Modern form.[138]

FIGURE 13–17.
Barbed bone point from Middle Stone Age deposits by the Semliki River in Zaire near the Ugangan border excavated by Alison Brooks and John Yellen. (Drawn by Kay Clahassey after Shreeve, 1992.)

THE ORIGIN OF COOKING

There was another cultural development at this time, also originally a part of the formal complex designated Mousterian, and this was eventually to change the face of humanity in a literal sense. This was the beginning of culinary elaboration.[139] We are not really attuned to thinking of gastronomy as a Neanderthal invention, and perhaps it would be stretching things a bit to make such a claim, but there is reason to believe that the northern Neanderthals were the ones who pioneered the use of cooking as a regular means of preparing food.

Hearths appear in abundance in the northern Mousterian. Their frequency and extent clearly attest to their much greater importance, in contrast to the evidence from earlier habitation sites, and also in contrast with the sites in the Middle Stone Age in Africa.[140] It is also clear that they were being used for more than just keeping people warm. Further, the "hearths" that appear in some European Mousterian sites were obviously different in kind from those used for open campfires. Even after 50,000 years or more, the swirl of ashes and fire-blackened cobbles of a northern Mousterian hearth are preserved to a depth indicating that in original form it had been more than just a surface phenomenon. In fact, the remains look remarkably like those of recently used earth ovens ("roasting pits") of the kind still relied on in modern Polynesia and elsewhere.[141] Their construction and use follow this pattern: a pit is scooped out in the ground, a collection of fist-sized rocks is placed in the bottom, and a fire is built over the rocks. When the fire has consumed the fuel, the rocks are raked aside and the object to be cooked is placed in the bottom of the pit. The rocks are then pushed up against and over the food item, the whole is covered with a skin, or leaves, or grass (or burlap or canvas today) and dirt shoveled over everything. The overlying dirt provides an insulating blanket that keeps the heat within, and, with the heat provided by the rocks, the food steams in its own juices.[142] Aficionados of the New England clambake or the Polynesian luau claim that there is no tastier way of preparing food. The food is not only delicious, but it is also remarkably tender.

Most treatises on gastronomy and the culinary arts today stress the importance of the cooking process in producing the tastes that we value, but a good case can be made that it is the reverse. We do indeed value the tastes produced by the cooking process, but the point of that process had nothing to do with the generation of a particular taste in the first place.[143] The reason that things are cooked is to render them ingestible and digestible. Many vegetable foods cannot be handled by the human digestive system until they are chemically altered by the application of heat. Meat, on the other hand, does not have to be cooked at all to make it digestible. But after it has been sitting around for a while, particularly in warm weather and in the absence of refrigeration, it has to be cooked quite thoroughly or else it can cause considerable gastric distress, at the very least.[144]

Spoiled meat was probably not much of a problem for the Late Pleistocene hunters during their glacial winters, but frozen meat almost certainly was. Even the hungriest of Neanderthal bands could hardly have consumed more than a fraction of a woolly rhinoceros before the rest of it froze. Without some way of thawing it, the bulk of its meat would have been unusable, and no sapient Neanderthal would have undertaken the exertion, let alone the risk of tangling with a Pleistocene rhinoceros merely for the sake of a single meal. The Neanderthals of the last glaciation obviously had to have used some sort of regular cooking techniques in order to make use of the majority of the meat acquired by their hunting efforts. I have referred to this as "obligatory cooking."[145] The earth oven method is not only a logical candidate, but it is the one that makes the most efficient use of fuel. And then there are those Mousterian "hearths" that look so remarkably like the remains of earth ovens. Surely this is more than meaningless coincidence.

COOKING AND DENTAL REDUCTION

An incidental consequence of obligatory cooking was a substantial reduction in the amount of chewing necessary. This being the case, we could predict that the probable mutation effect would then be allowed to operate without detriment and that dental reduction would shortly ensue. Again, this appears to have been the case. The largest collection of Neanderthal teeth is from the site of Krapina in Yugoslavia, which comes from the time just at or before the beginning of the onset of the last glaciation. The molars are fully as large as those of the Pithecanthropines a million years earlier, and the front teeth, reflecting the importance of their manipulative function, are even larger.[146] Furthermore, the raised ridges on the lingual (tongue-side) surface of the incisors produce a form that has been called "shovel-shaped." This appears to be a morphological development designed to resist wear. While it has been uncritically taken as an Asian population marker in Modern *Homo sapiens,* it was generally present among the Pithecanthropines and achieves its greatest development in the incisors of the early Neanderthals in the North as exemplified at Krapina.

By the time of the Würm Neanderthals of Belgium and France, maybe 40,000 years more recently, tooth reduction had proceeded to such an extent that, in gross size, they were closer to the average for Upper Paleolithic populations. It would appear that the reductions that served to produce Modern face form had already begun in the Neanderthal groups in the northern parts of their area of occupation, and it may very well have been the result of their innovative culinary practices.

As with the advance from the Australopithecine to the Pithecanthropine Stages, the development from the Pithecanthropine to the Neanderthal Stage took place simultaneously throughout the inhabited parts of the Old World. The reason this happened was because the same kinds of cultural adaptations were used throughout the range of hominid habitation, and the same overall kinds of selective pressures influenced all extant human populations. This picture of relative uniformity began to change during the Neanderthal Stage, since inventions in one part of the world led to changes in selective forces that allowed biological changes to occur there before they

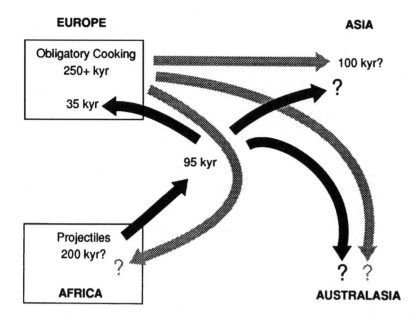

FIGURE 13–18. A diagrammatic depiction of the spread of projectile usage from its African area of origin to the rest of the Old World shown in contrast to the opposite direction of spread of cooking technology. (Brace, in press[d].)

had had time to spread to other parts of the world. Projectiles in the South, for example, led to the earlier appearance of Modern post-cranial morphology in Africa, while obligatory cooking in the North led to the earlier appearance of dental reduction in Europe (see Figure 13–18). Eventually, of course, projectiles spread North and cooking spread South, and the reductions in biological robustness that these portended followed suit. Modern form, then, emerged in a mosaic and piecemeal fashion rather than all at once in all parts of the world.

NEANDERTHAL DISTRIBUTION AND CLASSIFICATION

As an indicator of the geographical distribution of the Neanderthal Stage, human skeletal material is almost better than the archaeological record—far less complete of course, but more clearly indicative. The European skeletal material is represented by the original Neanderthaler, the Spy remains, the "Old Man" of La Chapelle-aux-Saints, skeletal remains from La Ferrassie, Gibraltar, Atapuerca, Monte Circeo, and a great many other less complete finds. (see Figure 13–19). Relatively abundant remains have been discovered in southern Russia and the Middle East, with perhaps the most exciting (and datable) remains coming from Shanidar cave in Iraq. One of the most com-

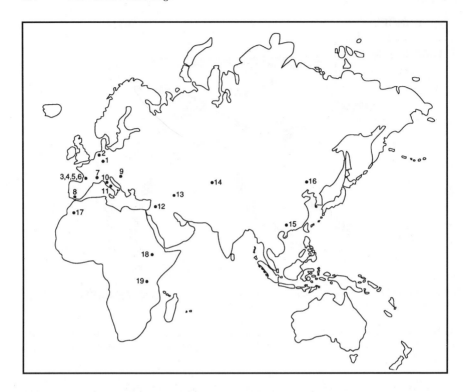

FIGURE 13–19.   Neanderthal distribution as represented by the locations of the more important discoveries. 1. Neanderthal. 2. Spy. 3. La Chapelle-aux-Saints. 4. Le Moustier. 5. La Ferrassie. 6. La Quina. 7. Hortus. 8. Atapuerca. 9. Gibraltar. 10. Krapina. 11. Saccopastore. 12. Monte Circeo. 13. Mount Carmel. 14. Shanidar. 15. Teshik Tash. 16. Jebel Ighoud. 17. Ngaloba 18. Jinniu Shan. 19. Maba.

plete skeletons is the female from the Tabūn cave on Mount Carmel in Israel, which shows that sexual dimorphism was still pronounced, although perhaps just a little less so than it had been during the Middle Pleistocene.

Skeletal remains of the Neanderthal Stage from the rest of the Old World are much less abundant, although the available fragments allow the inferences of distribution to be made. In China, for example, besides the Dali specimen that shows the Pithecanthropine-to-Neanderthal transition, there is a later full Neanderthal specimen from Maba in northern Guangdong (Canton) Province and an even more complete one from Jinniu Shan some 250 miles north of Beijing in Liaoning Province. In Africa, the Ngaloba skull from Laetoli works as a sub-Saharan African Neanderthal, as does the newly described ER-3884 specimen from East Turkana, and Jebel Ighoud is a fine representative of a North African Neanderthal.[147] The Narmada skull from central India may indicate the Pithecanthropine-to-Neanderthal transition there, but there are no skeletal remains as yet to go along with the Middle

Stone Age tools to tell us that there were indeed people there at the right time. We can predict that when the skeletons are eventually found, they will prove to be Indian Neanderthals.

The foregoing should suffice to indicate the form, the dating, and the distribution of the Neanderthal Stage. Because full modern cranial capacity and more had been attained, presumably indicating intellectual capabilities at least the equivalent to those of modern humans, it would not be justifiable to regard the Neanderthals as specifically distinct from people of today. Formally, then, this makes them *Homo sapiens* with at most a subspecific appendage of *neanderthalensis*.[148]

CHAPTER THIRTEEN NOTES

[1]In fact, the great majority of the students of the human fossil record, from Marcellin Boule (1913, 1921; Boule and Vallois, 1957) and, via Sir Arthur Keith (1915), right up to the present day (Howells, 1993; Stringer and Gamble, 1993) have rejected anything so "crude" and "bestial" as a Neanderthal as a possible Modern human ancestor.

[2]Of course, "this opinion is not accepted by the majority of palaeo-anthropologists" (Jelínek, 1978:419).

[3]Even this is denied by orthodox paleoanthropologists. The very idea of using the first discovered representative—Neanderthal—of Modern predecessors with robust faces, teeth, and bodies but with brains of fully Modern size as a representative of a named Stage in human evolution has been summarily dismissed. "The result is a monster of which the morphological character is merely large cranial size and large brows, and of which the range of variation is simply illegitimate" (Howells, 1976:9).

[4]Trinkaus and Shipman, 1992.

[5]The two specimens in question are the partial cranium from Maba in Guangdong (southern China) found in 1958 (Woo and Peng, 1959; Wu and Wu, 1985), and the more complete skull with parts of the rest of the skeleton from Jinniu Shan, Yingkou County of Liaoning Province north of Beijing, found in 1984 (Lü, 1984, 1990). The latter evidently is what was intended when the name "Yinnu Shan," was used (Wolpoff, 1989:82, 83). Jinniu Shan means "Gold Ox Hill," while "Yinnu Shan," depending on how the tones are rendered, could be translated as the "Hill of the eternal female principle." Although there are many forgiveable lapses in attempts to render Chinese in the Roman alphabet, and Jinniu Shan has acceptable variants, every effort should be made to avoid the kind of creative spelling that could confuse a woman with an ox. Uranium series dates have been produced for the sediments at Maba (119,000 to 140,000 years) and Jinniu Shan (210,000 to 300,000 years), and these span the range from early Neanderthals right back to Pithecanthropine levels (Chen and Zhang, 1988:68, 64). As always, these need refinement and confirmation.

[6]In sub-Saharan Africa, the continuing field work of Mary Leakey at Laetoli resulted in the find, in 1976, of a relatively complete skull, LH 18, along with Middle Stone Age artifacts of about 120,000 years antiquity in the Ngaloba Beds (Day et al., 1980; Magori and Day, 1983; Hay, 1987:45). Although the nasal skeleton was not preserved, the remaining part of the maxilla indicates that the nasal part of the face was short and nonprojecting, as it is in living Africans. The heavy brows, robustness, and prominent muscle markings on the occiput clearly show Middle Pleistocene ties, but with a capacity of 1,350 cc. (Stringer and Gamble, 1993:127), it is a splendid candidate for an African Neanderthal. A less complete skull recently described from the Ileret area east of Lake Turkana—ER-3884—would also appear to qualify (Bräuer et al., 1992). North Africa had previously given us a good candidate. In 1961, a robust skull was found in a Middle Paleolithic context in a Moroccan barium mine half way between Safi and Marrakesh at Jebel Ighoud (it is spelled Irhoud in the French literature, but the guttural French "r" has no equiva-

lent in English, and a gargled "gh" is about as close as we can come). Subsequently, other less complete pieces confirmed and augmented the picture presented by Ighoud I (Ennouchi, 1962; Hublin and Tillier, 1981; Hublin, 1993). The possible age range is somewhere between 130,000 and 190,000 years ago (Grün and Stringer, 1991:186), brain size at 1,480 cc. is fully up to Modern levels (Ennouchi, 1962:297); and the presence of thickened skull walls, heavy muscle markings, and enlarged brow ridges (Ennouchi, 1962:283), plus the association with Middle Paleolithic tools (Hublin, 1993:121), combine to make it a splendid representative of the Neanderthal Stage in North Africa. It lacks the elevation and elongation of the nasal bones so visible in Neanderthal and Modern Europeans, but then it evidently was not ancestral to the people who have continued to inhabit Europe.

[7]Grün and Stringer, 1991:164.

[8]Straus, 1989:489–90.

[9]Grün and Stringer, 1991:170.

[10]de Lumley, 1972:366.

[11]I must record my gratitude to Mme. M. A. de Lumley for allowing me to make my own measurements and observations on the dental remains from the Hortus site at the Laboratoire de Paléontologie Humaine et de Préhistoire at the Université de Marseille, September 30, 1992.

[12]Lévêque and Vandermeersch, 1980.

[13]Bordes, 1958; Lévêque and Vandermeersch, 1981:244; Stringer and Gamble, 1993:181.

[14]Mercier et al., 1991.

[15]Howells, 1993:153.

[16]I am greatly indebted to M. le Professeur Bernard Vandermeersch for allowing me to make my own observations and measurements on the Saint-Césaire specimen at the Laboratoire d'Anthropologie at the Université de Bordeaux, September 22, 1992.

[17]Trinkaus, 1977b:10, 1983b:468.

[18]Some of these are mentioned in Day (1986:109).

[19]Mercier et al., 1992; Aitkens and Valladas, 1993:30.

[20]Stringer and Gamble, 1993:121.

[21]Valladas et al., 1987.

[22]Ibid.

[23]Mellars, 1986; Kuhn, 1990; Lewis R. Binford, public lecture, Ann Arbor, Michigan, January 19, 1990.

[24]"Neander" actually means "new man" in Greek, and the composer's grandfather had changed the family name from Neumann to Neander. According to legend, his famous grandson, Joachim Neander (1650–1680), spent the summer of 1677 living in a cave, the "Neanderhöhle," in a wild and lovely stretch of the valley between Elbersfeld upstream and Düsseldorf on the Rhine. There, so the story goes, he composed the hymns for which he is famous. The best known of these is still a part of the Protestant hymnal and is known by its first line, translated from the German as "Hail to the Lord, the Almighty, the king of creation" (*Allgemeine Deutsche Biographie,* 1970, vol. 23, p. 329). After his untimely death at thirty, the people of the area named the gorge "Neumann's Valley," or, Neanderthal.

[25]The history of this change is spelled out in footnote 1 in Howells (1976:17).

[26]Neander's Valley did adopt the change, and it is now officially spelled "Neandertal" in Germany (Bürger, 1956).

[27]Vallois, 1951.

[28]My preference has recently received support in the form of a splendidly self-assured declaration that, "*The New York Times,* founded five years before the first Neanderthal fossil was discovered, has stayed with the original spelling" (Browne, 1993:21).

[29]Tattersall, 1986b; Stringer, 1987; Howells, 1993; Rak, 1993; Stringer and Gamble, 1993.

[30]Clark and Lindly, 1989a, b.

[31]Oddly enough, they are able to accept specimens such as Kabwe and Petralona as "Archaic *Homo sapiens,*" even though their brow ridges are enormous, their skulls heavy and thick, and

they have not quite achieved Modern levels of brain size, and yet they will not allow Neanderthals to qualify, even though brain size is fully Modern, brow ridge and skull wall thickness have started to reduce, and the evidence for cultural sophistication is an order of magnitude greater than it was in the Middle Pleistocene (see Stringer and Gamble, 1993).

[32]Brace and Hunt, 1990; Brace and Tracer, 1992; Brace, in press (c).

[33]Brace, 1991:186.

[34]There are some serious intellectual drawbacks to the "parsimony" approach. The desire for certitude in classifying individuals and groups expressed by Andrews in his advocacy of using an arbitrary cladistic approach rather than grappling with the issues of evolutionary dynamics (Andrews, 1984:168) is a classic illustration of the preference felt by orthodox paleoanthropology for the eternal verities assumed by the medieval church than for the "fuzzy set" messiness that characterizes the real biological world (Van Valen, 1988). Ironically, that urge for certitude in classification is doomed both for mathematical and, more tellingly, for logical reasons. The sheer number of possible parsimonious solutions quickly becomes astronomical with the increase in numbers of variables and specimens (Cartmill, 1981:90)—see the tens of thousands of equally parsimonious mtDNA trees recognized by Templeton (1993)—while the very process of making logical distinctions between taxa and character states leads to the conclusion that there can be no answer since the possibilities are literally infinite (Eco, 1984a:68; Brace, 1988). As Cartmill put it, "dogmatic insistence on an illusory rigor is an evasion of responsibility" (1981:92). Cladistics can be a useful tool, especially for indicating relationships, but unless used in conjunction with a treatment of adaptation, it can actually prevent an understanding of the course and dynamics of organic evolution, as it has done in the study of our own lineage. Some of this was evidently perceived by that deservedly obscure wordsmith I. Wright Drivell who, like his cousin Doolittle Wright, crossly put his thoughts into verse. Unlike Wright who preferred limerick form, the effusions of Drivell were usually couched in Burns's favorite choice of meter. The stanzas that follow are taken from the latter part of his "Punctured Cladomania," which I have previously pirated for use (1988:133–34):

> To get the right Platonic name,
> Where sister species rank the same;
> Synapomorphies rule the game,
> > By which one gets,
> A branching ranked dendritic frame,
> > Of nested sets.

> Thus each new cladistic tree,
> Disguises with sadistic glee,
> The quintessential mystic plea,
> > That's no excuse,
> For such a casuistic spree,
> > Of little use.

It seems appropriate to end this with an especially killjoy outburst of Drivell's recorded in his "Owed to Trees" (pirated by Brace, 1981:426).

> As we survey the path we've trod,
> Of knowledge gained by labored plod;
> Now each aspiring learned clod,
> > Will try to see,
> How he can be a bit like God
> > And make a tree.

> The record shows that those who strived,
> Produced results that look contrived;
> Are twigs then based on traits derived,
> > To make a clade?
> Do branches show the route arrived,
> > To reach a grade?

However much they try to please,
The schemes expand by twos and threes;
The viewer then who thinks he sees,
    Can only fail,
To tell the forest from the trees
    —To no avail.

[35]Brace, 1991:187.

[36]While the attribution of a "bent-knee-gait" to the Neanderthals did not originate with Marcellin Boule, it was his emphasis of this along with a "long series of primitive or pithecoid traits" (1913:240) that fixed this as part of the Neanderthal caricature, which was adopted with such conviction by professional anthropologists and the public at large (Keith, 1915:157; Quennell and Quennell, 1922:99; Smith, 1924:87; and many more).

[37]Trinkaus, 1983a, 1987, 1989.

[38]Trinkaus, 1983a:169.

[39]Lovejoy and Trinkaus, 1980:467.

[40]Ben-Itzhak et al., 1988.

[41]The so-called dorsal axillary sulcus of the Neanderthal scapula has sometimes been called "Boule's sulcus" because of the attention it drew in his description of the skeleton from La Chapelle-aux-Saints (Boule, 1913:123; McCown and Keith, 1939:135), although it was first given general recognition by Gorjanović-Kramberger in his description of the Croation Neanderthal collection from Krapina (1906:216). Gorjanović-Kramberger also was the first to point out that the early Upper Paleolithic specimens from Předmost in Czechoslovakia displayed what he referred to as a Chancelade form of double sulcus, which is intermediate between the Neanderthal and Modern condition (Gorjanović-Kramberger, 1914:232, 1926:90–91). This has subsequently been confirmed by several independent studies (Endo and Kimura, 1970:242; Trinkaus, 1977a:232–234; Frayer, 1992:36). The details of muscle attachments of the Neanderthal shoulder are clearly related to maintaining the integrity of the shoulder joint and preventing dislocations under circumstances of heavy stress (Trinkaus, 1977, 1987, 1989; Churchill and Trinkaus, 1990:157). Details of the muscle attachments of the arms are treated by Trinkaus (1987, 1989), and the characteristics of Neanderthal hand anatomy and capabilities are treated by Musgrave (1971, 1973) and Trinkaus (1987, 1989).

[42]Stewart, 1960; Rak and Arensburg, 1987; Rak, 1990.

[43]Trinkaus, 1984.

[44]Weidenreich, 1941:325; Smith 1986:327, 1991a:167–68; Tillier, 1992.

[45]Rosenberg, 1986, 1988.

[46]Garn et al., 1977:136; Garn, 1980:279.

[47]Ruff, 1993:54, 57.

[48]Trinkaus, 1981.

[49]Brace, 1979b.

[50]Boule, 1913:44; Hublin, 1978; Tattersall, 1986b:171.

[51]Brace, 1991, in press(d); Brace and Tracer, 1992:448–54. As I was working through northwestern European collections in the autumn of 1987 measuring Danish crania in the Panum Institute in Copenhagen, I began to see that the whole configuration of the rear part of the skull looked more than faintly like dilute Neanderthal form. That feeling became stronger as I worked on the medieval Norwegian crania at the Institute of Anatomy in Oslo and on the seventeenth century London plague-pit material at the British Museum (Natural History) and the Duckworth collection in Cambridge. I was hardly the first person to notice these characteristics, since the describer of the English specimens commented that they were "remarkable for their low retreating foreheads" (Hooke, 1926:54), and, at the turn of the century, the distinguished Edinburgh anatomist, Sir William Turner, commented that "it would be possible to arrange a series of modern British skulls in which variation from a well-marked occipital bulging to a form closely approaching that of the Neanderthal skull could be seen" (Turner, 1908:399). Again, as in the demonstration that Kabwe and Petralona are further removed from Modern European craniofacial form than are the "classic" Neanderthals, the use of thin plate splines and their partial warps to analyze what kind of Cartesian deformation would transform a Neanderthal into a

Norwegian shows that Neanderthals either share characteristics with Kabwe and Petralona or differ from them in the Modern direction. In no case were Neanderthals uniquely different from Modern human form, and, all together, they make a perfectly splendid intermediary between their slightly smaller-brained predecessors and their smaller-faced successors—or descendants, as I would prefer to regard them (Yaroch, 1994).

[52]See note 51.

[53]Gorjanović-Kramberger, 1902, 1906.

[54]Marcellin Boule was properly skeptical of the claims for brachycephaly at Krapina (Boule, 1913:220), but he did not have direct experience with the specimens themselves. When I worked on the collection in the autumn of 1959—evidently the first person to do so since before World War II—it was clear that when the cranial outlines were plausibly completed the width was not notably great in proportion to the length (Brace et al., 1971:108, 1979:110). The drawings on which this judgment was made were used by Smith to illustrate that point (Smith, 1976:116, 120, 122).

[55]Arsuaga et al., 1993.

[56]Bermudez de Castro, 1993:339. Stringer and Gamble state that the date was "probably . . . over 200,000 years ago" (1993:68).

[57]Bermudez de Castro, 1993:352–53.

[58]Of the three specimens found in July of 1992, one was an early adolescent, one was a complete cranial vault without a face, and the other was the better part of a cranial vault plus a complete face. The faceless adult had a cranial capacity of 1,390 cm.^{3} and a cranial width of 164 mm., while the other adult had a capacity of 1,125 cm^3 and a width of 145 mm. (Arsuaga et al., 1993:534). Those widths are extraordinarily large by any hominid standards, and would suggest a high width/length ratio by themselves alone. Lengths were not published, but it was possible to measure both length and width in relative fashion from the photo of the top view of the larger skull, cranium 4, and the ratio is approximately eighty-four, which is well within the broad-headed range characteristic of the living populations of central and eastern Europe.

[59]As one of the foremost authorities has put it, Neanderthals had the "largest hominid nasal apertures known" (Trinkaus, 1987:124).

[60]Coon, 1962:533.

[61]Howells, 1989; Brace et al., 1991.

[62]Brace et al., 1993.

[63]Negus, 1965:184; Slonim and Hamilton, 1987:47.

[64]Brace, in press(d).

[65]Trinkaus, 1989:57, 62.

[66]Trinkaus, 1987:123; Franciscus and Trinkaus, 1988. No primate has either the circulatory machinery or the internal nasal anatomy associated with the dissipation of significant amounts of heat via the respiratory passages (Baker, 1982, 1993; Baker and Chapman, 1977), as do carnivores and certain artiodactyls, and the idea that humans use the nose as a heat dissipating mechanism is rejected by respiratory physiologists (Negus, 1958:185). Humans dissipate heat through the surface of the skin by sweating, and those human populations under stress to get rid of the heat generated by metabolic activity display elongated distal segments of the limbs in a fashion exactly opposite to that seen in the Neanderthals. The idea of reclaiming the water whose evaporation presumably was responsible for reducing body heat is a physiological impossibility even if the nasal epithelium were capable of absorbing any significant amount of ambient moisture (Negus, 1958:270).

[67]Negus, 1965:143; Slonim and Hamilton, 1987:47.

[68]The model for this passage is in Psalms 4:5 and 6. I used it in the text of a presentation given at the 50th annual meetings of the American Association of Physical Anthropologists in Detroit, Michigan, April 23, 1981, and the title was "The Total Morphological Neanderthal as Rumpelstilzchen" in honor of the figure in the story who became so irate when Rapunzel guessed his name. The endless wrangling about the right name for this or that fossil is simply a continuation of the same tradition where knowing the right name gives one power over the designated object (Brace, 1981b). As has been said, "Neanderthals are what we make them" (Stringer and Gamble, 1993:15), and it is clear that many of the anthropologists who study them would like to make

them into the embodiment of the bestial—essence of ogre—rather than prehistoric human beings worthy of sympathetic study.

[69]This is derived from the definition that I first offered thirty years ago (Brace, 1964:18) and that I have used in all the previous editions of this book.

[70]"The keys to the appearance of modern form . . . have to be in the Mousterian itself" (Brace, 1992:4); and, "If the Mousterian refinements in hunting and food preparation techniques represent changes in the selective forces operating on the portions of the physique previously necessary for the performance of these activities, then wherever we find Mousterian, or its functional counterparts elsewhere in the world, we should expect the beginnings of modern morphology to emerge in the course of time" Brace, 1992:20–21).

[71]The rock shelter where the first Mousterian tools were identified was excavated in the autumn of 1863, over forty-five years before the famous skeleton was found in the lower shelter at the same locality (Lartet and Christy, 1864a:141, 1864b:238; Klaatsch and Hauser, 1909; Peyrony, 1930:50 ff.).

[72]Bar-Yosef, 1987, 1990–91; Dibble and Mellars (eds.), 1992.

[73]The late François Bordes objected to using the term for anything more than the late Middle Pleistocene and early Late Pleistocene stone tool traditions of Europe, North Africa, and the Middle East. Outside of this area, he would use the term "Mousterioid" (1977:39). Although it had fallen out of favor a generation ago, there has been an increasing tendency to use the term "Middle Paleolithic" to refer to those functionally similar but stylistically different regional contemporaries of the Mousterian (Dibble and Mellars [eds.], 1992; Marks, 1992:241, 244; Stringer and Gamble, 1993:151).

[74]Clark, 1988; 1993. At least one experienced archaeologist has referred to the Middle Stone Age material in East and South Africa as "Mousterian-like industries" (Bar-Yosef, 1993:139), and he has privately told me that if archaeologists with field experience in Europan Mousterian sites had actually been the ones exploring and describing their temporal counterparts in Africa, those would have been called Mousterian without any hesitation (Dec. 11, 1992).

[75]In assessing the temporal equivalents in China, two broadly knowledgeable archaeologists commented that "we saw nothing comparable to a European Mousterian or an African Middle Stone Age" (Clark and Schick, 1988:445).

[76]Brace, 1967, 1971:185, 1979b:531–32; Brace and Montagu, 1977:334.

[77]Hrdlička, 1920.

[78]Hrdlička, 1920:441.

[79]Brabant and Ketelbant, 1975.

[80]Lü, 1990:901.

[81]Under such circumstances, the worn top of the root is elevated to serve as the functioning part of the occlusion. A substantial portion of the tooth roots, then, represents potentially functional occlusal surface. With this as a perspective, it is obviously no accident that Neanderthal tooth roots are even larger in comparison with those of their Modern descendants than are Neanderthal tooth crowns.

[82]Eskimos have been observed using their teeth on a regular basis to untie frozen cord, hold the bit-block of a bow-drill, soften frozen boots, hold the towline of a harpooned seal while paddling a kayak, and crushing birds' heads, among many other manipulative tasks (de Poncins, 1941:39, 54, 94). Reflecting their entry into the industrialized world, they have put their teeth to such uses as prying the lids from gasoline drums (de Poncins, 1941:94) and pulling the toggle to start an outboard motor.

[83]Ryan, 1980:166–71, 183–84.

[84]Brace, 1962a, 1967, 1979a, b; Brace et al., 1987, 1991. For years, I have noted that the dentition formerly served as a combination of "vise, pliers, clamp and snippers" (Brace, 1971:185). Among the very few who have commented on those efforts at interpretation, the most recent has referred to the use of the teeth as a "vice"—presumably one of those sins that invoked Divine displeasure and hastened the extinction of its practitioners (Stringer and Gamble, 1993:37, 83).

[85]Humphrey, 1976, 1978, 1983; Alexander, 1990; Dunbar, 1993.

[86]Romer, 1966.

[87]Wallace, 1875:343. Although Wallace clearly understood natural selection, he lost his nerve when it came to applying it to such things as the origins of life and mind. At that point, he reverted to a mystical vitalism in classic fashion: "mind is essentially superior to matter and distinct from it" and therefore one "cannot believe that life, consciousness, mind are products of matter" (1903:319).

[88]Humphrey, 1983; Donald, 1991.

[89]As Diamond has perceptively observed, "Under hunter-gatherer conditions, the knowledge possessed by even one person over the age of seventy could spell the difference between survival and starvation for a whole clan" (1992:123). Mayr has even gone to the extent of allowing that, within the cultural context, "group selection does occur in the human species, as has often been demonstrated in the decimation or even extinction of human ethnic groups by others" (Mayr, 1992:24–25). Among other things, it has been suggested that the value to a group conveyed by the reservoir of knowledge represented by post-reproductive women may have been related to the generation of a long potential post-menopausal life span and also to the phenomenon of menopause itself (Dawkins, 1976:135–36; Alexander, 1990:13).

[90]The details of the saga were collected by the late Norman B. Tindale and related by Birdsell (1979:147–48). Diamond has provided comparable information concerning survival knowledge that had been given to him by one old man who remembered how his group had been able to survive the effects of the cyclone that hit Rennell Island in western Polynesia around 1905 when he was a child (Diamond, 1992:50).

[91]Hunters and gatherers have sometimes been portrayed as representatives of "the original affluent society" (Sahlins, 1960, 1972:1–39), living in a world of abundance, indolence, and ease. Others have spoken of the "monotony and redundancy of the hunting-gathering lifestyle," noting that "the civilizations of Australian and Tasmanian aborigines have remained unchanged for tens of thousands of years" (Donald, 1991:320, 169). Both such generalizations are more in the nature of manifestations of ethnocentrism and ignorance. There are always those years when the essentials are there in plenty, but a group need only starve once in a generation to fail to survive. And the resource utilization and technical knowledge of the aboriginal Australians is far in advance of what was available during the Pleistocene. They were, in fact, living at a sophisticated Mesolithic level comparable to that of the Late Pleistocene and post-Pleistocene in other parts of the world (McCarthy, 1940, 1974; Tindale, 1975).

[92]This point has been made explicitly in the last two editions of this book (Brace, 1988:116, 1991:150).

[93]Language, in the words of one of our most respected linguists, is "the most valuable single possession of the human race" (Hockett, 1958:1).

[94]Walkhoff, 1902, 1904. Telling rebuttals to Walkhoff's claims were written by Fischer (1903) and Weidenreich (1904), but the influence of that view has tended to linger almost indefinitely.

[95]Lieberman and Crelin, 1971; Lieberman, 1975; Donald, 1991:116–17; Lieberman et al., 1992. This inspired the following limerick by the ever-inept I. Doolittle Wright:

> His speech was a series of howls,
> And semi-articulate growls,
>   Cause the shape of his jaw,
>   Restricted his maw,
> To a limited number of vowels.

[96]Arensburg et al., 1985.

[97]Houghton, 1993:139.

[98]Boule, 1913:240.

[99]Boule and Anthony, 1911; Boule, 1921:228–37.

[100]As one of the most experienced of paleoneurologists has put it, "Certainly no significant convolutional details, or shape patterns, differ between ourselves and Neanderthals" (Holloway, 1982:220). Holloway concluded, "I see no evidence of any significant evolutionary change from Neanderthal, or archaic *Homo sapiens* of perhaps 120,000 years ago, to modern *Homo* in brain organization and size" (Ibid., p. 223). In any case, any possible question concerning Neanderthal capabilities has been removed by the skillful new reconstruction of the La Chapelle-aux-Saints by Jean-Louis Heim in Paris (Heim, 1989, 1993).

[101]Boule, 1913:62.

[102]Boule, 1913:227.

[103]Boule, 1921:236, 237.

[104]Stringer and Gamble, 1993:217.

[105]Stringer and Gamble, 1993:201. In restricting them to purely imitative capabilities, they have been treated in the same way as Australian aborigines hopping around their campfires in totemic ceremonies of a purely mimetic nature and of timeless antiquity stretching back to before the use of symbolic communication. Much of that erroneous picture of Australian behavior was the product of observers who never learned the aboriginal languages well enough to have any idea of the real information being conveyed in those ceremonies, and, as noted above, that information could spell the difference between survival and oblivion.

[106]Stringer and Gamble, 1993:207. This, in fact, denies the Neanderthals even the ability to appreciate the symbolic significance of a home base that is clearly possessed by the major carnivores with whom the Neanderthals were competing.

[107]Binford, 1981:296, 1985:321, 1987.

[108]Trinkaus, 1987:124.

[109]Trinkaus, 1989:55–58.

[110]Trinkaus, 1987:123–24, 1989:55–58.

[111]The ever skeptical I. Wright Drivell was moved to his own efforts at versified random bumbling:

> In a common view that's offered now,
> Nature never did endow
> Neanderthals with brains enow
>   To frame the thought
> Of hunting plans that would allow
>   For dinner caught.
>
> In addled search to gain his fare,
> He rushes forth he knows not where,
> Blunders here and stumbles there,
>   And hopes, this way,
> By random luck and wear and tear,
>   To find his prey.
>
> But random hunts are ever vain;
> And surely that expanded brain
> Suggests there was no mental strain
>   Behind the hunch
> That led to plans that let them gain
>   The sought-for lunch.

[112]Deacon, 1988.

[113]This essentially combines the perspectives of Walker (1984:144) and Jerison (1988:9–10).

[114]Chomsky, 1972:97; Bickerton, 1981:315, 1990:196; Stringer and Gamble, 1993:204.

[115]Pandolf et al., 1988: Chapters 9 and 10.

[116]Evidence for fire has been suggested for as long ago as 1.5 million years (Gowlett et al., 1981), and there have been repeated claims that fire was being used in the 300,000 to 500,000 year range (de Lumley, 1969:43; Perlès, 1977; Christen, 1979; de Beaune and White, 1993:108). However, the longtime claim that fire was used by the Pithecanthropines at Zhoukoudian in China, (Breuil, 1931) in that age range, has been convincingly challenged (Binford and Ho, 1985), and the question of whether those other purported traces of fire at half a million or more years of antiquity were the products of nature or of human intent has yet to be resolved. So far, the earliest solid evidence for the regular human use of fire has come from sites in France (Pech de l'Azé) and the island of Jersey off the French coast (La Cotte de Saint-Brelade), with dates in the 200,000 to 250,000+ year range (Straus, 1989).

[117]Barry et al., 1975; Imbrie and Imbrie, 1986; Broecker and Denton, 1990.

[118]Brace, in press (d).

[119]Brace and Brace, 1976.

[120]At one time, there was an attempt to attribute the idea of a "home base" to hominids at the Australopithecine stage (Isaac, 1971, 1976, 1978), but it has not withstood scrutiny (Binford, 1985; Stringer and Gamble, 1993:168). By the Neanderthal Stage, however, even though this has been denied by some of those critics (Binford, 1985:321, 1987; Stringer and Gamble, 1993:207), this would seem to be more of a vestige of the assumption that they were more beasts than human beings. The evidence is overwhelming that Neanderthals were repeatedly kindling their fires in the same hearths at the same caves over prolonged periods of time (Bar-Yosef et al., 1992).

[121]Some feel that the earlier focus on hunting as central to earlier hominid survival (Washburn and Lancaster, 1968) may have glorified the male role at the expense of the female one (Lee and DeVore [eds.], 1976). There have been attempts to balance this (Isaac, 1971:279; Zihlman, 1981). The importance of the hunting versus the gathering component of human subsistence in the societies where this was practiced varied greatly depending on the area of habitation, but the division of labor by sex along male hunting and female gathering lines was the standard pattern. Throughout the reproductive years, females were either pregnant or suckling infants, and this simply prohibited prolonged participation in hunting activities. Female roles in gathering, nurturing, and enculturating, however, were always at least as important as male actions as hunters and defenders of group territory.

[122]McCarthy and McArthur, 1960; Lee and DeVore (eds.), 1976; Binford, 1978; Brody, 1987.

[123]Weiss, 1984:642.

[124]Brace in press (c).

[125]Ofer Bar-Yosef, personal communication, December 11, 1992, and see Bar-Yosef, 1990–91, 1992:197, 1993:139.

[126]Ikawa-Smith, 1986:202; Serizawa, 1986:192.

[127]Bordes, 1968:146; Marks, 1992:241.

[128]Livingstone, 1974:294; Calvin, 1990:276.

[129]It was none other than Charles Darwin who observed that human beings alone were capable of throwing projectiles with any sort of aim and effect (1871, I:134; Brace, 1992:17).

[130]Brooks, 1988:347; Shea, 1988:448.

[131]Observations on leopard killing behavior recorded by Brain (1981) are consistent with the suffocation technique generally used by the big cats for killing prey that is larger than themselves (Macdonald, 1992:67). Interestingly enough and contrary to common assumption, the canine teeth often do not even break the skin and serve mainly to keep the jaws anchored over the muzzle or clamped on the windpipe (Ibid. p. 64).

[132]In a televised interview on The Learning Channel (September 5, 1993), Erik Trinkaus observed that the kinds of healed injuries visible on Neanderthal skeletons bore a strong resemblance to what one sees in professional rodeo participants in western North America. While it is Trinkaus's interpretation that the evidence for enlarged muscle attachments and reinforced skeletons among the Neanderthals indicated their predilection for cavorting in frantic and witless fashion—"scrambling around on the landscape, rather than strolling or even walking briskly from place to place" (Trinkaus and Shipman, 1992:368)—it is much more likely that both their robustness and the evidence for a high frequency of healed injuries were related to their literally coming to grips with their prey. If they were bringing home the bacon by bull-dogging animals to the ground and strangling them, even though they were more heavily muscled and skeletally reinforced than the most macho rodeo participant, it is no surprise to find similar tell-tale scars preserved on their skeletons.

[133]Fischer et al., 1984:24–25; Shea, 1989:616.

[134]These have been discovered as the result of fieldwork done by Alison Brooks and John Yellen as reported in Shreeve (1992) and Bar-Yosef (1993:143). Barbed bone points are well known from the later Upper Paleolithic of western Europe, where they also occur in conjunction with spear throwers (Garrod, 1955; de Sonneville-Bordes, 1963). Although this was some thousands of years after the time of the Cro-Magnons, these tools inevitably get attributed to them and cited with ethnocentric European pride as demonstrative of the superiority of their "noble" creators. For example, "Cro-Magnon tools were the first to show real innovation. This antler har-

poon was state of the art 30,000 years ago" (Diamond, 1989:60). Ignoring the errors in time and associations in this statement, it is clear that the European "state-of-the-art" was 100,000 years and perhaps a lot more behind what had been going on in Africa.

[135]Clark, 1988:239,291.

[136]Shea, 1988:445.

[137]The association of Modern morphology with thrown projectiles has also been mentioned by Churchill and Trinkaus (1990:158), but they have reversed the cause and effect. They evidently operate under the assumption that Modern shoulder form was selected for because it somehow improved the ability to throw. Just how Modern form made throwing easier remains a mystery. On the other hand, the reinforced Neanderthal shoulder was evidently put together in such a way that it resisted dislocation, and, as Baden-Powell observed (1924:287), shoulder dislocations are "a very common accident" when people hunt boars with hand-held spears. The appearance of Modern shoulder form was not selected for to improve throwing efficiency; it was what occurred when the hunter no longer had to come to grips with a stuck pig on a regular basis because he could impale it from a distance.

[138]Brace in press (d).

[139]I have even gone so far as to label this the "culinary revolution" (1979b:546). None other than James Boswell, the chronicler of the famous Dr. Samuel Johnson, recognized the fact that human beings alone of all the creatures of the world tend to modify their food extensively before eating it. He went on to say, "My definition of *Man* is, 'a cooking animal'" (in Hill [ed.] 1887, vol. 5:33). Perhaps the most sophisticated recognition of the modification of food as a measure of the distinction between the human and the nonhuman has been the treatment by the French structuralist, Claude Lévi-Strauss (1964, 1965, 1968).

[140]I am indebted to Dr. Alison S. Brooks, Chair of Anthropology, George Washington University, Washington D.C., for the information on the MSA of Africa. She tells me that traces of fire are present, but that there is nothing comparable to the extensive hearths in the sites of the northern Mousterian.

[141]Graebner, 1913.

[142]Brace, 1979b:545–46, 1992:16–17; Brace et al., 1988:713–14.

[143]As I put it in the first place, "I suspect that we like the taste of the food we cook as opposed to the situation of cooking the food to the taste we like" (1979b:546).

[144]Observers who recorded the cooking and eating of a kangaroo in the tropical north of Australia noted that an eighty-pound animal was only cooked for thirty-five to forty-five minutes in an earth oven and felt that "we would call it underdone." The Australians hung it in a tree over night, and, before using it for breakfast, brushed the flies off, singed off the greenish parts, and put it back into the earth oven for another roasting before they ate it again. One large kangaroo might be eaten for four meals or so and cooked anew each time, so that, although Europeans might consider it on the "underdone" side the first time around, surely when it had been cooked for the fourth time it would have long since achieved a state that even the most fastidious would label "well done" (McArthur, 1960:118–19).

[145]Brace, in press (d).

[146]Brace, 1979b.

[147]Its first describers mentioned "a blending of Neanderthal and modern traits" (Day et al., 1980), and it has recently been regarded as existing on the borderline of *Homo sapiens* but not properly *Homo sapiens sapiens* (Howells, 1993:132; and see the similar position of Stringer and Gamble, 1993:117). That, of course, is just what I am accepting as what one would expect to find for a representative of the Neanderthal Stage. Similar words are also used by the describers of ER-3884 from the Ileret area of East Turkana (Bräuer et al., 1992), and for the same reason it too should qualify as an African Neanderthal.

[148]Boule, on the contrary, staunchly defended the idea that Neanderthals warranted a specific title and that *Homo "Neanderthalensis"* was an archaic species that had disappeared (1913:240,242). Establishment paleoanthropology agrees completely (Tattersall, 1986b, 1992:83; Howells, 1993:215, 217; Stringer and Gamble, 1993:26), although the latter try to make the claim that their reasons were entirely different from Boule's. In their words, the Neanderthals were "too primitive or specialized to be closely related to living humans, particularly the supposedly highly

advanced white European race" (Stringer and Gamble, 1993:14). Those reasons, however, are exactly the same as Boule's, and it is evident that whatever differences they represent are only in trivial details, since the basic assumptions are essentially identical. To repeat once more, Stringer and Gamble have cogently noted that "Neanderthals are what we make them" (1993:15), and it is clear that they share Boule's wish to make them into the essence of the subhuman.

chapter fourteen

The Modern Stage

THE MYTH OF TRADITIONAL ANTHROPOLOGY

Fifty years ago, the appearance of modern humanity would have been presented in phrases such as these: "Sweeping into Europe from out of the East came a new type of man, tall and straight, with strong but finely formed limbs, whose superiority is proclaimed in the smooth brow and lofty forehead, and whose firm and prominent chin bespeaks a mentality in no way inferior to that of ourselves. In this fine and virile race we can recognize our own ancestors who suddenly appear upon the scene and replace the degenerate and inferior Neanderthals, perhaps as a result of bloody conflict in which the superior mentality and physique of the newcomers tipped the balance. Whatever the cause, the lowly Neanderthals disappear forever and the land henceforth becomes the never-to-be-relinquished home of our own lineage, the creator of the culture which is our own patrimony, and the originator of what has been built to the heights of Western civilization."[1]

While this paragraph is pure invention, it nevertheless captures some of the flavor of the interpretive accounts of human evolution written a half century ago. Their appeal to the imagination of the literate Western world was immense. In the first place, this is a wondrously ethnocentric outlook where Europe alone is considered to be the stage on which the drama of human change took place. The reference to an Eastern origin strikes a powerful chord in the mind of the Western reader who is conditioned from infancy to regard all that is civilized and sanctified in antiquity to have had its origins "in the East."[2] To these holy overtones are added the implications of the mysterious Orient. But this is just the beginning. The appeal to the lofty brow, often accompanied by explicit statements concerning the degree of development of the frontal lobes of the brain, caters to a folk belief, dating from the phrenology of the early nineteenth century and still current, that this is somehow indicative of superior mental ability.[3] The portrayal of our own ancestors in terms that correspond to the stereotypically idealized picture of European masculinity—tall, straight-limbed, and with a prominent chin, to which hints of blue eyes and fair hair are often added—stimulates a conscious pride in belonging to such a line, a view that contains not a little racism as well. (Figure 14–1 provides an example.) To complete the scene with all the components of a good, old-fashioned melodrama, the Neanderthals are brought in as the embodiment of the villain. They are depicted as hairy, strong and dangerous, violent and bestial, dwarfed and physically "inferior," and crafty but not really intelligent. In spite of adversities, good prevails and evil is vanquished, with the Neanderthals disappearing forever.[4] As an added attraction to our already potent little drama, all direct relationship between the Neanderthals and the invading Moderns is either flatly denied[5] or pushed so far back in time that it is lost in the mist of remote antiquity, which of course means that even people who are uneasy about accepting an evolutionary account of modern human origins can accept this story without any qualms.[6]

Since I outlined this scenario in the first edition of this book, using the mixture of the prejudice and prolixity that sometimes characterized the liter-

FIGURE 14–1.
An Upper Paleolithic Hunter, the first of the Modern Stage. Neatly dressed and clean shaven, he strides forth confidently to fulfill the destiny that his clear vision tells him is to be his future. Actually, the archaeological evidence does provide support for the existence, if not the invention, of tailored clothing and compound weapons in the Upper Paleolithic, but the lofty brow and "noble" expression are quite unwarranted idealizations.

ary style of past generations, two authors have taken note and rendered my little Paleolithic melodrama in modern dress—or rather, undress, since that sells a lot more books, and a pot-boiler laced with a lot of explicit and steamy sex will find a far bigger market than elegantly phrased musings on the shape of brows and chins, even though both approaches may be expressing the same assumptions. Jean Auel's *Clan of the Cave Bear,* for example, recounts in graphic detail the brutal lust of the dim-witted Neanderthal who has his way with the "Modern" heroine.[7] And in a much more literate version of Neanderthal/Modern encounters, the late Björn Kurtén depicts the lust of a female Neanderthal for the "Modern" object of her affections in his *Dance of the Tiger.*[8] In both instances, however, the poor dim Neanderthals have not quite gotten the hang of fully articulate speech, their technology is backward, and their impending doom is near.[9] Even the hybrid offspring that result from the torrid scenes are at best sterile and cannot perpetuate themselves.

Although the style of popular presentation has gone through a quantum change in the past two generations, underneath it all there is little, if any, modification in the basic message being conveyed, and the public is just as happy with it now as it was then. Dazzled by such dramatics, few people have been disturbed by the total lack of any reason for such a picture of invasion, of any source for the invaders, or of any perspectives on what they evolved out of and why.[10] Analogous to the legend in which Athena sprang fully armed from the brow of Zeus, it would seem that twentieth century prehistorians have tried to solve their headache concerning human origins by projecting a modern human stereotype, fully formed from their own inner consciousness, smack into the early Pleistocene—thereby creating their own anthropological mythology.[11] Even in the recent work specifically entitled *The Myths of Human Evolution* by Niles Eldredge and Ian Tattersall, the "myth" referred to in the title is not the scenario just presented—which they accept as demonstrated truth—but the possibility that modern human form could have evolved by natural means from its immediate predecessors.[12]

MITOCHONDRIAL DNA: IMMACULATE CONCEPTION IN THE GARDEN OF EDEN

If the standard anthropological myth regarding human origins can be compared for amusement to one of the best-known tales from Greek mythology, it is considerably more instructive, if no less amusing, to realize that its intellectual orientation actually owes much more to the biblical story of creation than it does to science.

"In the beginning, God created . . . " virtually everything simply by command.[13] Creation was instantaneous, miraculous, and divine. Since, in effect, there was no process, and because it was miraculous, there are no mechanics to discover and it cannot be studied and understood. The phenomenon of creation simply has to be accepted on faith.[14] This is the position taken by the proponents of "scientific" creationism, which is precisely why it cannot be called science. To start by denying that process can be studied and understood, and that aspects of understanding can be accepted or rejected on the basis of rigorous tests, is to deny the underlying conception of a scientific approach.[15] When dogmatic fundamentalists, whether they be Christian, Islamic, or other, declare that humans came into being instantaneously by an act of divine creation, they reject the very possibility of science.

It is interesting to note that the field of paleontology—including paleoanthropology—has its own fundamentalists, representatives of a strain of pre-Darwinian Neoplatonism with strong medieval roots. These are the particularly dogmatic "Hennigians" who have been called "transformed cladists,"[16] and they too deny that evolutionary process should or even can be studied.[17] Species are said to arise by "speciation events" that take place effectively instantaneously, no dynamics are ever considered, and natural selection is mentioned only to be denounced.[18]

The traditional biblical view, based on the the account in Genesis, traces human origins back to the Garden of Eden, reputed to be somewhere in the Middle East. Traditional anthropological accounts also tended to look to the origin of Modern human form somewhere in the Middle East.[19] The strength of these assumptions faded somewhat with the surge of evolutionary thinking that penetrated into anthropology from the biological sciences following World War II.[20] Recently, however, the old traditional medieval outlook has enjoyed a major resurgence and has re-established itself as the current majority view.[21]

It has done this with help from an unexpected source—molecular biology. As the study of the mechanics of inheritance advanced over the last quarter century, it became clear that some extra-nuclear DNA was not inherited in the usual fashion; that is, half from each parent of a fertilized egg. The exceptional DNA was that found in those tiny organelles in the cytoplasm named mitochondria, the so-called "power-plants" of the cell.[22] Mitochondrial DNA—mtDNA—makes up only one-tenth of one percent of the DNA in the whole genome, but it has some characteristics that make it a most fascinating and instructive molecule.[23]

Mitochondrial DNA does not come from the nucleus of the cell. Instead, it is a small, double-stranded, circular molecule of just under 17,000 base pairs, and it is inherited by each cell in the body directly from the cytoplasm of the original fertilized egg. That cytoplasm comes from the mother who produced the egg before it was fertilized. Mitochondrial DNA, then, is maternally inherited, or cloned.[24] It does not undergo crossover and recombination like ordinary strands of nuclear DNA, so it simply passes on in the female line from generation to generation, subject only to random loss when a given female line dies out or when mutations alter the identity of specific nucleotides. The mutation rate in mtDNA is many times more rapid than the mutation rate of nuclear DNA, but it is not the same in all regions of the mtDNA ring, and one of the problems that affects our ability to understand the meaning of mtDNA differences is the serious disagreements that exist concerning what the relevant mutation rates actually are.

The exciting thing about the study of mtDNA, however, is the realization that differences between the mtDNA configuration in each of the major population blocks of Modern *Homo sapiens* are proportional to the time since they shared a common ancestor—in this case, an original maternal ancestor. Researchers from the laboratory of the late Allan Wilson, at the University of California, Berkeley, have defended the view that the mtDNA configuration, which represents a survival of the oldest sequence still present in Modern human populations, is found today in sub-Saharan Africa.[25] The patterns found in such places as Europe and Asia, then, can be seen as differing from the African pattern strictly in proportion to the length of time since the ancestors of those various groups left Africa. Here is where the arguments about mtDNA mutation rate have led to so much disagreement.

The original group at the Berkeley laboratory, those who suggested this as a technique for measuring the age of divergence of Modern human populations, produced estimates that ranged in time from 50,000 years to three or four times that much. If the minimal estimate were true, this would mean that none of the fossil hominids in Europe, China, and Southeast Asia back in the Middle Pleistocene could be ancestral to the modern inhabitants in those regions. Indeed, one of the more publicized reports suggested that "*Homo erectus* was replaced without much mixing with the invading *Homo sapiens.*"[26] The cladistic representatives of hominid catastrophism, not surprisingly, were delighted with this. Two of them, Peter Andrews and Christopher B. Stringer at the British Museum of Natural History, immediately tried to gerrymander the available skeletal evidence so that it could be made to fit.[27]

Obviously this has created something of a furor. In fact, those of us who deal first with the skeletal and archaeological record could only splutter that something must be wrong. The evidence for regional continuity in cranial traits in Europe for over 100,000 years, in China for over 200,000 years, and in Southeast Asia for nearly a million years simply does not fit with such a suggestion. If the skeletal evidence does not fit, the much more abundant archaeological evidence fits even less well. There is virtually no archaeological evidence for the movement of any population out of Africa after the original spread of *Homo erectus* and its Lower Paleolithic culture late in the Lower Pleistocene about a million years ago.[28] In fact, the archaeological record is very clear that there were no major population movements from that time until 50,000 years ago when humans crossed the eastern Indonesian water gaps and got into New Guinea/Australia, and then at the end of the Pleistocene just over 10,000 years ago when people finally managed to cross the Bering Strait and spread out in the Western Hemisphere.[29] Subsequently, archaeology provides abundant evidence for the movement of Neolithic and, later, Bronze Age farmers out of the areas where major plant domestication had taken place and into the areas sparsely populated by hunting-and-gathering groups.

Other research teams have now entered the mtDNA field and, predictably, there are almost as many different views as there are research groups involved. One group even challenged the "out-of-Africa" view and suggested that Southeast Asia was a more likely spot for the hypothetical *Homo sapiens* Eden. Then several other groups, using different clustering algorithms, produced literally tens of thousands of alternate schemes that were even more likely than the one that had defended the recent "out-of-Africa" model.[30] After a long, hard look at the available evidence and the various schemes that have been offered, the most cogent appraisal suggests that mtDNA analysis has yet to give us a plausible hint of where or even how long ago Modern human differentiation began. The best that can be concluded is that there has been a "restricted but non-zero gene flow throughout the entire time period tracing back to the common mitochondrial ancestor with an overlay of a few recent population expansions of limited geographical range."[31] The ball is back in the court of the paleoanthropologists and the archaeologists now, and we can return to dealing with the tangible data available to us.

Certainly the study of mtDNA holds a great deal of promise. At the moment, it is producing very plausible pictures of the length of time since the recent divergence of populations such as Asians and Amerindians—plausible in that they agree with the archaeological and linguistic evidence.[32] And it is also producing estimates of post-Pleistocene population relationships in parts of the Pacific basin where there have been many questions in the past.[33] But these do not rely on calculating mtDNA mutation rates since the lengths of time are so short. Eventually, we can hope that the various calibration problems will be ironed out, and we will be able to rely on the projections it can produce to resolve our questions about the remote past.

For the moment, mtDNA analysis has captured a great deal of attention. The idea that it can pinpoint an original Modern home which might just involve an African Eve in an African Eden is something that has caught the imagination of the reading public. That heritage, passed on without male input, suggests a genesis that carries overtones of "immaculate conception." The whole package not only has great public appeal, it has been seized with enthusiasm by those anthropologists who have never felt very comfortable about dealing with the mundane mechanics by which human form was slowly shaped into the state we call "Modern."

THE MOSAIC NATURE
OF THE NEANDERTHAL-TO-MODERN TRANSITION

It scarcely needs to be said that this book does not subscribe to such a relapse into prescientific traditions. The attitude behind our approach is based on the assumption that the hominid fossil record can be comfortably accommodated within the framework of standard evolutionary theory as it is applied to the human world. Noting that the Neanderthals have an antiquity demonstrably greater than that of Moderns and that nothing but Modern skeletal material is evident since about 35,000 years ago, it is important to place both Stages within the same evolutionary framework. If, as is claimed, the Neanderthals simply evolved into Modern form, then structurally and temporally intermediate forms should be apparent, and some rationale should be available to account for the change. Fortunately for the present scheme, both can be produced, although, as we shall see, the emergence of Modern form was not something that took place in a lockstep kind of way everywhere it occurred. Instead, it happened in a decidedly mosaic and piecemeal fashion.

In the early 1930s, excavations in the rock shelter of Skhūl on the slopes of Mount Carmel in Israel (near the cave of Tabūn, which yielded a full-scale Neanderthal) produced a population of what has been called "Neanderthaloids" because they recall genuine Neanderthals in many respects, but, in other features, they deviate in the Modern direction (see Figure 14–2).[34] The dentition and the entire surrounding face has been somewhat reduced, leaving the forehead and sides of the cranial vault more vertical and producing the first vestiges of a distinct chin—formerly regarded as the "hallmark" of Modern form. Reductions in the robustness of ribs, long bones, and other aspects of the postcranial skeleton also show modification in the Modern direction.[35]

Also in the early-to-mid 1930s, excavations at the cave of Jebel Qafzeh, just over twenty miles to the east and north of Skhūl near the town of Nazareth, unearthed human skeletons, which, like those at Skhūl, have been referred to as "Modern," although with some archaic features retained (see Figure 14–3).[36] A third of a century later, excavations were resumed under the direction of Bernard Vandermeersch who used the results as the basis for his doctoral dissertation at the University of Paris.[37] Well over a dozen individuals are represented by the fragments, and some are complete enough so that decent statistical comparisons can be made. This makes it possible to come to conclusions that differ somewhat from the conclusions proposed by those who have been closest to the initial work of excavation and analysis.

For example, the fact that both Skhūl and Qafzeh show clear modifications in the Modern direction as compared with Neanderthals has led many scholars to lump them together as a single putative "Skhūl-Qafzeh population," in spite of the fact that each group is Modern in a way that is very different from the Modern nature of the other. The commingled group has

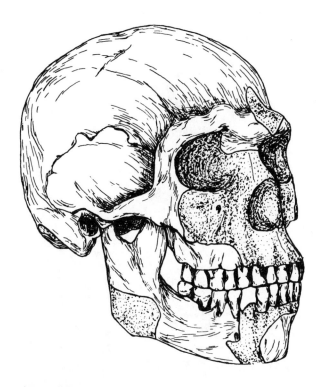

FIGURE 14–2.   A Neanderthaloid skull, Skhūl V, the best-preserved representative from a group of ten individuals found in a rock shelter on the slopes of Mount Carmel, Israel, in the early 1930s. (Drawn from a cast by M. L. Brace.)

been referred to as "Proto-Cro-Magnon" and even as an out-and-out "Cro-Magnon" form of hominid.[38] Presumably their descendants moved West from the Middle East and gave rise to the Cro-Magnons proper in western Europe somewhat over 25,000 years ago.[39] However, there are some problems with these assumptions. For one thing, the Qafzeh dentition is distinctly larger than that of the classic Neanderthals, and it would take less of a change to produce a Modern European set of teeth from a Neanderthal predecessor than from the jaws and teeth found at Qafzeh. Skhūl, on the other hand, has teeth that cannot be distinguished in size and form from the earliest Upper Paleolithic representatives of Modern humans in Eastern Europe.[40]

In the Skhūl specimens, the dentition has begun to reduce in the direction of the Modern inhabitants of a transect from western Europe to the Middle East (although the teeth are still closer to classic Neanderthal in size than they are to Modern Europeans). Qafzeh, on the other hand, has retained a full-sized set of Middle Pleistocene teeth at the same time that reinforcements of the post-cranial skeleton and skull have reduced to the extent that the specimens look distinctly Modern, if robust.[41] The Modern form

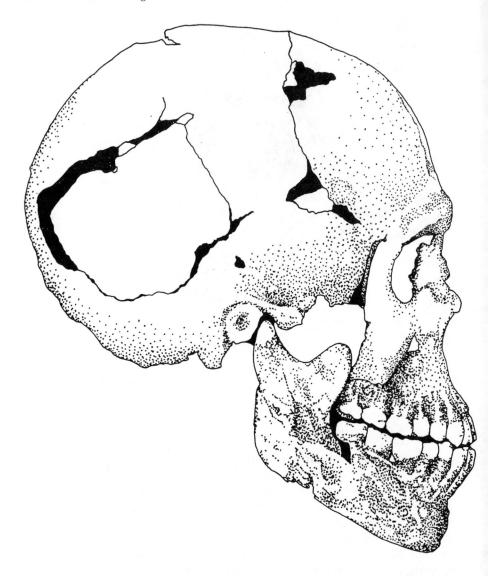

FIGURE 14–3. Qafzeh 9, a female skull from early in the Late Pleistocene of Israel, showing "Modern" sub-Saharan African cranial morphology and a Middle Pleistocene-sized dentition. (Drawn by Kay Clahassey after Plate 1 in Vandermeersch 1981.)

that they approximate, however, is not Modern European but Modern sub-Saharan African![42] Skhūl, on the other hand, has retained clear if reduced traces of Neanderthal form in the brow ridges and muscle markings of the skull and in the shoulder blades and pelvic form of the post-cranial skeleton.[43]

WHY iSRAEL?

As of yet, no sequence of fossils representing all of the steps by which the various regional Neanderthals became transformed into recognizably Modern form is available for any of the major geographical provinces where the archaeological record shows that human occupation has been continuous. Many scholars have taken this absence of transitional forms to indicate that in effect Moderns emerged instantaneously by some sort of "punctuation event," and that this is just the way evolution works. However, it was none other than Charles Darwin who realized that the vast majority of the individuals who lived in the past have left no trace of their existence and that, by its very nature, the fossil record is only a tantalizingly incomplete series of vignettes of what had once been a living continuum. For those who understand the nature of Darwinian process and use it to interpret the fossil record, "Absence of evidence is absence of evidence and not evidence of absence."[44]

Prehistoric humans may have left abundant evidence of their presence in the form of the imperishable stone tools they left behind, but, in contrast to the herd animals they hunted, the humans themselves were relatively rare creatures and there are long stretches of time where we simply have no tangible evidence for human form itself. When one really gets down to it, the famous Cro-Magnon specimen from the abundantly researched Upper Paleolithic is just about the only specimen known for a span of about 20,000 years from the end of the Mousterian to the later Magdalenian in western Europe.

While we cannot ignore that specimen and what it represents, there is no justification for the suggestion that it indicates stasis over that time stretch. When we examine the most abundant surviving pieces of the people who lived over that 20,000 year stretch—namely, the collections of teeth—it is clear that reduction in size and form was proceeding at a regular pace, and that the rate of change was quite sufficient to convert a Neanderthal into a Modern if it had continued from the time of full classic Neanderthals 50,000 years ago right up to the end of the Pleistocene and on to the present.[45] When the details of post-cranial robustness and muscle markings are examined, it is evident that they also show a gradual and unbroken gradation from full Neanderthal form through transitional manifestations in the Upper Paleolithic and on to the Modern state again, simply as the consequences of reduction.[46]

The evidence from other regions of the world is much less well-known than the European picture, but, where there are sequential pieces preserved—as with the collected dental evidence—the trajectory in each case is identical. The latter stages of the picture can be traced in Japan, China, Southeast Asia, and the Middle East, and in each case it seems clear that the

Modern state is achieved by reduction from what had been a much more robust condition in the past right there where the test is made. The only place where this evident course of *in situ* continuity seems to be contradicted by the material available is Israel where Skhūl and Qafzeh—both considered to be Modern if a bit on the "archaic" side—are so different from each other that it would be difficult if not impossible to derive them in place from the same more robust ancestor.

The answer has to be that their respective ancestors came from different parts of the world, and this is what makes the case of Israel and the early manifestations of Modern form there so interesting. Israel, unlike such places as southern Africa, western Europe, or eastern Asia, is right at the crossroads of the areas of human habitation and not at the ends. Any movement out of Africa to anywhere else in the world had to go through Israel. Any movement from the other parts of the world to sub-Saharan Africa also had to go through Israel. Recently it has been possible for Europe and Asia to make contact directly, but during earlier parts of the Pleistocene when the North Temperate Zone was only tentatively and intermittently exploited, that direct contact was much less likely. The more probable route, then, was through the Middle East and, inevitably, it included the area where Israel is located.

Israel, as a crossroads, is more likely than any of the other areas mentioned to have been graced by the occasional presence of representatives of one or another of the major continental regions inhabited. Of course, the continuously resident population would tend to prevail, as is generally the case with people at the same level of technological sophistication. The long-term residents of a given region know its resources and rhythms better than newcomers, and, unless there are other factors to be considered, major population displacements simply do not occur at the hunting-and-gathering level.[47]

One of those other factors, in the case of Israel, was the climatic alternation during the latter part of the Pleistocene between periods of more boreal (northern) conditions with occasional extensions of ecological conditions from south of the Sahara right up into Israel and the Middle East.[48] Israel, then, was both an obvious crossroads and a demonstrable zone of contact between a boreal and a more tropical ecology. It would hardly be surprising, then, if the remains of people found there showed the stamp of shaping influences that characterized markedly different parts of the world, namely the effects of adaptation to life in the North on the one hand and demonstrable ties with an African milieu on the other. In the long run, one would expect the features of northern origin to be more evident in the continuing population, but it is not only possible but likely that cultural elements that had their origin in those separate areas were adopted by those who had not been the first to develop them.

TIMING AND MECHANISM

For many years, the suggestion was made that the Mount Carmel material belonged in the last interglacial, which would have made it older than the full Neanderthals dated to the Würm glaciation in Europe and recently confirmed at Shanidar in Iraq.[49] To explain this mixture of traits, the interpretation was advanced that the people of Mount Carmel were hybrids between a fully Neanderthal group (initially represented by Tabūn, but now by Shanidar and a number of others) and a fully modern group for which such vague fragments as Piltdown were advanced as documentation.[50] When ^{14}C techniques were applied, the Mount Carmel caves were seemingly brought into line with European expectations, but it was eventually shown that radiocarbon was simply inadequate to deal with strata that proved to be twice as old as or even older yet than had been anticipated in either the Eurocentric view or in the assumptions that Modern human form had emerged in coordinated fashion.

Just recently, however, the electron-spin-resonance (ESR) and the thermoluminescence (TL) techniques have been used to date the Skhūl site.[51] Both ESR and TL have also been used to date Qafzeh,[52] and both sites are being given ages near 100,000 years.[53] This is substantially older than full-scale Neanderthal form in both Europe and the Middle East and has been regarded as proof for the view that Neanderthals could not have given rise to the Modern Stage of human evolution. With the hints of African affinities so obvious in Qafzeh, there seemed to be real justification for tracing it to sub-Saharan African origins and using it to indicate that all of what are now the various regional manifestations of Modern human form ultimately came out of Africa within the last 100,000 years.[54]

There were several additional matters that appeared to give support to this view. First, the faunal remains in the layers with the human skeletons at Qafzeh showed clear evidence for an incursion of sub-Saharan African forms.[55] Two species of sub-Saharan African mouse were among those faunal remains, and it seems clear that if ecological circumstances had allowed mice to make it all the way to Israel from south of the Sahara there is nothing that would have prevented people from coming along as well. Second, the stone flakes used as tools at Qafzeh were strikingly similar to those in the Middle Stone Age of sub-Saharan Africa, both in form and in the nature of their use-induced damage.[56] Finally, fragments of human skeletons from the southern part of Africa dating back to the end of the last interglacial or the beginning of the last glaciation have been called "Modern," and this has been taken to indicate the reservoir from which all subsequent Modern human form was derived.[57]

There is a counter to each of these points. This does not prove that the picture is necessarily incorrect, but, as we shall see, there simply is a better ex-

planation for the emergence of Modern human form that does not just derive it in black-box fashion from an African source. First, sub-Saharan African
mice do get up into the Middle East at the end of the Middle Pleistocene,
which clearly indicates that there was an open faunal avenue. Humans could
indeed have been part of that faunal connection, and I would argue that the
Qafzeh population actually did have a sub-Saharan origin not too far in its
past. The mice, however, never got any farther than Israel, and failed to perpetuate themselves in the face of competition from northern mice.

It is also true that the reductions in the Middle Pleistocene degrees of
cranial reinforcements and post-cranial robustness, which actually produced
Modern form, took place earlier in Africa than anywhere else. This evidently
was in response to the lessening of the selective forces that had maintained
those Middle Pleistocene amounts of robustness. However, characteristics
that have no obvious survival value and are shared by the inhabitants of a geographic province solely because of common inheritance will continue
through time in spite of major amounts of adaptive change. This is why the
measurable characteristics of the Qafzeh crania cannot be distinguished
from the configuration found in living people in sub-Saharan Africa, but
could never occur in Cro-Magnon of 25,000 years ago or in any more recent
East Asian, Middle Eastern, or European group. Regional patterns of craniofacial configuration appear to have a stability that runs through many tens of
thousands of years, although there have only been a few attempts to test
this.[58] Qafzeh is clearly a step in the direction of Modern form, but that form
is found only in living Africans and not Europeans, Asians, or any of the
other regionally identifiable clusters of Modern groups.[59]

The final reason it seems unlikely that the morphological moderniza-
tion that occurred earlier in Africa was the source of the Modern morphology that eventually emerged elsewhere is suggested by the very tools that
Qafzeh shared with its African contemporaries and predecessors. The key element is a long and elegant stone flake made by what is called the Levallois
technique,[60] and the reason this is a "key" is that these were hafted and used
as projectile points in the Middle Stone Age of Africa all the way from Klasies
River Mouth at the Cape of Good Hope to Qafzeh in Israel.[61] That means that
Africans from the beginning of the Middle Stone Age and perhaps up to
200,000 years ago were impaling their prey from a distance while their northern neighbors were still coming to grips with them with their hands. The relaxation of selective forces that this represents for the spear-throwers allowed
a reduction of robustness to occur through time, and the consequence was
the Modern aspects of form seen in the Qafzeh skeletons. When they got as
far as Israel, however, the people who were already there immediately copied
those projectiles and adopted them as their own.

Some 50,000 years later, the good Neanderthals at Kebara in Israel were
using the same kind of projectile points that had appeared at Qafzeh before
the last glaciation was fully under way. Of course, after adopting projectile us-

age, the people in the North subsequently underwent the same kind of reductions in robustness that had occurred earlier in Africa, and the consequence was the emergence of a northern version of Modern form. In the other direction, the phenomenon of obligatory cooking in the North had contributed to the prior reduction of jaw and tooth size, as can be seen at Skhūl. Subsequently the African immigrants at Qafzeh became acquainted with what had already produced a measurable degree of reduction in the jaws and teeth of their northern neighbors. At the moment, we are still unsure about the timing of just what occurred when, and the specimens illustrating the consequences are still skimpy and not entirely securely anchored in time. However, some version of this scenario has to have occurred to explain the survival of markedly larger jaws and teeth in sub-Saharan Africa to this day, while at the same time the vestiges of brow ridge enlargement remain more commonly observed in individuals from northern populations in Europe.

EARLY MODERNS BY REGION

Modern form emerged as a result of reductions in the levels of robustness present in Middle Pleistocene hominids, but this happened in piecemeal fashion in the various parts of the world—a classic case of mosaic evolution. In spite of some half-hearted attempts to claim that it is somehow more advantageous to be weaker, with bones that break more easily and joints that are more prone to dislocation and failure, it is hard to find a plausible biological justification for the "less is more" sentiments that are just about the only kinds of reasons offered to explain why those reductions should be regarded as adaptively advantageous.[62] Instead, it just seems more plausible to regard it as a case of "evolution by entropy"[63]; that is, in the absence of selection, things just tend to run down, which is just another way of saying that it is the product of the probable mutation effect.

Where specific technological innovations reduce the intensity of the selective forces that once maintained those portions of the anatomy that performed the functions for which those technological items are a substitute, then variations in those particular anatomical features will not be screened by selection. Since the vast majority of randomly occurring mutations will produce varying degrees of interference with the development of the traits that they control, where selection is reduced or suspended the traits in question will undergo a reduction through time. With human ingenuity increasingly finding ways to make survival easier, the prediction follows that technological refinements should presage reductions in just those anatomical features that no longer have to be quite as durable as they were before those particular aspects of technology were invented.

Modern human form, then, is the inevitable consequence of increasing refinements in the technological aspects of culture. It follows that early Moderns should display more archaic features than more recent Moderns, and the survival of an archaic feature in an otherwise Modern human population should be an indication that the population in question has possessed the relevant aspect of technology for a proportionately shorter period of time. The relevant technological innovations appeared at different times in different parts of the world, and the various manifestations of morphological reduction should be in proportion to the length of time that the innovation has been present in each area in question. As we shall see, these are testable predictions, and can be corroborated by an assessment of regional archaeological records and the anatomical features of the populations that were associated with their production.

Europe

I mention this region first, not because Modern human form first occurred there or that it was in any way central to the genesis of Modern form since this was clearly not the case, but principally because, in spite of its small area compared to the other major regions of the world, more work has been done in Europe and consequently more relevant specimens have been found there than in any other area no matter how large. Late in the last century, excavators in Moravia (northwestern Czechoslovakia) uncovered the remains of possibly more than two dozen early Upper Paleolithic individuals in an open air site near Předmost, fifty miles East of Brno (see Figure 14–4).[64] This is the largest assemblage of early Modern skeletal material that has ever been found—about half a dozen of the skulls were preserved well enough so that a real assessment of their form was possible (see Figure 14–5).[65] Unfortunately, the Germans commandeered the collection when they invaded Czechoslovakia early in World War II, and removed it to the castle in Mikulov. At the end of the war, the castle was set on fire before the German troops evacuated, and the entire collection along with some other similar and equally remarkable early Modern specimens were lost.[66]

The Předmost collection was associated with Early Upper Paleolithic tools of the same time and technological level as the Aurignacian in western Europe.[67] With samples of males and females from a wide range of ages, it is really the only picture we have of an Early Upper Paleolithic population in Europe. And a fascinating picture it is. Hrdlička regarded it as the "much searched-for bridge between the Neanderthal and recent man,"[68] and at least two of his contemporaries agreed with him.[69] Předmost obviously shows reductions from full Neanderthal form, but it retains an average degree of robustness that is missing from living Europeans. The jaws and teeth are exactly the same size as the jaws and teeth of Skhūl; that is, intermediate between Neanderthal and Modern European size, although quite a bit closer to Neanderthal than living Europeans.[70]

There was another collection of Aurignacian-level material that was also

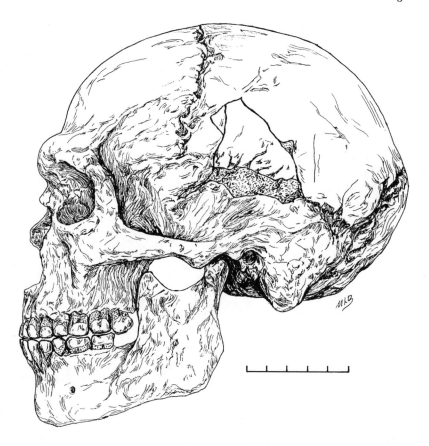

FIGURE 14–4. An Upper Paleolithic skull, Předmost III, a male from a large collection excavated in western Czechoslovakia in the late nineteenth and early twentieth centuries. The originals were destroyed with the castle at Mikulov prior to the German retreat from Czechoslovakia at the end of World War II. A lingering robustness of brow ridges, facial skeleton, and muscle markings recall earlier conditions in human evolution. (Drawn from a cast by M. L. Brace.)

recovered in Moravia, Czechoslovakia, late in the last century. Among the human bone fragments were half a dozen skulls—unfortunately missing their faces—from a small cave in a stone quarry at Mladeč.[71] Like Předmost, the date is approximately 30,000 and, also like Předmost, the traces of reinforcements over the brows and where the neck muscles attach to the back are half way between Neanderthal and Modern form. Some of the Mladeč specimens also were stored in the castle at Mikulov, along with the Předmost collection, and suffered the same fate.[72]

Still in eastern Europe, there is a collection of skeletal fragments from late Mousterian levels (dating some 10,000 years earlier) in northern Croatia at the site of Vindija that show characteristics of being in between Neanderthal and Modern degrees of robustness.[73] Objections have been raised

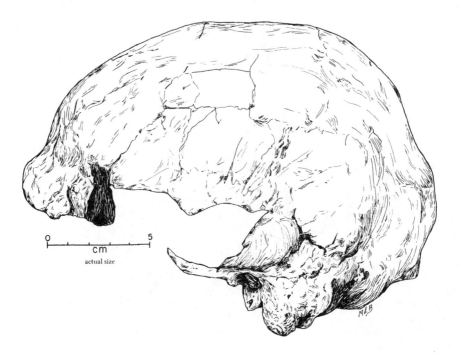

0 | 5
cm
actual size

FIGURE 14–5. An early Upper Paleolithic skull, Brno II, from Czechoslovakia, showing more than traces of Neanderthal form in the area of neck muscle attachments and in the brow ridges. Found in 1891 during sewer excavations in central Brno, the drawing (by M. L. Brace) is of the reconstruction made by Prof. Jan Jelínek (1959) and reproduced in Brace et al., 1979:151.

that the material is too incomplete to make a "convincing case,"[74] but the thinning of the brow ridges towards the lateral borders in what should have been a late Neanderthal context is just what one would expect if the transition from Neanderthal to Modern form were actually taking place. If those features had been found in association with Aurignacian tools, no one would have hesitated to ascribe them to a robust, early manifestation of Modern form. Like the features of Hortus and Saint-Césaire in the late Mousterian of southern France, they simply show that the reductions that ultimately led to Modern appearance were well under way in the late Mousterian.[75]

The last European specimens to be considered are the famous Grimaldi "Negroids." The Grimaldi Caves were investigated starting in 1872, prompted by the construction of avenues for transportation between Marseilles and Genoa along the shore of the Riviera. This is the portion of the Mediterranean coast where France abuts on Monaco, and Monaco abuts on Italy. An abundance of Paleolithic artifacts and some accompanying human skeletal remains were discovered over the course of the next thirty years in five different caves in the "commune of Grimaldi." On June 3, 1901, excavations at the Grotte des Enfants produced two human skeletons right on top of a Mousterian hearth at the bottom of the Upper Paleolithic.[76] These have proven to be Aurignacian burials—an "old" woman, and a youth on the threshold of his teens.

The adult female was not well-enough preserved to allow much in the way of detailed comparisons, but the youth attracted all kinds of attention, and has become what could only be called an icon in western folklore. When his face was reconstructed, he gave the appearance of having a dentition that projected forward in the middle of a rather short face in the fashion perceived in stereotype to be typical of the inhabitants of sub-Saharan Africa. This perception was enhanced by claims that the arms and legs had African proportions, and that there were African characteristics in other aspects of the facial skeleton.[77] The thing that impressed most observers, however, was the presence of an obviously large set of teeth in a short and not very robust face.

As it happens, this was the first Aurignacian skeleton to be discovered that had an intact and unworn set of teeth. Also, the skeleton was just on the threshold of adolescence, and, therefore, not fully developed. To make it more comparable to adult form, the deciduous molars were removed and the unerupted permanent maxillary premolars were elevated to what would be proper occlusal relationships for an adult. This, of course, meant that the bones of the facial skeleton were compressed and reshaped.[78] It was the indications of "inferiority" seen in the jaws and teeth as much as anything else that led to the judgment by Verneau and Boule that the Grimaldi skeletons were "Négroïdes."[79] In fact, the size and the form of the Grimaldi teeth puts them right in the range of the late Neanderthals. If those teeth alone had been found in a Mousterian layer, no one would have thought twice: They would have been immediately accepted as late Neanderthals. The shovel is considerably reduced from its early Neanderthal manifestations, and the lingual tubercle, just like that at Hortus and Saint-Césaire, has ceased to be a separate morphological element, but, unlike Modern African teeth, it retains vestiges of the earlier Neanderthal form.[80]

Even though the Grimaldi youth was barely at the beginning of adolescence, his craniofacial measurements were tested against those from a sampling of the populations of the world.[81] The results are not really conclusive because this involves comparing the suspect reconstruction of an immature specimen with groups of adults, but the tentative answer that emerges when the statistics are calculated is that he cannot be distinguished from recent Europeans, and that it would be most unlikely to find such a configuration in an African population.[82] Those aspects of dental robustness that drew such attention from his describers in fact were just what one would expect for a 30,000-year-old Modern who was less than 10,000 years removed from the Neanderthal-to-Modern transition.

There are several other less complete specimens from various places in Europe that are tentatively associated with the earlier part of the Upper Paleolithic just after the end of the Mousterian. Like the ones already discussed, they invariably show a greater degree of robustness than is true for the average living European, and the suggestion is difficult to avoid that their own ancestors were yet more robust. In many instances, it would not take much more robustness to put them comfortably within the Neanderthal range. The origin of Modern form as a consequence of reductions in Neanderthal robustness, then, is not contradicted by the available fossil evidence. When this is added to the expectations based on evolutionary theory and an appraisal of the archaeological record, then the *in situ* conversion of Neanderthal to Modern form is exactly what should have occurred.

Africa

In the whole continent of Africa, there is nothing like the quantity of archaic Modern specimens known for Europe. This does not mean that they were not there, it is just that Africa has only a very small fraction of the number of professional prehistorians that flourish in Europe. In Europe, also, the public at large is aware of the issues involved, and whenever new specimens are found as the result of farming or construction activities, even in the most rural locales, the matter quickly comes to the attention of the appropriate professionals. In much of Africa, however, comparable levels of literacy and awareness of local history/prehistory are still a long way from being achieved.

There are a number of finds worth mentioning, however, and the first of these is the partial skull found in 1932 in a warm spring deposit, Florisbad, north of Bloemfontein in the Orange Free State of the Transvaal in South Africa (see Figure 14–6).[83] The general morphology of the preserved parts of the nose, cheekbone, eye socket, and brow all recall Modern sub-Saharan African form, although the thickening of the supraorbital part of the brow is evidently greater than would be expected in living Africans. Attempts to date Florisbad using ^{14}C suggested an antiquity in the 30,000 to 40,000 year range, but that was just because the radiocarbon techniques of the time could go back no further than that. As it happens, Florisbad is way beyond the capabilities of ^{14}C and may well have a date between 100,000 and 200,000 years ago.[84]

If these dates are correct estimations, and that seems reasonable considering the associated artifacts,[85] then Florisbad was a contemporary of the early Neanderthals of Europe. But that also makes it a contemporary of the Neanderthaloids—the archaic Moderns at Skhūl and Qafzeh in Israel—and also of Border Cave and Klasies River Mouth. A more than Modern degree of robustness has been noted for the approximately contemporary fragments from both Border Cave and Klasies River Mouth,[86] and Florisbad itself has been regarded as "archaic" *Homo sapiens* even if not so archaic as full Neanderthal form.[87]

In June of 1967, a team headed by the young Richard Leakey was inves-

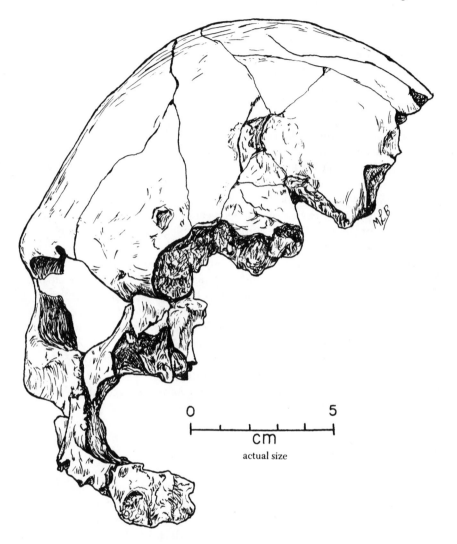

0   5
├──┴──┴──┴──┴──┤
cm
actual size

FIGURE 14–6.   Florisbad, an archaic Modern from near Bloemfontein in the Transvaal of South Africa, possibly early in the Late Pleistocene. Nuances of form are shared with living sub-Saharan Africans, but it is noticeably more robust. (Drawn by M. L. Brace from a photograph taken in the Nasionale Museum in Bloemfontein, Brace et al., 1979:157.)

tigating prehistoric deposits in southwestern Ethiopia in the Omo River area. The attraction, as far as fieldwork was concerned, was the discovery of fauna, Oldowan tools, and ultimately Australopithecines in the Shungura Formation of Pliocene age more than two million years ago.[88] The family heritage of "Leakey's Luck" held true, and team members found fragments of two crania, not from the Shungura Formation, however, but from the Kibish Formation early in the Late Pleistocene.[89] Uranium-Thorium dates from above the level of the cranial remains yielded a date of 130,000 years,[90] which puts the Omo Kibish material in the same time range as specimens from Klasies River to Qafzeh. Morphologically, too, the two crania have been regarded as archaic Modern, but Omo II is so archaic that it even verges on the degree of robustness seen in Ngaloba and ER-3884, the only known African Neanderthals.[91]

If one takes all the available evidence from sub-Saharan Africa, it would appear that archaic Modern form follows the African Neanderthal Stage (based on Ngaloba, ER-3884). Such specimens as Omo II are robust enough so that they evidently overlap the Neanderthal range of variation, but others range on towards robust versions of Modern form. All the specimens mentioned, however, are in excess of 100,000 years old when nothing but Neanderthals were present in Europe and comparable areas of the North (with the exception of Israel).

Evidently, Modern form emerged out of its Neanderthal predecessor earlier in Africa than elsewhere, and the suggestion has already been proposed that this was the result of a change in hunting technology symbolized by the presence of projectile points in the African Middle Stone Age. The reductions in cranial reinforcements and post-cranial robustness allowed by the use of projectiles led to the earlier emergence of Modern form from a Neanderthal ancestry in Africa. The subsequent spread of that technology to the North produced a somewhat later change in the nature of selection there as well, and the consequence was a somewhat later *in situ* emergence of Modern morphology out of northern Neanderthal ancestors.

East Asia

The evidence for Late Pleistocene human form is even skimpier in the Far East than in Africa, but there is at least a trace, which is more than can be said for South Asia or anywhere else between the western edges of the Old World and points farther East. In 1930, while the excavations that yielded the Pithecanthropines at Zhoukoudian was being undertaken, the site that was to produce early Modern human remains and an associated collection of Late Pleistocene artifacts was located in what is referred to as the "Upper Cave" at Zhoukoudian. When this was excavated in 1933, it yielded traces of seven individuals, including three skulls that were complete enough for productive study.[92] Figure 14–7 provides an example.

Of the three crania surviving, only one is complete and undistorted enough to allow reliable quantitative comparisons. Various authors have reported seeing aspects of such populations as Australians, Eskimos, Melanesians, Ainu, and Cro-Magnon in the Upper Cave individuals.[93] Whenever actual statistical treatment is undertaken, the conclusion has always been reached that, although it is not close to the Modern Chinese, it does display

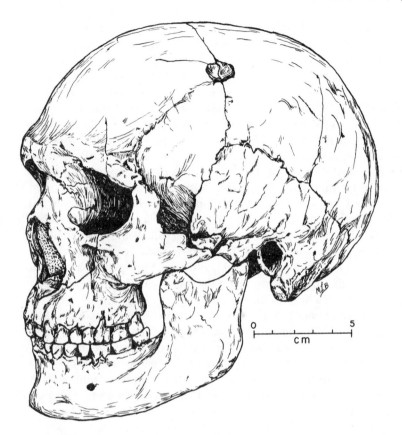

FIGURE 14–7. The "Old Man"—specimen 101—from the Upper Cave of Zhoukoudian, a Chinese contemporary of Cro-Magnon of Europe. (Drawn by M. L. Brace from the photograph of a cast, Brace et al., 1979:165.)

the pattern found among the survivors of the aboriginal population of Japan, the Ainu, and their prehistoric ancestors, the Jōmon. The Jōmon had been the original inhabitants of the Japanese archipelago when the ancestors of the modern Japanese invaded from the mainland somewhat over 2,000 years ago.[94]

The main difference between the Upper Cave and the prehistoric and living populations to which it is most closely related is its greater robustness and the fact that the dentition is measurably larger.[95] Dates now being cited are in the 25,000 year range, which makes it roughly contemporary with the overworked Cro-Magnon specimen from western Europe.[96] The actual proportions are quite unlike the Cro-Magnon pattern,[97] but, like Cro-Magnon, it differs from its most closely related modern counterparts principally in its greater robustness. If that tells us anything at all, it demonstrates that robustness decreased late in the Pleistocene in eastern Asia just the way it did in Europe, and suggests that a yet earlier ancestor was even more robust—in fact, enough so to qualify as a Neanderthal.

Early Modern status has also been claimed for a skeleton from Liujiang County in Guangxi Zhuang Autonomous Region, the southernmost Province of China. Found in 1958, it includes the skull and pieces of the postcranial skeleton of a middle-aged male.[98] A Uranium series date of 67,000 years has been given for strata at the site,[99] although the original describer suspected that it was not as old as the other elements of the site and its stratigraphic position "cannot be confirmed."[100] If the age is in the correct range, that would make Liujiang by far the least robust Late Pleistocene specimen ever found. Some have claimed to see hints of Australian or even African form in Liujiang, but these are not based on any kind of metric analysis.[101] Standard quantitative testing against samples representing the living human world show that Liujiang is excluded from all but eastern Asian groups. In that context, it is somewhat closer to the Ainu and prehistoric Jōmon of Japan than to any other populations, and in this sense it behaves somewhat like specimens from the Upper Cave of Zhoukoudian.[102]

There is one other site in East Asia that has produced convincing Late Pleistocene remains of Modern form. That is Minatogawa, a quarry some six miles southeast of Naha City on Okinawa, the largest island in the Ryukyu chain to the south of Japan.[103] Remains of two individuals were found in 1967, and they have been studied and published with promptness and skill. At 16,000 to 18,000+ years, they are clearly Late Pleistocene,[104] and they show in somewhat more rugged form the same kind of characteristics that were apparent in the post-Pleistocene Jōmon populations of Japan.[105]

Evidently, Minatogawa was part of that same network of late Pleistocene people in the Far East who inhabited the eastern edge of the continent and the adjacent islands. These included the Upper Cave people near Beijing in North China and Liujiang in the South—if Liujiang is indeed Pleistocene—and they gave rise to the population that constituted the original inhabitants of the Japanese archipelago from Hokkaido in the North to Okinawa in the Ryukyus in the South. They also gave rise to the people who first entered the western hemisphere at the end of the Pleistocene and to the groups who moved out into the small islands of the Pacific within the last 4,000 years.[106] However, they were not closely related to the people who are now the predominant inhabitants of eastern Asia. So far, we have no candidates for the Late Pleistocene ancestors of these latter Asians who obviously accompanied the spread of agriculture and largely obliterated the traces of the Upper Cave-Minatogawa configuration to the extent that their only obvious survivors are the remaining Ainu on Hokkaido, the northernmost of the Japanese islands.

Australia

To complete the picture of the appearance of early Modern form, we can turn to the fourth corner of the Old World—Australia. No other area better illustrates the mosaic nature of what constitutes Modern form and how it emerged. Australia was not continuously inhabited from the Lower Pleistocene on, as was true for the rest of the Old World South of the equator; nor was it inhabited from the Middle Pleistocene on, as was tentatively true for the more temperate areas. Instead, the first humans to get to Australia did so in the middle of the Late Pleistocene, about 50,000 years ago.[107] At that time, the inhabitants of Europe still fully qualified as Neanderthals and, as we shall see, there is more than a little reason to contemplate referring to the first entrants into the land "down under" as Australian Neanderthals.

Before 50,000 years ago, human beings, like other land mammals, could only extend their range as far as they could walk, and the permanent water barriers of eastern Indonesia kept them from moving into the realm of the marsupials in New Guinea and Australia. As long ago as 1860, Darwin's contemporary, Alfred Russel Wallace, had observed that, in regard to natural history, "South America and Africa, separated by the Atlantic, do not differ so widely as Asia and Australia." The faunal discontinuity in eastern Indonesia appears between Bali and the island immediately to the east and runs north between Borneo on the West and Sulawesi (Celebes), and it was christened "Wallace's Line" by another of their great contemporaries, Thomas Henry Huxley.[108] The faunal separation that it represents goes back to the split-up of the great southern continent, Gondwanaland, in the Mesozoic before the Age of Mammals,[109] and except for bats that flew and a few rodents that drifted, the only "native" placental mammals that live East of Wallace's Line today are *Homo sapiens* and the dogs they brought.

Evidently by 50,000 years ago, human beings had acquired the requisite technological capabilities to navigate across expanses of water that were never less than forty miles wide even at the time of the lowest sea levels during the height of the last glaciation.[110] Once they had gotten from eastern Indonesia to New Guinea, however, the rest was easy. During periods of lower sea level, New Guinea and Australia simply coalesced into one larger land mass and the Torres Strait that separates them today completely disappeared. The people who had made it across the crucial water gaps at that time were *Homo sapiens*, like all the inhabitants of the world at that time and ever since, and the chief thing that made them sapient was the possession of a fully Modern-sized brain. In their other traits, however, we can guess that they may have retained a fair measure of the robustness of their Middle Pleistocene ancestors.

If they were able to get across at that early time level, then repeated encounters across that gap must have occurred intermittently ever since. People engaged in reproductive behavior every time that happened, and the consequence was that specific unity was maintained right on through time to the present day. Some aspects of cultural exchange also must have taken place, but, even so, those water barriers represented a major buffer, and cultural innovations from the rest of the world were slow getting to and taking hold in Australia. Agriculture, metallurgy, pottery, and bows and arrows were unknown in Australia at the time of first European contact within the last 500 years, and, from the distribution of other cultural elements such as netting technology and the use of spear-throwers,[111] it is evident that things had been trickling into the continent from the North and slowly spreading out southwards.

A generation or two ago it was fashionable to denigrate Australian aboriginal culture as a Stone Age survival of an unchanged Pleistocene way of life—positively Paleolithic, in fact.[112] The producers of that "backward" culture, the aborigines themselves, were regarded by their European conquerors as the epitome of the "primitive." In the words of one widely used textbook in anthropology, "Physical anthropologists are in general agreement that the Australoid race is retarded in biological evolution and physically more primitive than other races."[113]

Unfortunately, this view is still alive and well in some quarters,[114] but, in fact, when they were forced to interact with the rest of the world, Australians were pursuing a very sophisticated Mesolithic subsistence economy.[115] The whole tenor of their way of life was post-Pleistocene, and there were areas that even verged on horticultural practices.[116] To be sure, they lacked some of the important innovations that have arisen elsewhere in the last 10,000 years and could be regarded as "behind" other parts of the world in that respect, but a lag of 10,000 years is miniscule when one contemplates the earlier time differential between the beginnings of projectile use and obligatory cooking at the western edge of the world.

As far as the impact on the selective forces that maintain aspects of anatomical robustness made by the relevant technological elements is concerned, obviously the time depth in Australia has to be far less than is true for any other part of the world. Even if we had no evidence to test our expectations, we could predict that Australians should have retained specific aspects of an earlier level of robustness to an extent not found in any other human population. We could even predict that there should be a gradient in Australia itself, with the greatest degree of retained robustness evident in the South, which the incoming aspects of technology reached last. These predictions are clearly borne out by the evidence available to us even though, as elsewhere in the world, the record is skimpy and incomplete and much more discovery and testing remains to be done.

Australia had to have been populated by people who came from an area West of Wallace's line, but the difference in craniofacial configuration between the living inhabitants of Bali, Java, and Sumatra—the islands immediately to the West—and the Australians is so marked that it is clear that the roots of those different patterns go back further than the emergence of Modern human form. The fact that living Indonesians do not have the intensity of skin pigmentation of people with long-term association with the Tropics suggests that their own ancestry should be traceable to the North, and indeed their craniofacial characteristics cluster with those of the Asian mainland right up through China.[117] The available evidence suggests that agriculturalists from the North moved down into the Tropics of peninsular Southeast Asia and Indonesia within the last 5,000 years, absorbing the original nonagricultural inhabitants and reflecting only subtle traces of the features of those aborigines except, increasingly, in the eastern islands of the Indonesian chain closest to New Guinea.[118]

If the living inhabitants of Indonesia largely show their debt to the Asian populations in the North, their predecessors should give us a picture of the probable ancestors of the aboriginal Australians, and indeed they do. Franz Weidenreich was quite explicit in noting that the late Middle Pleistocene Solo (Ngandong) specimens shared a whole series of traits with Australians. Furthermore, they also shared many of these details with the preceding Pithecanthropines.[119] This makes the sequence from the Javanese Pithecanthropines through the Solo transitional forms to the Modern Australians as good a picture of the emergence of a regional configuration of Modern *Homo sapiens* as we have for anywhere in the world.[120]

That being the case, prehistoric Australians should look even more like the Solo specimens, and this is evidently true. Living Australians have the largest brow ridges, jaws, and teeth of any Modern humans, but prehistoric Australians had larger ones yet.[121] Skulls are thicker, muscle attachments are more prominent, and long bone shafts are stouter.[122] More than 100 specimens have been found near the Willandra Lakes of western New South Wales, and the most robust of these has an ESR date of 29,000,[123] which makes him a contemporary of the Cro-Magnons of Europe. This specimen, WLH 50, has a cranial profile that duplicates the group average for the Solo (Ngandong) specimens of Java.[124] With a fully Modern brain but unreduced Middle-Pleistocene-level face and skeleton, this should qualify as a good Australian Neanderthal.

Of course, other individuals of that time are not so robust and would not immediately merit the designation Neanderthal. It just so happens that sexual dimorphism is more pronounced in living Australians than in other Modern populations, and this was apparently even more the case in the past.[125] The very fact that some members of a population are robust enough to earn the label Neanderthal while others in the same population would not is a good example of how arbitrary this business of assigning names can be.

But if there were people in Australia 30,000 years ago who would warrant being called Australian Neanderthals, and if that should mean that the items of technology that led to the reduction of Neanderthal form in a modern direction had not had enough time to have had a measurable effect, then this should agree with what we can see in the archaeological record. At contact, the use of projectiles in hunting and the use of earth ovens for cooking was universal in Australia. Because many Australians used wooden spears with fire-hardened points as projectiles, there is no good way of telling how far back in time projectile usage went. Since robustness and muscularity decrease through time, there is some reason to suspect that the first entrants to cross Wallace's line brought their throwing spears with them.[126]

There is also evidence that the first entrants brought fire with them as well,[127] but, like the inhabitants of Africa during the Middle Stone Age, they may well have had control of fire but not have used it in cooking. Certainly the terminal Pleistocene Kow Swamp and Coobool Crossing people continued to have teeth of Middle Pleistocene size, and, although there are traces of earth ovens that go back 15,000 to 30,000 years,[128] the evidence pales beside its ubiquitous presence and use after the end of the Pleistocene.[129] It was during this later period also that tooth size in the Murray River Basin of New South Wales and South Australia underwent a reduction at the same rate that characterized its diminution in the change from Neanderthal-sized to Modern-sized teeth in Europe.[130] However, instead of a span of 50,000 years, as was the case in Europe, it was only on the order of 10,000 years and it lacked a final 10,000 years where the use of pottery doubled the rate of reduction, as was the case all across the northern part of the Old World.

The use of food preparation techniques, including grinding and pounding as well as earth-oven cooking, evidently got into Australia from the North and reduced the selection maintaining Pleistocene-sized teeth first in the North and then progressively towards the South. One can surmise that it was also accompanied by gene flow from people in New Guinea and points West who had enjoyed the benefits of those techniques and who had started to undergo dental reduction as a consequence. At the moment, there is no way to say how much Australian tooth size reduction was the consequence of gene flow from an area of prior reduction and how much was the result of selection force relaxation *in situ*.

In any case, the prediction that emerges is that there should have been a tooth size gradient—a cline—running from North to South, with the largest teeth evident in the southern reaches that were the last to adopt the incoming techniques. This is indeed the case, and, correcting for body size, the smallest teeth were to be found in the North, where they were the size of late Upper Paleolithic teeth in Europe, while the teeth in the heart of the Murray River basin in the Southeast were still larger than those of the classic European Neanderthals.[131]

THE UPPER PALEOLITHIC

Several generations of scholars now have noted that, in Europe, the appearance of Modern form is correlated with the appearance of Upper Paleolithic tool-making traditions, although the modernity of that form is generally overemphasized. From the time of Marcellin Boule on, many interpreters have assumed that there was something inherent in Modern form that led to the production of Upper Paleolithic cultural manifestations.[132] At the same time, there is the often stated opinion that human biological evolution ceased at this point and that the rest was all culture.[133] There is a wondrous European ethnocentrism in this which is confounded by the fact that what counts as Modern human form actually appears in Africa as much as 100,000 years earlier. Rather than Modern morphology somehow entailing the production of Upper Paleolithic tools, it was elements of Mousterian technology that changed the nature of selective forces and allowed those reductions in robustness to accumulate, which generated what we complacently refer to as Modern human form.[134]

The advance in technological complexity of the Upper Paleolithic over the Mousterian has often been regarded as comparable to the advance that the Mousterian showed over the Lower Paleolithic. Refinements in tool-making were signalled by the technique of preparing flint cores so that long narrow spalls, technically called *blades,* could be detached.[135] (Samples of Upper Paleolithic flint tools are shown in Figure 14–8.) This increased the number of tools that a given amount of raw material could yield. Furthermore, the tools thus produced could be worked into a greater variety of functionally distinct forms than was previously the case. However, this did not occur in the earlier part of the Upper Paleolithic. Instead, at the beginning of the Upper Paleolithic, subsistence techniques and residence sites continued to be largely the same as they had been in the previous Mousterian.[136] Indeed, some of the early Upper Paleolithic local traditions were simply transformations *in situ* of Mousterian predecessors.

Evidently the big technological advance in Europe occurred, not between the Mousterian and the beginning of the Upper Paleolithic, but between the early and the late Upper Paleolithic.[137] Points, knives, and scrapers were refined, and to these were added a variety of gouging tools called burins. Evidently these were used in working bone and antler, and they coincide with the appearance of an extensive bone industry: harpoon points, awls, and needles with eyes in them.[138]

From the appearance of those needles, we can infer that shaped and sewn (tailored) clothing was being made. Light harpoon heads were added to the roster of heavy bone spear points, and it is obvious that European hunters were now using the technique of hurling projectiles at prey. This is further supported by the appearance of spear-throwers, (*atlatls,* to give them their Mexican name), which, by acting as an extension of the arm, significantly increased the power of propulsion and added to the effective range over which a spear could operate. Certainly the vast quantities of animal remains found in Upper Paleolithic sites attest to the effectiveness of hunting techniques, and we can assume that a higher level of social cooperation lay behind their evident ability to drive game in quantity.

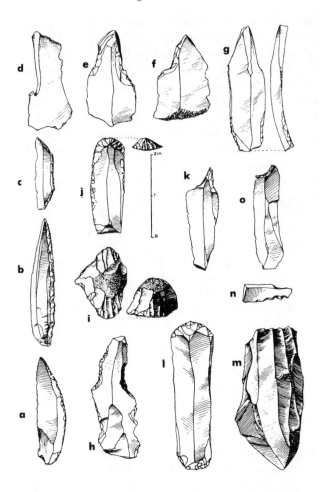

FIGURE 14–8. European Upper Paleolithic flint tools: (a) and (b), "knife points"; (d–g), gravers or burins; (i), (j), (l), (o), scrapers; (k), a piercer; (c), (h), (n), miscellaneous tools; (m), a core from which blades have been struck. (By permission of the British Museum of Natural History.)

The picture that is usually developed of the Upper Paleolithic is based largely upon work that has been done in Europe over the last century and a third. It depicts adaptation to circumstances associated with the presence of the last stretch of glacially affected climate, and it is not really appropriate to use it as the measure for trying to understand how people in other parts of the world were living, although it does afford some insight into the adaptations of people at the same latitude. For example, while China was not glaciated the same way that Europe was, it was distinctly colder than at present. The presence of eyed bone needles in the Upper Cave of Zhoukoudian indicates that sewn clothing was being used, but the overall impression recorded by comparative archaeological assessment is that the cultural traditions there were "deeply rooted in the earlier Pleistocene of China."[139]

In the Middle East, the roots of the Upper Paleolithic in the preceding Levalloiso-Mousterian are clearly indicated,[140] and in sub-Saharan Africa the Later Stone Age, which starts somewhat less than 40,000 years ago,[141] clearly emerges from the preceding Middle Stone Age. In Europe also, although there may be elements that were adopted from outside, there is much that simply appears to be *in situ* continuity.[142] As with the skeletal evidence itself, the cultural sequence in each region shows a picture of continuation in place leavened by aspects of novelty that spread from elsewhere and was grafted onto what was already there.

THE ORIGIN OF ART

It has often been assumed that with the advent of the Upper Paleolithic, we can see the first manifestations of human artistic capabilities used solely for esthetic purposes.[143] In fact, the beginnings of the modification of the surfaces of stone and bone for nonutilitarian purposes clearly go back to the Mousterian and are not greatly advanced over that level in the early Aurignacian of Europe.[144] In those assemblages called Châtelperronian, which grew directly out of the Mousterian, it is clear that items such as animal teeth were being modified for use as pendants.[145] For those who are convinced that the Neanderthals were too dense to have conceived of this themselves, the answer is that they were imitating their early Aurignacian contemporaries.[146] The only problem with this is that the Aurignacian itself is relatively "impoverished" in regard to what we would call objects of art.[147]

The big change, as was true for subsistence technology, did not come when the Upper Paleolithic succeeded the Mousterian but when the early Upper Paleolithic was succeeded by the late Upper Paleolithic.[148] Animal outlines engraved on bone and stone surfaces clearly depict forms that can be identified as to species. Along with equally realistic three-dimensional sculptures using bones and pebbles, these objects constitute what has been termed "portable art." Later still in the Upper Paleolithic, extraordinarily realistic and often life-sized polychrome paintings of Pleistocene animals were applied to the walls of caves in western Europe.[148] Although artistic technology did not change the nature of the selective forces that affected human survival, it does give us just a glimpse into a realm of culture that is less tangible but no less important than the one preserved in the abundant pieces of stone and bone.

The fieldwork of ethnologists—social/cultural anthropologists—among Modern groups who lack writing, but whose artistic accomplishments display similar levels of sophistication, shows that the other perishable areas of cultural achievement are equally well-developed. Amerindians of the Northwest coast of North America, the Dogon and Benin of West Africa, the Melanesians of New Britain and New Ireland, and the Maori of New Zealand, among others, have all been rightly celebrated for their spectacular artistic productions.[149]

We know also that these accomplishments are paralleled by equal levels of sophistication in cultural traditions that include myths, legends, orally recounted history, codes dictating social behavior, case law, and a knowledge of natural history that regularly astonishes professional biologists.[150] Many of these aspects of culture are of essential value for human survival. So, although our glimpse into the realm of unpreserved cultural behavior of the Upper Paleolithic does not go much beyond the visually decorative—however spectacular that may be—it does suggest to us that other aspects of culture had developed to a comparable extent.

STRING AND WHAT IT IMPLIES

As the Upper Paleolithic progressed from its early to its later phases, not only is it evident that the people of the Upper Paleolithic were able to hunt large game with greater efficiency, but, for the first time in prehistory, they were able to acquire small game in great and increasing quantities. Vast amounts of rabbit-sized mammals, birds, and fish were now being utilized, as attested to by the quantity of their bones in later Upper Paleolithic sites. Of course, it is possible to spear a fish, a bird, or a rabbit individually, but it is a laborious and time-consuming process and it does not yield the quantities to which the archaeological record now attests. What is indicated is the development of one of those things that we now take for granted but which might be called an "unobvious" element of technology—string.[151] The concept of string is indicated by the presence of eyed needles and the even earlier appearance of drilled beads that were obviously used as necklaces and other decorative arrangements that were made by stringing them in loops.[152]

But string can also be used to make fish lines, noose snares, and nets. And with nets, flocks of birds and schools of fish become available sources of food to an extent previously impossible. Since birds, fish, and small mammals represent an edible biomass that is as great as or greater than that represented by large game, the subsistence base in the Upper Paleolithic was greatly expanded, and at far less risk than had previously been the case. Casting a net over a flock of feeding quail or drawing a seine around a school of fish requires only a fraction of the raw muscle required to impale 100 or 200 hundred pounds of deer or wild pig and then survive the thrashings of the wounded prey.

String in network form can also be used as a container to increase the efficiency of the gatherer. Mesh bags make it possible to collect things in quantity that would otherwise be impossible. Roots, nuts, berries, fruit, eggs, shellfish, and the like could be brought back by the kilogram instead of by the handful.[153] Other containers such as woven baskets can also serve the same purpose. At the moment, we cannot say which came first—the bag or the basket—but the masses of snail and clam shells in late Upper Paleolithic sites indicate that some sorts of such containers were now being used for the first time.

With the advent of net-assisted hunting, the selective pressures that had long maintained Middle Pleistocene levels of skeletomuscular robustness were now markedly reduced. We could predict that the probable mutation effect would produce an immediate consequent reduction in that degree of robustness. This, in fact, is precisely what happens and the predictable result is "Modern" form.[154]

MOUSTERIAN CONTINUITY

Initially, the Upper Paleolithic appeared in the same area where the Mousterian had flourished before it. The same caves were utilized as shelters and the same kinds of animals continued to be hunted.[155] Some Upper Paleolithic traditions in western Europe—the Châtelperronean, for example—are simply modified continuations of the local Mousterian. All told, the Upper Paleolithic can be regarded as a refined outgrowth—a culminating perfection—of the cold-climate adaptation of which the Mousterian represents the beginning stage.[156] New technological items were added, although many are simply refinements of the cruder Mousterian counterparts. The complex of refined cold-climate technological items and the hunting life-way associated with them spread across the northern reaches of the entire Old World. After the end of the Pleistocene, they spread East across the Bering Sea to North America, and their culmination could be seen in the extraordinary arctic hunting culture of the Eskimos from Alaska to Greenland, which lasted into the twentieth century, vestiges of which survive today. Obviously, this was a remarkably successful cultural adaptation.

Survival in the North Temperate Zone during the Late Pleistocene depended upon the cultural developments that started in the Mousterian and continued without break in the Upper Paleolithic. Because cultural changes, even at the Australopithecine level, represent alterations in the selective forces that affect the hominids involved, we should expect to find some sort of reflected change to have occurred in the anatomy of the beneficiaries. I have already mentioned the consequences of the development of projectiles, obligatory cooking, and string technologies. Another of the most obvious differences which set apart the Mousterian and the Upper Paleolithic from the preceding Lower Paleolithic is the appearance of a profusion of special cutting tools. From the choppers and bifaces (hand-axes) and the crude flakes of the pre-Würm cultures, one goes to a variety of points, scrapers, and knives of the Mousterian to the even more elaborate stone technology of the Upper Paleolithic. Obviously the ability to manipulate the surrounding world has been one of the prime factors in the successful survival of the human line, but equally obvious is the fact that a technological basis for any extensive manipulating did not exist prior to the Mousterean.

CHANGES IN SEXUAL DIMORPHISM

We have already noted that one of the main consequences of this increase in technological sophistication was a relaxation of the forces of selection for maintaining Middle Pleistocene levels of muscularity and robustness. The thrown spear meant that prey could be dispatched from a distance. Snares and nets later reduced the amount of muscular effort on the part of the hunters still further. The changes in the impact of the relevant selective forces, then, should have had greater consequences for the maintenance of the male than of the female physique. We could predict that a reduction in male size and robustness should have been more marked than would have been true for females. This, in fact, is exactly what happened. The consequence is that the marked degree of sexual dimorphism preserved throughout the Middle Pleistocene and clearly visible in the Neanderthals underwent a clear-cut decrease.[157]

Sexual dimorphism decreased throughout the Late Pleistocene, and it has continued to decrease in the post-Pleistocene. The switch from a hunting-and-gathering life-way to farming took place in some parts of the world as much as 10,000 years ago, and, while the work associated with tilling the soil is justly recognized, it does not require those periodic bursts of high-energy output and athletic ability that characterized the life of a Pleistocene hunter. We could predict that, among the living people of the world today, the minimum surviving degree of sexual dimorphism should be visible among those whose ancestors were the first to switch to farming as a means of subsistence. There is some incidental evidence to support such a prediction,[158] but the question has not been investigated in a systematic fashion, and, at the moment, no definitive statement can be made.

DENTO-FACIAL REDUCTION

From the extraordinary wear visible on the front teeth of the Neanderthals and their predecessors,[159] we can suggest that the dentition bore the brunt of the finer manipulations and itself served as a sort of general all-purpose tool—the original built-in, as we have previously noted. With the appearance of an adequate cutlery at the beginning of the Mousterian, the significance of possessing large and powerful front teeth was substantially decreased. This would have allowed the probable mutation effect to operate throughout the early Würm, resulting in the reduction of the forward part of the dental arch and the supporting parts of the face. Furthermore, the process must have been speeded up as technological refinement advanced toward the Upper Paleolithic level. In similar fashion, the continuation of the cookery traditions that began in the Mousterian relaxed the selective pressures that had formerly maintained a Middle-Pleistocene-sized set of molars. The modern face, then, took shape as a result of reductions at both the front and back of the dental arch.[160]

The significance of this change in tooth use can be appreciated if one considers for a moment the characteristic mode of eating of modern hunting-and-gathering people. Meat is not daintily manicured into bite-sized portions with knife and fork before ingesting. Rather, a chunk is taken in one hand, thrust part way into the mouth, where it is held with the front teeth, and then sawed off at lip level by means of a cutting implement—the "stuff-and-cut" school of etiquette, as it has been called.[161] As practiced by modern hunters and a variety of peasants throughout the world, it is aided by the use of metal knives, but, even so, the effect is sufficient to produce a substantial amount of flat wear on the incisors and canines, resulting in the "edge-to-edge" bite characteristic of so many of the nonwestern peoples of the world. In fact, before the refinements of eating habits indicated by the adoption of chopsticks in Asia, and later by the knife and fork in the West, the edge-to-edge bite was the universal human condition.[162] Before the development of metallurgy, this form of tooth wear was even more extensive; we can just imagine the burden placed on the front teeth *before* the development of even adequate *stone* cutlery.

The heavy wear apparent on the front teeth of many of the Neanderthals indicates that the burden was only gradually shifted from teeth to tools. For this reason, the reduction of the full Neanderthal face is only halfway accomplished in the Skhūl population at Mount Carmel and remained incomplete in the early Upper Paleolithic, which suggests that the teeth were still important for more than simply processing food. The curious rounding wear of Neanderthal incisors and the details of the manifestation of that wear revealed by the scanning electron microscope suggest that they were using their teeth to process leather in a fashion similar to that of the modern Eskimo.[163] This is consistent with the view presented previously that the Neanderthals were utilizing skins for clothing. This brings up another area of cultural adaptation and leads to another suggestive, if unproven, speculation.

THE START OF DEPIGMENTATION

Recall that the development of a hairless and heavily pigmented skin was suggested for the hunters early in the Pithecanthropine Stage. From this we must assume that the early Neanderthals, who first successfully adapted to the North Temperate Zone prior to the Würm, were dark brown or "black," as a correlate with the general human tropical physiology. The use of clothing, among other things, was of great importance in the success of their adaptation to the northern areas of habitation. By covering the skin with clothes, the importance of the epidermal pigment melanin as an ultraviolet filter was drastically reduced. Once again, the probable mutation effect operating over a substantial period of time would serve to reduce the structure whose importance had decreased.[164] In this case, the "structure" is melanin, the principal pigment in the human skin. The consequence of its reduction, of course, is depigmentation. It is of more than passing interest to note that, in general, those parts of the world where the amount of pigment in the human skin is at a minimum are also just those areas where Mousterian scrapers and Neanderthal teeth indicate that clothing has been utilized for the longest period of time. The picture evoked by a blond Neanderthaler is somewhat contrary to the usual stereotype, but it is quite possible that the invention of clothing by the Neanderthals prior to the Würm was the source of the depigmentation phenomenon that allows some of the peoples of the world today to be described by the euphemism "white."[165]

Now, if it was conditions in the North Temperate Zone that led to the amount of depigmentation that lets some people be called "white," then why are not all of the people who are long-term residents of North Temperate latitudes equally depigmented? Why, for example, are there no native blonds in China or Mongolia? The answer has to be that their ancestors have just not been at that latitude for as long a stretch of time as have the residents at comparable latitudes at the western edge of human habitation. Eventually this guess can be tested archaeologically. In this case, the current absence of evidence may really mean that there were no people there from the penultimate glaciation on, although that might be just because not as much archaeological research has been undertaken in those portions of eastern Asia.

Compared to the residents of the Tropics, the inhabitants of the temperate portions of eastern Asia have undergone a major degree of depigmentation from our assumed common tropical ancestor. It just has not proceeded quite so far as depigmentation in Europe, and this should mean that the ancestors of Europeans were permanent residents at that latitude before the last interglacial. The archaeological record says that there were people there over 200,000 years ago, but the tools were Mousterian and the people were Neanderthals. For that matter, the inhabitants of China at that time were also Neanderthals, albeit Chinese Neanderthals. If the European Neanderthals gave rise to Modern Europeans, then we can guess that it took something more than 200,000 to 250,000 years for a European amount of depigmentation to occur.

On that scale, the maximum amount of Asian depigmentation should have needed between 150,000 to 200,000 years to take place. These estimates of pigment change fit with the rates observed in the only two instances where dated test cases are known. One of these is the spread of long-term tropic dwellers into Australia 50,000 years ago. Australia extends down almost as far south of the equator as China does north, and, if our predictions hold, depigmentation should have become apparent in the descendants of the first occupants of the South Temperate Zone in Australia. This has indeed taken place, and the great majority of southern Australian aborigines can be described as light brown or lighter, while those in the north are "chocolate" or darker.[166] Depigmentation in the South is indeed evident, but not to nearly the extent that is found in China, where it has been taking place three times as long or more.

The other test case is the Western Hemisphere, where the maximum human antiquity does not go back demonstrably more than 12,000 years.[167] The arrivals came from the Northeast portion of the Asian coast from ancestors who had been undergoing depigmentation for maybe 150,000 years or more, and they quickly spread throughout the length and breadth of the New World. It tells us something about how long it takes for selection to produce significant amounts of skin color change when we note that, even though people have been in the Tropics of the New World for over 10,000 years, there is still no significant difference in skin pigment between the inhabitants at the equator and those in either the North or South Temperate Zone extremes. Evidently 50,000 years is long enough to produce a clearly evident pigment change, but 10,000 years is not.

GRINDING STONES, POTS, AND CONTINUING EVOLUTION

Many have assumed that once Modern form was achieved, "we" had arrived, evolution had stopped, and we should live happily ever after, virtually unchanged, world without end, amen.[168] The truth, however, is quite otherwise. The changes that produced early Modern out of Neanderthal form have continued in the same direction and, if anything, have actually speeded up. In fact, some aspects of dental and facial reduction are now proceeding at between double and triple the rate that served to convert Neanderthal into Modern form.

Late in the Pleistocene, the herds of large-sized game animals began to disappear. Some have suggested that the efficiency of the Upper Paleolithic hunters had gotten so great that they were cropping the herds faster than they could reproduce.[169] In any case, big game hunting became a less and less important aspect of human subsistence activities. Many an archaeologist, relishing the dramatic imagery conjured up by the Pleistocene mammoth hunters, has felt that the culture of the succeeding Mesolithic represented a "decline" from the heights of art and technology that had previously been achieved. Again, this simply is not the case. During the Mesolithic, the further concentration on nets and traps emphasized the shift in focus from the disappearing large game. Furthermore, the development of mortars and pestles and various forms of grinding technology allowed the people of the Mesolithic to begin to utilize an even more significant source of foods than had been possible before—namely, grains. The seeds of the grass family— wheat, oats, millet, barley, rice, and the like—as well as pulses such as lentils and peas, represent an enormous dietary resource that had previously been unavailable. Their exploitation led to a substantial population increase.[170]

By the end of the Pleistocene, just over 10,000 years ago, the use of grains as a subsistence base had advanced to the extent that they were being deliberately planted and tended in the Middle East and in South China/Southeast Asia, and the gathering of the Mesolithic had been transformed to the full-fledged farming of the Neolithic.[171] Shortly thereafter, the discovery and manufacture of pottery further reduced the already lessened survival value in the possession of a large and well-formed dentition. In cooking pots, food can be simmered to drinkable consistency, at which point the edentulous can ingest their calories as easily as those who still possess a veritable Pithecanthropine dental arch. It is no accident that the populations with the smallest and fewest teeth in the world today are those associated with the areas where the Neolithic and preceding Mesolithic go back farthest in time.[172]

With the suggestion that changes in the cultural adaptive mechanism are responsible for changes in face form, skin color, skeletomuscular robustness, and sexual dimorphism, it should be possible to account for some of the major visible differences between the living peoples of the world in the same way. Some of this has already been mentioned briefly, although to go into this in any detail is beyond the scope of this book. In the area where technological complexity has been having its impact for the greatest length of time, we would expect dental reduction to have proceeded to its greatest extent—and, as can be seen, these expectations are fulfilled. The most striking example occurs in Australia, where the facial form of the aborigines shows less reduction than in any of the other modern human groups. Even within Australia, however, there is a remarkable North-South gradient. Mesolithic culture elements such as nets and seed grinders clearly came in from the North after the end of the Pleistocene.[173] These altered conditions for the inhabitants, who had been living there for up to 50,000 years, to such an extent that, at the time of contact with the incoming Europeans, tooth size of the northernmost aborigines had reduced to the level visible in the European Upper Paleolithic. That reduction was less apparent towards the South, where the incoming cultural elements had much less time depth. By the time one gets down to the Murray River basin in southern Australia, one finds that tooth size had reduced only slightly from the Middle Pleistocene level of the fossil Murray inhabitants of only 10,000 years ago, and, at least in their molars, tooth size was distinctly larger than it had been for the "classic" Neanderthals of western Europe 50,000 years back.

Differences in the modern range of dento-facial robustness can be seen in the illustrations of male and female European skulls (in this case, Germans)[174] and the contrasting male and female Australian aborigines (southern Australians from the Murray River basin).[175] (Figures 14–9 and 14–10 provide examples of the Australian male and female.) Admittedly I chose one of the most robust Australian males for the example so the brow ridge

FIGURE 14–9.   Southern Australian male. (Drawn by M. L. Brace at the Department of Anatomy, University of Edinburgh Medical School, courtesy of Professor George. J. Romanes.)

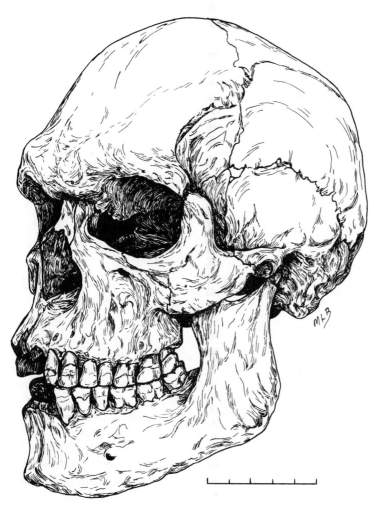

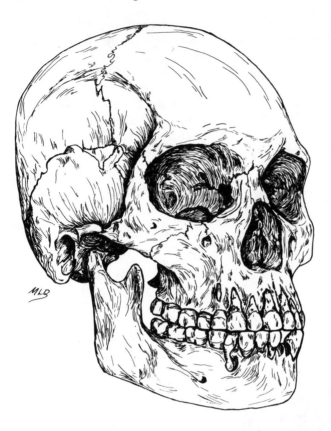

FIGURE 14–10. Southern Australian female. (Drawn by M. L. Brace at the American Museum of Natural History, New York, courtesy of Dr. Ian Tattersall.)

shown actually represents the extreme of the Australian range of variation. Even so, the degree of sexual dimorphism among the southern Australian aborigines is considerably greater than that normally seen among the other modern human populations of the world. In this respect also, they have retained more of the characteristics generally found some 50,000 years ago.[176]

The Europeans, on the other hand, do not represent the maximum degree of facial reduction among living human populations because, as can be clearly seen, they retain quite substantial noses, showing in this instance a greater degree of retention from the past than is true for many of the other peoples of the world (see Figures 14–11 and 14–12). The contrast between southern Australian and European tooth size and robustness, however, does

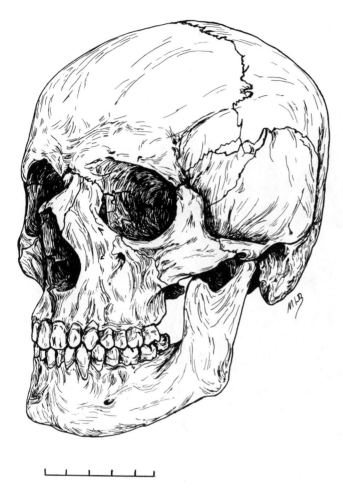

FIGURE 14–11. German male from Bavaria. (Drawn by M. L. Brace at the American Museum of Natural History, New York, courtesy of Dr. Ian Tattersall.)

come close to illustrating the extremes visible in the modern spectrum. The southern Australians are clearly the least reduced in this respect, while the Europeans vie with just a few other groups as representing the most reduced (see Figure 14–13). The illustration showing the contrast in the Australian and European conditions in fact displays, side-by-side, the dental arches of the same female Australian and European individuals used to demonstrate the contrast with male cranial form depicted in the previous pictures. Not only are the teeth of the European markedly reduced in size, but the third molars (or so-called "wisdom" teeth) are congenitally missing, which reflects a kind of ultimate reduction. Australians, like all humans over 30,000 and

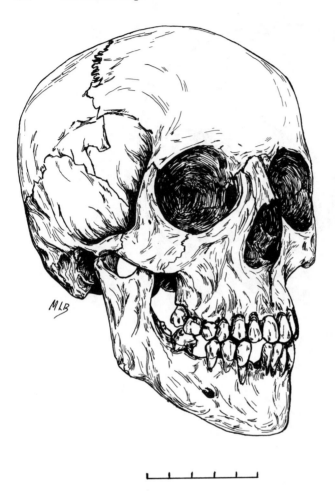

FIGURE 14–12. German female from Bavaria. (Drawn by M. L. Brace at the American Museum of Natural History, New York, courtesy of Dr. Ian Tattersall.)

more years ago, very rarely lack third molars. In contrast, among modern Europeans and Chinese, as many as half of the individuals examined will lack one or more third molars.[177]

Using the arguments just developed, we can suggest that the human diversity visible in the world today is largely a product of events that have occurred during the last 100,000 to 200,000 years or so. It is only during this time that the archaeological record yields clear signs of functional differentiation in the cultural adaptive mechanism between one area of the world and another. As has been suggested, important aspects of this were initiated by the survival problems posed by the periglacial areas. Solutions to these problems had a number of important consequences. One of these was the ability

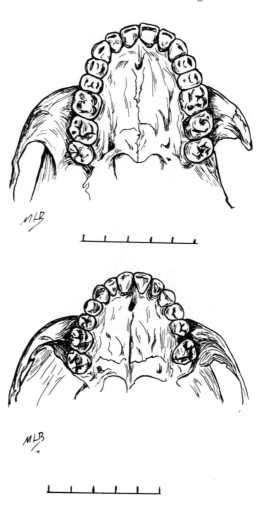

FIGURE 14–13.
Size and robustness contrasts in modern human palates and teeth. The large one is a southern Australian female, and the small one is a Bavarian German female. These are the same individuals that were used to represent the contrast in facial appearance in the previous illustrations. (Drawn by M. L. Brace at the American Museum of Natural History in New York, courtesy of Dr. Ian Tattersall.)

to thrive in the more northern areas even during the height of the last Pleistocene glaciation. (Figure 14–14 illustrates the area occupied.)

As the last glacial stage came to an end, the massive continental ice sheets at the northwestern section of the Old World began to melt and retreat. As they followed these North, people at the Upper Paleolithic level of cultural development spread throughout the whole vast Eurasian steppe of the Old World and, at the eastern extremity, crossed the land bridge between Siberia and Alaska producing the initial population of the New World. Except for the move into Australia 40,000 years earlier, this was the only large-scale spread into previously unoccupied territory to have occurred since the expansion of the Pithecanthropine Stage throughout the Old World tropics over nearly two million years back.

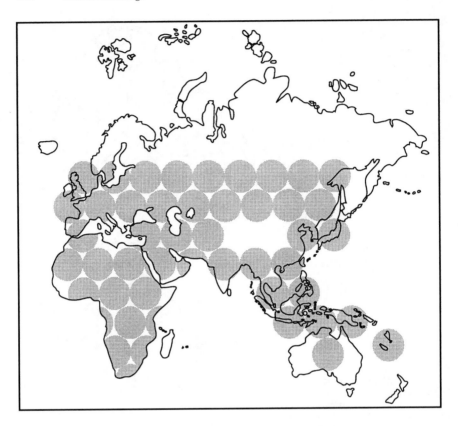

FIGURE 14–14. The area successfully occupied by people with an Upper Paleolithic level of technology during the height of the last glaciation.

It was people at a developed level of this same general stage of complexity who were able to domesticate plants and animals, thus assuring their food sources and creating the foundation for the still greater cultural disparities that followed. (This food-producing or Neolithic "revolution" occurred about 10,000 years ago in the Middle East and Southeast Asia, and, independently, somewhat more recently in Meso-America.) The effects of these various developments slowly diffused into other parts of the world, but a detailed discussion of the events involved and their impact is the subject of other books by other authors.

One is tempted to speculate that the increasing technical and medical ingenuity of developing world culture will further reduce or suspend the adaptive significance of many other human features. Reduction of these features as a result of the probable mutation effect would then follow, and it is possible to suggest that people in the future will be somewhat puny and underendowed by today's standards. Each era creates its own values, however, and the Neanderthals might very well have had the same feelings about ourselves, could they have known that we, their remote descendants, should be so much less robust than they. Perhaps our own hypothetical descendants of 1,000,000 A.D.—should we call them *Homo "durabilis," "the man who endures?"*—will look back at the people of the twentieth century with feelings of repugnance and disgust (see Figure 14–15). Tempting as such excursions may be, they do not properly belong in a book about the human past. In fact, they hardly belong to the realm of "science," and are included here only to lead the reader to realize that human evolution is not just something that occurred long ago: It has been continual, it is happening right now, and it will go on in the future as long as people shall exist.

If evolution goes on as a matter of course, that does not mean that things get better and better. Evolution is simply a matter of change. Things become different, and that is neither better nor worse. To speak of evolutionary "advance" is to attach human value judgments on a process that is purely opportunistic. The only thing about which we can be certain is that our descendants will not be the same as we.

FIGURE 14–15.
The "man" of the future (we are tempted to call him *Homo "durabilis,"* or the man who endures). Although it is perhaps unwarranted to visualize our distant descendants as puny, balding, myopic, and toothless little "men(?)," there is reason to suspect that some such trends may occur. Note that in the previous stages of human evolution the cultural element symbolizing human adaptation was held in the hand of the man in question, whereas in this portrayal it is hung around his neck. Actually, my symbolism is already hopelessly obsolete, since the punch card with its "do not fold, spindle, or mutilate" implications is now unknown to the CD-ROM generation.

> *"Homo durabilis"* Ho!
> Spindle-shanked, missing a toe;
>   Hollow of chest,
>   Weak-eyed and depressed,
> Is this really the way we shall go?
>
> Our grip gets progressively limper,
> Our defiance of fate but a whimper;
>   Bald, blind, and toothless,
>   Our end shall be ruthless,
> And not with a fang but a simper.
>
>   *I. Doolittle Wright scribit*

Owed on Modern Form[178]
I. W. Drivell

The Modern form we designate refined,
Emerged when bulk of tooth and bone declined.

We denigrate the hulks that went before,
And preen ourselves by thinking less is more.

Neanderthal with brutal strength indued,
We look down upon as primitive and crude;

How crass that sloping forehead beetle-browed,
And chinless jaw with massive teeth endowed;

The presence of a low and thickened skull,
We assume denotes a brain that's dim and dull.

But brawn itself need not mean lack of mind,
Nor mighty hands deny a skill refined.

Neanderthals produced those early tools,
That changed the evolutionary rules;

Inventions took the burden from our frame,
And selective forces ceased to be the same;

Where once it needed strength to get along,
Now the weak could thrive as well as could the strong.

A spear that's launched from several yards away,
Will keep the thrower distant from his prey.

No more the close-in tussle at the kill,
Where muscle is a substitute for skill;

The need for force was lessened further yet,
When strings were tied together in a net

Which needed little effort to produce,
And gained an ample harvest by its use.

Then countless more inventions would abate
The value to possess a given trait.

As selective forces ceased to claim their due,
Then chance alone would generate the new;

When mutations change the nature of a form,
A smaller trait becomes the future norm;

The present, but a shadow of the past;
A fleeting figure destined not to last;

Our modern shape, so elegant and slim,
A weakened trunk atop a feeble limb;

The upright brow we think betokens mind,
Is nothing but a vestige left behind;

Projecting nose above a relic chin,
Survives when cheeks and teeth have shrunken in.

What is left is just a hint of what has gone;
A remainder of that prehistoric brawn.

It's perversity that's heard each time we speak,
And declaim why it is better to be weak.

Complacency alone is in the view,
Our Modern form is better 'cause it's new.

CHAPTER FOURTEEN NOTES

[1]The inspiration for this kind of orotund phraseology comes largely from the writings of Marcellin Boule and the picture he portrayed in his monograph on La Chapelle-aux-Saints (1913). After depicting the Neanderthals as the embodiment of the bestial, Boule declaimed: "What a contrast with the men of the following geological and archaeological period, the men of the type of Cro-Magnon with a more elegant body, finer head, a broad and upright forehead, who . . . left such evidence of their manual skills, of the resources of their inventive spirit, their artistic and religious preoccupation, their faculty for abstract thought, and who were the first to merit the glorious title *Homo sapiens*" (1913:227). This was quoted verbatim years later with evident relish by the equally orotund Sir Arthur Keith (McCown and Keith, 1939:360–61), and it has characterized the thinking of much of paleoanthropology and those who have uncritically accepted its conclusions ever since. Only a decade ago, the eminent science writer, Stephen Jay Gould, followed in step in extending his accolades to the "Cro-Magnon people of 50,000 years ago" and concluded that "They were us" (quoted in Gleick, 1983:64)—never mind the fact that he has nearly doubled the actual antiquity of Cro-Magnon. The same glorified view of Cro-Magnon also underlies the thesis of the "great leap forward" articulated by another successful popularizer of anthropological themes, the physiologist and science writer, Jared Diamond (1992:13).

[2]The famous seven volume treatise, *The History of the Decline and Fall of the Roman Empire*, by the eighteenth century historian, Edward Gibbon (1737–1794), is a monument to the recognition given by western Europeans to the eastern roots of their civilization (Burgess, 1988). The Romans in earlier times had celebrated the Greek and Middle Eastern roots of their own civilization (Moore, 1961:12), and the Greeks had been "profoundly impressed" by Egyptian civilization to the extent that Herodotus himself had recorded his "veneration for the wisdom and antiquities of Egypt" (Breasted, 1909:578; Bowman, 1986:22). The survival of the view *ex oriente lux* in classical and even in prehistoric archaeological circles has been explicitly recognized by the late François Bordes (1919–1981) (1972:211).

[3]Erickson, 1977.

[4]Keith, 1915:136, 1925, I:199; Smith, 1924:90; McCown and Keith, 1939:18; Eldredge and Tattersall, 1982:151; Diamond, 1992:41; Howells, 1993:217. The general reading public had been introduced to these themes in detail in the fanciful historical reconstruction, "The grisly folk," by H. G. Wells (1966[1927]) and its book-length counterpart written for the children's market (Quennell and Quennell, 1922).

[5]Boule, 1913:248; Stringer and Gamble, 1993:194.

[6]As you might expect, I. Doolittle Wright could not resist attempting a versified presentation of this theme, and there is something about the inherent simple-mindedness of his "poetic" skill that is curiously appropriate to use in representing the level of intellectual sophistication inherent in the views expressed. It is part of what he had called:

Neanderthrall

O come all and take a good gander
At this curious archaic Neander-
    thal, not in the stream
    Of true Moderns 'twould seem,
But a backwards and stagnant meander.

Because tromping from out of the East—
A hunter of man and of beast—
    Cro-Magnon came on,
    Like a true paragon,
Supplanting the low-browed deceased.

Cro-Magnon the hunter supreme;
That ancestral cream-of-the-cream;
    No Neanderthal kin,
    He did all of them in,
And fathered the Caucasoid dream.

[7]Auel, 1980.

[8]Kurtén, 1980.

[9]The late Nobel laureate, Sir William Golding (1911–1993), had used this condescending view of the Neanderthals in his novel, *The Inheritors* (1955). The Nobel Committee obviously overlooked this in assessing the literary merits of his body of work. That may have helped him win the Nobel Prize, but it left anthropology with a work by an internationally esteemed literary figure that has been assessed as "nothing short of insulting" (these are the words of Terry Southern who reviewed it in *Nation* [1962], 195:332). Golding actually was following up on a theme articulated by H. G. Wells in his story "The grisly folk" (1966[1927]) which itself was an exercise in historical interpretation inspired by the picture presented by Marcellin Boule. With this as his inspiration, Golding adopted the assumption that the Neanderthals were largely restricted to monosyllables strung together with a minimal grammar. If the accepted ground rules specify monosyllables in a rudimentary grammatical arrangement, it is evident that even a Nobel Prize winner in literature will be defeated in his efforts to come up with anything that could be called scintillating dialogue. The resultant lumpen prose can generate nothing more than the most simple-minded of caricatures. Not only is it a dull and plodding book, but Golding also incorporated a bit of the anti-Irish prejudice of an earlier generation when Pruner-Bey had insisted that the original Neanderthal skull was that of *"a Celt"* like the *"modern* Irish Celt" (Pruner-Bey, 1864a:145, 146). His English correspondent had felt that it was our "duty" to test the hypothesis that the skull was that of "a powerfully organised Celt of low mental organisation" (Blake, 1864:cliv). Golding, in his turn, depicted his inarticulate Neanderthal as having red hair and freckles.

[10]Those questions were asked pointedly and cogently by Aleš Hrdlička two generations ago (1927), and, lacking any vestige of an answer, he concluded that there was no reason why Neanderthals should not be regarded as the ancestors of Modern human beings. I repeated his queries a generation ago (1964) and again recently (1992), and, lacking any cogent reply, I have been constrained to agree with Hrdlička's conclusion. Where the western Neanderthals are concerned, I remarked that: "For those of us of Western European ancestry contemplating the possible fate of the 'classic' Neanderthals, we might well sum it up with the phrase, 'We have met their descendants and they are us'" (1991:192; slightly modified from the remark by Pogo's friend Porky Pine, in Kelly, 1970:128).

[11]Brace, 1964:19.

[12]Eldredge and Tattersall, 1982.

[13]Genesis 1:1.

[14]Morris, 1974:104; Gish, 1979:21.

[15]Federal District Judge William R. Overton, in overturning Arkansas Act 590 on January 5, 1982, said "'creation science' . . . is simply not science" (1982:938).

[16]Dawkins, 1986:279.

[17]Hennig, 1966:194. As one observer has noted, "cladists . . . study the pattern rather than the process of evolution" (Carson, 1989:872).

[18]Gaffney, 1979:100. Others have declared it as a matter of faith that "natural selection is not the driving force in evolution" (Wiley and Brooks, 1982:6–7); and "We believe that Darwinism . . . is . . . a theory that has been put to the test and found false" (Nelson and Platnick, 1984:143). An attempt to defend the Darwinian outlook has been offered by Brace (1988, 1989, and in press [a]) among others (for example, Mayr, 1974, 1992; Rose and Bown, 1993; Szalay, 1993).

[19]Blumenbach, 1795 (1865).

[20]Brace, 1981a.

[21]Diamond, 1992; Howells, 1993; Stringer and Gamble, 1993.

[22]The mitochondrion is a fascinating phenomenon in itself. It is an "organelle," that is, a discrete body with its own special function and it almost leads a separate kind of existence within the cytoplasm of the cell. Evolutionary biologists suspect that mitochondria may be the remains of what had once been separate and independent organisms early in the history of life on earth which became associated with other independent single-celled organisms in a kind of symbiosis where each benefited from the contribution of the other (Margulis, 1971). In time, they became integral parts of the cells with which they were associated, although they retained their own DNA and continued to be responsible for their own replication as the cells in which they were located underwent mitosis (cell division) (Wagner, 1969). Mitochondria play an important role in the the famous Krebs cycle, and serve to convert cellular nourishment into adenosine-triphosphate (ATP) which is the main source of energy tapped for running the metabolism (Lehninger, 1964).

[23]Nei, 1985; 1987; Stoneking, 1993.

[24]While this is supposed to be the way things happen in theory, in fact it is not quite so clear-cut. The sperm theoretically contributes only DNA to the egg it fertilizes, but photomicrographs show that other parts of the sperm also can be found in the egg being fertilized, and it seems that a low but not insignificant amount of paternal mtDNA also gets transmitted between generations (Phillip V. Tobias and Morris Goodman, personal communications, October 8, 1993, Detroit Michigan).

[25]Cann et al., 1987; Cann, 1988; Stoneking and Cann, 1989: Stoneking, 1993; Stoneking et al., 1993.

[26]Cann et al., 1987:35.

[27]Stringer and Andrews, 1988.

[28]The spread of such things as projectiles from South to North and, later, cooking from North to South was not an indication of population movement. These were only culture elements and not whole cultures, and those elements were simply adopted by the *in situ* residents as their advantages became obvious.

[29]Brace and Tracer, 1992.

[30]Hedges et al., 1992; Maddison et al., 1992; Templeton, 1992.

[31]Templeton, 1992:69; 1994.

[32]Wallace et al., 1985; Hertzberg et al., 1991; Ward et al., 1991; Horai et al., 1993.

[33]Horai, 1992.

[34]McCown and Keith, 1939:17; Hooton, 1946:334. As the self-proclaimed "language maven" William Safire has recently advised, -*oid* is a Greek suffix that "usually means 'similar but not the same' when applied to a noun" (1993:32), and, like "factoid," he notes the aura of the ersatz that inheres in the various "oids."

[35]McCown and Keith, 1939:135; Tillier, 1992:24; Trinkaus, 1992:282.

[36]Mellars, 1989:378.

[37]Vandermeersch, 1981; Trinkaus and Shipman, 1992:358; Bar-Yosef and Vandermeersch, 1993:96.

[38]Vandermeersch, 1981:5, 9, 300, 1989:157; Valladas et al., 1988; Howells, 1993:148; Schwarcz and Grün, 1993:44.

[39]Vandermeersch, 1981:9. Brace in press (b).

[40]Qafzeh, for example, has a summary tooth size figure (calculated as described in Brace, 1979b:530) of 1494 mm.^{2} (from the data in Vandermeersch, 1981:176–77), while "classic" Neanderthals had a TS = 1415 mm.^{2} (as calculated by Brace, 1979b: 533, 542, from Wolpoff, 1971:176–85). For Skhūl, TS = 1358 mm.^{2} (calculated from McCown and Keith, 1939:212–13), which is practically identical for the Aurignacian-equivalents at Předmost in Czechoslovakia with 1349 mm.,^{2} (calculated from Matiegka, 1934:142–43). Both of the latter are well over 100 mm.^{2} smaller, and this "almost certainly has some basic biological meaning" (Brace, 1980:144).

[41]Tillier, 1992:24; Trinkaus, 1992:282.

[42]Braüer, 1984; Brace., 1991:189–91, in press (b).

[43]McCown and Keith, 1939:85, 135.

[44]Gingerich, 1984:338.

[45]Brace, 1979b; Brace et al., 1987, 1991.

[46]Gorjanović-Kramberger, 1914, 1926. The first and still the clearest development of the view that Modern human form emerged simply as a result of a reduction in Neanderthal levels of robustness was written over sixty years ago by the Czech-born American biological anthropologist Aleš Hrdlička (1930:347). Hrdlička's treatment of the issues has rarely even been discussed let alone refuted by mainstream biological anthropology, although it has played a major part in shaping my own approach (Brace, 1964, 1992, and all of the editions of this book).

[47]Krantz, 1976.

[48]Tchernov, 1988, 1992.

[49]Garrod, 1958.

[50]Ashley-Montagu, 1940:521; Hooton, 1946:337–38; Howells, 1959:189, 228.

[51]Stringer et al., 1989; Aitken and Valladas, 1993.

[52]Grün and Stringer, 1991; Schwarcz and Grün, 1993.

[53]The Qafzeh date estimates have varied between just over 92,000 years to up to 120,000 years, and the Skhūl dates have recently been put around 120,000 years (Mercier et al., 1992). There can be no doubt that the populations from both sites—neither being anything like unmodified Neanderthal form—clearly predate full-scale Neanderthals such as La Chapelle-aux-Saints in France and Kebara in Israel at 60,000 years (Valladas et al., 1987).

[54]Braüer, 1984, 1989; Stringer and Andrews, 1988; Stringer, 1990; Stringer and Gamble, 1933.

[55]Tchernov, 1988:216, 1992:179.

[56]Brooks, 1988:347; Shea, 1989:616–17; Bar-Yosef, 1990–91:583.

[57]The two sites prominently mentioned are Border Cave in Natal and Klasies River Mouth right near the eastern tip of the Cape of Good Hope. Both have been dated by ESR, among other techniques (Grün et al., 1990a, b), both contain the Howiesons Poort manifestation of the Middle Stone Age (Singer and Wymer, 1982; Klein, 1989a, and both have human skeletal remains that have been called Modern (Rightmire, 1979, 1983, 1989).

[58]Brace, 1991, in press (d).

[59]Brace in press (c).

[60]The Levallois technique was first described in 1931 and involved the careful preparation of a large blank of flint or other fine-grained stone from which a large, leaf-shaped flake was detached (Breuil and Koslowski, 1931:454; Bordes and Bourgon, 1951:1; Bordes, 1961:17–20; Bar-Yosef et al., 1992:544). From the traces of impact damage and basal use modification, it has been shown that Levallois flakes were being used as projectile points at Klasies River Mouth and elsewhere in the African Middle Stone Age before they appear in Israel at Qafzeh, Tabūn, Hayonim, and other northern sites early in the Late Pleistocene (Brooks, 1988:347; Shea, 1988:448, 1989:617, 1992:147). Neanderthals clearly were making and using Levalloisian flakes as projectile points (for example, at Kebara [Shea, 1992:147]), and this has been offered in support of the suggestion that Neanderthals were just as intelligent and dexterous as the Moderns who owed their very form to its development and use. "Production of these Levallois flakes requires a *high* degree of precision, intelligence and training . . . even *today, there are few students of lithic technology that ever achieve a Neandertal's level of expertise*" (Hayden, 1993:118). I am arguing that it was the adoption of this technology by northern Neanderthals, who were smart enough to know a

good thing when they saw it, that changed the nature of selection, allowing the emergence of Modern postcranial form from preceding Neanderthal levels of robustness.

[61]Shea, 1988:448.

[62]The phrase "less is more," while not original to it, was one of the artistic dicta of the "Bauhaus School" of architecture in Weimar Germany between the end of World War I and the beginning of Nazi control in the early 1930s (Barth, 1986). One attempt to look on the positive side was called "the somatic budget effect," which suggested that the energy saved by producing a smaller end-product represented a competitive advantage in vying for scarce resources (Jolly, 1970:14). When the amount of dental reduction in France since the end of the Pleistocene is calculated, it amounts of $0.21mm.^2$ per generation, and there is a legitimate reason to "doubt that the energy required to grow two-tenths of a millimeter of tooth area could amount to a discernible nutritional differential" (Brace et al., 1991:41).

[63]Brace in press (d).

[64]Předmost can also be spelled Předmostí, and both are evidently correct in Czech. I have spelled it Předmost since that is the way the Czech-born American anthropologist, Aleš Hrdlička, chose to render it (cf. Hrdlička, 1914:550–51). The "ř" is a retroflex "r," as in Chinese, and it has no counterparts in western European languages. The Germans simply give up and pronounce it Shedmost just because the "sh" sound in German is always rendered by "sch"). This is comparable to using a "z" to pronounce the hard "th" in English which makes this and that come out *zis* and *zat*. It works, but it is obviously a fudge. Předmost is better off pronounced with the ordinary English "r" sound. At least that way we are not imitating the German inability to imitate the actual Czech pronunciation.

[65]The study was meticulously performed by Professor Jindrich Matiegka (1862–1941), who included a long synopsis in French and used French labels on the tabular material so his monograph can be used by those who do not read Czech (Matiegka, 1934).

[66]Dokládal and Brožek, 1961:456.

[67]Absolon, 1957:8; Jan Jelínek, personal communication, April 16, 1991, Ann Arbor, Michigan.

[68]Hrdlička, 1914:551.

[69]Bonnet, 1921:134; Weidenreich, 1928:11.

[70]Matiegka, 1934:142–43; McCown and Keith, 1939:212–13; Brace, 1979b.

[71]Bayer, 1922; Szombathy, 1925; Jelínek, 1969.

[72]The Mladeč collection was never given the systematic treatment applied to Předmost, and some of it, too, was lost at Mikulov when the castle was set on fire in 1945 (Vallois and Movius, 1953:228–29). Some of the material was preserved in the Natural History Museum in Vienna, however, and a new study is in preparation by David W. Frayer, Milford H. Wolpoff, Jan Jelínek, Fred H. Smith, and Nancy Minugh.

[73]Malez et al., 1980; Smith et al., 1985.

[74]Stringer and Gamble, 1993:183.

[75]See notes 13 and 16 in Chapter 13.

[76]Verneau, 1906; Boule, 1921:272–83. At first, Boule regarded the Grimaldi "Negroids" as contemporaries with the Neanderthals in the Mousterian (1913:243), but even later when he had to concede that the field notes clearly indicated that they had been buried from the layer above, he felt that they represented an immediate and sudden "anthropological" change just as the Aurignacian represented a cultural discontinuity (Boule, 1921:274).

[77]Verneau, 1902:583, 1906:202; Boule, 1921:274–76.

[78]It was none other than Marcellin Boule who was entrusted with the job of reconstructing the facial skeleton in the Muséum d'Histoire Naturelle in Paris, which he did under the direction of Albert Gaudry and René Verneau (Gaudry, 1903:3). He also later repeated Gaudry's observations that the teeth were not only large and set in jaws that were "less widely divergent than in the higher races," but that the distal molars retained a full complement of cusps, as in the Australian aboriginal dentition depicted—all of which gave "an indication of inferiority" (Boule, 1921:279–80). While Boule simply categorized the Grimaldi remains as categorically distinct from subsequent Europeans, and allied by their large teeth with the geographically nearest "inferior" race (that is, Africans), Verneau took a less typological view and tried to put them into a

more Darwinian perspective. European form, he suggested, may have arisen by reduction from earlier more robust stages, and Grimaldi might just be that more robust manifestation prior to Cro-Magnon. In effect, he was suggesting a "Negroid" phase in human evolution preceding Cro-Magnon and still more reduced living Europeans (1906:202–23). Like Boule, he assumed the "Negroid" nature of Grimaldi was "inferior," but he put it in a temporal context where everything earlier and more "primitive" was by definition "inferior." This contained the implication that the living Africans are representatives of an earlier phase of evolution, which would account for the "inferiority" that he and his contemporaries took as a given. Eventually Verneau came to regard Grimaldi as a link between an earlier Neanderthal and a later Cro-Magnon stage in the evolution of Modern European form (1924:225, 229).

[79]Verneau, 1902:582–83; 1906:202; Boule, 1921:274ff.

[80]I am grateful to Mme. S. Simone and to M. J. F. Bussière of the Musée d'Anthropologie préhistorique de la Principauté de Monaco for making it possible for me to collect my own measurements and observations on the Grimaldi specimens, October 2, 1992.

[81]Ibid.

[82]The burgeoning new movement called "Afrocentrism" has adopted Grimaldi with enthusiasm as indicating the importance of an African strain in the ancestry of Europeans (Diop, 1985:26; Finch, 1985:22). Europeans certainly had African ancestors at some time in the Middle Pleistocene, but an actual examination of the evidence provides no support for such an interpretation for any time after the Neanderthals developed the cultural capacity to survive in the North Temperate Zone at the time of the penultimate glaciation over 200,000 years ago. Grimaldi, at possibly 30,000 years ago, just represented indigenous Europeans at a point where there still were obvious traces of their recent emergence from a Neanderthal past.

[83]Dreyer and Ariëns-Kappers, 1935; Clarke, 1985; Kuman and Clarke, 1986.

[84]Clarke, 1985; Kuman and Clarke, 1986:123; Smith, 1993:238; Stringer and Gamble, 1993:127.

[85]Meiring, 1956; Kuman and Clarke, 1986:111–12,120.

[86]Smith, 1993:242.

[87]Rightmire, 1978:475; Kuman and Clarke, 1986:121.

[88]Arambourg and Coppens, 1967; Chavaillon, 1971.

[89]Butzer, 1969; Day, 1969; R. Leakey, 1984:91. The Omo Kibish remains, presumably because the Shungura level hominids were all Australopithecines, became known informally as "Homo Omo," although that designation has no defenders. It continues to be used in almost derogatory fashion by insiders in the business, however, not to indicate any taxonomic preference, but just as a familiar term the way "Zinj" continues to be used.

[90]Cole, 1975:289.

[91]Klein, 1983:35.

[92]Pei, 1934; Weidenreich, 1938–1939.

[93]More than one author has commented on the presumed resemblance to both "Palaeolithic man of Europe" and "the aboriginal Australian" (Pinkley, 1935–1936:189; Weidenreich, 1938–1939:169). It was Weidenreich who compared the two distorted female crania to an Eskimo and a Melanesian (1938–1939:167–70), while he noted the resemblance between the relatively undistorted male cranium and Ainu form evident in the photographs and measurements sent to him by the brilliant anatomist-anthropologist at the University of Tokyo Medical School, Yoshikiyo Koganei (1859–1944) (1938–1939:169). For years, textbook writers also have opined about the extent to which the Upper Cave male recalls Upper Palaeolithic European form, especially Cro-Magnon (Hooton, 1946:402; Howells, 1959:300; Lasker, 1973:319), and the latest version of this is the declaration that it looks "more like Cro-Magnons" than intermediaries between ancient and modern Chinese (Stringer and Gamble, 1993:139).

[94]Coon had chided Weidenreich about the various names he had used to describe the morphology of the Upper Cave sample, and felt that the sooner all that talk about Eskimos, Melanesians, and Ainus be forgotten the better (Coon, 1962:475), but it would seem that Weidenreich's judgment concerning the one undistorted specimen, the so-called "Old Man," Number 101, was remarkably close to what can be shown by modern multivariate analysis. That specimen can easily be eliminated from samples of all the living representatives of Modern humans with the sole exception of the Ainu (Kamminga and Wright, 1988, Kamminga 1992; Brace, in press [d]). The Ainu in turn cannot be separated from the prehistoric Jōmon, and specimen 101 from the Up-

per Cave clearly cannot be distinguished from the spectrum represented by those prehistoric and living samples.

[95]Weidenreich did not include tooth measurements in his original study, and, since the specimens were lost in World War II, the only available source is from the casts. Fortunately an excellent set is preserved in the Institute of Vertebrate Paleontology and Paleoanthropology in Beijing, and I was able to measure them, courtesy of Professors Wu Rukang and Wu Xinzhi. The Upper Cave dentition is larger than the living population (its evident descendant) by exactly the same amount that the Upper Paleolithic European teeth are larger than those of living Europeans (Brace et al., 1984:501).

[96]The deposits at the Upper Cave have been subjected to radiocarbon dating using the recently refined "accelerator mass spectrometry" technique, and the dates range from 13,000 to 32,000 years ago with most of them in the 23,000 to 26,000 year range (Hedges et al., 1988:300). Uranium series dates of 19,000 and 21,000 years have also been determined (Chen and Zhang, 1991:149), but the dates of the actual culture-bearing layers have not yet been run. In any case, the Upper Cave is not terminal Pleistocene Mesolithic as was once assumed (Chang, 1968:33, 67–68), being instead the Chinese equivalent of the European Upper Paleolithic.

[97]The same battery of craniofacial measurements was taken on both Cro-Magnon 1 and a cast of the Upper Cave 101 specimen and tested by Fisher's discriminant function against the same sampling of the living populations of the world as well as the prehistoric Jōmon of Japan (which were lumped with living Polynesians from which they are not clearly distinguishable). The Cro-Magnon specimen was excluded from all the test samples except living northwest Europeans, and the Upper Cave specimen was excluded from all—including northwest Europeans—except the Jōmon-Pacific sample (Brace in press [d]). Except for the fact that this analysis included a treatment of Cro-Magnon, the conclusions were almost exactly the same as those independently reached on the basis of another set of multivariate tests using a different measurement battery (Kamminga and Wright, 1988:748, 762).

[98]Woo, 1959.

[99]Wu, 1992:376.

[100]Woo, 1959:116; Chen and Zhang, 1991:150. Kamminga and Wright are also highly skeptical of the antiquity of Liujiang and are inclined to consider it "recent prehistoric rather than Pleistocene in age" (Kamminga and Wright, 1988:763). On the basis of form alone, that would be my conclusion also.

[101]Coon, 1962:469; Aigner, 1973:25; Stringer, 1990:104.

[102]Brace and Tracer, 1992:453; Brace in press (d). The measurements I used to run Fisher's discriminant function were actually taken on the cast at the Institute of Vertebrate Paleontology and Paleoanthropology in Beijing, since I was not able to get access to the original.

[103]Suzuki, 1981, 1982; Baba and Endo, 1982.

[104]Matsu'ura, 1982:207.

[105]This was clearly described by the late Hisashi Suzuki, and was definitively confirmed by testing with Fisher's discriminant function (Brace and Tracer, 1992:453). Once again, the independent analysis of Kamminga and Wright has reached essentially the same conclusion (Kamminga and Wright, 1988:760, 762).

[106]Brace and Tracer, 1992.

[107]Roberts et al., 1990.

[108]Quoted in Mayr, 1944:1.

[109]Zinmeister, 1986:62.

[110]Birdsell, 1977:121.

[111]Davidson, 1933, 1936; Bowdler, 1976.

[112]I was guilty of that condescending stance in the first edition of this book (1967:105) and was justly put in my place as a consequence (Wright, 1976:268). Meanwhile, my research trip to Australia in 1973–1974 had proven to be a revelation and made me realize how parochial my previous views had been.

[113]Hoebel, 1958:139.

[114]Donald, 1991:169.

[115]McCarthy, 1970, 1974; White and O'Connell, 1979.

[116]Campbell, 1965.

[117]Brace and Hunt, 1990; Brace and Tracer, 1992.

[118]Brace and Hinton, 1981; Brace et al., 1984.

[119]Weidenreich, 1943:248–50, 1945:30–31, 1951:239.

[120]Wolpoff, 1989:80; Kramer, 1991.

[121]Hrdlička, 1928; Brace, 1980; Brace and Ryan, 1980.

[122]Brown, 1981, 1993; Webb, 1990.

[123]Webb, 1990:403.

[124]This is based on work that Alan Thorne is preparing for publication, but which he used for a presentation at the University of Michigan in Ann Arbor, November 20, 1990.

[125]Brace and Ryan, 1980.

[126]The thrown spear was universal in Australia and Tasmania, but the use of the spear-thrower as a propulsive device had not reached all parts of the continent. Spear-throwers were used by preference throughout the desert heart of Australia, but they were absent in parts of the well-watered areas of the Darling and Murray drainage, they had only recently been adopted at the southeastern and southwestern edges of the continent, and they were entirely missing from Tasmania (Davidson, 1936; Davidson and McCarthy, 1957:197–98). Since Tasmania had been cut off from Australia by the post-Pleistocene rise in sea level just under 10,000 years ago (Jennings, 1971:9, 1974:37; Pardoe, 1991), it would appear that spear-throwers have not been in Australia for more than 5,000 or 6,000 years. It is just possible that they came along with what has been called the "small tool tradition," which appeared about 7,000 years ago in the North and spread South very slowly (Allen, 1974:317; Golson, 1974:380). Spear-throwers extend the range over which a spear can be hurled, but they cannot be used with a spear as heavy as the hand-thrown spear. With a lighter spear, the strain on the shoulder and arm muscles is less than that exerted by the heavy hand-thrown spear, which continued to be preferred for intergroup conflict in the Southeast, while the lighter spear and spear-thrower were used for hunting. The superficial impression one gets from the distribution of Australian aboriginal body build is that the groups who continued to use the heavy hand-thrown spear were more robust—particularly in the shoulders and chest—while those who relied most extensively on the spear-thrower were much more slender (Brace, 1980:149). This would be a fascinating topic to explore further, but so far it has not aroused much interest. Of the two papers that treat projectile use and body build, one does not deal with the mechanics of how differential survival would effect a change in physique (Brues, 1959), and the other is committed to the idea that reductions have to be the result of selection even if no logical reason can be discerned by which smaller is better (Frayer, 1981).

[127]Jones, 1989:767.

[128]Gill, 1974; Pretty, 1977.

[129]Moore, 1973:78.

[130]Brace, 1979b, 1980. At the end of the Pleistocene in the Murray Basin, the robust inhabitants of Kow Swamp and Coobool Crossing had summary tooth-size figures that ran on the average between 1544 and 1588 mm.^{2}, while the people whom the incoming Europeans encountered at contact had a TS of 1429 mm.^{2} (Brace, 1980:147; Brace and Ryan, 1980:432).

[131]Brace, 1980; Brace et al., 1991. A sample from Cairns towards the northern edge of Australia measured 1272 mm.^{2} (Brace, 1980:145) while the late Upper Paleolithic of Europe had a TS of 1235 mm.^{2} (calculated from Frayer, 1976:140)—at that, a noticeable reduction from the 1349 mm.^{2} figure for Předmost in the early Upper Paleolithic. The teeth of the Walbiri, half way between the North and the South, were exactly the same size as the Předmost teeth—1350 mm.^{2} (Brace, 1980:147). The Murray Basin figure of 1429 mm.^{2} (Brace and Ryan, 1980:432) is slightly larger than the "classic" Neanderthal figure of 1415 (calculated from Wolpoff, 1971:176–85). I. Doolittle Wright evidently understood this when he penned that bit of doggerel on the Australian aboriginal dentition:

> Australian teeth show a grade,
> From the north where reduction's displayed,
>   To those in the south
>   Where the typical mouth
> Has a Pleistocene dental arcade.

> Quoted in Brace, 1980:141.

[132]Boule, after having said that "There is hardly a more rudimentary and miserable industry than that of our Mousterian man" (1921:248), went on to extoll the Upper Paleolithic as illustrating the physical and psychic superiority of its makers: "their manual dexterity, the resources of their inventive spirit, their artistic and religious preoccupations, their faculties of abstraction, all of which truly earn for them the glorious title of *Homo sapiens!*" (*idem.*) Essentially the same view is currently being promoted by authors such as Gould (in Gleick, 1983:64, Klein (1985:7) and Diamond who has referred to those cultural emanations illustrating Modern superiority as "the great leap forward" (Diamond:1989a; 1992:53). To be sure, one recent work that has started from Boule's operating assumption of Neanderthal as "degenerate" (Boule, 1921:245), at least recognizes that Modern human form predates the appearance of the European Upper Paleolithic by some tens of thousands of years. To these authors, Culture arose *sui generis,* "adapting to the anatomy of modern humans," and then "spread like a virus among the host populations" (Stringer and Gamble, 1993:218). In this view, the poor, dim Neanderthals never did catch it and only produced a poorly understood imitation (Ibid., p. 207).

[133]Again, Boule was the first to state this in so many words (1921:248), and ever since then it has continued to be assumed as a kind of given without any consideration of the dynamics involved (e.g., Huxley, 1953:114; Fishbein, 1976:84; Gould, in Gleick, 1983:64; Klein, 1985, 1992:12).

[134]"The keys to the appearance of modern form . . . have to be in the Mousterian itself" (Brace, 1992:4), and "wherever we find Mousterian, or its functional counterparts elsewhere in the world, we should expect the beginnings of modern morphology to emerge in the course of time" (Ibid., p. 21). Since Modern form emerges by different patterns of reduction in different parts of the world, there can be no given configuration that by itself defines the Modern condition. One percipient observer has noted that, as a consequence, "any morphological definition is unlikely to be valid" (Wolpoff, 1986:51).

[135]Actually, Upper Paleolithic blade production was pioneered by the technology that produced Levallois points in the Middle Stone Age of Africa and the Mousterian elsewhere (Clark, 1993:153).

[136]Hrdlička, 1927:271; Clark and Lindly, 1989a:642, 1989b:972.

[137]The big change occurred about 20,000 years ago (Clark and Lindly, 1989a:643; Clark, 1992:197).

[138]Traditional European ethnocentrism is evident in the depiction of a late Upper Paleolithic harpoon point pushed back into the Aurignacian with the explanation: "Cro-Magnon tools were the first to show real innovation. This antler harpoon was state of the art 30,000 years ago" (Diamond, 1989a:60). In fact, very similar harpoon points were in use in Africa in the Middle Stone Age (Shreeve, 1992; Bar-Yosef, 1993:143; Brace in press [d]). The dates of those African bone points are not firmly established yet, but the Middle Stone Age goes back nearly 200,000 years, which makes the European "state of the art" very much an afterthought.

[139]Clark and Schick, 1988:446.

[140]Bar-Yosef, 1993:141; Clark, 1993:153.

[141]Klein, 1983:33.

[142]As the late François Bordes put it, "there must have been many points of transition, and many and varying origins" (1968:220). And he added, "it seems increasingly certain that the transition from Middle to Upper Palaeolithic . . . took place at various places and at various times within a period that would appear to fall between 40,000 and 35,000 years before our era" (Ibid., p. 224; and essentially repeated in 1972:214, 216). An almost identical position has been clearly spelled out recently by Clark and Lindly (1989a:642).

[143]Boule, 1921:238–48; Diamond, 1992:13.

[144]Peyrony, 1934:33; Simek, 1992:241.

[145]Simek, 1992:238.

[146]Stringer and Gamble, 1993:207.

[147]The continuities between the Mousterian and the early Upper Paleolithic have been well documented (Bordes, 1972:214). It has been further noted that, "If an artistic explosion occurred, it was later during the Upper Paleolithic and probably had little to do with the biological shift from Neandertals to modern humans" (Simek, 1992:240). Hayden (1993:118–20) is in essential argreement.

[148]Caves with spectacular wall paintings began to be discovered towards the end of the nineteenth century in southwestern France and Spain. Polychrome rendering of extinct bison on the ceiling of the Spanish cave of Altamira and the more-than-life-sized bulls on the ceilings of the French cave of Lascaux, discovered near Montignac in 1940, date from the Magdalenian of 17,000 years ago (Leroi-Gourhan, 1982:104, 106). These are gloriously portrayed in works such as Breuil (1952), Leroi-Gourhan (1967), White (1986), and Ruspoli (1987). Alas, exposure to twentieth century air and tourists has led to the deterioration of some of the most spectacular representatives such as Altamira and Lascaux. Just recently, however, a cave was discovered near Marseilles in southeastern France that can only be reached by scuba divers through a tunnel that runs up from over 100 feet below the surface of the Mediterranean. This is the Grotte Cosquer named after the diving instructor, Henri Cosquer, who first put his searchlight on the specimens in July of 1991. In addition to pictures of bison, horses, antelope, and deer, there is one depiction of what looks like a penguin. In fact, it is a picture of the Great Auk, a flightless marine bird that still existed in the North Atlantic when the United States was still a new nation. During the late Pleistocene, however, their range extended down to the Mediterranean, and, at that time of lower sea levels, the entrance to the cave was on dry land and not beneath the water. Still, it was well over 500 feet from the entrance slanting up to the chamber with the paintings (Simons, 1992; Clottes and Courtin, 1993). The paintings are older than those at Lascaux, but they are a good 10,000 years younger than the Aurignacian Cro-Magnons, who will surely be be declared to have been the artists. Because of the difficulty of access, it is much more likely to survive intact without the deterioration progressively affecting some of the other famous painted caves.

[149]Price, 1967; Schrempp, 1992.

[150]Burt, 1988; Haskell, 1993; Dornan, 1925:110–111; Stephenson, 1982; Diamond, 1989b.

[151]As Brian Hayden noted, it was not until late in the Upper Paleolithic that people began to make use of such "unobvious resources" as grass seeds, insects, rodents, and so forth, which require special equipment to collect and process (1981:525). Until their efficiency is demonstrated, things like mortars or nets just do not automatically suggest themselves to potential users which is why I have called them, in parallel fashion, "unobvious" elements of technology.

[152]White, 1989, 1993.

[153]Bowdler, 1976.

[154]I. Wright Drivell phrases these thoughts in his own infelicitous fashion. I quote from the latter part of his "strange device," "Reductior," which is somewhat typical of the unregenerate Drivell:

> When our hunter came to know
> That, from a distance, he could throw
> A spear that dealt a lethal blow;
>   And so could duck
> A tussle that might lay him low;
>   He was in luck.
>
> An even more important thing
> Would come when he invented string;
> Snares and nets could quickly bring
>   Him lots of fish,
> And hare and fowl, and bird on wing,
>   If he should wish.
>
> Selection then began to ease
> The need for rugged joints and knees,
> Or limbs that had the strength of trees;
>   And so no harm
> Will follow when, in time, one sees
>   A weakened arm.
>
> Since most mutations tend to slow
> The rate at which a trait will grow;
> When selective force lets go,

It's hardly strange
That size reduction tends to show
    The course of change.

The gristle that was once imbued
Will change when people cook their food;
The consequences will intrude
    And make a stew;
When fiber starts to come unglued,
    There's less to chew.

Inventions ease our former fate;
Selective forces then abate;
Mutations change that early state,
    And thus bequeath,
A modern form emerging late,
    With feeble teeth.

Although there's no predestined goal,
When muscles lack their former role,
Mutations take their usual toll;
    And puny form
Has come to be, however droll,
    The Modern norm.

[155]Hrdlička, 1927; Straus, 1983; Clark and Lindly, 1989a.

[156]The transition from the Mousterian to the Upper Paleolithic appears to have occurred more than 10,000 years earlier in the Middle East than it did in western Europe (Bar-Yosef, 1993:141) and only slightly less early in eastern Europe (Mellars, 1993:202). Innovations spreading from the Middle East appear to have influenced the local Mousterian in eastern Europe, Italy, and France to produce the Szelitian, Uluzzian, and Châtelperronian respectively (Mellars, 1993:199–209). Arguments have continued about how much population movement accompanied that technological diffusion, and we are not yet in a position to provide an appropriate test. The analogous instance of the spread of spear-throwers and netting techniques into post-Pleistocene Australia makes an interesting comparison (Davidson, 1933, 1936). Gene flow clearly accompanied that spread, and the time differential was roughly the same, but there apparently was nothing like population replacement, and it seems unlikely that this would happen at the hunting and gathering level (Krantz, 1976). The most significant population changes in the area from the Middle East to Europe since the initial occupation by the early Neanderthals came after the end of the Pleistocene with the spread of farming (Brace and Tracer, 1992).

[157]Brace, 1973, 1979a.

[158]Brace and Ryan, 1980.

[159]Brace, 1962; Ryan, 1980; Brace et al., 1981.

[160]It is an interesting thing to contemplate that the living western Europeans have a tooth-size profile that is exactly parallel to that of the European Neanderthals but at a smaller size, and the living people of West Africa have a tooth-size profile that is exactly parallel to that of the Qafzeh population about 100,000 years ago, but also at a smaller size. The European and West African profiles, however, are not parallel, and the Neanderthal and Qafzeh profiles also fail to be parallel in exactly the same way. In proportion to their molars, Europeans still maintain relatively larger incisors just as the earlier European Neanderthals did, while the living Africans retain relatively larger molars in proportion to their incisors, just as was true for Qafzeh (Brace in press [b]).

[161]Brace, 1977:199.

[162]Brace, 1977:200.

[163]Ryan, 1980.

[164]The argument has been raised that pigment in the skin was actively selected against in the North, since a noncarcinogenic level of ultraviolet penetration was necessary in order to produce the amounts of Vitamin D needed for bone growth and to prevent rickets (Loomis, 1967,

1970). This was based on the observation that "black" people residing in northern Europe in the late nineteenth and early twentieth centuries had markedly higher incidences of rickets than their aboriginal European counterparts. Lack of adequate amounts of sunlight was implicated, and the deficiency in the amount of Vitamin D normally synthesized in the skin could be made up by dietary supplements. To the English who ran the studies, however, all people with dark skin were "black," and they did not distinguish between those of African/West Indies origin and those from Pakistan. As it happened, the latter were less heavily pigmented but much more prone to rickets, which accounted in part for the high incidents of rickets among "black" residents in English cities. But the Pakistani diet was not the same as that of other residents and included a higher percentage of chapatis, which are made with a flour that tends to bind calcium (Robins, 1991:199). Although skin pigment does retard the penetration of UV differentially in European and more heavily pigmented tropical populations, the mechanism of Vitamin D synthesis in the skin of all humans works the same way (Holick, 1987), and it does not take many days of exposure to the sun to produce enough Vitamin D to be stored in fat and muscle tissue for a whole year (Webb et al., 1988). As Robins put it, "given the prolonged hours of sun exposure in the northern summer and the body's remarkable potential for storing the compound, early pigmented humans would have manufactured and stored the vitamin as efficiently as their depigmented counterparts" (1991:208). Reduction of pigment in the North, then, was not produced by selection for Vitamin D synthesis.

[165]I suspect that it is no accident that all of those populations containing numbers of people who can be described as "blonds" are long-term residents of just those areas where the first inhabitants were Mousterian Neanderthals. Interestingly enough, after this suggestion had appeared in the first two editions of *The Stages* (1967:105; 1979:100), it was picked up by Björn Kurtén (1980) who, in depicting his fair-haired but inarticulate Neanderthal heroine, may have portrayed the earliest-yet version of that classic stereotype, the "dumb blond."

[166]Birdsell, 1967:120.

[167]Hoffecker et al., 1993:51.

[168]See note 133.

[169]Martin and Klein, eds., 1984.

[170]Clarke, 1976.

[171]Zvelebil (ed.), 1986; Chang, 1987; McCorriston and Hole, 1991: Thomas, 1991.

[172]Brace, 1977, 1979b; Brace et al., 1987, 1991:47–48, 50–51.

[173]See notes 111, 126, and 131.

[174]The specimens pictured are part of the von Luschan collection in the Department of Anthropology at the American Museum of Natural History in New York. The individuals came from Heidenheim in the Swabian Jura.

[175]The male specimen, admittedly an extreme example, was part of the collection in the Department of Anatomy at the Edinburgh University Medical School. It has been returned for reburial in Australia.

[176]Brace and Ryan, 1980.

[177]As chance would have it, the third molar is even more a target for recent reduction/elimination in Chinese than in European dental arches. Systematically collected data are not available, but, in gathering dental measurements from regional representatives of all of the world's populations, I have been struck by how small my samples of Chinese third molars actually are. While I was making measurements on the dental casts of entering students at the Department of Orthodontics of Beijing University in June of 1992, I was hard put to get a single instance of both an upper and a lower third molar from the male and female samples. The Liu Jiang specimen—whether Pleistocene or not—lacks third molars, and the best-preserved Chinese Neanderthal, Jinniu Shan, has markedly reduced third molars.

[178]Speaking of owing, this obviously has roots in the *Essay on Man* of the brilliant Enlightenment poet, Alexander Pope. In its abbreviated length as well as in its lack of polish, it is a verbal illustration of the probable mutation effect at work—compare to Pope (1734 [1969]). Drivell actually produced this in response to the challenge from his cousin that he do something other than imitate the rhythms of Robert Burns. The reader will recognize that, hidden in the iambic pentameter of the heroic couplet is a secondary rhythm of anapestic trimeter—evidently a sly corruption of the clunkety-thump of Wright's limericks. In what is obviously typical Drivell, the worst of each is preserved.

chapter fifteen

Epilogue/Summary

Almost half a century ago, Franz Weidenreich generated his famous diagram depicting the "Stages of Human Evolution" with lines of regional continuity through time linking representative fossils in sequence (see Figure 15–1).[1] Many more fossils have been discovered and integrated into the picture since his pioneering effort, and it seems high time to try to bring it up to date. I have tried to do that here, preserving the original vision of specific unity maintained between the regions at any one time by gene flow indicated by the horizontal and diagonal lines, and adding dates and fossils that have become known since his first attempt.[2] Gene flow alone, however, is not the source of the change that characterizes the sequence of Stages depicted. The next diagram attempts to put labels on those cultural elements that actually changed the nature of selection in such a way that morphology responded as a consequence (see Figure 15–2).

In summary, the Figures 15–2 and 15–3 present a supersimplified picture of the changes occurring in the entire span of human evolution, with their suggested causal correlates. The second figure, Figure 15–3, presents a record of hominid evolution seen from the point of view of tooth size alone. The vertical scale represents the average cross-sectional area in square millimeters of all of the teeth in the dental arch summed together. The robust Australopithecines had obviously become very large of tooth prior to their

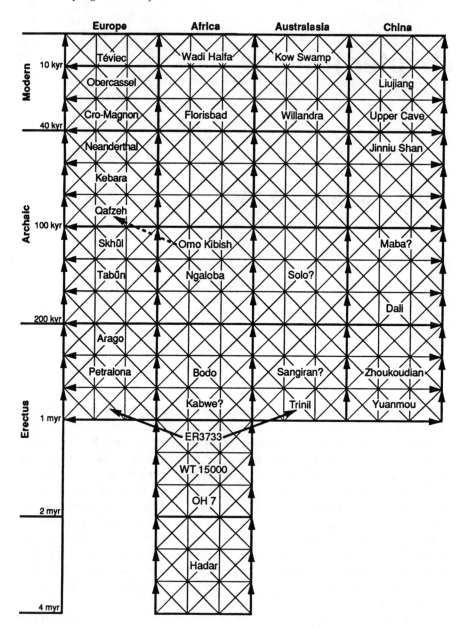

Figure 15–1.   Weidenreich's famous diagram updated to accommodate the fossils and dates found since his pioneering effort.

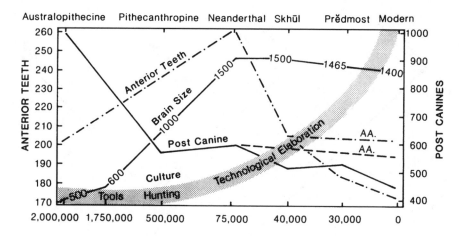

Figure 15–2. Human evolution graph.

extinction. The spread at the *sapiens* end of the graph reflects the fact that within the last 100,000 years, the teeth of some human populations have undergone a marked degree of reduction, whereas those of others, the large-toothed southern Australian aborigines, have scarcely been altered.

Finally, for the cladists who feel that the hominid fossil record does *not* represent the course of hominid evolution, Figure 15–4 displays a cladogram showing the four grades discussed in the preceding chapters as though they

Figure 15–3. Tooth size graph.

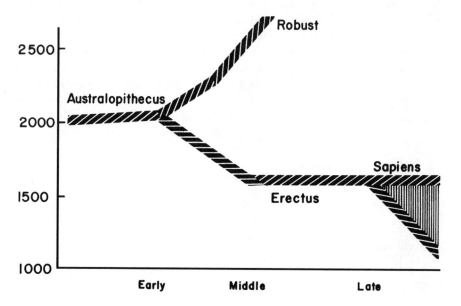

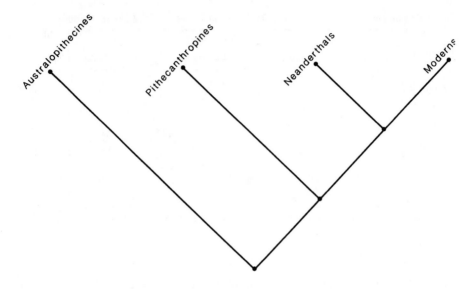

Figure 15–4.   The Stages of Human Evolution arranged in the form of a cladogram.

had branched from as-yet-undiscovered ancestors in the sequence shown. My own view, however, is represented by the final unilinear arrangement, shown in Figure 15–5. The Australopithecines evolved into the Pithecanthropines, which in turn evolved into the Neanderthals throughout the whole of the inhabited Old World, and these finally became transformed into the various modern populations alive today. I have left off the Australopithecine twig that became hyper-robust and died out before the Middle Pleistocene just to give a streamlined version of my general view.

There is another message from the study of the cumulative record for human existence since "the beginning," and that is the picture of a population whose growth has gotten out of control. Before the Pithecanthropines spread from Africa a million years ago, there may have been a total *Homo erectus* population of 500,000 individuals. Paleodemographers have estimated

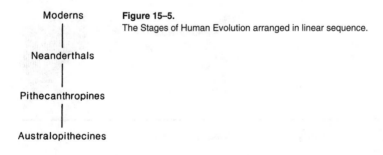

Moderns

Figure 15–5.
The Stages of Human Evolution arranged in linear sequence.

Neanderthals

Pithecanthropines

Australopithecines

that, during the Middle Pleistocene some half a million years ago, Pithecan-thropine population size stabilized at 1.3 million. There it remained through the transition from *erectus* to *sapiens* and on through the Neanderthals of 100,000 years ago towards the end of the Pleistocene. Throughout most of the existence of the genus *Homo*, then, the entire population of the world at any one time was somewhat less than a million and a half people.[3]

During the Neolithic, between five and ten thousand years ago, human population size had multiplied nearly fivefold to number more than six million. Obviously the effort to assure a future food supply inherent in the farmer's way of life permanently upset the balance that had existed between the human species and the rest of the natural world for the previous million years and more. By the time of the Roman Empire, 0 A.D., there were 300 million people in the world. By the year 1800, the figure had reached one billion.[4] By 1950, it was 2.5 billion, and by 1987 the total was 5 billion.[5]

As one demographer has noted, if this rate were to continue, the mass of humanity would outweigh the earth in just over a thousand years. And in less than 6,000 years, the teeming mass of people would form a sphere of flesh expanding at the speed of light![6] Alan Gregg, a former vice president of the Rockefeller Foundation, compared human population increase to a cancer, noting that cancerous growths demand food but are never cured by getting it.[7] Obviously the food resources available to support human life will have been exhausted long before the point, some six or seven hundred years from now, when, given our present rate of increase, there would be one human body for every square foot of earth on the globe.[8]

Whatever else this picture can be construed to mean, it has the inevitable implication that the structure of human social life as we now know it will be changed beyond recognition in the not-so-distant future. What will it be like? Will the human species survive? Will life on earth continue in anything like its present form? These are questions that we cannot begin to answer, but we are forced to ask them because, if we don't, the answers will be furnished for us—or rather, for our descendants—and those answers will almost certainly be other than what we/they would choose.

It does not take an expert to recognize that more than the usual amount of speculation has been included in this book. The major pieces of evidence have been presented, and evolutionary theory has been considered. The speculation entered when theory rather than solid evidence was used to support the interpretations offered, and it should be clearly recognized that this cannot constitute proof. As more fragments of human fossils are found in the years to come, the level of probability that one interpretation or another is correct will increase, but this is not proof either. Ultimately, it is impossible to "prove" the validity of any interpretation, because proof assumes an absolute certainty that can only occur in the realms of logic, mathematics, and religion, and not, in a formal sense, in science. At best, science can produce varying degrees of probability that its findings are to be believed. Where it is a matter of interpreting the course of human evolution, the theoretical consistency of the scheme presented here should be justification enough for its development. The future alone can decide the probability of its rectitude.

CHAPTER FIFTEEN NOTES

[1]Weidenreich, 1946:30, 1947a:201; reprinted in Brace, 1981:424.
[2]The present attempt is a modification of Brace in press(d).
[3]Weiss, 1984:642.
[4]Coale, 1974:43.
[5]Keyfitz, 1989:119.
[6]Coale, 1970:134, 1974:51.
[7]Lerner and Libby, 1976:275.
[8]See note 6.

Sources Cited

Absolon, Karel. 1957. Recherches d'ethnographie préhistorique dans les stations diluviales de Moravie. *Mélanges Pittard*, Chastrusse et Cie, Brive (Corrèze), pp. 5–12.

Ackerknecht, Erwin H. 1953. *Rudolf Virchow: Doctor, Statesman, Anthropologist.* Madison: University of Wisconsin Press. 304 pp.

Adam, Karl Dietrich. 1985. The chronological and systematic position of the Steinheim akull. In Eric Delson (ed.). *Ancestors: The Hard Evidence.* New York: Alan Liss, pp. 272–76.

Agassiz, Louis. 1860. Prof. Agassiz on *The Origin of Species. American Journal of Science and Arts* 30:142–54.

Aigner, Jean S. 1973. Pleistocene archaeological remains from South China. *Asian Perspectives* 16(1):16–38.

Aitken, Martin J. 1985. *Thermoluminescence Dating.* Orlando: Academic Press. 359 pp.

Aitken, Martin J., Christopher B. Stringer, and Paul A. Mellars (eds.). 1993. *The Origin of Modern Humans and the Impact of Chronometric Dating.* Princeton: Princeton University Press. 248 pp.

Aitken, Martin J., and Helène Valladas. 1993. Luminescence dating relevant to human origins. In M. J. Aitken, C. B. Stringer, and P. A. Mellars (eds.), *The Origin of Modern Humans and the Impact of Chronometric Dating.* Princeton: Princeton University Press, pp. 27–39.

Aldrich, Michele L. 1974. United States: Bibliographic Essay. In Thomas F. Glick (ed.), *The Comparative Reception of Darwinism.* Austin: University of Texas Press, pp. 207–26.

Alexander, Richard D. 1978. Evolution, creation, and biology teaching. *The American Biology Teacher* 40(2):91–107.

————. 1979. Sexual dimorphism and breeding systems in Pinnipeds, Ungulates, Primates and Humans. In N. C. Chagnon and W. Irons (eds.), *Evolutionary Biology and Human Social Behavior: An Anthropological Perspective.* Duxbury Press, North Scituate, MA: pp. 402–435.

————. 1990. How did humans evolve? Reflections on the uniquely unique species. *The University of Michigan Museum of Zoology, Special Publications,* no. 1, pp. 1–38.

Alexeev, Valeriĭ. 1986. *The Origin of the Human Race.* Translated from the Russian by H. Campbell Creighton. Moscow: Progress Publishers. 355 pp.

Alland, Alexander, Jr. 1967. *Evolution and Human Behavior.* Garden City, NY: Natural History Press. 259 pp.

Allen, Harry. 1974. The Bagundji of the Darling basin: Cereal gatherers in an uncertain environment. *World Archaeology* 5(3):309–22.

Allen, Lucia L. 1982. Evolutionary change in *Homo erectus. American Journal of Physical Anthropology* 57(2):166.

Alvarez, Luis W., Walter Alvarez, Frank Asaro, and Helen V. Michel. 1980. Extraterrestrial cause for the Cretaceous-Tertiary extinction. *Science* 208:1095–1108.

Alvarez, Walter, and Frank Asaro. 1990. An extraterrestrial impact. *Scientific American* 263(4):78–84.

Alvarez, Walter, Erle G. Kauffman, Finn Surlyk, Luis W. Alvarez, Frank Asaro, and Helen V. Michel. 1984. Impact theory of mass extinctions and the invertebrate fossil record. *Science* 223:1135–40.

Andrews, Peter. 1984. An alternative interpretation of the characters used to define *Homo erectus.* In P. Andrews and J. L. Franzen (eds.), *The Early Evolution of Man With Special Emphasis on Southeast Asia and Africa. Courier Forschungs-Institut, Senckenberg* 69:167–75.

Andrews, Peter, and Lawrence Martin. 1987. Cladistic relationships of extant and fossil hominoids. *Journal of Human Evolution* 16(1):101–18.

Andrews, Peter, and Judith A. H. Van Couvering. 1975. Paleoenvironments in the East African Miocene. In Frederick S. Szalay (ed.), *Approaches to Primate Paleobiology.* S. Karger, Basel: *Contributions to Primatology* 5:62–103.

Andrews, Roy Chapman. 1926. *On the Trail of Ancient Man: A Narrative of the Field Work of the Central Asiatic Expeditions.* Garden City, NY: Garden City Publishing Company. 375 pp.

Anfinsen, Christian B. 1959. *The Molecular Basis of Evolution.* New York: John Wiley & Sons. 228 pp.

Appel, Toby A. 1987. *The Cuvier-Geoffroy Debate: French Biology in the Decades Before Darwin.* New York: Oxford University Press. 305 pp.

Aquinas, Thomas 1923. *The Summa Contra Gentiles.* Literally translated by the English Dominican Fathers from the latest Leonine Edition. London: Burns Oates & Washbourne. 4 vols.

Arambourg, Camille. 1954. L'hominien fossile de Ternifine (Algérie). *Comptes Rendus des Séances de l'Académie des Sciences de Paris* 239(15):893–95.

Arambourg, Camille, and Yves Coppens. 1967. Sur la découverte, dans le Pleistocène inférieur de la vallée de l'Omo (Éthiopie), d'une mandibule d'Australopithécien. *Comptes Rendus des Séances de l'Académie des Sciences de Paris* Série D, 265:589–90.

Arensburg, Baruch, Ofer Bar-Yosef, Mario Chech, Paul Goldberg, Henri Lavelle, Liliane Meignen, Yoel Rak, Eitan Tchernov, Ann-Marie Tillier, and Bernard Vandermeersch. 1985. Une sépulture néandertalienne dans la grotte de Kébara (Isräel). *Comptes Rendus des Séances de l'Académie des Sciences de Paris,* Série 2, 300(6):227–30.

Armstrong, Este. 1983. Relative brain size and metabolism in mammals. *Science* 220:1302–04.

Arnold, Matthew. 1869. *Culture and Anarchy: An Essay in Political and Social Criticism.* London: Smith, Elder and Company. 212 pp.

Arsuaga, Juan-Luis, Ignacio Martínez, Ana Gracia, José-Miguel Carretero, and Eudald Carbonell. 1993. Three new human skulls from the Sima de los Huesos Middle Pleistocene site in Sierra de Atapuerca, Spain. *Nature* 362:534–37.

Ashley-Montagu, Montagu Francis. 1935. The premaxilla in the Primates. *Quarterly Review of Biology* 10(1):32–59; 10(2):181–208.

———. 1940. Review of *The Stone Age of Mount Carmel,* vol. II, by T. D. McCown and A. Keith. *American Anthropologist* 42(3):518–22.

Auel, Jean M. 1980. *The Clan of the Cave Bear: Earth's Children.* New York: Crown Publishers. 468 pp.

Ayala, Francisco J. 1972. Competition between species. *American Scientist* 60(2):348–57.

———. 1974. Biological evolution: natural selection or random walk? *American Scientist* 62(6):692–701.

Baba, Hisao, and Banri Endo. 1982. Postcranial skeleton of the Minatogawa Man. In Hisashi Suzuki and Kazuro Hanihara (eds.), *The Minatogawa Man: The Upper Pleistocene Man from the Island of Okinawa.* The University Museum, The University of Tokyo, Bulletin No. 19, pp. 61–195.

Badash, Lawrence. 1989. The age-of-the-earth debate. *Scientific American* 261(2):90–96.

Baden-Powell, Robert S. S. 1924. *Pig-Sticking or Hog-Hunting: A Complete Account for Sportsmen—and Others.* Revised edition. London: H. Jenkins. 312 pp.

Baker, Mary Ann. 1982. Brain cooling in endotherms in head and exercise. *Annual Review of Physiology* 44:85–96.

———. 1993. A wonderful safety net for mammals. *Natural History* 102(8):63–64.

Baker, M. A., and L. W. Chapman. 1977. Rapid brain cooling in exercising dogs. *Science* 195:781–83.

Baker, Robert J., Michael J. Novacek, and Nancy B. Simmons. 1991. On the monophyly of bats. *Systematic Zoology* 10(2):216–31.

Bakker, Robert T. 1986. *The Dinosaur Heresies: New Theories Unlocking the Mystery of the Dinosaurs and Their Extinction.* New York: William Morrow. 481 pp.

Baksi, A. K., V. Hsu, M. O. McWilliams, and E. Farrar. 1992. $^{40}Ar/^{39}Ar$ dating of the Brunhes-Matuyama geomagnetic field reversal. *Science* 256:356–57.

Balout, Lionel. 1955. *Préhistoire de l'Afrique du Nord: Essai de Chronologie.* Paris: Arts et Métiers Graphiques. 536 pp.

Barry, Roger G., J. T. Andrews, and M. A. Mahaffy. 1975. Continental ice sheets: Conditions for growth. *Science* 190:979–81.

Barth, John. 1986. A few words about minimalism. *The New York Times Book Review,* Dec. 28, pp. 1, 2, 25.

Barthélemy-Madaule, Madeleine. 1982. *Lamarck the Mythical Precursor: A Study of the Relations Between Science and Ideology.* Translated from the French by M. H. Shank. Cambridge, MA: M.I.T. Press. 174 pp.

Bartholomew, George A., and Joseph B. Birdsell. 1953. Ecology and the protohominids. *American Anthropologist* 55(4):481–98.

Bar-Yosef, Ofer. 1987. Pleistocene connexions between Africa and Southwest Asia: An archaeological perspective. *The African Archaeological Review* 5:29–38.

———. 1990–91. Mousterian adaptations—A global view. *Quaternaria Nova* 1:575–91.

———. 1993. The role of western Asia in modern human origins. In M. J. Aitkens, C. B. Stringer, and P. A. Mellars (eds.), *The Origins of Modern Humans and the Impact of Chronometric Dating.* Princeton: Princeton University Press, pp. 132–47.

Bar-Yosef, O., B. Arensburg, A. Belfer-Cohen, P. Goldberg, H. Laville, L. Meignen, Y. Rak, J. D. Speth, E. Tchernov, A-M. Tillier, and S. Weiner. 1992. The excavations in Kebara Cave, Mt. Carmel. *Current Anthropology* 33(5):497–550.

Bar-Yosef, Ofer, and Bernard Vandermeersch. 1993. Modern humans in the Levant. *Scientific American* 268(4):94–100.

Bates, Marston. 1960. Ecology and evolution. In Sol Tax (ed.), *Evolution After Darwin: Vol. 1, The Evolution of Life.* Chicago: University of Chicago Press, pp. 547–68.

Bateson, William. 1894. *Materials for the Study of Variation Treated With Especial Regard to Discontinuity in the Origin of Species.* London: Macmillan. 598 pp.

Bather, F. A. 1925. The word "Australopithecus" and others. *Nature* 115:947.

Bayer, J. 1922. Das Aurignac-Alter der Artefakte und menschlichen Skelettreste aus der Fürst-Johanns-Höhle bei Lautsch in Mähren. *Mitteilungen der Anthropologischen Gesellschaft in Wien* 52(4):173–85.

de Beaune, Sophie A., and Randall White. 1993. Ice Age lamps. *Scientific American* 266(3):108–13.

de Beer, Gavin. 1954. Archaeopteryx lithographica. *A Study Based Upon the British Museum Specimen.* British Museum (Natural History), London. 68 pp.

Behrensmeyer, Anna K. 1976. Fossil assemblages in relation to sedimentary environments in the East Rudolf succession. In Yves Coppens, F. C. Howell, G. Ll. Isaac, and R. E. F. Leakey (eds.), *Earliest Man and Environments in the Lake Rudolf Basin: Stratigraphy, Paleoecology and Evolution.* Chicago: University of Chicago Press, pp. 383–401.

Ben-Itzhak, Sara, Patricia Smith, and R. A. Bloom. 1988. Radiographic Study of the humerus in Neandertals and *Homo sapiens sapiens. American Journal of Physical Anthropology* 77(2):231–42.

Bennett, Wendell C., and Robert M. Zingg. 1935. *The Tarahumara, An Indian Tribe of Northern Mexico.* Chicago: University of Chicago Press. 412 pp.

Berckhemer, F. 1933. Ein Menschen-Schädel aus den diluvialen Schottern von Steinheim a. d. Murr, ein vorläufiger Bericht. *Anthropologischer Anzeiger* 10(4):318–21.

Bergson, Henri. 1907. *L'Évolution Créatrice.* Paris: Felix Alcan. 403 pp.

Bickerton, Derek. 1981. *Roots of Language.* Ann Arbor, I: Kroma Publishers. 351 pp.

———. 1990. *Language & Species.* Chicago: University of Chicago Press. 297 pp.

Bilsborough, Alan, and Bernard A. Wood. 1988. Cranial morphometry of early hominids: Facial region. *American Journal of Physical Anthropology* 76(1):61–86.

Binford, Lewis R. 1978. *Nunamiut Ethnoarchaeology.* New York: Academic Press. 509 pp.

———. 1981. *Bones: Ancient Men and Modern Myths.* New York: Academic Press. 320 pp.

———. 1985. Human ancestors: Changing views of their behavior. *Journal of Anthropological Archaeology* 4(4):292–327.

———. 1987. The hunting hypothesis, archaeological methods, and the past. *Yearbook of Physical Anthropology* 30:1–9.

Binford, Lewis R., and Chuan Kun Ho. 1985. Taphonomy at a distance: Zhoukoudian, "The cave home of Beijing man"? *Current Anthropology* 26(4):413–42.

Birdsell, Joseph B. 1967. Preliminary data on the trihybrid origin of the Australian aborigines. *Archaeology and Physical Anthropology in Oceania* 2(1–2):100–55.

———. 1977. The recalibration of a paradigm for the first peopling of greater Australia. In Jim Allen, Jack Golson and Rhys Jones (eds.), *Sunda and Sahul: Prehistoric Studies in Southeast Asia, Melanesia and Australia*. London: Academic Press, pp. 113, 167.

———. 1979. Ecological influences on Australian Aboriginal social organization. In Irwin S. Bernstein and Euclid O. Smith (eds.), *Primate Ecology and Human Origins*. New York: Garland Press, pp. 117–51.

Black, Davidson. 1927. On a lower molar hominid tooth from the Chou Kou Tien Deposit. *Palaeontologia Sinica*, Series D. 7(1):1–28.

Blake, C. Carter. 1864. On the alleged peculiar characters, and assumed antiquity of the human cranium from the Neanderthal. *Journal of the Anthropological Society of London* 2:cxxxix–clvii.

Blumenbach, Johann Friedrich. 1795. *De Generis Humani Verietate Nativa*, 3rd ed. Translated by Thomas Bendyshe, 1865. London: Longman, Green, Longman, Roberts and Green. (*The Anthropological Treatises of Johann Friedrich Blumenbach*). 406 pp.

Blumenschine, Robert J. 1986. Carcass consumption sequences and the archaeological distinction of scavenging and hunting. *Journal of Human Evolution* 15(8):639–59.

———. 1987. Characteristics of an early hominid scavenging niche. *Current Anthropology* 28(4):383–407.

Blumenschine, Robert J., and John A. Cavallo. 1992. Scavenging and human evolution. *Scientific American* 267(4):90–96.

Boesch, Christophe, and Hedwige Boesch. 1981. Sex differences in the use of natural hammers by wild chimpanzees: A preliminary report. *Journal of Human Evolution* 10(7):585–93.

———. 1989. Hunting behavior in wild chimpanzees in the Taï National Park. *American Journal of Physical Anthropology* 78(4):547–73.

Boesiger, Ernest. 1980. Evolutionary biology in France at the time of the evolutionary synthesis. In E. Mayr and W. B. Provine (eds.), *The Evolutionary Synthesis*. Harvard Cambridge, MA: University Press, pp. 309–21.

Bonifay, Eugène. 1991. Les premères industries du Sud-est de la France et du Massif-central. In E. Bonifay and B. Vandermeersch (eds), *Les Premiers Européens*. Actes du 114ᵉ Congrès National des Sociétés Savantes, Paris, 3–9 avril, 1989. Editions du Comité des Travaux Historiques et Scientifiques, Paris. pp. 63–80.

Bonnet, R. 1919. Die Skelete. In M. Verworn, R. Bonnet, and G. Steinmann (eds.), *Der Diluviale Menschenfund von Obercassel bei Bonn*. Wiesbaden: Bergmann Verlag, pp. 11–185.

———. 1921. Der Lücke zwischen der Neandertal- und Cro-Magnongruppe, sowie dem Skelett von Combe Capelle. *Verhandlungen der anatomische Gesellschaft* 30:134–35.

Bordes, François. 1958. Le passage du Paléolithique moyen au Paléolithique supérieur. In G. H. R. von Koenigswald (ed.), *Hundert Jahre Neanderthaler.*: Utrecht: Kemink en Zoon N. V., pp. 175–81.

———. 1961. *Typologie du Paléolithique Ancien et Moyen,* Mémoire N° 1, Institut de Préhistoire de l'Université de Bordeaux. Bordeaux: Delmas. 85 pp.

———. 1968. *The Old Stone Age.* Translated from the French by J. E. Anderson. New York: World University Library (McGraw-Hill). 255 pp.

———. 1972. Du paléolithique moyen au paléolithique supéreiur: Continuité ou discontinuité? In François Bordes (ed.), *The Origin of Homo Sapiens.* Paris: UNESCO, pp. 211–18.

———. 1977. Time and space limits of the Mousterian. In R. V. S. Wright (ed.), *Stone Tools as Cultural Markers.* Australian Institute of Aboriginal Studies, Canberra, pp. 37–39.

Bordes, François, and Maurice Bourgon. 1951. Le complexe Moustérien: Moustérien, Levalloisien et Tayacien. *L'Anthropologie* 55(1–2):1–23.

Bortz, Walter M., II. 1985. Physical exercise as an evolutionary force. *Journal of Human Evolution* 14(2):145–55.

Bouchud, Jean. 1965. Remarques sur les fouilles de L. Lartet à l'abri de Cro-Magnon (Dordogne). *Bulletin de la Société d'Études et de Recherches Péhistoriques et Centre d'Études de Préhistoire et d'Art Préhistorique, Les Eyzies* 15:28–36.

Boule, Marcellin. 1913. *L'Homme Fossile de La Chapelle-aux-Saints.* Reprinted from *Annales de Paléontologie,* vols. 6–8. Masson & Cie. 278 pp.

———. 1915a. La guerre et M. Hauser. *L'Anthropologie* 26:169–182.

———. 1915b. La paléontologie humaine en Angleterre. *L'Anthropologie* 26:1–67.

———. 1921. *Les Hommes Fossiles: Éléments de Paléontologie Humaine.* Paris: Masson & Cie. 491 pp.

———. 1929. Le "Sinanthropus." *L'Anthropologie* 39(5–6)455–60.

———. 1937. Le Sinanthrope. *L'Anthropologie* 47(1–2):1–22.

Boule, Marcellin, and Raoul Anthony 1911. L'encéphale de l'homme fossile de la Chapelle-aux-Saints. *L'Anthropologie* 22:129–95.

Boule, Marcellin, and Henri V. Vallois. 1957. *Fossil Men.* Translated by Michael Bullock. New York: Dryden Press. 535 pp.

Bouyssonie, Amédée, Jean Bouyssonie, and Louis Bardon. 1908. Découverte d'un squelette humain moustérien à La Chapelle-aux-Saints. *Comptes Rendus des Séances de l'Académie des Sciences de Paris* 147(25):1414–15.

Bowdler, Sandra. 1976. Hook, line and dillybag: An interpretation of an Australian coastal shell midden. *Mankind* 10(4):248–58.

Bowman, Alan K. 1986. *Egypt After the Pharaohs 332 B.C.–A.D. 642: From Alexander to the Arab Conquest.* Berkeley: University of California Press. 264 pp.

Bowman, Sheridan. 1990. *Radiocarbon Dating.* Berkeley: University of California Press. 54 pp.

Bowring, Samuel A., John P. Grotzinger, Clark E. Isachsen, Andrew H. Knoll, Shane M. Pelechaty, and Peter Kolosov. 1993. Calibrating rates of early Cambrian evolution. *Science* 261:1293–98.

Brabant, Hyacinthe, and R. Ketelbant. 1975. Observations sur la frequence de certains caractères Mongoloides dans la denture permanente de la population Belge. *Bulletin du Groupement européen pour la Recherche scientifique en Stomatolotie & Odontologie* 18(3–4):121–34.

Brace, C. L. 1962a. Cultural factors in the evolution of the human dentition. In M. F. A. Montagu (ed.), *Culture and the Evolution of Man.* New York: Oxford University Press Galaxy Book, pp. 343–54.

———. 1962b. Refocusing on the Neanderthal problem. *American Anthropologist* 64(4): 729–41.

———. 1963. Structural reduction in evolution. *The American Naturalist* 97:39–49.

———. 1964. The fate of the "classic" Neanderthals: A consideration of hominid catastrophism. *Current Anthropology* 5(1):3–43.

———. 1967. Environment, tooth form, and size in the Pleistocene. *Journal of Dental Research* 46(5), (Supplement): 809–16.

———. 1971. *Homo sapiens.* In *Anthropology Today.* Del Mar, CA: CRM Books, pp. 175–87.

———. 1973. Sexual dimorphism in human evolution. *Yearbook of Physical Anthropology, 1972* 16:31–49.

———. 1977. Occlusion to the anthropological eye. In James A. McNamara, Jr. (ed.), *The Biology of Occlusal Development.* Center for Human Growth and Development, the University of Michigan, Ann Arbor. Craniofacial Growth Series Monograph No. 7, pp. 179–209.

———. 1979a. Biological parameters and Pleistocene hominid life-ways. In I. S. Bernstein and E. O. Smith (eds.), *Primate Ecology and Human Origins: Ecological Influences on Social Organization.* New York: Garland Press, pp. 263–89.

———. 1979b. Krapina, "classic" Neanderthals, and the evolution of the European face. *Journal of Human Evolution* 8(5):527–50.

———. 1980. Australian tooth-size clines and the death of a stereotype. *Current Anthropology* 21(2):141–64.

———. 1981a. Tales of the phylogenetic woods: The evolution and significance of phylogenetic trees. *American Journal of Physical Anthropology* 56(4):411–29.

———. 1981b. The total morphological Neanderthal as Rumpelstilzchen. *American Journal of Physical Anthropology* 54(2):204.

———. 1988. Punctuationism, cladistics and the legacy of Medieval Neoplatonsim. *Human Evolution* 3(3):121–38.

———. 1989. Medieval thinking and the paradigms of paleoanthropology. *American Anthropologist* 91(2):442–46.

———. 1991. Monte Circeo, Neanderthals, and continuity in European cranial morphology, a rear end view. In Marcello Piperno & Giovanni Scichilone (eds.), *The Circeo 1 Neandertal Skull: Studies and Documentation.* Libreria Dello Stato, Rome, pp. 175–95.

———. 1992. *Modern Human Origins: Narrow Focus or Broad Spectrum?* The David Skomp Lecture. Department of Anthropology, Indiana University, Bloomington, Indiana. 30 pp.

———. In press (a). The creation of specific hominid names: *Gloria in excelsis Deo?* or Ego? or Praxis? *Human Evolution.*

———. In press (b). Cro-Magnon and Qafzeh: Vive la différence. *L'Anthropologie.*

———. In press (c). A four-letter word called "race." In L. J. Reynolds and L. Lieberman (eds.), *Race and Other Miscalculations, and Mismeasures: Papers in Honor of Ashley Montagu.* Dix Hills NY: General Hall Publishers.

———. In press (d). Modern human origins and the dynamics of regional continuity. In T. Akazawa and E. Szathmary (eds.), *Prehistoric Mongoloid Dispersals.* New York: Oxford University Press.

Brace, C. Loring, and Mary L. Brace. 1976. Monkey business and bird brains. In Eugene Giles and Jonathan S. Friedlaender (eds.), *The Measures of Man.* Cambridge, MA: Peabody Museum Press, pp. 54–71.

Brace, C. Loring, and Robert J. Hinton. 1981. Oceanic tooth size variation as a reflection of biological and cultural mixing. *Current Anthropology* 22(5):549–69.

Brace, C. Loring, and Kevin D. Hunt. 1990. A non-racial craniofacial perspective on human variation: A(ustralia) to Z(uni). *American Journal of Physical Anthropology* 88(3):341–60.

Brace, C. Loring, Paul E. Mahler, and Richard B. Rosen. 1973. Tooth measurements and the rejection of the taxon *"Homo Habilis."* *Yearbook of Physical Anthropology 1972* 16:50–68.

Brace, C. Loring, and M. F. Ashley Montagu. 1965. *Man's Evolution: An Introduction to Physical Anthropology.* New York: Macmillan. 352 pp.

Brace, C. Loring, and Ashley Montagu. 1977. *Human Evolution: An Introduction to Biological Anthropology,* 2nd ed. New York: Macmillan. 493 pp.

Brace, C. Loring, Harry Nelson, and Noel Korn. 1971. *Atlas of Fossil Man.* New York: Holt, Rinehart and Winston. 150 pp.

Brace, C. Loring, Harry Nelson, Noel Korn, and Mary L. Brace. 1979. *Atlas of Human Evolution,* 2nd ed. New York: Holt, Rinehart and Winston. 178 pp.

Brace, C. Loring, Karen R. Rosenberg, and Kevin D. Hunt. 1987. Gradual change in human tooth size in the late Pleistocene and post-Pleistocene. *Evolution* 41(4):705–20.

Brace, C. Loring, and Alan S. Ryan. 1980. Sexual dimorphism and human tooth size differences. *Journal of Human Evolution* 9(5):417–35.

Brace, C. Loring, Alan S. Ryan, and B. Holly Smith. 1981. Comment of P-F. Puech "Tooth wear in La Ferrassie man." *Current Anthropology* 22(4):426–30.

Brace, C. Loring, Shao Xiang-qing, and Zhang Zhen-biao. 1984. Prehistoric and modern tooth size in China. In F. H. Smith and F. Spencer (eds.), *The Origins of Modern Humans: A World Survey of the Fossil Evidence.* New York: Alan Liss, pp. 485–516.

Brace, C. Loring, Shelley L. Smith, and Kevin D. Hunt. 1991. What big teeth you had Grandma! Human tooth size past and present. In Marc A. Kelley and Clark Spencer Larsen (eds.), *Advances in Dental Anthropology.* New York: Wiley-Liss, pp. 33–57.

Brace, C. Loring, and David P. Tracer. 1992. Craniofacial continuity and change: A comparison of Late Pleistocene and Recent Europe and Asia. In T. Akazawa, K. Aoki and T. Kimura (eds.), *The Evolution and Dispersal of Modern Humans in Asia.* Tokyo: Hokusen-Sha, pp 439–71.

Brace, C. Loring, David P. Tracer, Lucia Allen Yaroch, John Robb, Kari Brandt, and A. Russell Nelson. 1993. Clines and clusters versus "Race": A test in ancient Egypt and the case of a death on the Nile. *Yearbook of Physical Anthropology* 37:1–31.

Brain, Charles K. 1981. *The Hunters or the Hunted? An Introduction to African Cave Taphonomy.* Chicago: University of Chicago Press. 365 pp.

Bräuer, Günter. 1984. The "Afro-European *sapiens*-hypothesis," and hominid evolution in East Asia during the late Middle and Upper Pleistocene. In P. Andrews and J. L. Franzen (eds.), *The Early Evolution of Man With Special Emphasis on Southeast Asia and Africa.* Courier Forschungsinstitut, Senckenberg 69:145–65.

———. 1989. The evolution of modern humans: A comparison of the African and non-African evidence. In P. Mellars and C. Stringer (eds.), *The Human Revolu-*

tion: *Behavioural and Biological Perspectives on the Origins of Modern Humans.* Edinburgh: Edinburgh University Press, pp. 123–54.

Bräuer, Günter, Richard E. Leakey, and Emma Mbua. 1992. A first report on the ER-3884 cranial remains from Ileret/East Turkana, Kenya. In G. Bräuer and F. H. Smith (eds.), *Continuity or Replacement: Controversies in Homo sapiens Evolution.* Rotterdam: A. A. Balkema, pp. 111–19.

Breasted, James H. 1909. *A History of Egypt From the Earliest Times to the Persian Conquest.* New York: Charles Scribner's Sons. 364 pp.

Brennan, Mary U. 1991. *Health the Disease in the Middle and Upper Paleolithic of Southwestern France: A Bioarcheological Study.* Ph.D. Dissertation, New York University. 317 pp.

Breuil, Henri. 1931. Le feu et l'industrie lithique et osseuse à Choukoutien. *Bulletin of the Geological Society of China* 11(4):147–54.

———. 1952. *Four Hundred Centuries of Cave Art.* Centre d'Études et de Documentation Préhistorique, Montignac. 413 pp.

Breuil, Henri, and L. Koslowski. 1931. Études de stratigraphie Paléolithique dans le Nord de la France, la Belgique et l'Angleterre. *L'Anthropologie* 41(5–6)449–88.

Broca, Paul. 1868. Sur les crânes et ossements des Eyzies. *Bulletins de la Société d'Anthropologie de Paris.* Série 2, Tome 3:350–92.

———. 1870. Sur le transformisme. *Bulletins de la Société d'Anthropologie de Paris.* Série 1, Tome 5:168–242.

Brody, Hugh. 1987. *Living Arctic: Hunters of the Canadian North.* London: Faber and Faber. 254 pp.

Broecker, Wallace, and George H. Denton. 1989. The role of ocean-atmosphere reorganizations in glacial cycles. *Geochimica et Cosmochimica Acta* 53(10):2465–2501.

———. 1990. What drives glacial cycles? *Scientific American* 262(1):48–56.

Bromage, Timothy G., and M. Christopher Dean. 1985. Re-evaluation of the age of death of immature fossil hominids. *Nature* 317:525–27.

Brooks, Alison S. 1988. Middle Stone Age. In I. Tattersall, E. Delson and J. Van Couvering (eds.), *Encyclopedia of Human Evolution.* New York: Garland Publishing Company, pp. 346–349.

Brody, Hugh. 1990. *Living Arctic: Hunters of the Canadian North.* Vancouver: Douglas and McIntyre. 254 pp.

Broom, Robert. 1936. A new fossil anthropoid skull from South Africa. *Nature* 138:486–88.

———. 1938a. Further evidence on the structure of the South African Pleistocene anthropoids. *Nature* 142:897–99.

———. 1938b. The Pleistocene anthropoid apes of South Africa. *Nature* 142:377–79.

———. 1939. The dentition of the Transvaal Pleistocene anthropoids, *Plesianthropus* and *Paranthropus, Annals of the Transvaal Museum* 19(3):303–14.

———. 1947. Discovery of a new skull of the South African ape-man, *Plesianthropus. Nature* 159:672.

———. 1950a. Discovery of a new skull of the South African ape-man, *Plesianthropus. Nature* 159:672.

———. 1950b. *Finding the Missing Link.* London: Watts. 104 pp.

———. 1950c. The genera and species of the South African fossil ape-men. *American Journal of Physical Anthropology* 8(1):1–13.

Broom, Robert, and John T. Robinson. 1947. Further remains of the Sterkfontein ape-man, *Plesianthropus*. *Nature* 160:430–31.

———. 1949. A new type of fossil man. *Nature* 164:322–23.

———. 1950a. Man contemporaneous with Swartkrans ape-man. *American Journal of Physical Anthropology* 8(2):151–55.

———. 1950b. Notes on the pelves of the fossil ape-men. *American Journal of Physical Anthropology* 9(4):489–94.

Brown, Frank, John Harris, Richard Leakey, and Alan Walker. 1985. Early *Homo erectus* skeleton from West Lake Turkana, Kenya. *Nature* 316:788–92.

Brown, Peter. 1981. Sex determination of Australian Aboriginal crania from the Murray River Valley: A reassessment of the Larnach and Freedman technique. *Archaeology in Oceania* 16(1):53–63.

———. 1993. Recent human evolution in East Asia and Australasia. In M. J. Aitken, C. B. Stringer, and P. A. Mellars (eds.). *The Origins of Modern Humans and the Impact of Chronometric Dating*. Princeton: Princeton University Press, pp. 217–33.

Browne, Malcolm W. 1993. The way we were? Review of *In Search of the Neanderthals* by C. Stringer and C. Gamble; *The Neandertals* by E. Trinkaus and P. Shipman; and *What the Bones Tell Us* by J. H. Schwartz. *New York Times Book Review*, July 4, pp. 1, 21.

Brues, Alice M. 1959. The spearman and the archer—an essay on selection in body build. *American Anthropologist* 61(3):457–69.

Bunn, Henry T., and Ellen M. Kroll. 1986. Systematic butchery by Plio/Pleistocene hominids at Olduvai Gorge, Tanzania. *Current Anthropology* 27(5):431–52.

Bürger, Willy. 1956. *Johann Carl Fuhlrott der Entdecker des Neandertalmenschen Menschen*. Beiträge zur Geschichte und Heimatkunde des Wuppertals, Band 2, 3rd. Auflage, Abendland, Wuppertal: Verlag. 64 pp.

Burgess, Anthony. 1988. Mr. Gibbon and the Huns. *New York Times Book Review*. Feb. 28, pp. 1, 36–37.

Burkhardt, Richard W., Jr. 1977. *The Spirit of System: Lamarck and Evolutionary Biology*. Cambridge, MA: Harvard University Press. 286 pp.

Burt, Eugene C. 1988. *Ethnoart: Africa, Oceania, and the Americas*. New York: Garland. 191 pp.

Busk, George. 1864. Pithecoid Priscan Man from Gibraltar. *The Reader*, July 23, pp. 109–10.

———. 1865. On a very ancient human cranium from Gibraltar. *Report of the Thirty-Fourth Meeting of the British Association for the Advancement of Science*, held at Bath in September 1864. pp. 91–92.

Butler, Robert F. 1991. *Paleomagnetism: Magnetic Domains to Geologic Terranes*. Cambridge, MA: Blackwell Scientific. 319 pp.

Butzer, Karl W. 1969. Geological interpretation of two Pleistocene hominid sites in the lower Omo basin. *Nature* 222:1133–35.

Calvin, William H. 1990. *The Ascent of Mind: Ice Age Climates and the Evolution of Intelligence*. New York: Bantam Books. 302 pp.

Campbell, Alastair. 1965. Elementary food production by the Australian Aborigines. *Mankind* 6(5):207–11.

Campbell, Bernard G. 1966. *Human Evolution: An Introduction to Man's Adaptations*. Chicago: Aldine. 425 pp.

Cande, Steven C., and Dennis V. Kent. 1992. A new geomagnetic polarity for the late Cretaceous and Cenozoic. *Journal of Geophysical Research* 97(B 10):13917–51.

Cann, Rebecca L. 1988. DNA and human origins. *Annual Review of Anthropology* 17:127–43.

Cann, Rebecca L., Mark Stoneking, and Allan C. Wilson. 1987. Mitochondrial DNA and human evolution. *Nature* 325:31–36.

Carrier, David R. 1984. The energetic paradox of human running and hominid evolution. *Current Anthropology* 25(4):483–95.

Carrington, Richard. 1963. *A Million Years of Man: The Story of Human Development as a Part of Nature*, 1964 ed. New York: New American Library, Mentor Book. 304 pp.

Carson, Hampton L. 1989. Evolution: The pattern of the process. Review of *Speciation and Its Consequences*, Daniel Otte and John A. Endler (eds.). *Science* 245:872–873.

Cartmill, Matt. 1981. Hypothesis testing and phylogenetic reconstruction. *Zeitschrift für zoologische Systematik und Evolutionsforschung* 19(2):73–96.

Cerling, T. E., F. H. Brown, B. W. Cerling, G. H. Curtis, and R. E. Drake. 1979. Preliminary correlations between the Koobi Fora and Shungura Formations, East Africa. *Nature* 279:118–21.

Chang, Kwang-chih. 1968. *The Archaeology of Ancient China*, revised ed. New Haven: Yale University Press, 483 pp.

———. 1987. *The Archaeology of Ancient China*, 4th ed. New Haven: ed. Yale University Press. 450 pp.

Chavaillon, Jean. 1971. État actuel de la préhistoire ancienne dans la vallée de l'Omo. *Archéologia* 38:34–43.

Chavaillon, Jean, and Nicole Chavaillon. 1969. Les habitats oldowayens de Melka Kontouré (Ethiopie): Premiers résultats. *Comptes Rendus des Séances de l'Académie des Sciences de Paris* 268(24):2244–47.

Chen Tiemei and Yuan Sixun. 1988. Uranium-series dating of bones and teeth from Chinese Palaeolithic sites. *Archaeometry* 30(1):59–76.

Chen Tiemei and Zhang Yinyun. 1991. Palaeolithic chronology and possible coexistence of *Homo erectus* and *Homo sapiens* in China. *World Archaeology* 23(2):147–54.

Chomsky, Noam. 1972. *Language and Mind*. New York: Harcourt, Brace and World. 194 pp.

Christen, Yves. 1979. On tiendrait enfin le "chaînon manquant." *Le Figaro Magazine*, Feb. 3:40–44, 97–98.

Churchill, Steven E., and Erik Trinkaus. 1990. Neandertal scapular glenoid morphology. *American Journal of Physical Anthropology* 83(2):147–60.

Clark, Geoffrey A. 1988. Some thoughts on the Black Skull: An archaeologist's assessment of WT-1700 *(A. boisei)* and systematics in human paleontology. *American Anthropologist* 90(2):357–71.

———. 1992. Continuity or Replacement? Putting modern human origins in an evolutionary context. In Harold Dibble and Paul Mellars (eds.), *The Middle Paleolithic: Adaptation and Variability*. Philadelphia: University of Pennsylvania Museum, pp. 183–205.

Clark, Geoffrey A., and J. M. Lindly 1989a. The case for continuity: Observations on the biocultural transition in Europe and western Asia. In P. Mellars and C. Stringer (eds.), *The Human Revolution: Behavioural and Biological. Perspectives on the Origins of Modern Humans*. Edinburgh: Edinburgh University Press, pp. 626–76.

———. 1989b. Modern human origins in the Levant and western Asia: The fossil and archeological evidence. *American Anthropologist* 91(4):962–85.

Clark, J. Desmond. 1950. *The Stone Age Cultures of Northern Rhodesia: With Particular Reference to the Cultural and Climatic Succession in the Upper Zambezi Valley and its Tributaries.* The South African Archaeological Society, Claremont, South Africa. 157 pp.

———. 1959. *The Prehistory of Southern Africa.* Harmondsworth, Middlesex, England: Penguin Books. 341 pp.

———. 1975. Africa in prehistory: Peripheral or paramount? *Man* 10(2):175–98. The Huxley Memorial Lecture, 1974.

———. 1976. African origins of man the toolmaker. In G. Ll. Isaac and E. R. McCown (eds.), *Human Origins: Louis Leakey and the East African Evidence.* Menlo Park, CA: Benjamin, pp. 1–53.

———. 1988. The Middle Stone Age of East Africa and the beginnings of regional identity. *Journal of World Prehistory* 2(3):235–305.

———. 1993. African and Asian perspectives on the origins of modern humans. In M. J. Aitkens, C. B. Stringer, and P. A. Mellars (eds.), *The Origins of Modern Humans and the Impact of Chronometric Dating.* Princeton: Princeton University Press, pp. 148–78.

Clark, J. Desmond, and C. Vance Haynes, Jr. 1970. An elephant butchery site at Mwangande's Village, Karonga, Malawi, and its relevance for Paleolithic archaeology. *World Archaeology* 1(3):390–411.

Clark, J. Desmond, and Kathy D. Schick. 1988. Context and content: Impressions of Palaeolithic sites and assemblages in the People's Republic of China. *Journal of Human Evolution* 17(4):439–48.

Clark, Wilfrid E. Le Gros. 1928. Rhodesian man. *Man* 28(12):206–7.

———. 1950. *History of the Primates: An Introduction to the Study of Fossil Man.* British Museum (Natural History), London. 117 pp.

———. 1960. *The Antecedents of Man: An Introduction to the Evolution of the Primates.* Chicago: Quadrangle Books. 374 pp.

———. 1967. *Man-Apes of Ape-Men? The Story of Discoveries in Africa.* New York: Holt, Rinehart and Winston. 150 pp.

Clarke, David. 1976. Mesolithic Europe: The economic basis. In G. de. G. Sieveking, I. H. Longworth and K. E. Wilson (eds.), *Problems in Economic and Social Archaeology.* London: Duckworth, pp. 449–81.

Clarke, Ronald J. 1985. A new reconstruction of the Florisbad cranium, with notes on the site. In Eric Delson (ed.), *Ancestors: The Hard Evidence.* New York: Alan Liss, pp. 301–5.

Clottes, Jean, and Jean Courtin. 1993. Neptune's ice age gallery. *Natural History* 102(4):64–71.

Cloud, Preston, and Martin F. Glaessner. 1982. The Ediacarian Period and System: Metazoa inherit the earth. *Science* 217:783–92.

Clutton-Brock, Tim H. 1985a. Reproductive success in red deer. *Scientific American* 252(2):86–92.

———. 1985b. Size, sexual dimorphism and polygyny in primates. In William L. Jungers (ed.), *Size and Scaling in Primate Biology.* New York: Plenum, pp. 51–60.

Coale, Ansley J. 1970. Man and his environment. *Science* 170:132–36.

———. 1974. The history of the human population. *Scientific American* 231(3):40–51.

Cole, Sonia. 1975. *Leakey's Luck: The Life of Louis Seymour Bazett Leakey.* New York: Harcourt, Brace, Jovanovich. 448 pp.

Coleman, William R. 1964. *Georges Cuvier, Zoologist: A Study in the History of Evolution Theory.* Cambridge, MA: Harvard University Press. 212 pp.

Conroy, Glenn C., Clifford J. Jolly, Douglas Cramer, and Jon E. Kalb. 1978. Newly discovered fossil hominid skull from the Afar depression, Ethiopia. *Nature* 276:67–70.

Conroy, Glenn C., Martin Pickford, Brigitte Senut, John Van Couvering, and Pierre Mein. 1992. *Otavipithecus namibiensis,* first Miocene hominoid from southern Africa. *Nature* 356:144–48.

Cooke, H. B. S. 1978a. Pliocene-Pleistocene Suidae from Hadar, Ethiopia. *Kirtlandia: The Cleveland Museum of Natural History* 19:1–63.

———. 1978b. Suid evolution and correlation of African hominid localities: An alternative taxonomy. *Science* 201:460–63.

Coon, Carleton S. 1962. *The Origin of Races.* New York: Alfred A. Knopf. 724 pp.

Cope, Edward Drinker. 1887. *The Origin of the Fittest: Essays on Evolution.* London: Macmillan. 467 pp.

Coppens, Yves. 1983. Systematique, phylogénie, environement et culture des australopithèques, hypothèses et synthèse. *Bulletins et Mémoires de la Société d'Anthropologie de Paris,* Série 13, 10:273–84.

Courtillot, Vincent E. 1990. A volcanic eruption. *Scientific American* 263(4):85–92.

Courtillot, V., G. Féraud, H. Maluski, D. Vandamme, M. G. Moreau, and J. Besse. 1988. The Deccan flood basalts and the Cretaceous/Tertiary boundary. *Nature* 333:843–46.

Crompton, A. W., and Stephen M. Gatesy. 1989. A cold-eyed look at a treatise on warm-blooded dinosaurs: Review of *Predatory Dinosaurs of the World* by Gregory Paul. *Scientific American* 260(1):110–13.

Crompton, A. W., and Farish A. Jenkins, Jr. 1973. Mammals from the reptiles: A review of mammalian origins. In F. A. Donath, F. G. Stehli, and W. G. Wetherill (eds.), *Annual Reviews of Earth and Planetary Sciences.* CA: Palo Alto, pp. 131–55.

Cunningham, Daniel J. 1895. Dr. Dubois's so-called Missing Link. *Nature* 51:428–29.

Curtis, G. H., R. E. Drake, T. Cerling, and J. Hampel. 1975. Age of KBS Tuff, East Turkana, Kenya. *Nature* 258:395–98.

Curtis, Garniss H., and Richard L. Hay. 1972. Further geologist studies and potassium-argon dating at Olduvai Gorge and Ngorongoro Crater. In W. W. Bishop and J. A. Miller (eds.), *Calibration of Hominoid Evolution.* Edinburgh: Scottish Academic Press, pp. 289–301.

Cuvier, Georges. 1826. Discours sur les révolutions de la surface du globe. In *Recherches sur les ossemens fossiles,* 3rd edition. G. Dufour and Ed. D'Ocagne, Paris. 196 pp.

Czerkas, Sylvia J., and Everett C. Olson (eds.). 1987. *Dinosaurs Past and Present.* Natural History Museum of Los Angeles County,Los Angeles, California. 2 vols.

Daniel, Glyn. 1986. The fall of the House of Ussher. Review of *The Amateur and the Professional: Antiquarians, Historians and Archaeologists in Victorian England, 1838–1886,* by Philippa Levine. *Times Literary Supplement,* September 12, p. 1015.

Dart, Raymond A. 1925. *Australopithecus africanus:* The man-ape of South Africa. *Nature* 115:195–99.

———. 1948. The Makapansgat proto-human Australopithecus prometheus. *American Journal of Physical Anthropology* 6(3):259–81.

————. 1949. Innominate fragments of Australopithecus prometheus. *American Journal of Physical Anthropology* 7(3):301–32.

Dart, Raymond A., and Dennis Craig. 1959. *Adventures with the Missing Link*. New York: Harper & Brothers. 155 pp.

Darwin, Charles R. 1859. *On the Origin of Species by Means of Natural Selection, Or the Preservation of the Favoured Races in the Struggle for Life*. London: John Murray. 502 pp.

————. 1868. *The Variation of Animals and Plants Under Domestication*. London: John Murray. 2 vols.

————. 1871. *The Descent of Man and Selection in Relation to Sex*. London: John Murray. 2 vols.

Davidson, Daniel S. 1933. Australian netting and basketry techniques. *Journal of the Polynesian Society* 42:257–99.

————. 1936. The spearthrower in Australia. *Proceedings of the American Philosophical Society* 74(4):445–83.

Davidson, Daniel S., and Frederick D. McCarthy. 1957. The distribution and chronology of some important types of stone implements in Western Australia. *Anthropos* 52:390–458.

Davidson, Ian, and William Noble. 1989. The archaeology of perception: Traces of depiction and language. *Current Anthropology* 30(2):125–55.

Dawkins, Richard. 1976. *The Selfish Gene*. New York: Oxford University Press. 224 pp.

————. 1986. *The Blind Watchmaker: Why the Evidence of Evolution Reveals a Universe Without Design*. New York: W. W. Norton. 332 pp.

Dawson, John W. 1863. On the antiquity of man: A review of "Lyell" and "Wilson." *The Canadian Naturalist and Geologist* 8(2):113–35.

Day, Michael H. 1969. Omo human skeletal remains. *Nature* 222:1135–38.

————. 1977. *Guide to Fossil Man: A Handbook of Human Palaeontology*. 3rd edition. Chicago: University of Chicago Press. 346 pp.

————. 1984. The postcranial remains of *Homo erectus* from Africa, Asia, and possibly Europe. In P. Andrews and J. L. Franzen (eds)., *The Early Evolution of Man*. Courier Forschungsinstitut, Senckenberg 69:113–21.

————. 1986. *Guide to Fossil Man*, 4th ed., Chicago: University of Chicago Press. 432 pp.

Day, Michael H., Mary D. Leakey, and C. C. Magori 1980. A new hominid fossil skull (L.H.18) from the Ngaloba Beds, Laetoli, northern Tanzania. *Nature* 284:55–56.

Deacon, Terrence W. 1988. Human Evolution: II. Embryology and brain allometry. In Harry J. Jerison and Irene Jerison (eds.), *Intelligence and Evolutionary Biology*. New York: Springer Verlag, pp. 383–415.

Dean, M. Christopher 1985a. The eruption pattern of the permanent incisors and first permanent molars in *Australopithecus (Paranthropus) robustus*. *American Journal of Physical Anthropology* 67(3):251–57.

————. 1985b. Variation in the developing root cone angle of the permanent mandibular teeth of modern man and certain fossil hominids. *American Journal of Physical Anthropology* 68(2):233–38.

————. 1987. The dental developmental status of six East African juvenile fossil hominids. *Journal of Human Evolution* 16(2):197–213.

————. 1988. Growth of teeth and development of the dentition in *Paranthropus*. In Frederick E. Grine (ed.), *Evolutionary History of the "Robust" Australopithecines*. New York: Aldine de Gruyter, pp. 43–53.

Dean, M. C., A. D. Beynon, J. F. Thackeray, and G. A. Macho. 1993. Histological reconstruction of dental development and age at death of a juvenile *Paranthropus robustus* specimen, SK 63, from Swartkrans, South Africa. *American Journal of Physical Anthropology* 91(4):401–419.

Diamond, Jared. 1989a. The great leap forward. *Discover* 10(5)50–60.

―――. 1989b. This-fellow frog, name belong-him dakwo. *Natural History* 4:16–23.

―――. 1992. *The Third Chimpanzee:* The Evolution and Future of the Human Animal. New York: Harper Collins. 407 pp.

Dibble, Harold L., and Paul Mellars (eds.). 1992. *The Middle Paleolithic: Adaptation, Behavior, and Variability.* University Museum, Philadelphia. University Symposium Series Vol. 4, University Museum Monograph, 78. 216 pp.

di Gregorio, Mario A. 1984. *T. H. Huxley's Place in Natural Science.* Yale University Press, CN: New Haven. 253 pp.

Diop, Cheikh Anta. 1985. Africa: Cradle of humanity. In Ivan Van Sertima (ed.), *Nile Valley Civilizations.* Proceedings of the Nile Valley Conference, Atlanta, September 26–30. *Journal of African Civilizations* 6(2):23–28.

Dobzhansky, Theodosius. 1937. *Genetics and the Origin of Species.* New York: Columbia University Press. 364 pp.

―――. 1944. On species and races of living and fossil man. *American Journal of Physical Anthropology* 2(3):251–65.

Dokládal, Milan, and Josef Brožek. 1961. Physical anthropology in Czechoslovakia: Recent developments. *Current Anthropology* 2(5):455–77.

Donald, Merlin. 1991. *Origins of the Modern Mind: Three Stages in the Evolution of Culture and Cognition.* Cambridge, MA: Harvard University Press. 413 pp.

Dornan, S. S. 1925. *Pygmies & Bushmen of the Kalahari: An Account of the Tribes Inhabiting the Great Arid Plateau of the Kalahari Desert, Their Precarious manner of Living Their Habits, Customs and Beliefs, with some Reference to Bushmen Art, both early & recent date, & to the neighboring African Tribes.* London: Seeley, Service & Co. 318 pp.

Drake, Robert, and Garniss H. Curtis. 1987. K-Ar geochronology of the Laetoli fossil localities. In Mary D. Leakey and John M. Harris (eds.), *Laetoli: A Pliocene Site in Northern Tanzania.* Oxford: Clarendon Press, pp. 48–61.

Drennan, M. R. 1953. The Saldanha skull and its associations. *Nature* 172:791–93.

―――. 1955. The special features and status of the Saldanha skull. *American Journal of Physical Anthropology* 13(4):625–34.

Dreyer, J. F., and C. U. Ariëns-Kappers. 1935. A human skull from Florisbad, Orange Free State. *Proceedings of the Section of Sciences, Akademie van Wetenschappen te Amsterdam* 38(1):119–28.

Dubois, Eugène. 1894. Pithecanthropus erectus, *Eine Menschenänliche Uebergangsform aus Java.* Batavia: Landesdruckerei. 40 pp.

―――. 1895. Pithecanthropus erectus, betrachtet als eine wirkliche Uebergangsform und als Stammform des Menschen. *Verhandlungen der Berliner Gesellschaft für Anthropologie, Ethnologie und Urgeschichte,* Ausserordentliche Sitzung vom 14. December: 723–38.

―――. 1896. Pithecanthropus erectus, eine Stammform des Menschen. *Anatomischer Anzeiger* 12(1):1–22.

―――. 1935. On the gibbon-like appearance of Pithecanthropus erectus. *Proceedings. Koninklijke Akademie van Wetenschappen te Amsterdam* 38(6):578–85.

Dumond, Don E. 1980. The archeology of Alaska and the peopling of America. *Science* 209:984–91.

———. 1987. A reexamination of Eskimo-Aleut prehistory. *American Anthropologist* 89(1):32–56.

Dunbar, Robin I. M. 1993. Co-evolution of neocortex size, group size and language in humans. *Behavioral and Brain Sciences* 16(4): 681–94.

Dyck, Willy. 1967. Recent developments in radiocarbon dating: Their implications for geochronology and archaeology. *Current Anthropology* 8(4):349–51.

Earhart, Caroline M., and Ned K. Johnson. 1970. Sex dimorphism and food habits of North American owls. *The Condor* 72(3):251–64.

Eco, Umberto. 1983. *The Name of the Rose.* Translated from the Italian (1980) by William Weaver. San Diego: Harcourt, Brace, Jovanovich. 502 pp.

———. 1984a. *Postscript to the Name of the Rose.* Translated from the Italian (1983) by William Weaver. San Diego: Harcourt, Brace, Jovanovich. 84 pp.

———. 1984b. *Semiotics and the Philosophy of Language.* London: Macmillan. 242 pp.

von Eickstedt, Egon Freiherr. 1937. *Rassenkunde und Rassengeschichte der Menschheit.* 2nd ed. Vol. 1: *Die Forschung am Menschen,* Erste Lieferung. Stuttgart: Ferdinand Enke Verlag. 128 pp.

Eijgenraam, Felix. 1993. "Java man" gains (and loses) a consort. *Science* 261:297.

Eldredge, Niles. 1993. What, if anything, is a species? In W. H. Kimbel and L. B. Martin (eds.), *Species, Species Concepts, and Primate Evolution.* New York: Plenum Press, 3–20.

Eldredge, Niles, and Joel Cracraft. 1980. *Phylogenetic Patterns and the Evolutionary Process: Method and Theory in Comparative Biology.* New York: Columbia University Press. 350 pp.

Eldredge, Niles, and Stephen Jay Gould. 1972. Speciation and punctuated equilibria: An alternative to phyletic gradualism. In Thomas J. M. Schopf (ed.), *Models in Paleobiology.* San Francisco: Freeman, Cooper and Company, pp. 85–120.

Eldredge, Niles, and Ian Tattersall. 1982. *The Myths of Human Evolution.* New York: Columbia University Press. 197 pp.

Elliott, David K. 1987. A reassessment of *Astraspis desiderata,* the oldest North American vertebrate. *Science* 237:190–92.

Endo, Banri, and Tasuku Kimura. 1970. Postcranial skeleton of the Amud man. In Hisashi Suzuki (ed.), *The Amud Man and His Cave Site.* Tokyo: University of Tokyo Press, pp. 231–406.

Ennouchi, Émile. 1962. Un Néanderthalien: l'homme du Jebel Irhoud (Maroc). *L'Anthropologie* 66(3–4):279–99.

Erickson, Paul A. 1977. Phrenology and physical anthropology: The George Combe connection. *Current Anthropology* 18(1):92–93.

Eyre, Edward J. 1845. *Journals of Expeditions of Discovery Into Central Australia, and Overland from Adelaide to King George's Sound in the Years 1840–1841,* 2 vols. London: T. & W. Boone.

Falk, Dean. 1975. Comparative anatomy of the larynx in man and chimpanzee: Implications for language in Neanderthal. *American Journal of Physical Anthropology* 43(1):123–32.

———. 1983. Cerebral cortices of East African early hominids. *Science* 221:1072–74.

———. 1988. Enlarged occipital/marginal sinuses and emissary foramina: Their significance in hominid evolution. In Frederick E. Grine (ed.), *Evolutionary History of the "Robust" Australopithecines.* New York: Aldine de Gruyter, pp. 85–112.

———. 1990. Brain evolution in *Homo*: The "radiator" theory. *Behavioral and Brain Sciences* 13(2):333–81.

———. 1992. *Braindance.* New York: Henry Holt. 260 pp.

Falkner, Frank, and James. M. Tanner, (eds.). 1986. *Human Growth: A Comprehensive Treatise,* 3 vols. New York: Plenum.

Feduccia, Alan. 1980. *The Age of Birds.* Cambridge, MA: Harvard University Press. 196 pp.

———. 1993. Evidence from claw geometry indicating arboreal habitats of *Archaeopteryx. Science* 259:790–93.

Finch, Charles S. 1985. The evolution of the caucasoid. In Ivan Van Sertima (ed.), *African Presence in Early Europe,* incorporating *Journal of African Civilizations* 7(2):17–22.

Findlay, George H. 1972. *Dr. Robert Broom, F.R.S. Palaeontologist and Physician, 1866–1951: A Biography, Appreciation and Bibliography.* Cape Town: A. A. Balkema. 157 pp.

Fischer, Anders, Peter V. Hansen, and Peter Rasmussen. 1984. Macro and micro wear on lithic projectile points: Experimental results and prehistoric examples. *Journal of Danish Archaeology* 3:19–46.

Fischer, Eugen. 1903. Beeinflusst der M. Genioglossus durch seine Funktion beim Sprechen den Bau des Unterkiefers? *Anatomischer Anzeiger* 23(2–3):33–37.

Fishbein, Harold D. 1976. *Evolution, Development, and Children's Learning.* Pacific Palisades, CA: Goodyear Publishing. 332 pp.

Fisher, Charles D. 1970. *Geographic Variation and Evolution in the Australian Ringneck Parrots Barnardius.* Ph.D. Dissertation, Department of Zoology, University of Michigan, Ann Arbor. 242 pp.

Fisher, Helen E. 1983. Richard Leakey's time machine: Interview. *Omni* 5(6):94–104, 142–45.

Fisher, Ronald A. 1930. *The Genetical Theory of Natural Selection* Oxford: The Clarendon Press. 272 pp.

Fitch, Frank J., Ian C. Findlater, Ronald T. Watkins, and J. A. Miller. 1974. Dating the rock succession containing fossil hominids at East Rudolf, Kenya. *Nature* 251:213–15.

Fitch, Frank J., and J. A. Miller. 1969. Age determinations on feldspar from the lower Omo Basin. *Nature* 222:1143.

Fleagle, John G., Thomas M. Bown, John D. Obradovich, and Elwyn L. Simons. 1986. Age of the earliest African anthropoids. *Science* 234:1247–49.

Fleagle, John G., Elwyn L. Simons, and Glenn C. Conroy. 1975. Ape limb bone from the Oligocene of Egypt. *Science* 189:135–37.

Fleming, Stuart J. 1977. *Dating in Archaeology: A Guide to Scientific Techniques.* London: Dent. 272 pp.

Foley, Robert. 1987. *Another Unique Species: Patterns in Human Evolutionary Ecology.* New York: John Wiley. 313 pp.

Fox, Michael W. (ed.). 1975. *The Wild Canids: Their Systematics, Behavioral Ecology and Evolution.* New York: Van Nostrand Reinhold. 508 pp.

Fraipont Julien, and Max Lohest. 1886. La race humaine de Néanderthal ou de Canstadt en Belgique. *Bulletin de l'Académie Royale de Belgique* 12:741–84.

Franciscus, Robert G., and Erik Trinkaus. 1988. The Neandertal nose. *American Journal of Physical Anthropology* 75(2):209–10.

Frayer, David W. 1976. *Evolutionary Dental Changes in Upper Paleolithic and Mesolithic Human Populations.* Ph.D. Dissertation, Department of Anthropology, University of Michigan, Ann Arbor. 529 pp.

———. 1981. Body size, weapon use, and natural selection in the European Upper Paleolithic and Mesolithic. *American Anthropologist* 83(1):57–73.

———. 1992. Evolution at the European edge: Neanderthal and Upper Paleolithic relationships. *Préhistoire Européenne* 2:9–69.

Frayer, David W., Milford H. Wolpoff, Alan G. Thorne, and Geoffrey G. Pope. 1993. Theories of modern human origins: The paleontological test. *American Anthropologist* 95(1):14–50.

Fuhlrott, Johann C. 1857. Theilen des menschlichen skelettes im Neanderthal bei Hochdal. *Verhandlungen des naturhistorischen Vereins der preussischen Rheinlande und Westfalens, Korrespondenzblatt* 4:50.

Gaffney, Eugene S. 1979. An introduction to the logic of phylogeny reconstruction. In Joel Cracraft and Niles Eldredge (eds.), *Phylogenetic Analysis and Paleontology.* New York: Columbia University Press, pp. 79–111.

Garn, Stanley M. 1980. Human Growth. *Annual Review of Anthropology* 9:275–92.

Garn, Stanley M., Helen A. Shaw, and Kinne D. McCabe. 1977. Effects of socioeconomic status and race on weight-defined and gestational prematurity in the United States. In D. W. Reed and F. J. Stanley (eds.), *Epidemiology and Prematurity.* Baltimore: Urban and Schwarzenberg, pp. 127–143.

Garrod, Dorothy A. E. 1955. Palaeolithic spear-throwers. *Proceedings of the Prehistoric Society* 21(3):21–35.

———. 1958. The ancient shore-lines of the Lebanon, and the dating of Mt. Carmel Man. In G. H. R. von Koenigswald (ed.), *Hundert Jahre Neanderthaler.* Utrecht: Kemink en Zoon, N.V., pp. 182–83.

Gasman, Daniel. 1971. *The Scientific Origins of National Socialism: Social Darwinism in Ernst Haeckel and the German Monist League.* London: McDonald. 208 pp.

Gaudry, Albert. 1903. Contribution à l'histoire des hommes fossiles. *L'Anthropologie* 14:1–14.

Gause, G. F. 1934. *The Struggle for Existence.* Baltimore: Williams & Wilkins. 163 pp.

Ghiselin, Michael T. 1969. *The Triumph of the Darwinian Method.* Berkeley: University of California Press. 287 pp.

———. 1972. Review of *The Origins of Theoretical Population Genetics,* William B. Provine. *Science* 175:507.

Gibert, J. 1992. Age des gisements à presence humaine et à action anthropique de la région d'Orce (Grenade, Espagne). *Journal of the Israel Prehistoric Society,* Supplement 1: Program and Book of Abstracts, 3rd International Congress on Human Paleontology. p. 43.

Gibert, J., D. Campillo, B. Martinez, F. Sanchez, R. Caporicci, C. Jimenez, C. Fernandez, and F. Ribot. 1991. Nouveaux restes d'hominidés dans les gisements d'Orce et de Cueva Victoria (Espagne). In E. Bonifay and B. Vandermeersch (eds.), *Les Premiers Européens.* Paris: Comité des Travaux Historiques et Scientifiques, pp 273–82.

Gibert, J., C. Jimenez, A. Iglesias, and L. Gibert. 1992. Action anthropique dans le Pleistocene inférieur de la région d'Orce (Espagne). *Journal of the Israel Prehistoric Society,* Supplement 1: Program and Book of Abstracts, 3rd International Congress on Human Paleontology. p. 42.

Gieseler, Wilhelm. 1953. Allemagne. In H. V. Vallois and H. Movius (eds.), *Catalogue des Hommes Fossiles.* Macon: Protat Frères, p. 80.

Gillespie, R., R. E. M. Hedges, and J. O. Wand. 1984. Radiocarbon dating of bone by mass spectrometry. *Journal of Archaeological Science* 11(2):164–70.

Gingerich, Philip D. 1975a. Dentition of *Adapis parisiensis* and the origin of lemuriform primates. In I. Tattersall and R. Sussman (eds.), *Lemur Biology.* New York: Plenum, pp. 65–80.

———. 1975b. Systematic position of *Plesiadapis. Nature* 253:111–13.

———. 1976a. *Cranial Anatomy and Evolution of Early Tertiary Plesiadapidae (Mammalia, Primates).* Papers on Paleontology No. 15, Museum of Paleontology, University of Michigan, Ann Arbor. 141 pp.

———. 1976b. Paleontology and phylogeny: Patterns of evolution at the species level in early tertiary mammals. *American Journal of Science* 276(1):1–28.

———. 1977a. Patterns of evolution in the mammalian fossil record. In A. Hallam (ed.), *Patterns of Evolution.* Amsterdam: Elsevier Scientific Publishing Company, pp. 461–500.

———. 1977b. Radiation of Eocene Adapidae in Europe. *Géobios (Lyon), Mémoir Special* 1:165–82.

———. 1984. Punctuated equilibria—where is the evidence? *Systematic Zoology* 33(3):335–38.

———. 1986. *Plesiadapis* and the delineation of the order Primates. In B. Wood, L. Martin, and P. Andrews (eds.), *Major Topics in Primate and Human Evolution.* Cambridge: Cambridge University Press, pp. 32–46.

Gingerich, Philip D., and Elwyn L. Simons. 1977. Systematics, phylogeny, and evolution of early Miocene Adapidae (Mammalia, Primates) in North America. *Contributions of the Museum of Paleontology, University of Michigan* 24(22):245–79.

Girdler, R. W., and P. Styles. 1974. Two stage Red Sea floor spreading. *Nature* 242:244.

Gish, Duane T. 1979. *Evolution, The Fossils Say No!* 3rd ed. San Diego: Creation-Life Publishers. 198 pp.

———. 1985. *Evolution: The Challenge of the Fossil Record.* El Cajon. CA: Creation-Life Publishers. 277 pp.

Gittleman, John L. (ed.). 1989. *Carnivore Behavior, Ecology, and Evolution.* Ithaca, NY: Cornell University Press. 620 pp.

Gleick, James. 1983. Stephen Jay Gould: Breaking tradition with Darwin. *New York Times Magazine,* November 20, pp. 48–64.

Godfrey, Laurie (ed.). 1983. *Scientists Confront Creationism.* New York: Norton. 324 pp.

Golding, William. 1962. *The Inheritors.* New York: Harcourt, Brace and World. 233 pp.

Golson, Jack. 1974. Land connections, sea barriers and the relationship of Australian and New Guinea prehistory. In D. Walker (ed.), *Bridge and Barrier: The Natural and Cultural History of Torres Strait,* 2nd ed., Publication BG/3. Canberra: Australian National University, pp. 375–397.

Goodall, Jane M. 1963. Feeding behaviour of wild chimpanzees, a preliminary report. *Symposia of the Zoological Society of London* 10(1):399–48.

———. 1964. Tool using and aimed throwing in a community of free-living chimpanzees. *Nature* 201:1264–66.

———. 1986. *The Chimpanzees of Gombe: Patterns of Behavior.* Cambridge, MA: Belknap Press of Harvard University Press. 655 pp.

Goodman, Morris. 1975. Protein-sequence and immunological specificity: Their role in phylogenetic study of primates. In W. P. Luckett and F. S. Szalay (eds.), *Phy-*

logeny of the Primates: A Multidisciplinary Approach. New York: Plenum Press, pp. 219–48.

————. 1989. Update to "Evolution of the immunologic species specificity of human serum proteins." *Human Biology* 61(5–6):925–34.

Gorjanović-Kramberger, Karl Dragutin. 1902. Der paläolithische Mensch und seine Zeitgenossen aus dem Diluvium von Krapina in Kroatien. *Mittheilungen der Anthropologischen Gesellschaft in Wien* 32:189–216.

————. 1906. *Der Diluviale Mensch von Krapina in Kroatien: ein Beitrag zur Paläoanthropologie.* Wiesbaden: C. W. Kriedels Verlag. 277 pp.

————. 1914. Der Axillarand des Schulterblattes des Menschen von Krapina. *Hrvatsko Prirodoslovno Drustvo u Zagrebu Glasnik* 26:231–57.

————. 1926. Das Schulterblatt des diluvialen Menschen von Krapina in seinem Verhältnis zu dem Schulterblatt des rezenten Menschen und der Affen. *Vijesti Geološki Zavoda* 1:67–122.

Gould, Stephen Jay. 1974. Review of *By the Evidence,* L. S. B. Leakey. New York Times Book Review, November 17, p. 18.

————. 1977. *Ontogeny and Phylogeny.* Cambridge. MA: Belknap Press of Harvard University Press. 502 pp.

————. 1979. Piltdown revisited. *Natural History* 88(3):86–97.

————. 1990. Bully for *Brontosaurus. Natural History* 2:16–24.

————. 1992. We are all monkeys' uncles. *Natural History* 6:14–21.

Gould, Stephen Jay, and Richard C. Lewontin. 1979. The spandrels of San Marco and the Panglossian paradigm: A critique of the adaptationist programme. *Proceedings of the Royal Society of London, B* 205:581–98.

Gould, Stephen Jay, and Elisabeth Vrba. 1982. Exaptation—A missing term in the science of form. *Paleobiology* 8(1):4–15.

Gowlett, John A. J., J. W. K. Harris, D. Walton, and B. A. Wood. 1981. Early archaeological sites, hominid remains and traces of fire from Chesowanja, Kenya. *Nature* 294:125–29.

Graebner, F. 1913. Der Erdofen in der Südsee. *Anthropos* 8:801–9.

Grayson, Donald K. 1983. *The Establishment of Human Antiquity.* New York: Academic Press. 262 pp.

Gregory, William K., and Milo Hellman. 1938. Evidence of the Australopithecine man-apes on the origin of man. *Science* 88:615–16.

Grine, Frederick E. 1988a. Evolutionary history of the "robust" Australopithecines: A summary and historical perspective. In F. E. Grine (ed.), *Evolutionary History of the "Robust" Australopithecines.* New York: Aldine de Gruyter, pp. 509–20.

————. 1988b. New craniodental fossils of *Paranthropus* from the Swartkrans Formation and their significance in "robust" Australopithecine evolution. In F. E. Grine (ed.), *Evolutionary History of the "Robust" Australopithecines.* New York: Aldine de Gruyter, pp. 223–243.

Groves, Colin P. 1989. *A Theory of Human and Primate Evolution.* Oxford: Clarendon Press. 375 pp.

Groves, Colin P., and Vratislav Mazák. 1975. An approach to the taxonomy of the Hominidae: Gracile Villafranchian hominids of Africa. *Časopis Pro Mineralogii A Geologii* 20(3):225–46.

Grubb, Peter. 1982. Refuges and dispersal in the speciation of African forest mammals. In Ghillean T. Prance (ed.), *Biological Diversification in the Tropics.* New York: Columbia University Press, pp. 537–53.

Grün, Rainer, Peter B. Beaumont, and Christopher B. Stringer. 1990a. ESR dating evidence for early modern humans at Border Cave in South Africa. *Nature* 344:537–39.

Grün, Rainer, Nicholas J. Shackleton, and Hilary J. Deacon. 1990b. Electron-spin-resonance dating of tooth enamel from Klasies River Mouth Cave. *Current Anthropology* 31(4):427–32.

Grün, Rainer, and Christopher B. Stringer. 1991. Electron spin resonance dating and the evolution of modern humans. *Archaeometry* 33(2):153–99.

Gunnell, Gregg F. 1986. *Evolutionary History of the Superfamily Microsyopoidea and the Relationship Between Plesiadapiformes and Primates.* Ph.D. Dissertation in Paleontology, University of Michigan, Ann Arbor, Michigan. 630 pp.

Haeckel, Ernst 1870. *Natürliche Schöpfungsgschichte.* 2nd ed. Berlin: Georg Reimer. 688 pp.

Haldane, John B. S. 1929. Natural selection. *Nature* 124:444.

———. 1933. The part played by recurrent mutation in evolution. *The American Naturalist* 67:5–19.

Hallam, Anthony 1983. *Great Geological Controversies.* New York: Oxford University Press. 190 pp.

———. 1987. End-Cretaceous mass extinction event: Argument for terrestrial causation. *Science* 238:1237–42.

Hardin, Garrett. 1960. The competetive exclusion principle. *Science* 131:1292–98.

Hardman, John K., and Charles Yanofsky. 1967. Substrate binding properties of mutant and wild-type A proteins of *Escherischia coli* tryptophan synthetase. *Science* 156:1369–71.

Hardy, Sir Alister C. 1975. *The Biology of God: A Scientist's Study of Man the Religious Animal.* London: Jonathan Cape. 238 pp.

Hardy, Kenneth R. 1974. Social origins of American scientists and scholars. *Science* 185:497–506.

Harpending, Henry C., S. T. Sherry, A. R. Rogers, and M. Stoneking. 1993. The genetic structure of ancient human populations. *Current Anthropology* 34(4):483–96.

Harris, John W. K. 1983. Cultural beginnings: Plio-Pleistocene archaeological occurrences from the Afar, Ethiopia. *The African Archaeological Review* 1:3–31.

Harvey, Paul H., and Tim H. Clutton-Brock. 1985. Life history variation in primates. *Evolution* 39(3):559–81.

Harvey, Paul H., Michael Kavanagh, and Tim H. Clutton-Brock. 1978. Sexual dimorphism in primate teeth. *Journal of Zoology* 186(4):475–85.

Haskell, Francis. 1993. *History and its Images: Art and the Interpretation of the Past.* New Haven: Yale University Press. 558 pp.

Hauser, Otto. 1909. Découverte d'un squelette du type de Néandertal sous l'abri inférieur du Moustier, Station No 44, Commune de Saint-Léon (Dordogne). *L'Homme Préhistorique* 7:1–9.

Hay, Richard L. 1987. Geology of the Laetoli area. In Mary D. Leakey and John M. Harris (eds.), *Laetoli: A Pliocene Site in Northern Tanzania.* Oxford: Clarendon Press, pp. 48–61.

Hay, Richard L., and Mary D. Leakey. 1982. The fossil footprints of Laetoli. *Scientific American* 246(2):50–57.

Hayden, Brian. 1981. Research and development in the stone age: Technological transitions among hunter-gatherers. *Current Anthropology* 22(5):519–48.

————. 1993. The cultural capacities of Neandertals: A review and re-evaluation. *Journal of Human Evolution* 24(2):113–146.

Hedges, R. E. M., R. A. Housley, I. A. Law, C. Perry, and E. Hendy. 1988. Radiocarbon dates from the Oxford AMS System: Datelist 8. *Archaeometry* 30(2):291–305.

Hedges, S. Blair, Sudhir Kumar, Kichiro Tamura, and Mark Stoneking. 1992. Human origins and analysis of mitochondrial DNA sequences. *Science* 255:737–39.

Heim, Jean-Louis. 1989. La nouvelle reconstuction du crâne Néandertalien de La Chapelle-aux-Saints. Méthode et résultats. *Bulletins et Mémoires de la Société d'Anthropologie de Paris.* 1(1–2):95–118.

————. 1993. L'homme de Néandertal . . . a un nouveau visage. *Pour la Science* 192:26–28.

Hennig, G. J., W. Herr, E. Weber, and N. I. Xirotiris. 1981. ESR-dating of the fossil hominid cranium from Petralona Cave, Greece. *Nature* 292:533–36.

Hennig, Willi. 1966. *Phylogenetic Systematics.* D.D. Davis and R. Zangerl, trans. Urbana: University of Illinois Press. 263 pp.

Hertzberg, Mark, K. N. P. Mickleson, and Ron J. Trent. 1991. Polynesian origins and migrations: The story according to nuclear and mitochondrial DNA markers. *Bulletin of the Indo-Pacific Prehistory Association* 11(2)270–75.

Hesse, Henrike. 1966. Zum Schicksal des neandertales Fundes von le Moustier (Homo mousteriensis Hauseri). *Forschungen und Fortschritte* 40:347–48.

Hill, George Birbeck (ed.). 1887. *Boswell's Life of Johnson Including Boswell's Journal of a Tour to the Hebrides and Johnson's Diary of a Journey into North Wales,* vol. 5. Oxford: Clarendon Press. 460 pp.

Hillman, G.C., G.V. Robins, D. Oduwole, K.D. Sales, and D.A.D. McNeil. 1983. Determination of thermal histories of archeological cereal grains with electron spin resonance spectroscopy. *Science* 222:1235–37.

Hockett, Charles F. 1958. *A Course in Modern Linguistics.* New York: Macmillan. 621 pp.

————. 1978. In search of Jove's brow. *American Speech* 153(4):243–313.

Hoebel, E. Adamson. 1958. *Man in the Primitive World: An Introduction to Anthropology,* 2nd ed. New York: McGraw-Hill. 678 pp.

Hoffecker, John F., W. Roger Powers, and Ted Goebel. 1993. The colonization of Beringia and the peopling of the New World. *Science* 259:46–53.

Holden, Constance. 1979. Paul Maclean and the triune brain. *Science* 204:1066–68.

Holick, Michael E. 1987. Photosynthesis of vitamin D in the skin: Effect of environmental and life-style variables. *Federation of American Societies for Experimental Biology: Federation Proceedings* 46(5):1876–82.

Holloway, Ralph L. 1970. Australopithecine endocast (Taung specimen, 1924): A new volume determination. *Science* 168:966–68.

————. 1975. Early hominid endocasts: Volumes, morphology and significance for hominid evolution. In Russell H. Tuttle (ed.), *Primate Functional Morphology and Evolution.* Mouton, The Hague. pp. 391–415.

————. 1981. Revisiting the South African Taung Australopithecine endocast: The position of the lunate sulcus as determined by stereoplotting technique. *American Journal of Physical Anthropology* 56(1):43–58.

————. 1982. Human brain evolution: A search for units, models and synthesis. *Canadian Journal of Anthropology* 3(2):215–30.

Hooke, Beatrix G. E. 1926. A third study of the English skull with special reference to the Farringdon Street crania. *Biometrika* 18(1–2):1–55.

Hooton, Earnest A. 1946. *Up From the Ape,* 2nd ed. New York: Macmillan. 788 pp.

Horai, Satoshi. 1992. Human mitochondrial DNA: A clue to the development and dispersion of Asian populations. In Kazuro Hanihara (ed.), *Japanese as a Member of the Asian and Pacific Populations.* International Symposium 4, International Research Center for Japanese Studies, Kyoto, pp. 147–59.

Horai, S., R. Kondo, Y. Nakagawa-Hattori, S. Hayashi, S. Sonoda, and K. Tajima. 1993. Peopling of the Americas founded by four major lineages of mitochondrial DNA. *Molecular Biology and Evolution* 10(1):23–47.

Houghton, Philip. 1993. Neandertal supralaryngeal vocal tract. *American Journal of Physical Anthropology* 90(2):139–46.

Howell, F. Clark. 1965. *Early Man.* New York: Time Incorporated, Life Nature Library. 200 pp.

Howells, William. 1959. *Mankind in the Making.* New York: Doubleday. 382 pp.

———. 1976. Neanderthal man: Facts and figures. *Yearbook of Physical Anthropology, 1974* 18:7–18.

———. 1989. *Skull Shapes and the Map: Craniometric Analyses in the Dispersion of Modern Homo.* Papers of the Peabody Museum of Archaeology and Ethnology, Harvard University, Cambridge, Massachusetts, vol. 79. 189 pp.

———. 1993. *Getting Here: The Story of Human Evolution.* Washington, D.C.: The Compass Press. 261 pp.

Hrdlička, Aleš. 1914. The most ancient skeletal remains of man. *Annual Report of the Board of Regents of the Smithsonian Institution for the Year Ending 1913.* Government Printing Office, Washington, D.C. pp. 491–552.

———. 1920. Shovel-shaped teeth. *American Journal of Physical Anthropology* 3(4):429–65.

———. 1926. The Rhodesian man. *American Journal of Physical Anthropology* 9(2):173–204.

———. 1927. The Neanderthal Phase of Man. *Journal of the Royal Anthropological Institute* 57:249–69.

———. 1928. Catalogue of human crania in the United States National Museum collections: Australians, Tasmanians, South African Bushmen, Hottentots, and Negro. *Proceedings of the United States National Museum* 71(24):1–140.

———. 1930. *The Skeletal Remains of Early Man.* Smithsonian Miscellaneous Collections, Washington, D.C., vol. 83. 379 pp.

Hsü, Kenneth J. 1972. When the Mediterranean dried up. *Scientific American* 227(6):26–36.

———. 1983. *The Mediterranean Was a Desert: A Voyage of the Glomar Challenger.* Princeton: Princeton University Press. 197 pp.

Hsü, Kenneth J., William B. F. Ryan, and Maria B. Cita. 1973. Late Miocene dessication of the Mediterranean. *Nature* 242:240–44.

Hublin, Jean-Jacques. 1978. Quelques caractères apomorphes du crâne néandertalien et leur interprétation phylogénique. *Comptes Rendus des Séances de l'Académie des Sciences de Paris* Série D, 287(10):923–26.

———. 1993. Recent human evolution in northwestern Africa. In M. J. Aitkens, C. B. Stringer, and P. A. Mellars (eds.), *The Origin of Modern Humans and the Impact of Chronometric Dating.* Princeton: Princeton University Press, pp. 118–31.

Hublin, Jean-Jacques, and Anne-Marie Tillier. 1981. The Mousterian juvenile mandible from Irhoud (Morocco): A phylogenetic interpretation. In Christopher B. Stringer (ed.), *Aspects of Human Evolution.* London: Taylor and Francis, pp. 167–85.

Hulse, Frederick S. 1962. Race as an evolutionary episode. *American Anthropologist* 64(5):929–45.

———. 1963. *The Human Species: An Introduction to Physical Anthropology.* New York: Random House. 490 pp.

Humphrey, Nicholas K. 1976. The social function of intellect. In P. P. G. Bateson and R. A. Hinde (eds.), *Growing Points in Ethology.* New York: Cambridge University Press, pp. 303–18.

———. 1978. Nature's psychologists. *New Scientist* 78:900–903.

———. 1983. *Consciousness Regained: Chapters in the Development of Mind.* New York: Oxford University Press. 222 pp.

Hunt, Kevin D. 1989. *Positional Behavior in* Pan Troglodytes *at the Mahale Mountains and Gombe Stream National Parks, Tanzania.* Ph.D. Dissertation, Department of Anthropology, University of Michigan, Ann Arbor. 314 pp.

———. 1991a. Mechanical implications of chimpanzee behavior. *American Journal of Physical Anthropology* 86(4):521–36.

———. 1991b. Positional behavior in the Hominoidea. *International Journal of Primatology* 12(2):95–118.

———. 1992. Positional behavior of *Pan troglodytes* in the Mahale Mountains and Gombe Stream National Parks, Tanzania. *American Journal of Physical Anthropology* 87(1):83–105.

Huxley, Julian S. 1953. *Evolution in Action.* New York: New American Library. 141 pp.

———. 1958. Evolutionary processes and taxonomy with special reference to grades. In Olov Hedberg (ed.), *Systematics of Today: Proceedings of a Symposium Held at the University of Uppsala in Commemoration of the 250th Anniversary of the Birth of Carolus Linnaeus.* Uppsala Universitets Arrskrift 1958:6, pp. 21–39.

Huxley, Leonard (ed.). 1900. *Life and Letters of Thomas Henry Huxley,* 2 vols. New York: D. Appleton.

Huxley, Thomas H. 1887. On the reception of the "Origin of Species." In Francis Darwin (ed.), *The Life and Letters of Charles Darwin,* vol. I. New York: D. Appleton, pp. 533–58.

Hymes, Dell H. 1964. A perspective for linguistic anthropology. In Sol Tax (ed.), *Horizons in Anthropology.* Chicago: Aldine, pp. 92–107.

Ikawa-Smith, Fumiko. 1986. Late Pleistocene and early Holocene technologies. In R. L. Pearson, G. L. Barnes, and K. L. Hutterer (eds.), *Windows on the Japanese Past: Studies in Archaeology and Prehistory.* Center for Japanese Studies, University of Michigan, Ann Arbor. pp. 199–216.

Imbrie, John, and Katherine P. Imbrie. 1979. *Ice Ages: Solving the Mystery.* Cambridge, MA: Harvard University Press. 224 pp.

Isaac, Glynn Ll. 1971. The diet of early man: Aspects of archaeological evidence for Lower and Middle Pleistocene sites in Africa. *World Archaeology* 2(3):278–99.

———. 1972. Chronology and tempo of cultural change during the Pleistocene. In W. W. Bishop and J. A. Miller (eds.), *Calibration of Hominoid Evolution: Recent Advances in Isotopic and Other Dating Methods Applicable to the Origin of Man.* Edinburgh: Scottish Academic Press, pp. 381–430.

———. 1976. The activities of early African hominids: A review of archaeological evidence from the time span two and a half to one million years ago. In Glynn Ll. Isaac and Elizabeth R. McCown (eds.), *Human Origins: Louis Leakey and the East African Evidence.* Menlo Park, CA: W. A. Benjamin, pp. 483–514.

————. 1978. The food-sharing behavior of protohuman hominids. *Scientific American* 238(4):90–108.

Jablonski, Nina G. 1993. Introduction. In Nina G. Jablonski (ed.), *Theropithecus: The Rise and Fall of a Primate Genus*. New York: Cambridge University Press, pp. 1–12.

Jacob, Teuku. 1973. Palaeoanthropological discoveries in Indonesia with special reference to the finds of the last two decades. *Journal of Human Evolution* 2(6):473–85.

————. 1975. The Pithecanthropines of Indonesia. *Bulletins et Mémoires de la Société d'Anthropologie de Paris*. Série 13, 2:243–56.

Jacobs, John A. (ed.). 1987. *Geomagnetism*, 2 vols. Orlando, FL: Academic Press.

Jarvik, Erik. 1980. *Basic Structure and Evolution of Vertebrates*, 2 vols. London: Academic Press.

Jelínek, Jan. 1959. Bestattung und skelletmaterial. In J. Jelínek, J. Pališek, and K. Valoch (eds.), *Der fossile Mensch Brno II*. *Anthropos* (Brno) 9:17–22.

————. 1969. Neanderthal man and *Homo sapiens* in central and eastern Europe. *Current Anthropology* 10(5):475–503.

————. 1978. *Homo erectus* or *Homo sapiens*? In D. J. Chivers and K. A. Joysey (eds), *Recent Advances in Primatology*, vol. 3, pp. 419–29. London: Academic Press.

Jennings, J. N. 1971. Sea level changes and land links. In Derek J. Mulvaney and Jack Golson (eds.), *Aboriginal Man and Environment in Australia*. Canberra: Australian National University Press, pp. 1–13.

————. 1974. Some attributes of Torres Strait. In D. Walker (ed.), *Bridge and Barrier: The Natural and Cultural History of the Torres Strait*, 2nd ed., Publication BG/3. Canberra: Australian National University Press, pp. 29–38.

Jerison, Harry. 1988. Evolutionary biology of intelligence: The nature of the problem. In Harry J. Jerison and Irene Jerison (eds.), *Intelligence and Evolutionary Biology*. New York: Springer-Verlag, pp. 1–11.

Johanson, Donald C. 1976. Ethiopia yields first "family" of early man. *National Geographic Magazine* 150(6):790–811.

————. 1978. Our roots go deeper. *Science Year: The World Book Science Annual, 1979*. Chicago: Field Enterprises Educational Corporation, pp. 43–55.

————. 1986. Thoughts on the "Black Skull" from Kenya. *Institute of Human Origins Newsletter* 4(1):4–5.

Johanson, Donald C., and Maitland A. Edey. 1981. *Lucy: The Beginning of Humankind*. New York: Simon and Schuster. 409 pp.

Johanson, D. C., C. O. Lovejoy, W. H. Kimbel, T. D. White, S. C. Ward, M. E. Bush, B. M. Latimer, and Y. Coppens. 1982. Morphology of the Pliocene partial skeleton (A. L. 288–1) from the Hadar Formation, Ethiopia. *American Journal of Physical Anthropology* 57(4):403–52.

Johanson, D. C., F. T. Masao, G. G. Eck, T. D. White, R. C. Walter, W. H. Kimbel, B. Asfaw, P. Manega, P. Ndessokia, and G. Suwa. 1987. New partial skeleton of *Homo habilis* from Olduvai Gorge, Tanzania. *Nature* 327:205–9.

Johanson, Donald, and James Shreeve. 1989. *Lucy's Child: The Discovery of a Human Ancestor*. New York: William Morrow. 319 pp.

Johanson, Donald C., and Maurice Taieb. 1976. Plio-Pleistocene hominid discoveries in Hadar, Ethiopia. *Nature* 260:293–97.

Johanson, Donald C., and Tim D. White. 1979. A systematic assessment of early African hominids. *Science* 203:321–30.

Johanson, Donald C., Tim D. White, and Yves Coppens. 1978. A new species of the genus *Australopithecus* (Primates: Hominidae) from the Pliocene of eastern Africa. *Kirtlandia: The Cleveland Museum of Natural History* 28:1–14.

Jolly, Clifford D. 1970. The seed eaters: A new model of hominid differentiation based on a baboon analogy. *Man* 5(1):5–26.

———. 1993. Species, subspecies, and baboon systematics. In W. H. Kimbel and L. B. Martin (eds.), *Species, Species Concept, and Primate Evolution*. New York: Plenum Press, pp. 67–107.

Jones, Rhys. 1989. East of Wallace's Line: Issues and problems in the colonization of the Australian continent. In Paul Mellars and Chris Stringer (eds.), *The Human Revolution: Behavioural and Biological Perspectives on the Origins of Modern Humans.* Edinburgh: Edinburgh University Press, pp. 743–82.

Jungers, William L. 1982. Lucy's limbs: Skeletal allometry and locomotion in *Australopithecus afarensis*. *Nature* 297:676–78.

Kamminga, Johan. 1992. New interpretations of the Upper Cave, Zhoukoudian. In T. Akazawa, K. Aoki and T. Kimura (eds.), *The Evolution and Dispersal of Modern Humans in Asia.* Tokyo: Hokusen-Sha, pp. 379–400.

Kamminga, Johan, and R. V. S. Wright. 1988. The Upper Cave at Zhoukoudian and the origins of the Mongoloids. *Journal of Human Evolution* 17(8):739–67.

Kay, Lily E. 1993. *The Molecular Vision of Life: Caltech, The Rockefeller Foundation, and the Rise of the New Biology.* New York: Oxford University Press. 304 pp.

Kay, Richard F., and Frederick E. Grine. 1988. Tooth morphology, wear and diet in *Australopithecus* and *Paranthropus* from southern Africa. In F. E. Grine (ed.), *Evolutionary History of the "Robust" Australopithecines.* New York: Aldine de Gruyter, pp. 427–47.

Kehoe, Thomas F. 1978. Paleo-Indian bison drives: Feasibility studies. In Leslie B. Davis and Michael Wilson (eds.), *Bison Procurement and Utilization: A Symposium. Plains Anthropologist,* Memoir 14, part 2, pp. 79–83.

Keith, Arthur. 1895. Pithecanthropus erectus—a brief review of human fossil remains. *Science Progress* 3(17):348–69.

———. 1911. *Ancient Types of Man.* New York: Harper & Brothers. 151 pp.

———. 1915. *The Antiquity of Man.* London: Williams and Norgate. 519 pp.

———. 1946. *Evolution and Ethics.* New York: G. P. Putnam's Sons. 246 pp.

———. 1947. Australopithecinae or Dartians. *Nature* 159:377.

———. 1948. *A New Theory of Human Evolution.* London: Watts. 451 pp.

———. 1949. *A New Theory of Human Evolution.* New York: Philosophical Library. 451 pp.

———. 1950. *An Autobiography.* London: Watts & Company. 721 pp.

Kellog, Davida E. 1988. "And then a miracle occurs"—Weak links in the chain from punctuation to hierarchy. *Biology and Philosophy* 3(1):3–28.

Kelly, Walt. 1970. *Impollutable Pogo: Don't Tread on Me.* New York: Simon and Schuster. 128 pp.

Kennedy, Gail E. 1985. Bone thickness in *Homo erectus*. *Journal of Human Evolution* 14(8):699–708.

———. 1991. On the autapomorphic traits of *Homo erectus*. *Journal of Human Evolution* 20(5):375–412.

———. 1992. The evolution of *Homo sapiens* as indicated by features of the postcranium. In G. Bräuer and F. H. Smith (eds.), *Continuity or Replacement: Controversies in Homo sapiens Evolution* Rotterdam: A. A. Balkema, pp. 209–18.

Kennedy, James G. 1978. *Herbert Spencer.* Boston: Twayne Publishers. 163 pp.

Kennedy, Kenneth A. R., Arun Sonakia, John Chiment, and K. K. Verma. 1991. Is the Narmada hominid an Indian *Homo erectus? American Journal of Physical Anthropology* 86(4):475–96.

Kerr, Richard A. 1992. The earliest mass extinction? *Science* 257:612.

Keyfitz, Nathan. 1989. The growing human population. *Scientific American* 261(3):119–26.

Khatri, A. P. 1963. A century of prehistoric research in India. *Asian Perspectives* 6(1–2):169–85.

Kimbel, William H. 1991. Review of *A Theory of Human and Primate Evolution*, by Colin Groves. *Journal of Human Evolution* 20(3):355–71.

Kimbel, William H., Donald C. Johanson, and Yoel Rak. 1994. The first skull and other new discoveries of *Australopithecus afarensis* at Hadar, Ethiopia. Nature 368:449–51.

Kimbel, William H., and Lawrence B. Martin. 1993. Species and speciation: Conceptual issues and their relevance for primate evolutionary biology. In W. H. Kimbel and L. B. Martin (eds.), *Species, Species Concepts, and Primate Evolution.* New York: Plenum Press, pp. 539–53.

Kimbel, William H., and Yoel Rak. 1993. The importance of species taxa in paleoanthropology and an argument for the phylogenetic concept of the species concept. In W. H. Kimbel and L. B. Martin (eds.), *Species, Species Concepts, and Primate Evolution.* New York: Plenum Press, pp. 461–84.

Kimbel, William H., Tim D. White, and Donald C. Johanson. 1988. Implications of KNM-WT 1700 for the evolution of "robust" Australopithecines. In Frederick E. Grine (ed.), *Evolutionary History of the "Robust" Australopithecines.* New York: Aldine de Gruyter, pp. 259–68.

Kimura, Motoo. 1968. Evolutionary rate at the molecular level. *Nature* 217:624–26.

———. 1983. *The Neutral Theory of Molecular Evolution.* New York: Cambridge University Press. 367 pp.

King, Jack Lester, and Thomas H. Jukes. 1969. Non-Darwinian evolution. *Science* 164:788–98.

Klaatsch, Hermann, and Otto Hauser. 1909. Homo mousteriensis Hauseri. Ein altdiluvialer Skelettfund im Departement Dordogne und seine Zugehörigheit zum Neandertaltypus. *Archiv für Anthropologie* 7:287–97.

Klein, Richard G. 1983. The Stone Age prehistory of Southern Africa. *Annual Review of Anthropology* 12:25–48.

———. 1985. Breaking away. *Natural History* 94(1):4–7.

———. 1988. The causes of "robust" Australopithecine extinction. In Frederick E. Grine (ed.), *Evolutionary History of the "Robust" Australopithecines.* New York: Aldine de Gruyter, pp. 499–505.

———. 1989a. Biological and behavioural perspectives on modern human origins in southern Africa. In P. Mellars and C. Stringer (eds.), *The Human Revolution: Behavioural and Biological Perspectives on the Origins of Modern Humans.* Edinburgh: Edinburgh University Press, pp. 529–46.

———. 1989b. *The Human Career: Human Biological and Cultural Origins.* Chicago: University of Chicago Press. 524 pp.

———. 1992. The archaeology of modern human origins. *Evolutionary Anthropology* 1(1):5–14.

von Koenigswald, G. H. Ralph. 1949. The discovery of early man in Java and southern China. In W. W. Howells (ed.), *Early Man in the Far East: Studies in Physical An-*

thropology No. 1. The American Association of Physical Anthropologists, Detroit, pp. 83–98.

———. 1956. *Meeting Prehistoric Man,* Trans. Michael Bullock. London: Thames and Hudson. 216 pp.

Kokkoros, P. and A. Kanellis. 1960. Découverte d'un crane d'homme paléolothique dans la péninsule chalcidique. *L'Anthropologie* 64(5–6):438–46.

Köppel, R. 1935. Das Alter der neuentdeckten Schädel von Nazareth. *Biblica* 16:58–73.

Kortlandt, Adriaan. 1980. How might early hominids have defended themselves against large predators and food competitors? *Journal of Human Evolution* 9(2):79–112.

Kramer, Andrew. 1986. Hominid-pongid distinctiveness in the Miocene-Pliocene fossil record: The Lothagam mandible. *American Journal of Physical Anthropology* 70(4):457–73.

———. 1989. *The Evolutionary and Taxonomic Affinities of the Sangiran Mandibles of Central Java, Indonesia.* Ph.D. Dissertation in Anthropology, University of Michigan, Ann Arbor, 197 pp.

———. 1991. Modern human origins in Australasia: Replacement or evolution? *American Journal of Physical Anthropology* 86(4):455–73.

Krantz, Grover S. 1976. On the nonmigration of hunting peoples. *Northwest Anthropological Research Notes* 10(2):209–16.

Krishtalka, Leonard. 1989. *Dinosaur Plots & Other Intrigues in Natural History.* New York: Morrow. 316 pp.

———. 1993. Anagenetic angst: Species boundaries in Eocene primates. In W. H. Kimbel and L. B. Martin (eds.), *Species, Species Concepts, and Primate Evolution.* New York: Plenum, pp. 331–44.

Kroeber, Alfred L. 1948. *Anthropology,* 2nd ed. New York: Harcourt, Brace. 856 pp.

Kuhn, Steven L. 1990. Late Mousterian technology and foraging patterns at Grotta Breuil, Italy. *Anthroquest* 42:12–15.

Kuman, Kathleen, and Ronald J. Clarke. 1986. Florisbad—new investigations of a Middle Stone Age hominid site in South Africa. *Geoarchaeology* 1(2):103–25.

Kuper, Adam. 1993. Adaptable man. Review of *Why Humans Have Culture,* Michael Carrithers. *Times Literary Supplement,* July 16, p. 6.

Kurtén, Björn. 1980. *Dance of the Tiger: A Novel of the Ice Age.* New York: Pantheon. 255 pp.

Lancaster, Jane B. 1968. On the evolution of tool-using behavior. *American Anthropologist* 70(1):65–66.

Larson, James L. 1971. *Reason and Experience: The Representation of Natural Order in the Work of Carl von Linné.* Berkeley: University of California Press. 172 pp.

Lartet, Édouard. 1856. Note sur un grand singe fossile qui se rattache au groupe des singes supérieurs. *Comptes Rendus des Séances de l'Académie des Sciences, Paris* 43:219–23.

Lartet, Édouard, and Henry Christy 1864a. L'homme fossile dans le Périgord. Appendice IV, L'Homme Fossile en France, to *L'Ancienneté de l'Homme Prouvée par la Géologie,* Sir Charles Lyell. Paris: J. B. Baillière et fils, pp. 135–77.

———. 1864b. Sur des figures d'animaux gravées ou sculpltées, et autres produits d'art et d'industrie rapportables aux temps primordiaux de la période humaine. *Revue Archéologique* 9:233–67.

Lartet, Louis. 1868. Une sépulture des troglodytes du Périgord (crânes des Eyzies). *Bulletin de la Société d'Anthropologie de Paris.* Série 2, Tome 3:335–49.

Larwood, Gilbert P. (ed.). 1988. *Extinction and Survival in the Fossil Record.* New York: Clarendon (Oxford University Press). 365 pp.

Lasker, Gabriel Ward. 1961. *Physical Anthropology.* New York: Holt, Rinehart and Winston. 424 pp.

Latham, Alf G., and Henry P. Schwarcz. 1992. The Petralona hominid site: Uranium-series re-analysis of "layer 10" calcite and associated palaeomagnetic analyses. *Archaeometry* 34(1):135–40.

Laurin, Michel, and Robert R. Reisz. 1990. *Tetraceratops* is the oldest known therapsid. *Nature* 345:249–50.

Leakey, Louis S. B. 1948. Skull of *Proconsul* from Rusinga Island. *Nature* 162:688.

———. 1951. *Olduvai Gorge: A Report on the Evolution of the Hand-Axe Culture in Beds I-IV.* Cambridge: Cambridge University Press. 164 pp.

———. 1959. A new fossil skull from Olduvai. *Nature* 184:491–93.

———. 1965. *Olduvai Gorge 1951–1961, vol. I. A Preliminary Report on the Geology and Fauna.* Cambridge: Cambridge University Press. 118 pp.

———. 1974. *By the Evidence: Memoirs, 1932–1951.* New York: Harcourt, Brace, Jovanovich. 276 pp.

Leakey, Louis S. B., and Vanne Morris Goodall. 1969. *Unveiling Man's Origins: Ten Decades of Thought About Human Evolution.* Cambridge, MA: Schenkman Publishing Company. 220 pp.

Leakey, Louis S. B., Phillip V. Tobias, and John R. Napier. 1964. A new species of genus *Homo* from Olduvai Gorge. *Nature* 202:7–9.

Leakey, Mary D. 1966. A review of the Oldowan Culture from Olduvai Gorge, Tanzania. *Nature* 210:462–66.

———. 1971. *Olduvai Gorge. Vol. 3. Excavations in Beds I and II, 1960–1963.* New York: Cambridge University Press. 306 pp.

———. 1979a. 3.6 million years old footprints in the ashes of time. *National Geographic Magazine* 155(4):446–57.

———. 1979b. *Olduvai Gorge: My Search for Early Man.* Glasgow: William Collins Sons. 187 pp.

———. 1984. *Mary Leakey: Disclosing the Past.* Garden City, NY: Doubleday. 224 pp.

———. 1987. Introduction. In Mary D. Leakey and John M. Harris (eds.), *Laetoli: A Pliocene Site in Northern Tanzania.* Oxford: Clarendon Press, pp. 1–22.

Leakey, Mary D., and John M. Harris (eds.). 1987. *Laetoli: A Pliocene Site in Northern Tanzania.* New York: Clarendon Press (Oxford University Press). 561 pp.

Leakey, Mary D., R. L. Hay, G. H. Curtis, R. E. Drake, M. K. Jackes, and T. D. White. 1976. Fossil hominids from the Laetolil Beds. *Nature* 262:460–66.

Leakey, Meave G., and Richard E. Leakey (eds.). 1978. *Koobi Fora Research Project, vol. 1: The Fossil Hominids and an Introduction to their Context 1968–1974.* Oxford: Clarendon Press. 191 pp.

Leakey, Richard E. F. 1973. Evidence for an advanced Plio-Pleistocene hominid from East Rudolf, Kenya. *Nature* 242:447–50.

———. 1981. *The Making of Mankind.* New York: E. P. Dutton. 256 pp.

———. 1984. *One Life: An Autobiography.* Salem, NH: Salem House/Merrimack Publishers Circle. 207 pp.

Leakey, Richard E., and Meave G. Leakey. 1986a. A new Miocene hominoid from Kenya. *Nature* 324:143–46.

———. 1986b. A second new Miocene hominoid from Kenya. *Nature* 324:146-148.

———. 1987. A new Miocene small-bodied ape from Kenya. *Journal of Human Evolution* 16(2):369–87.

Leakey, R. E. F., J. M. Mungai, and A. C. Walker. 1971. New Australopithecines from East Rudolf, Kenya. *American Journal of Physical Anthropology* 35(2):175–86.

Leakey, R. E. F., and A. C. Walker. 1976. *Australopithecus, Homo erectus,* and the single-species hypothesis. *Nature* 261:572–74.

———. 1980. On the status of *Australopithecus afarensis. Science* 207:1103.

———. 1985. A fossil skeleton 1,600,000 years old. Homo erectus unearthed. *National Geographic Magazine* 168(5):624–29.

Lee, Richard B., and Irven DeVore (eds.). 1976. *Kalahari Hunter-Gatherers: Studies of the !Kung San and Their Neighbors.* Cambridge, MA: Harvard University Press. 408 pp.

Lehninger, Albert L. 1964. *The Mitochondrion: Molecular Basis of Structure and Function.* New York: W. A. Benjamin. 263 pp.

Lerner, I. Michael, and William J. Libby. 1976. *Heredity, Evolution and Society,* 2nd ed. San Francisco: Freeman. 432 pp.

Leroi-Gourhan, André. 1967. *Treasures of Prehistoric Art.* Trans. Norbert Guterman. New York: H. N. Abrams. 543 pp.

Leroi-Gourhan, Arlette. 1982. The archaeology of Lascaux cave. *Scientific American* 246(6):104–12.

Lévêque, François, and Bernard Vandermeersch. 1980. Découverte de restes humains dans un niveau castelperronien à Saint- Césaire (Charente-Maritime). *Comptes Rendus des Séances de l'Académie des Sciences de Paris,* Série D, 291(2):187–89.

———. 1981. Le néandertalien de Saint-Césaire. *La Recherche* 12(119):242–44.

Lévi-Strauss, Claude. 1964. *Le Cru et le Cuit.* Paris: Librairie Plon. 400 pp.

———. 1965. Le triangle culinaire. *L'Arc* 26:19–29.

———. 1968. *L'Origine des Manières de Table.* Paris: Librairie Plon. 478 pp.

Li, Tianyuan and Dennis A. Etler. 1992. New Middle Pleistocene hominid crania from Yunxian in China. *Nature* 357:404–7.

Lieberman, Daniel E., David R. Pilbeam, and Bernard A. Wood. 1988. A probabilistic approach to the problem of sexual dimosphism in *Homo habilis:* A comparison of KNM-ER 1470 and KNM-ER 1813. *Journal of Human Evolution* 17(5):503–11.

Lieberman, Philip. 1975. *On the Origins of Language: An Introduction to the Evolution of Human Speech.* New York: Macmillan. 196 pp.

Lieberman, Philip, and Edward S. Crelin. 1971. On the speech of Neanderthal man. *Linguistic Inquiry* 2(2):203–22.

Lieberman, Philip, J. R. Laitman, J. S. Reidenburg, and P. J. Gannon. 1992. The anatomy, physiology, acoustics and perception of speech: Essential elements in analysis of the evolution of human speech. *Journal of Human Evolution* 23(6):447–67.

Limoges, Camille. 1980. A second glance at evolutionary biology in France. In Ernst Mayr and William B. Provine (eds.), *The Evolutionary Synthesis: Perspectives on the Unification of Biology.* Cambridge, MA: Harvard University Press. pp. 322–28.

Lindroth, Sten. 1973. Linnaeus (or Von Linné), Carl. In Charles Coulston Gillispie (ed.), *Dictionary of Scientific Biography*, vol. 8. New York: Charles Scribner's Sons, pp. 374–81.

Livingstone, Frank B. 1974. Review of *Sexual Selection and the Descent of Man*, Bernard Campbell. *American Journal of Physical Anthropology* 40(2):293–95.

Loewe, Frederick, and Alan Jay Lerner. 1956. *My Fair Lady: Adapted from Bernard Shaw's Pygmalion*. New York: Chappell. 256 pp.

Loomis, W. Farnsworth. 1967. Skin-pigment regulation of vitamin-D synthesis in man. *Science* 157:501–6.

———. 1970. Rickets. *Scientific American* 223(6):76–91.

Lovejoy, Arthur O. 1936. *The Great Chain of Being: A Study of the History of an Idea*. Cambridge, MA: Harvard University Press. 382 pp.

Lovejoy, C. Owen 1974. The gait of australopithecines. *Yearbook of Physical Anthropology 1973* 17:147–61.

———. 1978. A biomechanical review of the locomotor diversity of early hominids. In Clifford J. Jolly (ed.), *Early Hominids of Africa*. New York: St. Martin's Press, pp. 403–29.

———. 1981. The origin of man. *Science* 211:341–50.

———. 1988. Evolution of human walking. *Scientific American* 259(5):118–25.

Lovejoy, C. O., K. Heiple, and A. H. Burstein. 1973. The gait of *Australopithecus*. *American Journal of Physical Anthropology* 39(3):757–80.

Lovejoy, C. and Erik Trinkaus. 1980. Strength and robusticity of the Neandertal tibia. *American Journal of Physical Anthropology* 53(4):465–70.

Lü Zun-er. 1984. Jinniu Shan. *China Daily* 4:1 (Nov. 20).

———. 1990. La découverte de l'homme fossile de Jing-niu-shan: Première étude. *L'Anthropologie* 94(4):899–902.

de Lumley, Henry. 1969. A Paleolithic camp at Nice. *Scientific American* 220(5):42–50.

———. 1972. Chronologie du Würmein II en Europe. In Henry de Lumley (ed.), *La Grotte de l'Hortus (Valflaunès, Hérault). Les Chasseurs Néandertaliens et leur Milieu et Vie. Élaboration d'une Chronologie du Würmein II dans le Midi Méditerranéen*. Éditions du Laboratoire de Paléontologie Humaine et de Préhistoire, Université de Provence, Centre Saint-Charles, Marseille. *Études Quaternaires, Géologie, Paléontologie, Préhistoire*. Mémoire n° 1:363–69.

de Lumley, Henry, and Marie-Antoinette de Lumley. 1971. Découverte de restes humains anténéndertaliens datés du début du Riss à la Caune de l'Arago (Tautavel, Pyrenées-Orientales). *Comptes Rendus des Séances de l'Académie des Sciences de Paris* 272(13):1739–42.

Lurie, Edward. 1960. *Louis Agassiz: A Life in Science*. Chicago: The University of Chicago Press. 449 pp.

Lyell, Charles. 1863. *The Geological Evidences of the Antiquity of Man, With Remarks on Theories of the Origin of Species by Variation*. London: John Murray. 520 pp.

McArthur, Margaret. 1960. Food consumption and dietary level of groups of aborigines living on naturally occurring foods. In Charles P. Mountford (ed.), *Records of the American-Australian Scientific Expedition to Arnhem Land*, vol. 2, *Anthropology and Nutrition*. Melbourne: Melbourne University Press, pp. 90–135.

McCarthy, Frederick D. 1940. Aboriginal Australian material culture: Causative factors in its composition *Mankind* 2(8):241–69; 2(9):294–320.

———. 1970. Prehistoric and recent change in Australian aboriginal culture. In Arnold R. Pilling and R. A. Waterman (eds.), *Diprotodon to Detribalization: Studies of Change Among Australian Aborigines.* East Lansing: Michigan State University Press, pp. 142–60.

———. 1974. Relationships between Australian aboriginal material culture, Southeast Asia and Melanesia. In A. P. Elkin and N. W. G. Macintosh (eds.), *Grafton Elliot Smith: The Man and His Work.* Sydney: Sydney University Press, pp. 210–26.

McCarthy, Frederick D., and Margaret McArthur. 1960. The food quest and the time factor in aboriginal economic life. In Charles P. Mountford (ed.), *Records of the American-Australian Scientific Expedition to Arnhem Land,* vol. 2, *Anthropology and Nutrition.* Melbourne: Melbourne University Press, pp. 145–94.

McCorriston, Joy, and Frank Hole. 1991. The ecology of seasonal stress and the origins of agriculture in the Near East. *American Anthropologist* 93(1):46–69.

McCown, Theodore D., and Arthur Keith. 1939. *The Stone Age of Mount Carmel: The Fossil Human Remains From the Levalloiso-Mousterian.* Oxford: Clarendon Press. 390 pp.

Macdonald, David W. 1992. *The Velvet Claw: A Natural History of the Carnivores.* London: BBC Books. 256 pp.

McDougall, I., R. Maier, P. Sutherland-Hawkes, and A. J. W. Gleadow. 1980. K-Ar age estimate for the KBS Tuff, East Turkana, Kenya. *Nature* 284:230–34.

Macfarlane, W. V. 1973. Functions of aboriginal nomads during summer. In Robert L. Kirk (ed.), *Human Biology of Aborigines in Cape York.* Australian Institute of Aboriginal Studies No. 44. Canberra. pp. 49–68.

———. 1976. Aboriginal palaeophysiology. In Robert L. Kirk and Alan G. Thorne (eds.), *The Origin of the Australians.* Australian Institute of Aboriginal Studies, Human Biology Series No. 6, Canberra. pp. 183–94.

McGrew, William C. 1992. *Chimpanzee Material Culture: Implications for Human Evolution.* New York: Cambridge University Press. 277 pp.

McHenry, Henry M. 1974. How large were the Australopithecines? *American Journal of Physical Anthropology* 40(3):329–40.

———. 1975a. Fossils and the mosaic nature of human evolution. *Science* 190:425–31.

———. 1975b. A new pelvic fragment from Swartkrans and the relationship between the robust and gracile australopithecines. *American Journal of Physical Anthropology* 43(2):245–62.

———. 1986a. The first bipeds: A comparison of the *A. afarensis* and *A. africanus* postcranium and implications for the evolution of human bipedalism. *Journal of Human Evolution* 15(3):177–91.

———. 1986b. Size variation in the postcranium of *Australopithecus afarensis* and extant species of Hominoidea. *Human Evolution* 1(2):149–56.

———. 1991. Sexual dimorphism in *Australopithecus afarensis. Journal of Human Evolution* 20(1):21–32.

McHenry, Henry M., and Robert S. Corruccini. 1978. Analysis of the hominoid os coxae by Cartesian coordinates. *American Journal of Physical Anthropology* 48(2):215–26.

Maddison, David R., Maryellen Ruvolo, and David L. Swofford. 1992. Geographic origins of human mitochondrial DNA: Phylogenetic evidence from control region sequences. *Systematic Biology* 4(1):111–24.

Magee, Donal F., and Arthur F. Dalley, II. 1986. *Digestion and the Structure and Function of the Gut.* Basel: Karger. 359 pp.

Maglio, Vincent J. 1970. Early Elephantidae of Africa and a tentative correlation of African Plio-Pleistocene deposits. *Nature* 225:328–32.

———. 1973. Origin and evolution of the Elephantidae. *Transactions of the American Philosophical Society* 63(3):1–149.

Magori, C. C., and Michael H. Day. 1983. Laetoli Hominid 18: An early *Homo sapiens* skull. *Journal of Human Evolution* 12(8):747–53.

Malez, Mirko, Fred H. Smith, Jakov Radovčić, and Darko Rukavina. 1980. Upper Pleistocene hominids from Vindija, Croatia, Yugoslavia. *Current Anthropology* 21(3):365–67.

Mania, Dietrich, and Emanuel Vlček. 1987. *Homo erectus* from Bilzingsleben (GDR)— His culture and his environment. *Anthropologie* 25(1):1-45.

Mann, Alan E., Michelle Lampl, and Janet M. Monge. 1990. Patterns of ontogeny in human evolution: Evidence from dental development. *Yearbook of Physical Anthropology* 33:111–50.

Mann, Alan E., Janet M. Monge, and Michelle Lampl. 1991. An investigation into the relationship between perikymata counts and crown formation times. *American Journal of Physical Anthropology* 86(2):175–88.

Manouvrier, Léonce. 1893. Étude sur la rétroversion de la tête du tibia et l'attitude humaine à l'époque quaternaire. *Mémoires de la Société d'Anthropologie de Paris* 4:219–64.

Margulis, Lynn. 1971. Symbiosis and evolution. *Scientific American* 225(2):48–57.

Marks, Anthony E. 1992. Upper Pleistocene archaeology and the origins of modern man: A view from the Levant and adjacent areas. In T. Akazawa, K. Aoki, and T. Kimura (eds.), *The Evolution and Dispersal of Modern Humans in Asia*. Tokyo: Hokusen-Sha, pp. 229–51.

Marks, Jonathan. 1993. Hominoid heterochromatin: Terminal C-bands as a complex genetic trait linking chimpanzee and gorilla. *American Journal of Physical Anthropology* 90(2):237–46.

Marston, Alvan T. 1935. Fossil human occipital bone from Thames gravels. *Nature* 136:637–38.

———. 1936. Preliminary note on a new fossil human skull from Swanscombe, Kent. *Nature* 138:200–201.

———. 1938. The Swanscombe skull. *Journal of the Royal Anthropological Institute* 67:339–406.

Martin, Lawrence, and Peter Andrews. 1984. The phyletic position of *Graecopithecus freybergi* KOENIGSWALD. In P. Andrews and J. L. Franzen (eds.), *The Early Evolution of Man*. Courier Forschungsinstitut, Senckenberg 69:25–40.

Martin, Paul S., and Richard G. Klein (eds.). 1984. *Quaternary Extinctions: A Prehistoric Revolution*. Tucson: University of Arizona Press. 892 pp.

Martin, Robert D. 1981. Relative brain size and basal metabolic rate in terrestrial vertebrates. *Nature* 293:57–60.

———. 1983. *Human Brain Evolution in an Ecological Context*, Fifty-Second James Arthur Lecture on the Evolution of the Human Brain, 1982. American Museum of Natural History, New York. 56 pp.

———. 1986. Primates: A definition. In B. A. Wood, L. B. Martin, and P. Andrews (eds.), *Major Topics in Primate and Human Evolution*. Cambridge: Cambridge University Press, pp. 1–31.

———. 1990. *Primate Origins and Evolution: A Phylogenetic Reconstruction*. Princeton: Princeton University Press. 808 pp.

Matiegka, Jindrich. 1934. *Homo Předmostensis. Fosilní, Clovek z Předmostí na Moravě.* Nákladem České Akademie Věd a Uměne, v Praze. 145 pp.

Matsu'ura, Shuji. 1982. Relative dating of the Minatogawa Man by fluorine analysis. In Hisashi Suzuki and Kazuro Hanihara (eds.), *The Minatogawa Man: The Upper Pleistocene Man from the Island of Okinawa.* The University Museum, The University of Tokyo, Bulletin No. 19. pp. 205–8.

Maugh II, Thomas H. 1992. Orangutans in the mist. *Los Angeles Times.* January 13, p. B3.

Mayer, August Franz Joseph Carl. 1864. Ueber die fossilen Ueberreste eines menschlichen Shädels und Skelettes in einer Felsenhöhle des Düssel- oder Neander-Thales. *Archiv für Anatomie, Physiologie und Wissenschaftliche Medecin* 1:1–26.

Mayr, Ernst 1942. *Systematics and the Origin of Species from the Viewpoint of a Zoologist.* New York: Columbia University Press. 334 pp.

———. 1944. Wallace's line in the light of recent zoogeographic studies. *The Quarterly Review of Biology* 19(1):1–14.

———. 1951. Taxonomic categories in fossil hominids. *Cold Spring Harbor Symposia on Quantitative Biology* 15:109–18.

———. 1960. The emergence of evolutionary novelties. In Sol Tax (ed.), *Evolution After Darwin,* vol. I: *The Evolution of Life: Its Origin, History and Future.* Chicago: University of Chicago Press, pp. 349–80.

———. 1963. The taxonomic evaluation of fossil hominids. In Sherwood L. Washburn (ed.), *Classification and Human Evolution.* Viking Fund Publications in Anthropology, No. 37. Wenner-Gren Foundation for Anthropological Research, New York. pp. 332–46.

———. 1974. Cladistic analysis or cladistic classification? *Zeitschrift für Zoologische Systematik und Evolutionsforschung* 12(2):94–128.

———. 1980. Curt Stern (Biographical Essay). In Ernst Mayr and William B. Provine (eds.), *The Evolutionary Synthesis: Perspectives on the Unification of Biology.* Cambridge, MA: Harvard University Press, pp. 424–29.

———. 1982. *The Growth of Biological Thought: Diversity, Evolution and Inheritance.* Cambridge, MA: Belknap Press/Harvard University Press. 974 pp.

———. 1991. *One Long Argument. Charles Darwin and the Genesis of Modern Evolutionary Thought.* Cambridge, MA: Harvard University Press. 195 pp.

———. 1992. Controversies in retrospect. In Douglas Futuyma and Janis Antonovics (eds.), *Oxford Surveys in Evolutionary Biology* 8:1–34. New York Oxford University Press.

Mech, L. David. 1970. *The Wolf: The Ecology and Behavior of an Endangered Species.* Garden City, NY: The Natural History Press. 384 pp.

———. 1972. Spacing and possible mechanisms of population regulation in wolves. *American Zoologist* 12(4):642.

———. 1975. Hunting behavior in two similar species of social canids. In Michael J. Fox (ed.), *The Wild Canids: Their Systematics, Behavioral Ecology and Evolution.* New York: Van Nostrand Reinhold, pp. 363–68.

———. 1988. *Arctic Wolf: Living With the Pack.* Stillwater, MN: Voyageur Press. 128 pp.

Meiring, A. J. D. 1956. The macrolithic culture of Florisbad. *Researches of the Nasionale Museum,* Bloemfontein, 1(9):205–37.

Mellars, Paul. 1986. A new chronology for the French Mousterian period. *Nature* 322:410–11.

———. 1989. Major issues in the emergence of modern humans. *Current Anthropology* 30(3):349–85.

———. 1993. Archaeology and the population-dispersal hypothesis of modern human origins in Europe. In M. G. Aitken, C. B. Stringer and P. A. Mellars (eds.), *The Origin of Modern Humans and the Impact of Chronometric Dating.* Princeton: Princeton University Press, pp. 196–216.

Mellars, P. A., M. J. Aitken, and C. B. Stringer. 1993. Outlining the problem: Summary. In M. J. Aitken, C. B. Stringer and P. A. Mellars (eds.), *The Origin of Modern Humans and the Impact of Chronometric Dating.* Princeton: Princeton University Press, pp. 3–11.

Mellars, Paul, and Chris Stringer (eds.). 1989. *The Human Revolution: Behavioural and Biological Perspectives on the Origins of Modern Humans.* Edinburgh: Edinburgh University Press. 800 pp.

Mercier, N., H. Valladas, J-L. Joron, J-L. Reyss, F. Lévêque, and B. Vandermeersch. 1991. Thermoluminescence dating of the late Neanderthal remains from Saint-Césaire. *Nature* 351:737–39.

Mercier, Norbert, Helène Valladas, Georges Valladas, and Arthur Jelinek. 1992. New Tabun cave chronology: TL dating of burnt flints from the Jelinek's excavation. *Journal of the Israel Prehistoric Society,* Supplement 1: Program and Book of Abstracts, 3rd International Congress on Human Paleontology, p. 80.

Mivart, St. George Jackson. 1871. *On the Genesis of Species.* London: Macmillan. 342 pp.

Montagu, M. F. Ashley. 1960. *An Introduction to Physical Anthropology,* 3rd ed. Springfield, IL: Charles C. Thomas. 771 pp.

Moody, Ernest A. 1935. *The Logic of William of Ockham.* New York: Sheed and Ward. 322 pp.

Moore, Edward Carter. 1961. *American Pragmatism: Peirce, James and Dewey.* New York: Columbia University Press. 285 pp.

Moore, Josselyn F. 1973. *The Archeological Hunting Bias: Suggestions from Australian Gathering Activities.* M.A. Thesis, Department of Anthropology, City University of New York, 120 pp.

Moreau, Reginald E. 1963. Vicissitudes of the African biomes in the Late Pleistocene. *Proceedings of the Zoological Society of London* 141(2):395–421.

———. 1966. *The Bird Faunas of Africa and Its Islands.* New York: Academic Press. 424 pp.

Morgan, Thomas Hunt. 1916. *A Critique of the Theory of Evolution.* Princeton: Princeton University Press. 197 pp.

Morris, Henry M. 1974. *The Troubled Waters of Evolution.* San Diego: Creation-Life Publishers. 247 pp.

de Mortillet, Gabriel. 1883. *Le Préhistorique: Antiquité de l'Homme.* Paris: C. Reinwald. 642 pp.

Muller, Hermann J. 1927. Artificial transmutation in the gene. *Science* 66:84–87.

———. 1928. The production of mutations by X-ray. Proceedings of the National Academy of Science, Washington, D. C. 14(9):714–16.

———. 1929. The method of evolution. *The Scientific Monthly* 29:481–505.

Murrill, Rubert I. 1981. *Petralona Man: A Descriptive and Comparative Study, With New Important Information of Rhodesian Man.* Springfield, IL: Charles C. Thomas. 284 pp.

Musgrave, Jonathan H. 1971. How dextrous was Neanderthal man? *Nature* 233:538–41.

———. 1973. The phalanges of Neanderthal and Upper Palaeolithic hands. In Michael H. Day (ed.), *Human Evolution*. London: Taylor and Francis, pp. 59–85.

Nei, Masatoshi. 1985. Human evolution at the molecular level. In Tomoko Ohta and Kenichi Aoki (eds.), *Population Genetics and Molecular Evolution*. New York: Stringer Verlag, pp. 41–64.

———. 1987. *Molecular Evolutionary Genetics*. New York: Columbia University Press. 512 pp.

Neel, James V. 1989. Human evolution and the "founder-flush" principle. In L. V. Giddings, K. Y. Kaneshiro, and W. W. Anderson (eds.), *Genetics, Speciation, and the Founder Principle*. New York: Oxford University Press, 299–313 pp.

Negus, Victor. 1958. *The Comparative Anatomy and Physiology of the Nose and Paranasal Sinuses*. Edinburgh: Livingstone. 402 pp.

———. 1965. *The Biology of Respiration*. Baltimore: Williams and Wilkins. 227 pp.

Nelkin, Dorothy. 1982. *The Creation Controversy: Science or Scripture in the Schools*, 2nd ed. New York: W. W. Norton. 242 pp.

Nelson, Gareth, and Norman Platnick. 1984. Systematics and evolution. In Mae-Wan Ho and Peter T. Saunders (eds.), *Beyond Neo-Darwinism:: An Introduction to the New Evolutionary Paradigm*. London: Academic Press, pp. 143–58.

Neuville, René, and Armand Ruhlmann. 1941. La place du paléolithique ancien dans le Quaternaire marocain. *Collection Hesperis, Institut des Hautes-Études Marocaines* (Casablanca) 8:1–156.

Nitecki, Matthew (ed.). 1984. *Extinctions*. Chicago: University of Chicago Press. 354 pp.

Oakley, Kenneth P. 1952. *Man the Tool-Maker*, 2nd ed. British Museum London: (Natural History). 98 pp.

———. 1957. Tools makyth man. *Antiquity* 31:199–209.

Odum, Eugene P. 1971. *Fundamentals of Ecology*, 3rd ed. Philadelphia: Saunders. 574 pp.

Ohno, Susumu. 1970. *Evolution by Gene Duplication*. New York: Springer-Verlag. 160 pp.

Olson, Todd R. 1981. Basicranial morphology of the extant hominoids and Pliocene hominids: The new material from the Hadar Formation, Ethiopia, and its significance in early human evolution and taxonomy. In Christopher B. Stringer (ed.), *Aspects of Human Evolution*. London: Taylor and Francis, pp. 99–128.

———. 1985. Cranial morphology and systematics of the Hadar Formation hominids and *"Australopithecus" africanus*. In Eric Delson (ed.), *Ancestors: The Hard Evidence*. New York: Alan R. Liss, 102–19.

Oppenoorth, W. F. F. 1932. Ein neuer diluvialer Urmensch von Java. *Natur und Museum* 62(9):269–79.

Osborn, Henry Fairfield. 1926. *Evolution and Religion in Education: Polemics of the Fundamentalist Controversy of 1922 to 1926*. New York: Charles Scribner's Sons. 240 pp.

Ostrom, John H. 1976. *Archaeopteryx* and the origin of birds. *Biological Journal of the Linnaean Society of London* 8(2):91–182.

———. 1979. Bird flight: How did it begin? *American Scientist* 67(1):46–56.

Overton, William R. 1982. Creationism in schools: The decision in McLean versus the Arkansas Board of Education. *Science* 215:934–43.

Ovey, Cameron D. (ed.). 1964. *The Swanscombe Skull: A Survey of Research on a Pleistocene Site.* Royal Anthropological Institute Occasional Paper No. 20. London: The Royal Anthropological Institute. 214 pp.

Oxnard, Charles E. 1987. *Fossils, Teeth and Sex: New Perspectives on Human Evolution.* Seattle: University of Washington Press. 281 pp.

Pan Yuerong. 1988. Small fossil primates from Lufeng, a latest Miocene site in Yunnan Province, China. *Journal of Human Evolution* 17(3):359–66.

Pan Yuerong and Nina G. Jablonski. 1987. The age and distribution of fossil cercopithecids in China. *Human Evolution* 2(1):59–69.

Pandolf, Kent B., Michael N. Sawka, and Richard R. Gonzalez (eds.). 1988. *Human Performance Physiology and Environmental Medicine at Terrestrial Extremes.* Indianapolis: Benchmark Press. 637 pp.

Pardoe, Colin. 1991. Evolution and isolation in Tasmania. *Current Anthropology* 32(1):1–21.

Partridge, T. C. 1982. The chronological positions of the fossil hominids of southern Africa. *1ᵉʳ Congrès International de Paléontologie Humaine, Nice.* Centre National pour la Recherche Scientifique, Paris, vol. 2:617–75.

Paterson, Hugh E. H. 1980. A comment on "mate recognition systems." *Evolution* 34(2):330–31.

———. 1985. The recognition concept of species. In Elisabeth S. Vrba (ed.), *Species and Speciation.* Transvaal Museum Monograph No. 4, Transvaal Museum, Pretoria, pp. 21–29.

Patterson, Bryan, Anna K. Behrensmeyer, and William D. Sill. 1970. Geology and fauna of a new Pliocene locality in Northwestern Kenya. *Nature* 226:918–21.

Patterson, Bryan, and William W. Howells. 1967. Hominid humeral fragment from early Pleistocene of northwestern Kenya. *Science* 156:64–66.

Pei, Wen-Chung. 1930. An account of the discovery of an adult *Sinanthropus* skull in the Chou Kou Tien deposit. *Bulletin of the Geological Society of China* 8(3):203–5.

———. 1931. Notice of the discovery of quartz and other stone artifacts in the Lower Pleistocene hominid-bearing sediments of the Chou Kou Tien deposit. *Bulletin of the Geological Society of China* 11(2):109—39.

———. 1934. A prliminary report on the Late Palaeolithic cave of Choukoutien. *Bulletin of the Geological Society of China* 13(3):327–58.

Perlès, Catherine. 1977. *Préhistoire du Feu.* Masson et Cⁱᵉ, Paris. 180 pp.

Pettigrew, John D. 1986. Flying primates? Megabats have the advanced pathway from eye to midbrain. *Science* 231:1304–06.

———. 1991. Wings or brain? Convergent evolution in the origin of bats. *Systematic Zoology* 10(2):199–216.

Peyrony, Denis. 1930. Le Moustier—Ses gisements, ses industries, ses souches géologiques. *Revue Anthropologique* 40(1–3):48–76.

———. 1934. La Ferrassie—Moustérien, Périgordien, Aurignacien. *Préhistoire* 3:1–92.

Pickford, Martin. 1986. On the origins of body size dimorphism in primates. *Human Evolution* 1(1):77–90.

Pilbeam, David. 1982. New hominoid skull from the Miocene of Pakistan. *Nature* 295:232–34.

———. 1984. The descent of hominoids and hominids. *Scientific American* 250(3):84–96.

———. 1986. Distinguished lecture: Hominoid evolution and hominoid origins. *American Anthropologist* 88(2):295–312.

Pinkley, G. 1935–1936. The Significance of Wadjak Man: A fossil *Homo sapiens* from Java. *Peking Natural History Bulletin* 10(3):183–200.

de Poncins, Gontran. 1941. *Kabloona.* New York: Reynal and Hitchcock, 339 pp.

Pope, Alexander. 1734 (1969). *An Essay on Man: Being the First Book of Ethic Epistles to Henry St. John, L. Bolingbroke.* Menston, England: The Scolar Press (A Scolar Press Facsimile). 75 pp.

Pope, Geoffrey G. 1988a. Jinniu Shan (Yingkou). In Ian Tattersall, Eric Delson, and John Van Couvering (eds.), *Encyclopedia of Human Evolution.* New York: Garland Publishing, p. 291.

———. 1988b. Recent advances in far eastern paleoanthropology. *Annual Review of Anthropology* 17:43–77.

———. 1989. Bamboo and human evolution. *Natural History* 10:48–57.

Popper, Karl. 1978a. Natural selection and the emergence of mind. *Dialectica* 32(3–4):339–55.

———. 1978b. *Unended Quest: An Intellectual Autobiography.* Glasgow: Fontana/Collins. 256 pp.

Potonie, Robert. 1958. Zur allgemeinen Bedeutung des Neandertal-Fundes. In G. H. R. von Koenigswald (ed.), *Hundert Jahre Neanderthaler.* Utrecht, Netherlands: Kemink en Zoon, pp. 277–86.

Poulianos, Aris N. 1967. The place of Petralonian man among the Palaeoanthropoi. *Anthropos* 19(II):216–21.

Price, Joseph H. 1967. *Political Institutions of West Africa.* London: Hutchinson. 266 pp.

Pruner-Bey, Franz Ignaz. 1863. Observations sur le crâne de Neanderthal. *Bulletin de la Société d'Anthropologie de Paris* 4:318–23.

———. 1864a. The Neanderthal skull. Letter, April 19, to C. Carter Blake. *The Anthropological Review* 2(5):145–46.

———. 1864b. The Neanderthal skull. Extract of a letter, July 9, to C. Carter Blake. *The Anthropological Review* 2(6):223.

de Puydt, Marcel, and Max Lohest. 1886. L'homme contemporain du Mammouth à Spy. *Annales de la Fédération Archéologique de Belgique* 2:207–35.

Pycraft, William P. 1928. Rhodesian man. Description of the skull and other human remains from Broken Hill. In W. P. Pycraft, G. E. Smith, M. Yearsley, J. T. Carter, R. A. Smith, A. T. Hopwood, D. M. A. Bate, and W. E. Swinton (eds.), *Rhodesian Man and Associated Remains.* London: British Museum (Natural History), pp. 1–51.

Quatrefages, Armand de, and Ernest T. Hamy. 1882. *Crania Ethnica: Les crânes des races humaines.* Baillière et fils, Paris.

Quennell, Marjorie C., and Charles H. B. Quennell. 1922. *Everyday Life in the Old Stone Age.* New York: G. P. Putnam's Sons, 210 pp.

Radinsky, Leonard B. 1973. *Aegyptopithecus* endocasts: Oldest record of a pongid brain. *American Journal of Physical Anthropology* 39(2):239–48.

———. 1979. *The Fossil Record of Primate Brain Evolution.* Forty-ninth James Arthur Lecture on the Evolution of the Human Brain, 1979. American Museum of Natural History, New York. 27 pp.

Rainger, Ronald. 1991. *An Agenda for Antiquity: Henry Fairfield Osborn and Vertebrate Paleontology at the American Museum of Natural History, 1890–1935.* University of Alabama Press, Tuscaloosa. 360 pp.

Rak, Yoel. 1990. On the differences between two pelvises of Mousterian context from the Qafzeh and Kebara caves, Israel. *American Journal of Physical Anthropology* 81(3):323–32.

———. 1993. Morphological variation in *Homo neanderthalensis* and *Homo sapiens* in the Levant: A biogeographic model. In W. H. Kimbel and L. B. Martin (eds.), *Species, Species Concepts, and Primate Evolution*. New York: Plenum Press, pp. 523–36.

Rak, Yoel, and Baruch Arensburg. 1987. Kebara 2 Neanderthal pelvis: First look at a complete inlet. *American Journal of Physical Anthropology* 73(2):227–31.

Raup, David M. 1986. *The Nemesis Affair: A Story of the Death of Dinosaurs and the Ways of Science*. New York: Norton. 220 pp.

Reed, Edward S. 1978. Darwin's evolutionary philosophy: The laws of change. *Acta Biotheoretica* 27(3/4):201–35.

Renne, Paul R., and Asish R. Basu. 1991. Rapid eruption of the Siberian traps: flood basalt at the Permo-Triassic boundary. *Science* 253:176–79.

Ricklan, D. E. 1987. Functional anatomy of the hand of *Australopithecus africanus*. *Journal of Human Evolution* 16(6/7):643–64.

Rightmire, G. Philip. 1978. Florisbad and human population succession in southern Africa. *American Journal of Physical Anthropology* 48(4);475–86.

———. 1979. Implications of Border Cave skeletal remains for later Pleistocene human evolution. *Current Anthropology* 20(1):23–35.

———. 1983. The fossil evidence for hominid evolution in southern Africa. In Richard G. Klein (ed.), *Southern African Prehistory and Palaeoenvironments*. Rotterdam: Balkema, pp. 147–68.

———. 1984. Comparisons of *Homo erectus* from Africa and Southeast Asia. In P. Andrews and J. L. Franzen (eds.), *The Early Evolution of Man With Special Emphasis on Southeast Asia and Africa*. Courier Forschungsinstitut, Senckenberg, 69:83—98.

———. 1988. *Homo erectus* and later Middle Pleistocene humans. *Annual Review of Anthropology* 17:239–59.

———. 1990. *Evolution of* Homo erectus: *Comparative Anatomical Studies of an Extinct Human Species*. Cambridge: Cambridge University Press. 260 pp.

Roberts, Richard G., Rhys Jones, and M. A. Smith. 1990. Thermoluminescence dating of a 50,000-year old human occupation site in northern Australia. *Nature* 345:153–56.

Robins, Ashley H. 1991. *Biological Perspectives on Human Pigmentation*. New York: Cambridge University Press. 153 pp.

Robinson, John T. 1954. Prehominid dentition and hominid evolution. *Evolution* 8(4):324–34.

———. 1956. *The Dentition of the Australopithecinae*. Transvaal Museum Memoir No. 9, Transvaal Museum, Pretoria. 179 pp.

———. 1961. The Australopithecines and their bearing on the origin of man and of stone tool-making. *South African Journal of Science* 57(1):3–13.

Romer, Alfred S. 1954. *Man and the Vertebrates*, 2 vols. England: Penguin Books, Harmondsworth.

———. 1966. *Vertebrate Paleontology* 3rd ed. Chicago: University of Chicago Press. 478 pp.

Romer, Alfred S., and Thomas S. Parsons. 1986. *The Vertebrate Body*, 6th ed. Philadelphia: Saunders. 679 pp.

Rona, E., and C. Emiliani. 1969. Absolute dating of Caribbean cores P6304-8 and P6304-9. *Science* 163:66–68.

Rose, Kenneth D., and Thomas M. Bown. 1993. Species concepts and species recognition in Eocene primates. In W. H. Kimbel and L. B. Martin (eds.), *Species, Species Concepts, and Primate Evolution.* New York: Plenum Press, pp. 299–330.

Rose, Kenneth D., and Alan Walker. 1985. The skeleton of early Eocene *Cantius,* oldest lemuriform primate. *American Journal of Physical Anthropology* 66(1):73–89.

Rosenberg, Karen R. 1986. *The Functional Significance of Neandertal Pubic Morphology.* Ph.D. Dissertation, Department of Anthropology, University of Michigan, Ann Arbor. 237 pp.

———. 1988. The functional significance of Neanderthal pubic length. *Current Anthropology* 29(4):595–617.

Rudwick, Martin J. S. 1972. *The Meaning of Fossils: Episodes in the History of Palaeontology.* London: Macdonald. 287 pp.

Ruff, Christopher B. 1993. Climatic adaptation and hominid evolution: The thermoregulatory imperative. *Evolutionary Anthropology* 2(2):53–60.

Ruff, Christopher B., Erik Trinkaus, Alan Walker, and Clark S. Larsen. 1993. Postcranial robusticity in *Homo.* I: Temporal trends and mechanical interpretation. *American Journal of Physical Anthropology* 91(1):21–53.

Ruff, Christopher B., and Alan Walker. 1993. Body size and body shape. In Alan Walker and Richard Leakey (eds.), *The Nariokotome* **Home erectus** *Skeleton.* Cambridge, MA: Harvard University Press, pp. 233–65.

Ruspoli, Mario. 1987. *The Cave of Lascaux: The Final Photographs.* New York: H. N. Abrams. 208 pp.

Rust, Alfred. 1956. *Artefakte aus der Zeit des Homo Heidelbergensis in Süd- und Norddeutschland.* Bonn: Rudolf Habelt Verlag. 43 pp.

Ryan, Alan A. 1980. *Anterior Dental Microwear in Hominid Evolution: Comparisons with Human and Nonhuman Primates.* Ph.D. Dissertation, Department of Anthropology, University of Michigan, Ann Arbor. 447 pp.

Ryan, Alan S., and Donald C. Johanson. 1989. Anterior dental microwear in *Australopithecus afarensis:* Comparisons with human and nonhuman primates. *Journal of Human Evolution* 18(3):235–68.

Sackett, James. 1981. The curious incident about Piltdown. *Diaspar* 22:5–20.

Safire, William. 1993. Safire on Language: Only the factoids. *New York Times Magazine,* December 5, pp. 32, 34.

Sahlins, Marshall D. 1960. The origin of society. *Scientific American* 203(3):76–87.

———. 1972 *Stone Age Economics.* Chicago: Aldine-Atherton. 348 pp.

Santa Luca, Albert P. 1980. *The Ngandong Fossil Hominids: A Comparative Study of a Far Eastern* **Homo erectus** *Group.* Yale University Publications in Anthropology. 78:1–175.

Sarich, Vincent M. 1971. Human variation in an evolutionary perspective. In Phyllis Dolhinow and Vincent M. Sarich (eds.), *Background for Man: Readings in Physical Anthropology.* Boston: Little, Brown, pp. 182–91.

Sartono, S., and D. Grimaud-Hervé. 1983a. Las pariétaux des Pithécanthropes Sangiran 12 et 17. *L'Anthropologie* 87(4):475–82.

———. 1983b. Les pariétaux de l'hominidé Sangiran 31. *L'Anthropologie* 87(4):465–68.

Schaaffhausen, Hermann. 1958. Zur Kentniss der ältesten Rassenschädel. *Archiv für Anatomie, Physiologie und Wissenschaftliche Medecin.* pp. 453–78.

Schaeffer, Bobb, Max K. Hecht, and Niles Eldredge. 1972. Phylogeny and paleontology. *Evolutionary Biology* 6:31–46.

Schaller, George B. 1965. *The Year of the Gorilla.* New York: Ballantine Books. 285 pp.

———. 1967. *The Deer and the Tiger: A Study of Wildlife in India.* Chicago: University of Chicago Press. 376 pp.

———. 1972. *The Serengeti Lion: A Study of Predator-Prey Relations.* Chicago: University of Chicago Press. 480 pp.

———. 1976. *The Mountain Gorilla: Ecology and Behavior.* Chicago: University of Chicago Press. 430 pp.

Schaller, George B., Hu Jinchu, and Pan Wenshi. 1985. *The Giant Pandas of Wolong.* Chicago: University of Chicago Press. 298 pp.

Schaller, George B., and Gordon R. Lowther. 1969. The relevance of carnivore behavior to the study of early hominids. *Southwestern Journal of Anthropology* 25(4):307–39.

Schick, Kathy D., and Nicholas Toth. 1993. *Making Silent Stones Speak: Human Evolution and the Dawn of Technology.* New York: Simon and Schuster. 352 pp.

Schiller, Francis. 1979. *Paul Broca: Founder of French Anthropology, Explorer of the Brain.* Berkeley: University of California Press. 350 pp.

Schoeninger, Margaret J. 1980. *Changes in Human Subsistence Activities From the Middle Paleolithic to Neolithic Period in the Middle East.* Ph.D. Dissertation, Department of Anthropology, University of Michigan, Ann Arbor. 270 pp.

———. 1982. Diet and the evolution of modern human form in the Middle East. *American Journal of Physical Anthropology* 58(1):37–52.

Schoetensack, Otto. 1908. *Der Unterkiefer des Homo Heidelbergensis Aus dem Sanden von Mauer bei Heidelberg: ein Beitrag zur Paläontologic des Menschen.* Wilhelm Engelmann, Leipzig. 67 pp.

Schrempp, Gregory A. 1992. *Magical Arrows: The Maori, The Greeks, and the Folklore of the Universe.* Madison: University of Wisconsin Press. 217 pp.

Schultz, Adolph H. 1963. Age changes, sex differences, and variability as factors in the classification of primates. In Sherwood L. Washburn (ed.), *Classification and Human Evolution.* Viking Fund Publications in Anthropology, No. 37. Wenner-Gren Foundation for Anthropological Research, New York, pp. 85–115.

Schwalbe, Gustav. 1906. *Studien zur Vorgeschichte des Menschen.* E. Schweizerbartsche Verlagsbuchhandlung (E. Nägele), Stuttgart. 228 pp.

———. 1913. Kritische Besprechung von Boule's Werk: "L'homme fossile de La Chapelle-aux-Saints." mit eigenen Untersuchungen *Zeitschrift für Morphologie und Anthropologie* 16(1):527–610.

Schwarcz, Henry P. 1993. Uranium-series dating and the origin of modern man. In M. J. Aitken, C. B. Stringer and P. A. Mellars (eds.), *The Origins of Modern Humans and the Impact of Chronometric Dating.* Princeton: Princeton University Press, pp. 12–26.

Schwarcz, Henry P., and Rainer Grün. 1993. Electron spin resonance (ESR) dating of the origin of modern man. In M. J. Aitken, C. B. Stringer and P. A. Mellars (eds.), *The Origin of Modern Humans and the Impact of Chronometric Dating.* Princeton: Princeton University Press, pp. 40–48.

Schwarcz, Henry P., Rainer Grün, Bernard Vandermeersch, Ofer Bar-Yosef, Helène Valladas, and Eitan Tchernov. 1988. ESR dates for the hominid burial site of Qafzeh in Israel. *Journal of Human Evolution* 17(8): 733–37.

Sergi, Sergio. 1953. I profanerantropi di Swanscombe e di Fontéchevade. *Rivista di Antropologia* 40:65–72.

Serizawa Chōsuke. 1986. The Paleolithic Age of Japan in the context of East Asia: A brief introduction. In R. J. Pearson, G. L. Barnes and K. L. Hutterer (eds.), *Windows on the Japanese Past: Studies in Archaeology and Prehistory.* Ann Arbor: Center for Japanese Studies, University of Michigan, pp. 191–97.

Shackleton, Nikolas J. 1975. The stratigraphic record of deep-sea cores and its implications for the assessment of glacials, interglacials, stadials and interstadials in the Mid-Pleistocene. In K. W. Butzer and G. Ll. Isaac (eds.), *After the Australopithecines: Stratigraphy, Ecology, and Culture Change in the Middle Pleistocene.* The Hague: Mouton, pp. 1–24.

Shackleton, Nikolas J., and N. N. Opdyke. 1976. Oxygen-isotope and paleomagnetic stratigraphy of Pacific core V28–239, late Pliocene to latest Pleistocene. *Memoirs of the Geological Society of America* 145:449–64.

Shapiro, Harry L. 1974. *Peking Man.* New York: Simon and Schuster. 190 pp.

Sharpton, Virgil L., K. Burke, A. Camargo-Zanguera, S. A. Hall, G. Suárez-Reynoso, J. M. Quezada-Muñeton, P. D. Spudis, and J. Urritia-Fucuguachi. 1993. Chicxulub multiring impact basin: Size and other characteristics derived from gravity analysis. *Science* 261:1564–67.

Shea, Brian T. 1989. Heterochrony in human evolution: The case of neoteny reconsidered. *Yearbook of Physical Anthropology* 32:69–101.

Shea, John J. 1988. Spear points from the Middle Paleolithic of the Levant. *Journal of Field Archaeology* 15(4):441–50.

———. 1989. A functional study of the lithic industries associated with hominid fossils in the Kebara and Qafzeh caves, Israel. In P. Mellars and C. Stringer (eds.), *The Human Revolution: Behavioural and Biological Perspectives on the Origins of Modern Humans.* Princeton: Princeton University Press, pp. 611–25.

———. 1992. Lithic microwear analysis in archaeology. *Evolutionary Anthropology* 1(4):143–50.

Shipman, Pat. 1986. Scavenging or hunting in early hominids: Theoretical framework and tests. *American Anthropologist* 88(1):27–43.

Shipman, Pat, and Jennie Rose. 1983. Early hominid hunting, butchering, and carcass-processing behaviors: Approaches to the fossil record. *Journal of Anthropological Archaeology* 2(1):57–98.

Shreeve, James. 1992. The dating game. *Discover* 13(9):76–83.

Simek, Jan F. 1992. Neanderthal cognition and the Middle to Upper Paleolithic transition. In G. Bräuer and F. H. Smith (eds.), *Continuity or Replacement: Controversies in Homo Sapiens Evolution.* Rotterdam: A. A. Balkema, 231–45 pp.

Simmons, Nancy B., Michael J. Novacek, and Robert J. Baker. 1991. Approaches, methods, and the future of the Chiropteran monophyly controversy. *Systematic Zoology* 10(2):239–43.

Simons, Elwyn L. 1965. New fossil apes from Egypt and the initial differentiation of Hominoidea. *Nature* 205:135–39.

———. 1967. The earliest apes. *Scientific American* 217(6):28–35.

———. 1972. *Primate Evolution: An Introduction to Man's Place in Nature.* New York: Macmillan. 322 pp.

———. 1984. Dawn ape of the Fayum. Tom, Dick, Harry, and Grant: The faces are familiar. *Natural History* 93(5):18–20.

———. 1987. New faces of *Aegyptopithecus* from the Oligocene of Egypt. *Journal of Human Evolution* 16(3):273–89.

———. 1989. Human origins. *Science* 245:1343–50.

———. 1993. Egypt's simian spring. *Natural History* 102(4):58–59.

Simons, Elwyn L, and David R. Pilbeam. 1965. Preliminary revision of the Dryopithecinae (Pongidae, Anthropoidea). *Folia Primatologia* 3(2/3):81–152.

Simons, Marlisle. 1992. Stone Age art shows penguins at Mediterranean. *New York Times*, October 20, B5, B6.

Simpson, George Gaylord. 1943. Criteria for genera, species and subspecies in zoology and paleozoology. *Annals of the New York Academy of Sciences* 44:145–78.

———. 1961. *Principles of Animal Taxonomy*. New York: Columbia University Press. 247 pp.

———. 1963. The meaning of taxonomic statements. In S. L. Washburn (ed.), *Classification and Human Evolution*. Viking Fund Publications in Anthropology, No. 37. Wenner-Gren Foundation for Anthropological Research, New York. pp. 1–31.

Singer, Charles. 1950. *A History of Biology: A General Introduction to the Study of Living Things*, 2nd ed. New York: Henry Schuman. 579 pp.

Singer, Ronald. 1958. The Rhodesian, Florisbad and Saldanha skulls. In G. H. R. von Koenigswald (ed.), *Hundert Jahre Neanderthaler*. Utrecht: Kemink en Zoon, pp. 52–62.

Singer, Ronald, and John Wymer. 1968. Archaeological investigations at the Saldanha skull site in South Africa. *South African Archaeological Bulletin* 23(3):63–74.

———. 1982. *The Middle Stone Age at Klasies River Mouth in South Africa*. The Chicago: University of Chicago Press. 234 pp.

Slonin, N. Balfour, and Lyle H. Hamilton. 1987. *Respiratory Physiology*, 5th ed. St. Louis: C. V. Mosby. 322 pp.

Smith, B. Holly. 1986. Dental development in *Australopithecus* and early *Homo*. *Nature* 323:327–30.

———. 1990. KNM-WT 15000 and the life history of *Homo erectus*. *American Journal of Physical Anthropology* 81(2):296.

———. 1991a. Dental development and the evolution of life history in the hominidae. *American Journal of Physical Anthropology* 86(2):157–74.

———. 1991b. Standards of human tooth formation and dental age assessment. In Marc A. Kelley and Clark S. Larsen (eds.), *Advances in Dental Anthropology*. New York: Wiley-Liss, pp. 143–68.

———. 1992. Life history and the evolution of human maturation. *Evolutionary Anthropology* 1(4):134–42.

———. 1993. The physiological age of KNM-WT 15000. In Alan Walker and Richard Leakey (eds.), *The Nariokotome* **Homo erectus** *Skeleton*. Cambridge, MA: Harvard University Press, pp. 195–220.

Smith, Fred H. 1976. *The Neandertal Remains from Krapina: A Descriptive and Comparative Study*. Department of Anthropology, The University of Tennessee, Knoxville, Tennessee. Report Number 15. 359 pp.

———. 1993. Models and realities in modern human origins: The African fossil evidence. In M. J. Aitken, C. B. Stringer, and P. A. Mellars (eds.), *The Origins of Modern Humans and the Impact of Chronometric Dating*. Princeton: Princeton University Press, pp. 234–48.

Smith, Fred H., Donna C. Boyd, and Mirko Malez. 1985. Additional Upper Pleistocene human remains from Vindija Cave, Croatia, Yugoslavia. *American Journal of Physical Anthropology* 68(3):375–83.

Smith, G. Elliot. 1924. *The Evolution of Man: Essays.* London: Humphrey Milford, Oxford University Press. 159 pp.

Solecki, Ralph S. 1963. Prehistory in Shanidar Valley, northern Iraq. *Science* 139:179–93.

———. 1971. *Shanidar: The First Flower People.* New York: Alfred A. Knopf. 302 pp.

Sollas, William J. 1908. On the cranial and facial characters of the Neanderthal race. *Philosophical Transactions of the Royal Society of London,* Series B: 199:281–339.

Sonakia, Arun. 1985. Skull cap of an early man from the Narmada Valley alluvium (Pleistocene) of central India. *American Anthropologist* 87(3):612–16.

de Sonneville-Bordes, Denise. 1963. Upper Paleolithic cultures in Western Europe. *Science* 142:347–55.

Spencer, Frank. 1990. *Piltdown: A Scientific Forgery.* New York: Oxford University Press. 272 pp.

Stanford, Dennis. 1987. The Ginsberg experiment. *Natural History* 96(5):10–14.

Stanford, Dennis, Robson Bonnichsen, and Richard E. Morlan. 1981. The Ginsberg experiment: Modern and prehistoric evidence of a bone-flaking technology. *Science* 212:438–40.

Stebbins, Robert E. 1974. France. In T. F. Glick (ed.), *The Comparative Reception of Darwinism.* Austin: University of Texas Press, pp. 117–63.

Stephenson, Robert O. 1982. Nunamiut Eskimos: Wildlife biologists and wolves. In Fred H. Harrington and Paul C. Paquet (eds.), *Wolves of the World: Perspectives of Behavior, Ecology and Conservation.* Park Ridge, NJ: Noyes Publications, pp. 434–440.

Stern, Jack T., and Randall L. Susman. 1983. The locomotor anatomy of *Australopithecus afarensis. American Journal of Physical Anthropology* 60(3):279–317.

Stewart, T. Dale. 1960. Form of the pubic bone in Neanderthal man. *Science* 131:1437–38.

Stoneking, Mark. 1993. DNA and recent human evolution. *Evolutionary Anthropology* 2(2):60–73.

Stoneking, Mark, and Rebecca L. Cann. 1989. African origin of human mitochondrial DNA. In P. Mellars and C. Stringer (eds.), *The Human Revolution: Behavioural and Biological Perspectives on the Origins of Modern Humans.* Edinburgh: Edinburgh University Press, pp. 17–30.

Stoneking, Mark, Stephen T. Sharry, Alan J. Redd, and Linda Vigilant. 1993. New approaches to dating suggest a recent age for the human mtDNA ancestor. In M. J. Aitken, C. B. Stringer, and P. A. Mellars (eds.), *The Origin of Modern Humans and the Impact of Chronometric Dating.* Princeton, NJ: Princeton University Press, pp. 84–103.

Straus, Lawrence Guy. 1983. From Mousterian to Magdalenian: Cultural evolution viewed from Vasco-Cantabrian Spain and Pyrenean France. In Erik Trinkaus (ed.), *The Mousterian Legacy: Human Biocultural Change in the Upper Pleistocene.* British Archaeological Reports International Series 164, Oxford. pp. 73–111.

———. 1985. Stone age prehistory of northern Spain. *Science* 230:501–07.

———. 1989. On early hominid use of fire. *Current Anthropology* 30(4):488–91.

Stringer, Christopher B. 1984. The definition of *Homo erectus* and the existence of the species in Africa and Europe. In P. Andrews and J. L. Franzen (eds.), *The Early Evolution of Man.* Courier Forschungsinstitut, Senckenberg 69:131–43.

———. 1986. An archaic character in the Broken Hill innominate E.719. *American Journal of Physical Anthropology* 71(1):115–20.

————. 1987. A numerical cladistic analysis for the genus *Homo. Journal of Human Evolution* 16(1):135–46.

————. 1988. Petralona. In I. Tattersall, E. Delson, and J. VanCouvering (eds.), *Encyclopedia of Human Evolution and Prehistory*. New York: Garland Press, p. 447.

————. 1990. The emergence of modern humans. *Scientific American* 263(6):98–104.

Stringer, Christopher B., and Peter Andrews. 1988. Genetic and fossil evidence for the origin of modern humans. *Science* 239:1263–68.

Stringer, Christopher, and Clive Gamble. 1993. *In Search of the Neanderthals*. London: Thames and Hudson. 247 pp.

Stringer, C. B., R. Grün, H. P. Schwarcz, and P. Goldberg. 1989. ESR dates for the hominid burial site of Es Skhul in Israel. *Nature* 338:756–58.

Stringer, Christopher B., F. Clark Howell, and J. K. Melentis. 1979. The significance of the fossil hominid skull from Petralona, Greece. *Journal of Archaeological Science* 6(3):235–54.

Stryer, Lubert. 1988. *Biochemistry*, 3rd ed. New York: Freeman. 1089 pp.

————. 1989. *Molecular Design of Life*. New York: Freeman. 215 pp.

Suzuki, Hisashi. 1981. Racial history of the Japanese. In Ilse Schwidetzky (ed.), *Rassengeschichte der Menschheit*. 8 Lieferung, *Asien I: Japan, Indonesien, Ozeanien*. München: R. Oldenbourg Verlag, pp. 7–69.

————. 1982. Skulls of the Minatogawa Man. In Hisahi Suzuki and Kazuro Hanihara (eds.), *The Minatogawa Man: The Upper Pleistocene Man from the Island of Okinawa*. The University Museum, The University of Tokyo, Bulletin No. 19 pp. 7–49.

Suzuki, Hisashi, and Fuyuji Takai (eds.), 1970. *The Amud Man and His Cave Site*. Tokyo: Keigaku Publishing Company. 530 pp.

Swadesh, Morris. 1971. *The Origin and Diversification of Language*, Joel Sherzer (ed.). Chicago: Aldine Atherton. 350 pp.

Swisher, C. C., III, G. H. Curtis, T. Jacob, A. G. Getty, A. Suprijo, Widiasmoro. 1994. Age of earliest known hominids in Java. *Science* 263:1118–21.

Swisher, Carl C., III, J. M. Grajaks-Nishimura, A. Montanari, S. V. Margolis, P. Claeys, W. Alvarez, P. Renne, E. Cedillo-Pardo, F. J-M. R. Maurasse, G. H. Curtis, J. Smit, and M. O. McWilliams. 1992. Coeval $^{40}Ar/^{39}Ar$ Ages of 65.0 million years ago from Chicxulub Crater melt rock and Cretaceous-Tertiary boundary tektites. *Science* 257:954–58.

Szalay, Frederick S. 1993. Species concepts: The tested, the untestable and the redundant. In W. H. Kimbel and L. B. Martin (eds.), *Species, Species Concepts, and Primate Evolution*. New York: Plenum Books, pp. 21–41.

Szalay, Frederick S., and Eric Delson. 1979. *Evolutionary History of the Primates*. New York: Academic Press. 580 pp.

Szombathy, Josef. 1925. Die diluvialen Menschenreste aus der Fürst-Johanns-Höhle bei Lautsch in Mähren. *Die Eiszeit* 2:1–34, 73–95.

Taieb, M., D. C. Johanson, Y. Coppens, R. Bonnefille, and J. Kalb. 1974. Découverte d'hominidés dans les séries Plio-Pleistocenes d'Hadar (Bassin de l'Awash: Afar, Éthiopie). *Comptes Rendus des Séances de l'Académie des Sciences de Paris*, Série D, 279:735–38.

Taieb, M., D. C. Johanson, Y. Coppens, and J. L. Aronson. 1976. Geological and paleontological background of Hadar hominid site, Afar, Ethiopia. *Nature* 260:289–93.

Tappen, Neil C. 1979. Studies on the condition and structure of bone of the Saldanha fossil cranium. *American Journal of Physical Anthropology* 50(4):591–94.

Tattersall, Ian. 1986a. A conspectus of primate evolution: Review of *Major Topics in Primate and Human Evolution*, Bernard Wood, Lawrence Martin, and Peter Andrews (eds.). *Journal of Human Evolution* 15(4):313–18.

———. 1986b. Species recognition in human paleontology. *Journal of Human Evolution* 15(3):165–75.

———. 1992. Evolution comes to life. *Scientific American* 267(2):80–87.

———. 1993. Speciation and morphological differentiation in the genus *Lemur*. In W. H. Kimbel and L. B. Martin (eds.), *Species, Species Concepts, and Primate Evolution*. New York: Plenum Press, pp. 163–76.

Taylor, Royal E. 1987. *Radiocarbon Dating: An Archaeological Perspective*. Orlando: Academic Press. 212 pp.

Tchernov, Eitan. 1988. The biogeographical history of the southern Levant. In Y. Yom-Tov and E. Tchernov (eds.), *The Zoogeography of Israel: The Distribution and Abundance at a Zoogeographical Crossroad*. Dordrecht: Dr. W. Junk, pp. 159–249.

———. 1992. Biochronology, paleoecology, and dispersal events of hominids in the southern Levant. In T. Akazawa, K. Aoki and T. Kimura (eds.), *The Evolution and Dispersal of Modern Humans in Asia*. Tokyo: Hokusen-Sha, pp. 149–88.

Teilhard de Chardin, Pierre, and Pei Wen-Chung. 1932. The lithic industry of the *Sinanthropus* deposits in Choukoutien. *Bulletin of the Geological Society of China* 11(4):315–58.

Templeton, Alan R. 1992. Human origins and analysis of mitochondrial DNA sequences. *Science* 255:737.

———. 1993. The "Eve" hypotheses: A genetic critique and reanalysis. *American Anthropologist* 95(1):51–72.

———. 1994. "Eve": Hypothesis compatibility versus hypothesis testing. *American Anthropologist.* 96(1):141–47.

Terrace, H. S., L. A. Petitto, R. J. Sanders, and T. G. Bever. 1979. Can an ape create a sentence? *Science* 206:891–902.

Theunissen, Bert. 1989. *Eugène Dubois and the Ape-Man from Java: The History of the First "Missing Link" and Its Discoverer*. Translated from the Dutch by Enid Perlin-West. Dordrecht: Kluwer Academic Publishers. 216 pp.

Thewissen, J. G. M., and S. K. Babcock. 1991. Distinctive cranial and cervical innervation of wing muscles: New evidence for bat monophyly. *Science* 251:934–36.

Thomas, Julian. 1991. *Rethinking the Neolithic*. Cambridge: Cambridge University Press. 212 pp.

Thomson, Keith Stewart. 1991. Piltdown man: The great English phylogeny. *Nature* 204:515–18.

Tillier, Anne-Marie. 1992. The origins of modern humans in Southwest Asia: Ontogenetic aspects. In T. Akazawa, K. Aoki, and T. Kimura (eds.), *The Evolution and Dispersal of Modern Humans in Asia*. Tokyo: Hokusen-Sha, pp. 15–28.

Tindale, Norman B. 1975. *Aboriginal Tribes of Australia: Their Terrain, Environmental Controls, Distribution, Limits and Proper Names*. Berkeley: University of California Press. 404 pp.

Tobias, Phillip V. 1967. *The Cranium and Maxillary Dentition of Australopithecus (Zinjanthropus) Boisei*. In L. S. B. Leakey (ed.), *Olduvai Gorge*, vol. 2. Cambridge: Cambridge University Press. 252 pp.

———. 1971. *The Brain in Hominid Evolution*, Thirty-Eighth James Arthur Lecture on the Evolution of the Human Brain, 1970. American Museum of Natural History. Columbia University Press, New York. 170 pp.

―――. 1973. Festschrift R. A. Dart. *Journal of Human Evolution* 2(6):417–577.

―――. 1976. White African: An appreciation and some personal memories of Louis Leakey. In Glynn Ll. Isaac and Elizabeth R. McCown (eds.), *Human Origins: Louis Leakey and the East African Evidence.* California: W. A. Benjamin, Menlo Park, pp. 55–74.

―――. 1980. *"Australopithecus afarensis"* and *A. africanus*: Critique and alternative hypothesis. *Palaeontologia Africana* 23:1–17.

―――. 1981. Emergence of man in Africa and beyond. *Philosophical Transactions of the Royal Society of London, Series B* 292:43–56.

―――. 1984. *Dart, Taung and the Missing Link: An Essay on the Life and Work of Emeritus Professor Raymond Dart.* Johannesburg: Witwatersrand University Press. 67 pp.

―――. 1987. The brain of *Homo habilis*: A new level of organization in cerebral evolution. *Journal of Human Evolution* 16(6/7):741–61.

Tobias, Phillip V., and G. H. Ralph von Koenigswald. 1964. A comparison between the Olduvai hominines and those of Java and some implications for hominid phylogeny. *Nature* 204:515–18.

Toth, Nicholas. 1985. Archaeological evidence for preferential right-handedness in the Lower and Middle Pleistocene, and its possible implications. *Journal of Human Evolution* 14(6):607–14.

―――. 1987a. Behavioral inferences from early stone artifact assemblages: An experimental model. *Journal of Human Evolution* 16(7/8):763–87.

―――. 1987b. The first technology. *Scientific American* 256(4):112–21.

Toth, Nicholas, and Kathy Schick. 1983. The cutting edge: An experimental elephant butchery with stone tools. *Interim Evidence* 5(1):8–10.

Trinkaus, Erik. 1977a. A functional interpretation of the axillary border of the Neandertal scapula. *Journal of Human Evolution* 6(3): 231–34.

―――. 1977b. An inventory of the Neanderthal remains from Shanidar cave northern Iraq. *Sumer* 33(1):9–33.

―――. 1981. Neanderthal limb proportions and cold adaptation. In C. B. Stringer (ed.), *Aspects of Human Evolution.* London: Taylor and Francis, pp. 187–224.

―――. 1983a. Neandertal postcrania and the adaptive shift to modern humans. In E. Trinkaus (ed.), *The Mousterian Legacy: Human Biocultural Change in the Upper Pleistocene.* British Archaeological Reports, Oxford. International Series 164:165–200.

―――. 1983b. *The Shanidar Neandertals.* New York: Academic Press. 502 pp.

―――. 1984. Neandertal pubic morphology and gestation length. *Current Anthropology* 25(4):509–13.

―――. 1987. Bodies, brawn and noses: Human ancestors and human predation. In M. H. Nitecki and D. V. Nitecki (eds.), *The Evidence for Human Hunting.* New York: Plenum, pp. 107–43.

―――. 1989. The Upper Pleistocene transition. In Erik Trinkaus (ed.), *The Emergence of Modern Humans: Biocultural Adaptations in the Early Pleistocene.* New York: Cambridge University Press, pp. 42–66.

―――. 1992. Morphological contrasts between the Near Eastern Qafzeh-Skhul and late archaic human samples: Grounds for a behavioral difference? In T. Akazawa, K. Aoki, and T. Kimura (eds.), *The Evolution and Dispersal of Modern Humans in Asia.* Tokyo: Hokusen-Sha, pp. 277–94.

Trinkaus, Erik, and William W. Howells. 1979. The Neanderthals. *Scientific American* 241(6):118–33.

Trinkaus, Erik, and Pat Shipman. 1992. *The Neandertals: Changing the Image of Mankind.* New York: Alfred A. Knopf. 454 pp.

Trinkaus, Erik, and Isabelle Villemeur. 1991. Mechanical advantages of the Neandertal thumb in flexion: A test of an hypothesis. *American Journal of Physical Anthropology* 84(3):249–60.

Turner, William. 1908. The craniology, racial affinities and descent of the Aborigines of Tasmania. *Transactions of the Royal Society of Edinburgh* 46 Part II(17): 365–403.

Tuttle, Russell H. 1988. What's new in African paleoanthropology. *Annual Reviews in Anthropology* 17:391–426.

Tylor, Edward Burnett. 1871. *Primitive Culture: Researches into the Development of Mythology, Philosophy, Religion, Language, Art, and Custom,* vol. I. London: John Murray. 453 pp.

Valladas, H., J. M. Geneste, J. L. Joron, and J. P. Chadelle. 1986. Thermoluminescence dating of Le Moustier (Dordogne, France) *Nature* 322: 452–54.

Valladas, H., J. L. Joron, G. Valladas, B. Arensburg, O. Bar-Yosef, A. Belfer-Cohen, P. Goldberg, H. Laville, L. Meignen, Y. Rak, E. Tchernov, A.-M. Tillier, and B. Vandermeersch. 1987. Thermoluminescence dates for the Neanderthal burial site at Kebara (Mount Carmel), Israel. *Nature* 330:159–60.

Valladas, H., J. Reyss, J. L. Joron, O. Bar-Yosef, and B. Vandermeersch. 1988. Thermoluminescence dating of "Proto-Cro-Magnon" remains from Israel and the origin of modern man. *Nature* 331:614–16.

Vallois, Henri-Victor. 1951. Néanderthal-Néandertal? *L'Anthropologie* 55(5–6):557–58.

Vallois, Henri-Victor, and Hallam L. Movius, Jr. 1953. *Catalogue des Hommes Fossiles.* Macon, France: Protat Frères. 318 pp.

Van den Broek, A. J. P. 1932. Comparison between the lower jaw of Heidelberg and a recent lower jaw. *Anthropologie* 10:144–60.

Vandermeersch, Bernard. 1966. Nouvelles découvertes des restes humaines dans les couches Levalloiso-Moustériennes du gisement de Qafzeh (Israël). *Comptes Rendus des Séances de l'Académie des Sciences de Paris* 262:1434–36.

———. 1969. Les nouveaux squelettes moustériens découverts à Qafzeh (Israël) et leur signification. *Comptes Rendus des Séances de l'Académie des Sciences de Paris* 268:2562–65.

———. 1970. Une sépulture moustérienne avec offrandes découverte dans la grotte de Qafzeh, *Comptes Rendus des Séances de l'Académie des Sciences de Paris* 270:298–301.

———. 1981. *Les Hommes Fossiles de Qafzeh (Israël).* Centre National de la Recherche Scientifique, Paris. 319 pp.

———. 1989. The evolution of modern humans: Recent evidence from southwest Asia. In Paul Mellars and Chris Stringer (eds.), *The Human Revolution: Behavioural and Biological Perspectives on the Origins of Modern Humans.* Edinburgh: Edinburgh University Press, pp. 155–64.

Van Valen, Leigh M. 1988. Species, sets, and the derivative nature of philosophy. *Biology and Philosophy* 3(1):49–66.

Verneau, René. 1902. Les fouilles du Prince de Monaco aux Baoussé-Roussé, un nouveau type humain. *L'Anthropologie* 13:561–85.

———. 1906. *Les Grottes de Grimaldi (Baoussé Roussé).* Tome II, *Anthropologie.* Imprimerie de Monaco. 212 pp.

———. 1924. La race de Néanterthal et la race de Grimaldi: leur rôle dans l'Humanité. *Journal of the Royal Anthropological Institute* 54:211–30. The Huxley Memorial Lecture for 1924.

Virchow, Rudolf. 1872. Untersuchung des Neanderthal-Schädels. *Verhandlungen der Berliner Gesellschaft für Anthropologie, Ethnologie und Urgeschichte* 4:157–65.

———. 1895. Pithecanthropus erectus Dub. *Verhandlungen der Berliner Gesellschaft für Anthropologie, Ethnologie und Urgeschichte.* Ausserordentliche Sitzung vom 14. December. pp. 744–47.

Vonk, H. J., and J. R. H. Western. 1984. *Comparative Biochemistry of Enzymatic Digestion.* Orlando: Academic Press. 501 pp.

Vrba, Elisabeth S. 1988. Late Pliocene climatic events and hominid evolution. In Frederick E. Grine (ed.), *Evolutionary History of the "Robust" Australopithecines.* New York: Aldine de Gruyter, pp 405–26.

———. 1993. The pulse that produced us. *Natural History* 102(5):47–51.

Wagner, Robert P. 1969. Genetics and phenogenetics of mitochondria. *Science* 163:1026–31.

Wagner, Rudolf. 1864. Ueber einige Sendungen von Schädeln, die in der letzten Zeit an die anthropologischen Sammlung des physiologische Instituts gemacht worden sind, und über eine besondere Forderung, welche man an unsere Alterthums-Vereine und die Geologen stellen muss. *Nachrichten von der Königlichen Gesellschaft der Wissenschaften und der Georg-August Universität zu Göttingen* 5:87–99.

Walker, Alan. 1980. 2,000,001 B.C.—Early human life in Plio-Pleistocene Africa. The Ermine Cowles Case Memorial Lecture, November 4, Ann Arbor, Michigan.

———. 1983. Fossil hunting indoors. *Interim Evidence* 5(1):5–7.

———. 1984. Extinction in hominid evolution. In Matthew Nitecki (ed.), *Extinctions.* Chicago: University of Chicago Press, pp. 119–52.

———. 1986. *Homo erectus* skeleton from West Lake Turkana, Kenya. *American Journal of Physical Anthropology* 69(2):275.

Walker, Alan, and Richard Leakey (eds.). 1993. *The Nariokotome* Homo erectus *Skeleton.* Cambridge, MA: Harvard University Press. 457 pp.

Walker, Alan, R. E. Leakey, J. M. Harris, and F. H. Brown. 1986. 2.5-Myr *Australopithecus boisei* from west of Lake Turkana, Kenya. *Nature* 322:517–22.

Walkhoff, Otto. 1902. Der Unterkiefer der Anthropomorphen und des Menschen in seiner functionellen Entwicklung und Gestalt. In Emile Selenka (ed.), *Studien über Entwicklungsgeschichte der Tiere: Menschenaffen* 9(4):209–327. (Wiesbaden).

———. 1904. Die menschliche Sprache in ihrer Bedeutung für die functionelle Gestalt des Unterkiefers. *Anatomischer Anzeiger* 24(5–6):129–39.

Wallace, Alfred Russel. 1875. The limits of natural selection as applied to man. In Alfred Russel Wallace, *Contributions to the Theory of Natural Selection.* London: Macmillan, pp. 332–71.

———. 1903. *Man's Place in the Universe: A Study of the Results of Scientific Research in Relation to the Unity or Plurality of Worlds.* London: Champan and Hall. 330 pp.

Wallace, Douglas C., Katherine Garrison, and William C. Knowler. 1985. Dramatic founder effects in Amerindian mitochondrial DNAs. *American Journal of Physical Anthropology* 68(2):149–55.

Walter, R. C., P. C. Manega, R. L. Hay, R. E. Drake, and G. H. Curtis. 1991. Laserfusion $^{40}Ar/^{39}Ar$ dating of Bed I, Olduvai Gorge, Tanzania. *Nature* 354:145–49.

Ward, Ryk H., B. L. Frazier, K. Dew-Jager, and S. Pääbo. 1991. Extensive mitochondrial diversity within a single Amerindian tribe. *Proceedings of the National Academy of Sciences* 88(19):8720–24.

Ward, Steven C., and Barbara Brown. 1986. The facial skeleton of *Sivapithecus indicus.* In D. R. Swindler and J. Erwin (eds.), *Comparative Primate Biology,* vol. 1: *Systematics, Evolution and Anatomy.* New York: Alan R. Liss, pp. 413–52.

Ward, Steven C., and William H. Kimbel. 1983. Subnasal alveolar morphology and the systematic position of *Sivapithecus American Journal of Physical Anthropology* 61(2):157–71.

Washburn, Sherwood L. 1951. The new physical anthropology. *Transactions of the New York Academy of Science* 13:298–304.

———. 1957. Australopithecines: The hunters or the hunted? *American Anthropologist* 59(4):612–14.

———. 1959. Speculations on the interrelations of the history of tools and biological evolution. *Human Biology* 31(1):21–31.

———. 1960. Tools and human evolution. *Scientific American* 203(3):63–75.

Washburn, Sherwood L., and Jane B. Lancaster. 1968. The evolution of hunting. In R. B. Lee and I. DeVore (eds.), *Man the Hunter*. Chicago: Aldine, pp. 293–303.

Washburn, Sherwood L., and Davida Wolffson. 1950. *The Shorter Anthropological Papers of Franz Weidenreich Published in the Period 1939–1948: A Memorial Volume*. New York: The Viking Fund. 267 pp.

Webb, Stephen. 1990. Cranial thickening in an Australian hominid as a possible palaeoepidemiological indication. *American Journal of Physical Anthropology* 82(4):403–11.

Weidenreich, Franz. 1904. Die Bildung des Kinnes und seine angebliche Beziehung zur Sprache. *Anatomischer Anzeiger* 24(21):545–55.

———. 1928. Entwicklungs- und Rassentypen des *Homo primigenius*. *Natur und Museum* 58(1):1–13, (2):51–62.

———. 1930. Lamarck, seine Persönlichkeit und sein Werk. Zur 100 Wiederkehr seines Todestages. *Natur und Museum* 60(6):326–33.

———. 1932. "Lamarckismus." *Natur und Museum* 62(9):298–300.

———. 1936a. Observations on the form and proportions of the endocranial casts of *Sinanthropus pekinensis*, other hominids and the great apes, a comparative study of brain size. *Palaeontologia Sinica* Series D, 7(4):4–50.

———. 1936b. Sinanthropus pekinensis and its position in the line of human evolution. *Peking Natural History Bulletin* 10(4):281–90.

———. 1937. The dentition of *Sinanthropus pekinensis*. *Palaeontologia Sinica* New Series D, 1:1–180.

———. 1938–1939. On the earliest representative of modern mankind recovered on the soil of East Asia. *Peking Natural History Bulletin* 13(3):161–74.

———. 1939. Six lectures on *Sinanthropus pekinensis* and related problems. *Bulletin of the Geological Society of China* 19(1):1–92.

———. 1940. Some problems dealing with ancient man. *American Anthropologist* 42(3):375–83.

———. 1941. The brain and its rôle in the phylogenetic transformation of the human skull. *Transactions of the American Philosophical Society* New Series 31(5):321–442.

———. 1943. The skull of *Sinanthropus pekinensis:* A comparative study on a primitive hominid skull. *Palaeontologia Sinica* New Series D, 10:1–484.

———. 1945. The Keilor skull: A Wadjak type from southeast Australia. *American Journal of Physical Anthropology* 3(1):21–32.

———. 1946. *Apes Giants and Man*. Chicago: University of Chicago Press. 122 pp.

———. 1947a. Facts and speculations concerning the origin of Homo sapiens. *American Anthropologist* 49(2):187–203.

———. 1947b. The trend of human evolution. *Evolution* 1(4):221–36.

————. 1951. Morphology of Solo Man. *Anthropological Papers of the American Museum of Natural History* 43(3):203–90.

Weiner, Joseph S. 1955. *The Piltdown Forgery*. London: Oxford University Press. 214 pp.

Weiner, Joseph S., and Bernard G. Campbell. 1964. The taxonomic status of the Swanscombe skull. In C. D. Ovey (ed.), *The Swanscombe Skull*. London: Royal Anthropological Institute, pp. 175–209.

Weiner, Joseph S., Kenneth Page Oakley, and Wilfrid E. Le Gros Clark. 1953. The solution of the Piltdown problem. *Bulletin of the British Museum (Natural History). Geology* 2(3):141–46.

Weinert, Hans. 1925. *Der Schädel des eiszeitlichen Menschen von le Moustier in neuer Zusammensetzung*. Berlin: J. Springer. 55 pp.

————. 1936. Der Urmenschenschädel von Steinheim. *Zeitschrift für Morphologie und Anthropologie* 35(3):463–518.

Weiss, Kenneth M. 1984. On the number of members of the genus *Homo* who have ever lived, and some evolutionary implications. *Human Biology* 56(4):637–49.

Wellnhofer, Peter. 1990. Archaeopteryx. *Scientific American* 262(5):70–77.

Wells, H. G. 1966. The grisly folk. In *The Complete Short Stories of H. G. Wells*. (First published in 1927). London: Ernest Benn, pp. 607–21.

Wheeler, Peter E. 1984. The evolution of bipedality and loss of functional body hair in hominids. *Journal of Human Evolution* 13(1):91–98.

————. 1985. The loss of functional body hair in man: The influence of thermal environment, body form and bipedality. *Journal of Human Evolution* 14(1):23–28.

————. 1990. The significance of selective brain cooling in hominids. *Journal of Human Evolution* 19(3):321–22.

————. 1993. Human ancestors walked tall, stayed cool. *Natural History* 102(8):65–67.

Whewell, William. 1832. Review of *Principles of Geology*, vol. 2, by Charles Lyell. *The Quarterly Review* 47:103–32.

Whitcomb, John C., and Henry M. Morris. 1961. *The Genesis Flood: The Biblical Record and Its Scientific Implications*. Philadelphia: The Presbyterian and Reformed Publishing Company. 518 pp.

White, Andrew Dickson. 1896. *A History of the Warfare of Science With Theology in Christendom*, 2 vols. New York: D. Appleton and Company.

White, J. Peter, and James F. O'Connell. 1979. Australian prehistory: New aspects of antiquity. *Science* 203:21–28.

White, Leslie A. 1959. *The Evolution of Culture*. New York: McGraw-Hill. 378 pp.

White, Nicholas P. 1979. *A Companion to Plato's Republic*. Indianapolis: Hackett Publishing Company. 275 pp.

White, Randall K. 1986. *Dark Caves, Bright Visions: Life in Ice Age Europe*. New York: W. W. Norton. 176 pp.

————. 1989. Production complexity and standardization in early Aurignacian bead and pendant manufacture: Evolutionary implications. In P. Mellars and C. Stringer (eds.), *The Human Revolution: Behavioural and Biological Perspectives on the Origins of Modern Humans*. Edinburgh: Edinburgh University Press, pp. 366–90.

————. 1993. The dawn of adornment. *Natural History* 102(5):60–67.

White, Tim D. 1980. Additional fossil hominids from Laetoli, Tanzania: 1976–1979 specimens. *American Journal of Physical Anthropology* 53(4):487–504.

————. 1981. Primitive hominid canine from Tanzania. *Science* 213:348–49.

————. 1984. Pliocene hominids from the Middle Awash, Ethiopia. In P. Andrews and J. L. Franzen (eds.), *The Early Evolution of Man With Special Emphasis on Southeast Asia and Africa. Courier Forschungs-Institut, Senckenberg* 69:57–68.

White, Tim D., and J. M. Harris. 1977. Suid evolution and correlation of African hominid localities. *Science* 198:13–21.

White, Tim D., and Gen Suwa. 1987. Hominid footprints at Laetoli: Facts and interpretation. *American Journal of Physical Anthropology* 72(4):485–514.

White, T. D., G. Suwa, W. K. Hart, R. C. Walters, G. WoldeGabriel, J. de Heinzelin, J. D. Clark, B. Asfaw, and E. Vrba. 1993. New discoveries of *Australopithecus* at Maka in Ethiopia. *Nature* 366:261–65.

Wible, John R., and Herbert H. Covert. 1987. Primates: Cladistic diagnosis and relationships. *Journal of Human Evolution* 16(1):1–22.

Wilberforce, Samuel. 1860. *Charles Darwin On the Origin of Species, by Means of Natural Selection; or the Preservation of Favoured Races in the Struggle for Life. The Quarterly Review* (London) 108:118–38.

Wiley, Edward O. 1978. The evolutionary species concept reconsidered. *Systematic Zoology* 27(1):17–26.

————. 1981. *Phylogenetics: The Theory and Practice of Phylogenetic Systematics.* New York: John Wiley & Sons. 439 pp.

Wiley, Edward O., and Daniel R. Brooks. 1982. Victims of history—a nonequilibrium approach to evolution. *Systematic Zoology* 31(1):1–24.

Wilford, John Noble. 1987. New fossil is forcing family tree revisions. *New York Times,* April 14, pp. 17, 21.

————. 1993a. Feathered dinosaur or a real bird? *New York Times,* February 5, p. A7.

————. 1993b. Skulls found in Spain are early Neanderthal. *New York Times,* April 20, pp. B5, B8.

————. 1993c. Just one big fossil family: Little Lucy and the big guys. *New York Times,* November 18, p. A10.

Williams, George C. 1992. *Natural Selection: Domains, Levels, and Challenges.* New York: Oxford University Press. 208 pp.

Wittgenstein, Ludwig. 1922. *Tractatus Logico-Philosophicus.* London: Kegan Paul, Trench, Trubner. 189 pp.

Wolpoff, Milford H. 1971. *Metric Trends in Hominid Dental Evolution.* Case Western Reserve Studies in Anthropology, No. 2. Case Western Reserve University Press, Cleveland: 244 pp.

————. 1979. Anterior dental cutting in the Laetolil hominids and the evolution of the bicuspid P_3. *American Journal of Physical Anthropology* 51(2):233–34.

————. 1980. *Paleoanthropology.* New York: Alfred A. Knopf. 379 pp.

————. 1984. Evolution in *Homo erectus*: The question of stasis. *Paleobiology* 10(4)389–406.

————. 1986. Describing anatomically modern Homo sapiens: A distinction without a definable difference. *Anthropos* (Brno):23:41–53.

————. 1989. Multiregional evolution: The fossil alternatives to Eden. In Paul Mellars and Chris Stringer (eds.), *The Human Revolution: Behavioural and Biological Perspectives on the Origins of Modern Humans.* Edinburgh: Edinburgh University Press, pp. 62–108.

————. In press. *Paleoanthropology,* 2nd ed. New York: McGraw-Hill..

Wolpoff, Milford H., Wu Xin Zhi, and Alan G. Thorne. 1984. Modern *Homo sapiens* origins: A general theory of hominid evolution involving the fossil evidence from East Asia. In F. H. Smith and F. Spencer (eds.), *The Origin of Modern Humans: A World Survey of the Fossil Evidence.* New York: Alan Liss, pp. 411–83. New York: A. Knopf.

Woo, Ju-Kang. 1959. Human fossils found in Liukiang, Kwangsi, China. *Vertebrata Palasiatica* 3(3):109–18.

Woo, Ju-Kang, and Ru-ce Peng. 1959. Fossil human skull of early paleoanthropic stage found at Mapa, Shaoquan, Kwangtung province. *Vertebrata Palasiatica* 3(4):176–82.

Wood, Bernard A. 1984. The origins of *Homo erectus.* In P. Andrews and J. L. Franzen (eds.), *The Early Evolution of Man. With Special Emphasis on Southeast Asia and Africa. Courier Forschungsinstitut, Senckenberg* 69:99–111.

Woodward, Arthur Smith. 1921. A new cave man from Rhodesia, South Africa. *Nature* 108:371–72.

Wright, Richard V. S. 1976. Evolutionary process and semantics: Australian prehistoric tooth size as a local adjustment. In Robert L. Kirk and Alan G. Thorne (eds.), *The Origin of the Australians.* Atlantic Highlands, NJ: Humanities Press, pp. 265–74.

Wright, Sewall. 1931. Evolution in Mendelian populations. *Genetics* 16(2):97–159.

————. 1943. Isolation by distance. *Genetics* 28(2):114–38.

————. 1946. Isolation by distance under diverse systems of mating. *Genetics* 31(1):38–59.

————. 1951. Fisher and Ford on "the Sewall Wright effect." *The American Scientist* 39(3):452–58, 479.

Wu Cheng-en. 1982. *Journey to the West,* trans. by W. J. F. Jenner from the 1955 Chinese ed., 3 vols. Beijing: Foreign Languages Press.

Wu Rukang, and Charles E. Oxnard. 1983. Ramapithecines from China: Evidence from tooth dimensions. *Nature* 306:258–60.

Wu Rukang, and John W. Olsen (eds.). 1985. *Palaeoanthropology and Palaeolithic Archaeology in the People's Republic of China.* Orlando: Academic Press. 293 pp.

Wu Rukang, and Xu Qinghua. 1985. *Ramapithecus* and *Sivapithecus* from Lufeng, China. In Wu Rukang and John W. Olsen (eds.), *Palaeoanthropology and Palaeolithic Archaeology in the People's Republic of China.* Orlando: Academic Press, pp. 53–68.

Wu Xinzhi 1992. The origin and dispersal of anatomically modern humans in East and Southeast Asia. In T. Akazawa, K. Aoki and T. Kimura (eds.), *The Evolution and Dispersal of Modern Humans in Asia.* Tokyo: Hokusen-Sha, pp. 373–78.

Wu Xinzhi, and Wang Linghong. 1985. Chronology in Chinese palaeoanthropology. In Wu Ru-kang and John W. Olsen (eds.), *Palaeoanthropology and Palaeolithic Archaeology in the People's Republic of China.* Orlando: Academic Press, pp. 29–51.

Wu Xinzhi, and Wu Maolin. 1985. Early *Homo sapiens* in China. In Wu Ru-kang and John W. Olsen (eds.), *Palaeoanthropology and Palaeolithic Archaeology in the People's Republic of China.* Orlando: Academic Press, pp. 91–106.

Wüst, K. 1951. Über den Unterkiefer von Mauer (Heidelberg) im Vergleich zu anderen fossilen und rezenten Unterkiefern von Anthropoiden und Hominiden. *Zeitschrift für Morphologie und Anthropologie* 42(1):1–112.

Wymer, John. 1958. Further work at Swanscombe, Kent. *The Archaeological NewsLetter* 6:190–91.

Yaroch, Lucia Allen. 1994. *Characterization of Neandertal Cranial Shape Using the Method of Thin-Plate Splines.* Ph.D. Dissertation, Department of Anthropology, University of Michigan, Ann Arbor. 303 pp.

Yellen, John E. 1990. The transformation of the Kalahari!Kung. *Scientific American* 262(4):96–105.

Young, John Z. 1971. *An Introduction to the Study of Man.* London: Oxford University Press. 719 pp.

Zihlman, Adrienne. 1981. Women as shapers of human adaptation. In Frances Dahlberg (ed.), *Woman the Gatherer.* New Haven, CN: Yale University Press, pp. 75–120.

Zihlman, Adrienne, and Lynda Brunker. 1979. Hominid bipedalism: Then and now. *Yearbook of Physical Anthropology 1979* 22:132–62.

Zinmeister, William J. 1986. Fossil windfall at Antarctica's edge. *Natural History* 95(5):60–67.

Zuckerkandl, Emile. 1987. On the molecular evolutionary clock. *Journal of Molecular Evolution* 26(1–2):34–46.

Zvelebil, Marek (ed.). 1986. *Hunters in Transition: Mesolithic Societies of Temperate Eurasia and Their Transition to Farming.* New York: Cambridge University Press. 194 pp.

Index